1 MON~

FREE
READING

at

www.ForgottenBooks.com

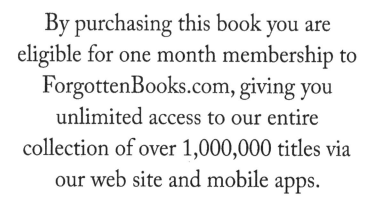

By purchasing this book you are eligible for one month membership to ForgottenBooks.com, giving you unlimited access to our entire collection of over 1,000,000 titles via our web site and mobile apps.

To claim your free month visit: www.forgottenbooks.com/free264081

ISBN 978-0-483-23672-1
PIBN 10264081

(Hanto)

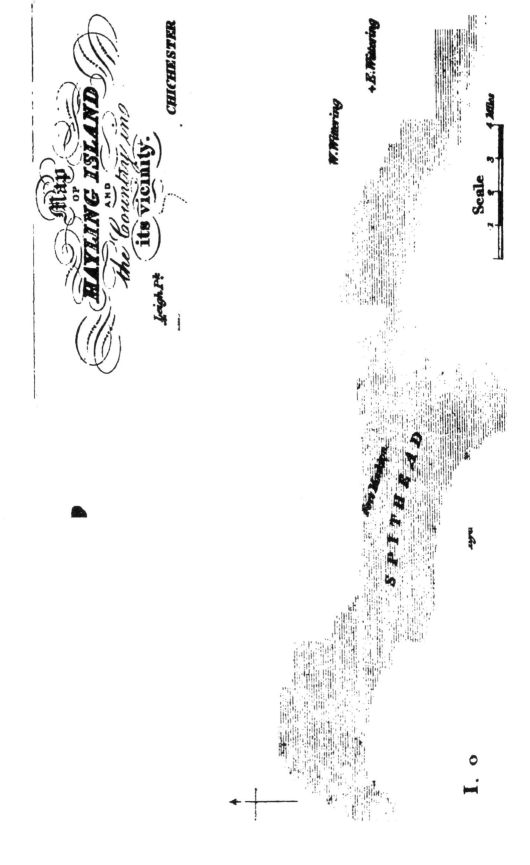

Map
OF
HAYLING ISLAND
AND
the Country in
its vicinity.

CHICHESTER

W. Wittering

+ E. Wittering

SPITHEAD

Scale

I. o

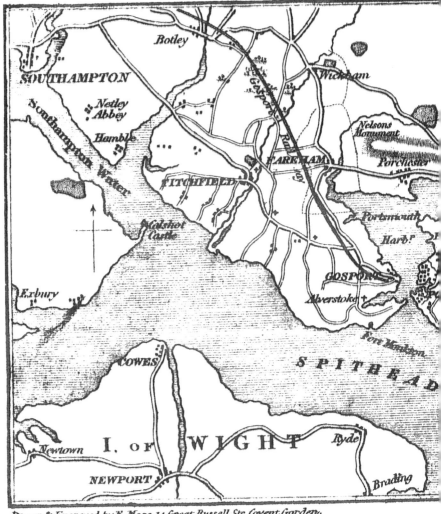

Drawn & Engraved by F. Mogg, 14 Great Russell Str. Covent Garden.

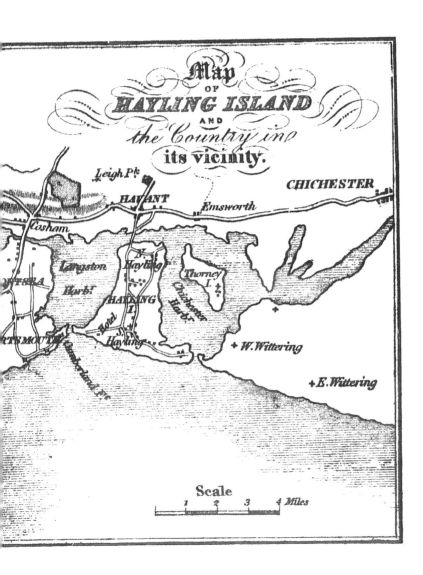

Map

OF

HAYLING ISLAND

AND

the Country in its vicinity.

Leigh Pk.

HAVANT

Emsworth

CHICHESTER

Cosham

Langston

Hayling

Thorney I.

PTSEA

Harbr.

Chichester Harbr.

HAYLING I.

RTSMOUTH

Hayling

W. Wittering

E. Wittering

Scale

1   2   3   4 Miles

TOPOGRAPHICAL ACCOUNT

OF THE

HUNDRED OF BOSMERE,

IN THE COUNTY OF

SOUTHAMPTON,

INCLUDING THE PARISHES OF

HAVANT, WARBLINGTON, AND HAYLING.

BY

CHARLES JOHN LONGCROFT.

LONDON:

JOHN RUSSELL SMITH,
36, SOHO SQUARE.

ANDREW NORTHCROFT,
18, TOOK'S COURT, CURSITOR STREET, CHANCERY LANE.

M.DCCC.LVII.

LONDON:
F. PICKTON, PRINTER,
PERRY'S PLACE, 29, OXFORD STREET.

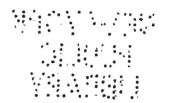

INTRODUCTION.

It has long been matter of regret, that a county like that of Southampton, rife with legend and local interest, should be without a history—a county containing, as it does, within its ambit, that most famous city, as Camden calls it, *Venta Belgarum*, with the Roman stations of Portchester, Bitterne, and Silchester; a county full of tradition of the obstinate resistance offered to the Roman general, Vespasian, whom the poet celebrates as—

> " Ille quidem nuper felici marte Britannos
> Fuderat "—

and around whose arm a snake is said to have wreathed its scaly coil without injury. Much might be said of the gentle Avon, and of Cerdic's Ford (contracted into Chardford), from the brave Saxon Cerdic; how he defeated the Britons under Natanleod, the most powerful of their kings, in a pitched battle, and not only extended his own frontier, but left an easy war to be conducted by his descendants. Much might be said of the Isle of Wight—of Carisbrook—of Quarr—of Christchurch, with its ancient castle, long since crumbled into dust, with its church of prebendaries, built in the Saxon days, repaired in those of William Rufus, and endowed by De Rivers, Earl of Devon. Of Southampton, the Clausentum of the *Itinerary*, where Canute checked the flattery of his courtiers, and, causing his chair to be placed on the shore, commanded the tide to stay its waves; and where, when the rippling surge had leapt upon his feet, he declared that none deserved the name of king but He to whose omnipotence the heaven and earth and sea were all obedient; and how from that moment he laid aside his crown, and placed it on the crucifix.

Much might be said of the Norman Conqueror, whose passion for the chase spread terror and destruction through lands since called the New Forest; of the sport of the royal huntsman, of his violent end, and of the curse pronounced upon his lifeless corpse, when Anselm Fitz-Arthur, the rightful lord of the soil, stood forth to deny him burial at the altar of St. Stephen's at Caen—a curse which they who heard it remembered well, when Rufus his son fell stricken from his horse with the arrow of Sir Walter Tyrrel, in the forest which the Conqueror had depopulated. Much again might be said in aftertimes of the Hospital of St. Cross—of the Crusaders, whose votive windows still adorn its beautiful church—of the princely magnificence of the prelates, Wykeham and Waynfleet, and many others, whose piety has come down to us in their colleges and foundations—of the Chancellor Wriottesley, who dismantled the Abbey of Titchfield, and erected the mansion sometime the shelter of the unfortunate Charles, but now in ruins—of Basyng, celebrated in the wars of the Commonwealth, and of numberless other men and places famous in story, whose incidents would go far to compile an extensive and highly interesting history.

INTRODUCTION.

It is, at least, singular that no one has yet been found to gather into shape this mass of neglected material; and, thinking that long ere this some Leland would be willing to undertake a task so congenial to the historian and the antiquary, I, some time since, commenced to make inquiry into the early records of the hundred in which I was born: this I have continued as opportunity offered, and the result has been, that notes have become the fragments of a narrative, and that the fragments themselves, in course of time, have assumed the shape of the present volume. It has little to recommend it, either in the style of diction or the arrangement of its details; but I have endeavoured to discover the truth, and to throw aside all for which no reasonable foundation existed. There are very few instances where I have not personally examined the original documents or attested copies, in order that mistakes might not occur; and where there is a doubt it will be found expressed.

At the request of those to whom the subject has been mentioned, I have been induced to place it in the hands of the printer; and in doing so I must seek for a justification in the fact, that collections once made and scattered are not easily regained, and that with each successive year the traditions of a neighbourhood pass away and are wholly lost. The preservation of obsolete customs and manners tends much to the illustration of history, and the gratification of individual curiosity. The fluctuations of property, the revolutions of fortunes in families, and the occurrences of the day, point oftentimes to the decay of population, the diversion of commerce, and the change in a locality; and without some knowledge of the past it is impossible to speculate with any degree of probability on the course of the uncertain future.

I can only hope that the little which I have done may stimulate others to a similar contribution, and that some association, like that of Sussex, may ere long be found for the preservation and publication of the private records which are to be found dispersed among the muniment rooms of the nobility and landowners of the county of Southampton.

The Plates with which the work is illustrated have been contributed by Mr. Padwick, the Lord of Hayling.

CHARLES JOHN LONGCROFT.

HAVANT,
January, 1856.

LIST OF PLATES.

ERRATA.

Page 119, *for* individuals have, *read* has.
,, 121, *for* entrenchment, *read* intrenchment.
,, 136, *for* and to keepe, *read* keep.
,, 137, *for* customary tenement, *read* tenements.
,, 191, *for* 6 Edw. 2, 1451, 6 Edw. 6, 1551.
,, 223, *for* Histoire de l'Abbay, *read* l'Abbaye.
,, 299, *for* others fleur, *read* fleurs.
,, 307, *for* with fleur, *read* fleurs.

MARY by the Grace of God of England France and Ireland Queen Defender of the Faith To ALL to whom these present Letters shall come Greeting KNOW YE that We in Consideration of yᵉ faithful Service which Our trusty and well beloved Cousin and Counsellor HENRY EARL OF ARUNDEL one of Our privy Council hath done us this last Civil War against the late Traitor Sir John Dudley Knight and for other Causes and Considerations of Our especial Grace certain Knowledge and mere Motion HAVE granted and Do by these presents for Us Our Heir and Successors grant to him yᵉ said Earl and his Heirs THAT they may for ever have and hold THE RETURN of All Writs Precepts Mandates and Bills of Us Our Heirs and Successors AND ALSO of the Summonses Estreats and Precepts of the Exchequer of Us Our Heirs and Successors And of the Estreats and Precepts of the Justices in Eyre of Us Our Heirs and Successors as well for Pleas of the Crown Common Pleas and Pleas of the Forest as of others the Justices whomsoever Of the Attainments as well of a Plea of yᵉ Crown as of others within the HUNDREDS of him yᵉ said EARL of Westburne Singelton Eseburne Box Stokebrugge Avesforde[1] Westsewrithe and Poling in Our County of SUSSEX AND in all and singular yᵉ Lordships Manors Lands Tenements Possessions Hundreds and Fees of him yᵉ said Earl in Our County of SALOP and in the MARCHES of WALES AND ALSO in his Hundred of Purslo in yᵉ same County of SALOP *And in his Lordships and Manors of Aulton and Hailinge* in the County of SOUTHAMPTON AND ALSO in his Hundreds of Aulton and Predebruge in the same County of Southampton AND ALSO that they yᵉ said Earl and his Heirs may have and hold a Court of his BOROUGH of ARUNDEL in yᵉ aforesaid County of Sussex And all things which to yᵉ same Court now do and hereafter shall belong AND shall and may of themselves and their Bailiffs for Ever hold that they yᵉ said Earl and his Heirs the SHERIFF'S TURN of yᵉ AFORESAID COUNTY of SUSSEX of the aforesaid Hundreds of Westburne Singelton Eseburne Box Stokkebrugge Avesforde[2] Westsewri the and Poling aforesaid being *within his aforesaid Liberty of Arundel* AND of the Hundreds of Dempforde *Manewood* and *Boseham* in yᵉ same county of Sussex being out of the aforesaid Liberty in like manner as the Sheriffs of the aforesaid County of Sussex have been accustomed to hold the Turn there And also that they the said Earl and his Heirs may yearly have and perceive all and all manner of Money for the Sheriff's Aid within

---

[1] Perhaps Anesforde.   [2] Perhaps Ancsforde.

1

the aforesaid Hundreds of Westburne Singelton Eseburne Box
Stokkebrugge Avesforde Westeswrithe and Poling AND within the
Court aforesaid And all other Things which to ye aforesaid Sheriff's
TURN now do and hereafter shall belong And that they ye said Earl
and his Heirs may by themselves their Bailiffs and Ministers have
in ye aforesaid Lordships Manors Lands tenements Possessions Fees
Hundreds and Courts aforesaid The execution and executions of
what sort soever of the aforesaid Writs Precepts Mandates Bills
Summonses and Estreats and of every of them and all other Things
whatsoever which to the office of Sheriff within ye Lordships Manors
Lands Tenements Possessions Fees Hundreds and Courts aforesaid
do and hereafter shall belong So as that no Sheriff Bailiff or other
Minister of Us Our Heirs or Successors may enter into ye Lordships
Manors Lands Tenements Possessions Fees Hundreds and Courts
aforesaid or any of them or any Parcel thereof to make or execute
Distresses and Attachments or Executions of the Writs Precepts
Mandates Bills Summonses and Estreats aforesaid or of any of
them NOR on Account of any Office or any Thing touching their
office NOR may in anywise interfere therein Unless for Default of
the aforesaid Earl and his Heirs and of their Ministers YIELDING
nevertheless to Us Our Heirs and Successors annually at ye Exchequer of Us Our Heirs and Successors for the aforesaid RETURN OF
WRITS and other the Premises within the aforesaid Hundreds of
Westburne Singelton Eseburne Box Stokkebrugge Avesforde[3] Westsewrithe and Poling And the aforesaid Court of his aforesaid
BOROUGH of Arundel aforesaid sixty and sixteen shillings and eight
pence AND for the aforesaid Sheriff's Turn of the aforesaid Hundreds
of Dempforde Manewode and Boseham aforesaid for the AMERCIA-
MENTS thereof forth-coming within ye same three Hundreds forty-
pence per Annum at ye customary Terms in like manner as y^e
aforesaid Earl of Arundel hath paid and been accustomed to pay
for the same severally in Times past SAVING to Us Our Heirs and
Successors ALL other Profits as well casual as others arising in y^e
said Hundreds of Dempforde Manewoode and Boseham aforesaid
Amerciaments AND that ye aforesaid Earl of Arundel and his Heirs
may for Ever have and perceive ALL and singular such Profits as are
called Mises[4] and other the Profits whatsoever of their Tenants in
the aforesaid County of Salop and in the Marches of Wales which
he ye said Earl and his Ancestors have in Times past had or been
accustomed to have at ye first Success and entry into their Lands
before the making of a certain Act set forth in the Session of Parliament holden by Prorogation at Westminster on ye 4th Day of
February in the 27th year of ye Reign of Our late most dear Father and
there continued and holden to and until ye 14th Day of April then next
ensuing concerning the administering of Laws and Justice in Wales
AND that they ye said Earl and his Heirs may have hold and keep

[3] Perhaps Anesforde.
[4] The Word *Mises* has various significations, one of which is (and will apply here)
a Customary Present given by the Welch to every new Prince of Wales.

within the Precinct of their said Lordships in ye said County of Salop and in the Marches of Wales[5] Courts Baron Leets and Views of Frankpledge And all and singular Things to the same Court appertaining And that they may have within the same Lordships and Views of Frankpledge Wayfe Shayfe Infanthef[6] Outfanthef[7] Treasure-trove Deodands Goods and Chattels of Felons and of Persons condemned or outlawed for Felony or Murther or of those put in Exigent for Felony or Murther *And also Wreck of the Sea Wharfage and Customs of Aliens in ye same Manor as he the said Earl and his ancestors have had in Times past before the making of the Act aforesaid The aforesaid Act or any Thing in ye same Act contained notwithstanding* We have also granted and Do by these Presents for Us Our Heirs and Successors grant to ye before named Earl and his Heirs That they may for Ever have All and all manner of Fines for Trespasses Contempts and other Offences whatsoever And Fines for Licence of Agreement Amerciaments and All Redemptions Issues and Penalties forfeited and to be from henceforth forfeited and All Forfeitures[8] whatsoever Year[8] Day and Waste and Strip And all Things that to Us Our Heirs and Successors might belong concerning such Year Day Waste and Strip as well of all their Men as all their Tenants Entire-Tenants and not Entire-Tenants Residents and Non-Residents and other Residents whomsoever of and in All ye Lordships Manors Lands Tenements Possessions Fees Hundreds and Hereditaments whatsoever of ye aforesaid Earl and his Heirs Although they ye same Men Tenants or Residents be the Tenants or Ministers of Us or of Our Heirs or Successors in what Courts soever of Us Our Heirs and Successors it shall happen that such Men or Tenants Residents and Non-Residents and other Residents shall be adjudged to be fined and amerced forfeit Issues and Penalties and Year Day and Waste and Strip and such like Forfeitures as well before Us Our Heirs and Successors and before Us Our Heirs and Successors in the Chancery of Us Our Heirs and Successors and before ye Treasurer and Barons of the Exchequer of Us Our Heirs and Successors And before ye Barons of the Exchequer of Us Our Heirs and Successors

---

[5] I have translated all these Words in the plural number though they are not terminated in ye Latin Exemplification of course they ascertain not whether the words apply to the singular or plural number. I suppos'd the Grant might mean a Court in each Lordship.

[6] *Infanthef* is a Privilege granted to Lords of Certain Manors to judge any Thief taken within their Fee.

[7] *Outfanthef*, a Privilege whereby a Lord can call any Man dwelling within his own Fee, and taken for Felony in any other place and to judge him in his own Court.

[8] *Year, Day, Waste, and Strip* " Year, Day, and Waste," is a part of the King's Prerogative whereby he challengeth the Profits of their Lands and Tenements for a Year and a Day who are attainted of petit Treason or Felony, whoever is Lord of ye Manor whereto ye Lands or Tenements belong; and he may in ye end *waste* ye Tenements, &c., Unless the Lord of the Fee agree with him for Redemption of such Waste *Strip* is ye Right of ye King to take Wood, &c., from off the premises during the Year and Day.

And also before the Justices of the Bench of Us Our Heirs and Suc-
cessors And before yᵉ Coroner or Coroners of Us Our Heirs and
Successors And before yᵉ Steward and Marshal and Clerk of the
Market of the Household of Us Our Heirs and Successors for the
Time being or any or either of them and in other yᵉ Courts of
Us Our Heirs and Successors whatsoever as before yᵉ Justices in
Eyre for Pleas of the Crown Common Pleas and Pleas of the
Forest the Justices for taking the Assizes and Goal-Delivery or
the Justices assigned to hear and determine Trespasses and Felonies
and other yᵉ Justices of Us Our Heirs and Successors as well in
the Presence as in the Absence of Us Our Heirs and·Successors
WHICH Fines Amerciaments Redemptions Issues and Penalties
Year Day Waste Strip and Forfeitures would have belonged to Us
Our Heirs and Successors if they had not been granted to the
before-named Earl and his aforesaid Heirs So AS THAT they yᵉ said
Earl and his Heirs may by themselves or by their Bailiffs and
Ministers for Ever levy perceive and have All and singular the
aforesaid Fines Amerciaments Redemptions Issues Penalties and
Forfeitures and each of them as well of such Men as of such
Tenants Entire-Tenants and not Entire-Tenants Residents and
Non-Residents and of other Residents whomsoever and of each of
them and all Things which to Us Our Heirs and Successors could
belong concerning Year Day and Waste or Strip aforesaid *without
the Interruption or Impeachment of Us Our Heirs or Successors
the Justices Escheators Sheriffs Coroners Bailiffs or other ye
Officers or Ministers of Us or of Our Heirs or Successors whomsoever* ALTHOUGH the same Men or Tenants Entire-Tenants and
not Entire-Tenants Residents and Non-Residents and other Residents *are or shall be the Officers or Ministers of Us Our Heirs and
Successors or could elsewhere* have in anywise held of Us Our
Heirs or Successors or of others WE HAVE ALSO granted and by
these Presents Do for Us Our Heirs and Successors grant to·yᵉ
aforesaid Earl of Arundel and his Heirs that they may for Ever
have the Chattels as well of their Men as of all their Tenants
Entire-Tenants and not Entire-Tenants Residents and Non-
Residents and of other Residents whomsoever of and in All and
singular their Lordships Manors Lands Tenements Hundreds
Liberties Franchises Possessions and Hereditaments whatsoever of
Heretics Lollards of Traitors as well for HIGH AS FOR PETIT TREASON[8]
of Murtherers Felons Fugitives Outlaws condemned attainted and
convicted persons and of those put in Exigent and of every of them
ALTHOUGH they the same Men Tenants and Residents shall be the
Tenants Ministers or Officers of Us Our Heirs or Successors So
AS that if any of the Men or Tenants Residents and Non-Residents
and other such Residents for any his Offence or Mis-Deed whatsoever of what Kind Nature or Sort soever it shall be ought to
lose Life or Limb or shall fly and will not abide Judgment or shall
commit any other crime whatsoever for which he ought to lose his

---

[8] " Proditorum, tam majorum quam minorum."

Goods and Chattels in what place soever Justice ought to be done
upon him whether in ye Court of Us Our Heirs or Successors or in
any Court whatsoever ALL AND SINGULAR the same Goods and
Chattels may be the aforesaid Earl's and his Heirs AND that they
ye said Earl and his Heirs may have the Chattels of Felons condemned or convicted for what Reason soever of Felons of themselves of Fugitives the Escapes of Felons and the Fines whatsoever
for the same Escapes in any of the Courts whatsoever of Us Our
Heirs and Successors as well before Us Our Heirs and Successors
as others the Justices Judges and Ministers of Us Our Heirs and
Successors whomsoever or any them to be assessed or made AND
ALSO the Chattels of any person soever put in Exigent for Felony
AND ALSO the Chattels of Fugitives Outlaws and condemned Per-
sons whomsoever and the Chattels of what Sort soever confiscated
as well of their Men as of all their Tenants Entire-Tenants
Residents and Non-Residents and of other Residents whomsoever
within all and singular their Lordships Manors Lands Tenements
Possessions and Hereditaments whatsoever ALTHOUGH the said
Tenants are not Entire-Tenants of him ye said Earl and of his
Heirs OR they the same Tenants or the said Men or the said
Residents or any of them may be the Tenants Officers or Ministers
of Us [9] our Heirs or Successors AND that those Goods and Chattels
be ye aforesaid Earl's and his Heirs AND that it be lawful for the
aforesaid Earl and his Heirs or their Ministers *without the
Hindrance of Us Our Heirs or Successors the Justices Escheators
Sheriffs Coroners or of others the Bailiffs or Ministers of Us Our
Heirs or Successors whomsoever to seize All and singular the
Goods and Chattels aforesaid and to take seize and retain them all
To the Use and Behoof of him ye said Earl and his Heirs
Although the same Goods and Chattels may have been before
seized by Us or the Ministers of Us Our Heirs or Successors*
WE HAVE ALSO GRANTED and Do by these Presents for Us AND [10]
Our Heirs grant to the aforesaid Earl of Arundel and his Heirs
THAT they shall and may for Ever have and hold VIEW OF FRANK-
PLEDGE [11] and whatsoever doth to such Views [11] belong or appertain
or which to Views of Frankpledge [11] may hereafter belong AND
that they may have All the Goods and Chattels which are called
Wayff or Strey Deodands Treasure-trove and other Things and
Chattels formed of and in All and singular the Lordships Manors
Lands Tenements Possessions Hundreds Liberties Franchises and
Hereditaments whatsoever of him ye said Earl and his Heirs AND
the Goods and Chattels called MANOUVRES [12] taken or to be taken
with any Person DISAVOWED [13] by such Person in any Place soever
within ye Lordships Manors Lands Tenements Possessions Hundreds Liberties Franchises Hereditaments aforesaid before any

---

[9] This Word is not in the Exemplification; supposed to be a mistake of the Clerk.
[10] This Word is not in the Exemplification.   [11] See note *five* in page 3.
[12] These were Goods taken in ye hands of an apprehended Thief.
[13] That is, who could not justify how they were come by.

Judge whomsoever *And that ye aforesaid Earl and his Heirs may for Ever have all Deodands within their Lorships Manors Lands Tenements Possessions Hundreds Liberties Franchises and Hereditaments whatsoever And also the Wreck of the Sea in any wise happening in any of the Coasts and Arms of the Sea adjoining to the aforesaid Lordships Manors Lands Tenements Possessions Hundreds Liberties Franchises and Hereditaments And all Things which to such Wrecks of the Sea and Deodands in ye same Lordships Manors Lands Tenements Possessions Hundreds Liberties Franchises and Hereditaments do belong And that such Goods and Chattels called Wayfe Straye Treasure-trove and other Things and Chattels found Goods and Chattels called Manouvres [14] Deodands and Wreck of the Sea and all Things which to such Deodands and Wreck of the Sea do belong be for Ever the aforesaid Earl's and his Heirs And that it may be lawful for them by themselves or by their Bailiffs or Ministers to seize and possess themselves of All and singular the aforesaid Goods and Chattels which are called Wayfe and Straye Treasure-trove and other Things or Chattels found Goods and Chattels called Manouvres [14] Deodands and Wreck of the Sea and of all Things to such Deodands and Wreck of the Sea belonging as often as and when they shall happen And all and singular the same to seize and take And ye same to retain To ye Use and Behoof of him ye said now Earl his Heirs and Successors without ye Disturbance Molestation or [16] Hindrance of Us Our Heirs or Successors the Justices Escheators Sheriffs Coroners or others ye Bailiffs of Us Our Heirs or Successors or of other Persons whomsoever* ALTHOUGH the same may have been seized by Us Our Heirs or Successors or any the Bailiffs Officers or Ministers of Us Our Heirs or Successors AND FURTHER We have granted and by these Presents for Us Our Heirs and Successors do grant to the before named Earl and his Heirs THAT they may by their proper Stewards and Bailiffs in all and singular their Lordships Manors Lands Tenements Possessions Hundreds Liberties Franchises and Hereditaments have and make the Assay and Assize of Bread Wine and Beer and of all sorts of other Victuals Weights and Measures whatsoever and of all other Things which now do or hereafter may belong to y⁰ Office of Clerk of the Market of the Houshold of Us Our Heirs or Successors with y⁰ Punishment thereof AND to do and exercise whatever now doth or hereafter may belong to that Office as often as and whensoever it shall be needful and necessary As FULLY as the same Clerk of the Market of the Houshold of Us Our Heirs or Successors should or ought to do in the presence of Us Our Heirs or Successors if this present Grant was not made to the aforesaid Earl and his Heirs AND that they y⁰ said Earl and his Heirs may have all manner of Amerciaments Fines and other Profits thence-coming to be taken and levyed by them and their Ministers without y⁰ Impeachment of Us Our Heirs or Successors the Clerk of the Market or others the Ministers of

---

[14] See note *twelve* in page 5.   [16] This Word is not in the Exemplification.

Us Our Heirs or Successors whomsoever So AS THAT ye aforesaid Clerk of ye Market of ye Houshold of Us Our Heirs or Successors may not enter the aforesaid Lordships Manors Lands Tenements Possessions Hundreds Liberties Franchises or Hereditaments to do or exercise any Thing therein that now doth or hereafter shall in anywise belong to his Office *And further We have granted and by these presents for Us Our Heirs and Successors Do grant to ye aforesaid Earl of Arundel and his Heirs that they may for ever have Free Warren in all their Lordships and Manors and in all and singular their Demesne Lands wheresoever they shall be And also Free Chace in All their Lordships and Woods Altho' ye same Lordships Manors Demesne Lands and Woods are or shall be within ye Metes of the Forests*[16] *of Us Our Heirs and Successors So as that no Justice of ye Forest Forester Officer or Minister of Us Our Heirs or Successors Nor any other Person may enter those Manors Lordships Lands or Woods to chace*[17] *or to take any Thing therein which to Warren or Chace doth belong Or to do*[18] *any Thing that to ye Office of Justice of the Forest or to ye Office of Forester or of any other Officer or Minister of Us Our Heirs and Successors of the Forests or Chaces of Us Our Heirs or Successors in anywise now doth or shall appertain without the Licence of the aforesaid Earl and his Heirs And further We being willing to give more ample Security of the Grants Liberties Franchises and Immunities aforesaid in form aforesaid by Us granted to him ye said Earl and his heirs for the Reasons aforesaid And that they ye said Earl and his Heirs may be able in future the more quietly and securely to use and enjoy the aforesaid Grants Liberties Franchises Acquittances and Immunities of Our more abundant Grace certain Knowledge and mere Motion aforesaid Have for Us Our Heirs and Successors granted to him ye said Earl and his Heirs That altho' they or their Heirs shall from henceforth upon any Contingency not use or shall abuse any of the Grants Liberties Franchises Acquittances and*[19] *Immunities aforesaid to them at present by Us granted Yet shall it be lawful for him ye said Earl and his Heirs to use and enjoy from Time to Time afterwards ye same Grants Liberties Franchises Acquittances and Immunities Wherefore We Will And do by these Presents for Us Our Heirs and Successors grant and command That ye aforesaid Earl and his Heirs may for ever have and hold All and singular the Gifts Grants Liberties Acquittances Franchises and Immunities aforesaid And that they may fully use and enjoy all and singular the same and every of them without the Impeachment Hindrance Disturbance Molestation or Grievance of Us Our Heirs or Successors the Justices Escheators Sheriffs or others ye Bailiffs or Ministers of Us or Our Heirs or Successors whomsoever*

---

[16] In ye plural Number in ye Exemplification.

[17] *Fugandum*, which implys also to *hunt*.

[18] The Word *facere*, or a Word of some such import, is wanting in the Exemplification.

[19] This Word is not in the Exemplification.

*And We Will and do for Us Our Heirs and Successors grant That
upon ye Exhibiting and Shewing of these Letters Patent or of ye
Inrolment thereof as well before Us in ye Chancery of us Our Heirs
and Successors as before ye Justices of either Bench of Us Our
Heirs and Successors and before ye Treasurer and Barons of ye
Exchequer of Us Our Heirs and Successors And also before ye
Justices and Commissioners of Us Our Heirs and Successors as
well in all and singular ye Courts and Places of Record of Us Our
Heirs and Successors as in all other Courts and Places whatsoever
throughout Our whole Kingdom of England concerning any Thing
or Things in ye same Our Letters Patent contained or specifyed
The same Letters Patent and all the Grants therein be forthwith
and imediately valid and allowed to the aforesaid Earl and his Heirs
And that they ye said Treasurers and Barons Justices Commissioners
and others whosoever to whom it appertains shall from Time to
Time make and cause to be made due Allowance of and in All and
singular the same Premises and that they ye said Earl and his
Heirs and every of them be from Time to Time towards Us Our
Heirs and Successors altogether discharged and do depart Quit of
all and all manner of Charges and Demands required of them in
any such Courts and places by the same Courts and Places contrary
to the Gifts Grants Confirmations Liberties Franchises Privileges
and Immunities aforesaid Any Variation Uncertainty Contrariety
Repugnance Neglect Omission undue or untrue Recital of ye Names
or Words Or any other Matter Cause or Thing whatsoever notwithstanding Although express Mention be not made in these Presents
of ye true yearly value or of any other Value or Certainty of the
Premises or of any of them or of other Gifts or Grants heretofore
made by Us or by any of Our Progenitors to ye before-named
Henry Earl of Arundel Or any Statute Act Ordinance Proviso or
Restriction made set forth ordained or provided Or any other
Matter Cause or Thing whatsoever to ye Contrary thereof in anywise
notwithstanding* IN TESTIMONY whereof We have caused these
Our Letters to be made patent WITNESS Ourself at Westminster
the 27th Day of February in the first year of Our Reign

P. Hare.

By the Queen herself and of the Date aforesaid By Authority
of Parliament.

Inrolled.

Indorsed thus:—

> This Charter is inrolled before the Lady the Queen at West-
> minster of Record in the Term of St. Hilary in the 32nd
> year of the Reign of the Lady Elizabeth now Queen of
> England among the Pleas of the Queen—*Roll* 3.
>
> Translated from the Original Exemplification under Seal y*
> 18 March 1784.

JOHN FURMAN.

Stationer, Inner Temple Lane.

MANOR ROYALTY AND FREE WARREN OF HAYLING, IN THE COUNTY OF SOUTHAMPTON.

COPY., CHARTER OF FREE WARREN.

Among the Records deposited in the Public Record Office, London, to wit: Patent Rolls, 14, James 1st, part 25, No. 4, it is thus contained :—

Of a Grant to Thomas Earl of Arundel, to him and his heirs. THE KING, to all to whom, &c., Greeting. Know ye that we, as well for and in consideration of the sum of twenty shillings of lawful money of England, at the receipt of our Exchequer at Westminster, well and faithfully paid to our use by our beloved and faithful subject and cousin Thomas Earl of Arundel and Surrey, Knight of the Illustrious Order of the Garter, and one of our Privy Council, whereof we confess ourselves to be fully satisfied and paid, and the same Thomas Earl of Arundel and Surrey, his heirs, executors, and administrators, to be thereof acquitted and discharged for ever by these presents as for divers other good causes and considerations us hereunto specially moving: Of our special grace and of our certain knowledge and mere motion, will and by these presents for us, our heirs and successors, do grant to the aforesaid Thomas Earl of Arundel and Surrey, his heirs and assigns, that he, his heirs and assigns, and every of them for ever, have free warren in their baronies, lordships, and manors of Greystock and Brough-upon-the-Sands, and in every of them, with all their rights, members, and appurtenances in our county of Cumberland, and in their manor or lordship of Rowcliff, otherwise Rocliff, with all its rights, members, and appurtenances in our said county of Cumberland, and in all other their lands, tenements, meadows, feedings, pastures, woods, underwoods, woodlands, wastes, furze, heaths, marshes, commons, and hereditaments in the baronies, manors, lordships, hamlets, vills, parishes, and places of Graystock, Brough-upon-the-Sands, and Rowcliff, otherwise Rocliff, and in each and every of them in our said county of Cumberland: And also in their manors or lordships of Doufton, Hoffe, and Drybeck, and in every

2

of them, with all their rights, members, and appurtenances in our
said county of Westmoreland, and in all other lands, tenements,
meadows, pastures, woods, underwoods, woodlands, wastes, furze,
heaths, marshes, commons, and hereditaments of the aforesaid
Thomas Earl of Arundel and Surrey, in the manors, lordships, vills,
parishes, hamlets, and places of Doufton, Hoff, and Drybeck aforesaid, and in each and every of them, in our said county of Westmoreland: And also free warren in their manors or lordships of
Keninghall, Lopham, Wynfarthing, Heywood, Halwick in Thetford,
Croxt on Santon, Shelfhanger, Faresfield, Boyland, Lancasters,
Banham, Hockam in Banham, Garboldsham, Pakenhams in Garboldsham, Little Framlingham, otherwise Earls Framlingham,
Ditchingham, Siseland, Loddon, Garsham, Harlston, Forrencett,
Acle, Harvergate, South Walsham, Suffield, Hanworth, Sheringham, Wells near the Sea, Castle, North Wotton, and Roydon, with
all their rights, members, and appurtenances in our county of
Norfolk, and in all other lands, tenements, meadows, feedings,
pastures, woods, woodlands, underwoods, wastes, commons, furze,
heaths, moors, marshes, and hereditaments of the aforesaid Thomas
Earl of Arundel and Surrey, in the manors, lordships, hamlets,
places, parishes, vills, and hundreds of Kenninghall, Lopham,
Wynfarthing, Heywood, Halwick in Thetford, Croxt on Santon,
Shelfhanger, Faresfield, Boyland, Lancasters, Banham, Hockham
in Banham, Garboldsham, Pakenham in Garboldsham, Little Framlingham, otherwise Earls Framlingham, Ditchingham, Siseland,
Loddon, Garsham, Harleston, Forencett, Acle, Halvergate, South
Walsham, Suffield, Hanworth, Sheringham, Wells, Castle Rysing,
North Wotton, Rydon, Guilcross, Lamdich, Southgrenehoe, Free-
bridge, Gallowe, Brothercrosse, and Smethdon, and in any and
every of them in our said county of Norfolk: And also free warren
in their manors or lordships of Bungay, Bungay Soke, Priorie,
Westwick, Channons, Downham, Merces, and Rushforth, and in
any and every of them in our county of Suffolk, and in all other
their lands, tenements, meadows, feedings, pastures, woods, underwoods, woodlands, furze, heaths, marshes, wastes, commons, and
hereditaments in the manors, lordships, vills, parishes, hamlets, and
places of Bungay, Bungay Soke, Priorie, Westwick, Channons,
Downham, Merces, and Rushforth, and in any and every of them
in our said county of Suffolk: And also free warren in their manor
or lordship of Glossop, otherwise Glossopdale, with all its rights,
members, and appurtenances in our county of Derby, and in all
their lands, tenements, meadows, feedings, pastures, woods, underwoods, woodlands, furze, heath, marshes, wastes, commons, and

hereditaments in Glossop, otherwise Glossopdale aforesaid, in our said county of Derby: And also free warren in their manors or lordships of Idsall with Shiffenhall, Wrockwardine, otherwise Rockward, Chesevardine, Tasley, Sutton, Maddock, Corpham, Wenne, Loppington, and Hinstock, and in any and every of them in our county of Salop, and in all other lands, tenements, meadows, feedings, pastures, woods, underwoods, woodlands, wastes, furze, heaths, marshes, commons, and hereditaments of the aforesaid Thomas Earl of Arundel and Surrey, in the manors, lordships, vills, parishes, hamlets, fields, and places of Idsall, with Shiffenhall, Wrockwardine, otherwise Rockwardine, Cheswardine, Tasley, Sutton, Maddock, Corpham, Wemm, Loppington, Hinstock Wick, Priors, Lee Woodhouses, Drayton, Haughton, Stanton, Upton, Lysiat, Snellsell, Burlangton, Ashton, Layes, Diddlebury, Lifton, Culmington, and Quicksall, and in any and every of them in our county of Salop. And also free warren in their manors or lordships of Arundel, Offham, Bury, Shellinglye, Wespham, Warming-camp, Little Hampton, Beeding, Almadington, and Preston, with all their rights, members, and appurtenances, in our county of Sussex, and all other the lands, tenements, meadows, feedings, pastures, woods, underwoods, woodlands, wastes, furze, heaths, marshes, commons, and hereditaments, of the aforesaid Thomas Earl of Arundel and Surrey, in the manors, lordships, vills, parishes, hamlets, and places of Arundel, Offham, Bury, Shellingley, Wepham, Warming-camp, Little Hampton, Beeding, Almardington, Preston, Medhome Park, Langhurst, Blackbrooke, Tamefold, Elmsdene, and Cudlowe, and in any and every of them in our said county of Sussex. And also free warren in their manor or lordship of Wiboston in all their lands and tenements in Wiboston aforesaid, in our said county of Bedford. And also free warren in their manors or lordships of Dowdikehall, in Sutterton and Digby, with all their rights, members, and appurtenances in our county of Lincoln, and in all their lands and tenements in Dowdikehall, in Sutterton and Digby, and in either or any of them in our said county of Lincoln. 𝕬𝖓𝖉 𝖆𝖑𝖘𝖔 free warren within their island called Haylinge, and in all the lands, tenements, meadows, feedings, pastures, woods, woodlands, wastes, furze, heaths, marshes, commons, and hereditaments, of the afore-said Thomas Earl of Arundel and Surrey, within the island afore-said, in our county of Southampton, being or not being parcel of our Duchy of Lancaster, any statute, act, ordinance, custom, law, or provision, to the contrary thereof, in anywise notwithstanding. And notwithstanding that our writs or writ of *ad quod dampnum* or *quo warranto*, or any other writ, therefore, heretofore, had or prosecuted, to be had or prosecuted, have or hath not first issued before the sealing of these our Letters Patent. Further, we give, and by these presents for us, our heirs and successors, of our more abundant special grace, and of our certain knowledge and mere motion do grant to the aforesaid Thomas Earl of Arundel and Surrey, his heirs and assigns, from time to time, for ever in all and singular, the said baronies, manors, and lordships, and in any and every of them, and in all and singular their lands, tenements, meadows, feedings, pastures, woods, wastes, furze, heaths, marshes, and hereditaments aforesaid, and in any part thereof full free and entire licence, power, and authority, from time to time, as and whensoever he, his heirs, or assigns shall please of reducing either, or any parcel thereof, into severality, and making park and parks, warren and warrens thereof, and of hedging and enclosing the same with ditches, hedges, walls, pales, or in any manner as a park or parks, warren or warrens and in the same park or in the same parks, warren, and warrens, and any and every of them so made and enclosed, to be made and enclosed, to have hold and enjoy the rights franchises, prerogatives, liberties, properties, and benefit of park, or free warren, in the same and any and every of them : Further we give, and by these presents for us, our heirs and successors, do grant to the aforesaid Thomas Earl of Arundel and Surrey, his heirs, and assigns, full free and entire liberty, licence, power, and authority, from time to time, to stock, fill, have, and keep all and singular the aforesaid baronies, manors, lordships, lands, tenements, wastes, commons, furze, heaths, marshes, and hereditaments, or any part or parcel of any or either of the same, as well enclosed as not enclosed with stags, deer, hares, rabbits, pheasants, partridges, wild ducks, and other beasts and birds of whatever kind in a wild state, at the will and pleasure of the same Thomas Earl of Arundel and Surrey, his heirs, and assigns for ever : And also that he, the afore-said Thomas Earl of Arundel and Surrey, his heirs, and assigns, may, and may be able to have, hold, and enjoy, in the same baronies, manors, lordships, and in any and every of them, and the lands, tenements, wastes, commons, furze, heaths, moors, and heredita-ments [aforesaid], the liberties, rights, privileges, properties, and benefit of park and parks, and free warren and warrens henceforth for ever : Also we give, and by these presents for us, our heirs, and successors, do grant, order, and command, that the aforesaid Thomas, Earl of Arundel and Surrey, his heirs, and assigns, may freely, lawfully, well and quietly have, and hold, use, and enjoy, and hence-forth for ever may, and may be able to have, hold, use, and enjoy, the aforesaid baronies, manors, lordships, lands, tenements, meadows, feedings, pastures, woods, wastes, commons, and hereditaments aforesaid, and every or any parcel thereof, park and parks, warren and warrens, together with all and singular liberties, privileges, rights, and commodities which to such park and free warren, or either of them appertain, or may appertain, in anywise howsoever: And if it shall happen that the aforesaid baronies, manors, lordships, parks, warrens, lands, tenements, meadows, feedings, pastures, woods, wastes, commons, and hereditaments, or any of them, or any parcel thereof, be within the metes and bounds of any our forests, parks or chase, or be to the prejudice of any of our liberties in the same, or be to the prejudice of any persons within any our manors, or that any one of our subjects having common in any such our manor be from the same common altogether excluded, then as to such parts or parcels thereof which are so within the metes and bounds of our forests, parks, or chases, or whereby any one of our subjects having common in any such our manor, may be from the same common altogether excluded, this our grant shall be void and of no force, as to that only; but as to the residue of the premises which are not within the metes and bounds of our forests, parks, or chases, nor whereby any one of our subjects having common in any such our manor, may be from the same common excluded: We will that this our grant shall stand and remain in full force and virtue, any thing in these presents to the contrary thereof in anywise notwithstanding: MOREOVER we will, and by these presents for us, our heirs and successors, do grant, order and command that no one enter, or presume to enter the park or parks, free warren or free warrens aforesaid, or either or any of them, to pursue, hunt, hawk, chase, torment, or in anywise disturb or take anything there which to such park or parks, warren or warrens appertain, or ought or might appertain, nor to do or commit anything in the same park or parks, warren or warrens, which may or might be to the loss, hurt, or prejudice of the park or parks, warren or warrens aforesaid, or the liberties, rights, or privileges of the same park or parks, warren or warrens, or either of them, without the will and licence of the aforesaid Thomas Earl of Arundel and Surrey, or the heirs or assigns of the same Thomas Earl of Arundel and Surrey, under the pain in the statutes and ordinance of this our Kingdom of England for conserving and keeping parks and free warrens passed and provided; and also under the pain of forfeiture to us of Ten Pounds of lawful money of England to the use of the aforesaid Thomas Earl of Arundel and Surrey, his heirs and assigns, in the name of us, our heirs and successors, to be levied, recovered and received by the hands of the

sheriffs of the several counties aforesaid severally and respectively
for the time being, so often as any such pain or pains shall happen
to be forfeited, and by the same sheriffs of the several counties
aforesaid severally and respectively for the time being, to be paid
and delivered to the aforesaid Thomas Earl of Arundel and Surrey,
his heirs and assigns.   Wherefore, we will and by these presents
grant, order, and for us, our heirs and successors, command the
sheriffs of the several counties aforesaid severally and respectively
for the time being, that when and so often as any such pain or pains
hereafter may or shall be lost or forfeited by any person or persons,
the same sheriffs of the several counties aforesaid respectively for the
time being, immediately after the collection or levying of the same
forfeiture, shall pay or cause to be paid the same Ten Pounds, or
any other pain so recovered from time to time, to the aforesaid
Thomas Earl of Arundel and Surrey, his heirs and assigns.   And
these our Letters Patent, or an enrolment of the same, shall be
from time to time a sufficient warrant and discharge to the aforesaid
sheriffs of the several counties aforesaid severally and respectively
for the time being in this behalf, against us, our heirs and successors, as well as in the Exchequer of us, our heirs and successors,
as in all other the courts of us, our heirs and successors whatsoever,
upon the sole shewing forth of these our Letters Patent, or an
enrolment of the same, without any other writ or warrant in this
behalf, to be sued forth, obtained or prosecuted from us, our heirs
or successors, in anywise howsoever.   And we will by these presents
grant to the aforesaid Thomas Earl of Arundel and Surrey, that he
may have, and shall have these our Letters Patent, in due manner
made and sealed, as well under our Great Seal of England as under
the seal of our Duchy of Lancaster, without fine in the hanaper,
&c.   Although express mention, &c.   In testimony, whereof, &c.
Witness, the King at Westminster, the 7th day of March.

BY WARRANT OF THE COMMISSIONERS.

THE SMUGGLERS.

A TALE.

AT the commencement of the latter half of the last century, and immediately after Byng's unhappy failure off Minorca, Ralph Rogers and Peter Crasler, two young men, natives of Hayling Island, once more visited this peaceful spot in the fond expectation of finding their much loved and never-forgotten home, after having passed many an eventful year, and experienced many a hardship together, as seamen, on board one of His Majesty's ships, then just returned from a foreign station. A singular fatality attended them both. Parents and near kindred were all gone; the unsparing hand of death had swept them all away, some in the fulness of age, and others in the greenness of youth; and their home—that only solace in the hour of toil and peril, the endearing remembrance of which had been unction to their wearied and troubled spirits whilst bending beneath the lash of the task-master and the frown of despotism—was in the hands of strangers, and refused them a shelter. Such of their more distant kindred as survived, looked upon them with eyes of suspicion, and disowned consanguinity. None would entertain the remotest recollection of them, save one innocent maiden, who, previous to Ralph's departure, had, in modest simplicity, plighted her troth with him. To the dwelling of Jane Pitt, therefore, Ralph's steps instinctively wandered; and from her kindness, and from the frank and hearty welcome of her parents, his generous heart soon learned to forget its grievous disappointment, and to infuse some portion of its altered feeling into that of his brother adventurer.

At this time smuggling was carried on to an immense height on the southern shores of Britain: large gangs of daring and outrageous characters violated the laws at mid-day, and set the constituted authorities for its suppression at defiance. It was no uncommon occurrence for the "gauger" and his military assistants to be dragged from their posts, and, under horrible threats of prompt and fearful vengeance, compelled to assist in performing that which they were employed to prevent. Government, too, weakened by the distractions of its counsels, and the struggles of party, had lost the energy requisite to cope with these depredators on its resources;

and instead of pursuing the prompt and decisive measures which
the crisis required, depended mostly upon the aid of informers,
secretly hired and paid, who were either the very lowest assistants
to the illicit trader, or men who had been actively employed in
more prominent situations, but whose notorious deficiency of
"honesty among thieves," had rendered them outcasts even from
their former associates. Little good, however, resulted from this
measure, for the information obtained from these impure sources
was often found not only to be erroneous, but the very reverse of
the actual fact: after various weak devices, therefore, which
strengthened rather than remedied the evil, the expedient was
adopted of offering the smuggler an amnesty for past aggression,
if he entered within a given period, as a common seaman, into the
naval service.*

Hayling Island, from its proximity to that hot-bed of illegal
traffic, the Isle of Wight, has ever been found a convenient
receptacle for contraband articles, and, at the period of which we
are speaking, formed the depôt from whence they were distributed
through all the eastern part of Hampshire and western portion of
Sussex. It is not therefore to be wondered at, that Ralph and
Peter should, in the absence of more honest means of gaining a
livelihood, look to this employment as most suitable to their
tempers, soured as they were by bitter disappointment, and congenial to their acquired habits of hardihood. It moreover presented
to their perverted ideas, an opportunity, as they thought, of
retaliating upon the government, for the hardships and severities
they had endured in its service; for they had both been impressed
into it, and had served under a severe disciplinarian. After remaining, therefore, a few days with Goodman Pitt, they joined one of
the most numerous and daring gangs of smugglers on the coast,
and shortly afterwards found themselves in a comfortable, though
rather awkward berth on board the Susan, commanded by the
notorious Will Watch. This man, who, for a series of years was
one of the most successful smugglers ever known, after pursuing a
career unprecedented in the annals of his vocation, eventually fell
in an engagement with one of His Majesty's Sloops of war off the
back of the Isle of Wight. His real name was Gill Brown, and
his memory has been kept alive, and will long remain so, by an

* Smollet, in his continuation of Hume, highly praises this measure, though, in the
same chapter, he acknowledges that the condition of English seamen at that period
presented anything but an incentive to exchange liberty and unbounded freedom of
action, for virtual imprisonment, and strict discipline. Indeed the offer was only
accepted by the actual outlaw; to others, it betrayed a weakness of which they did not
fail to take advantage.

excellent and well-known song, composed in commemoration of his fate. His ship, the Susan, which was named after his sweetheart, Susan Guy, of Leigh, near Havant, carried eighteen brass guns, was amply manned by a crew of desperate outlaws, and altogether admirably adapted for the employment in which she was engaged: she was the fastest sailer then known, and this circumstance, joined to Will's perfect knowledge of the Dutch and English coasts, had rendered him an object of intense anxiety to every British commander in the English seas. Will, however, by address and stratagem worthy of a better cause, contrived for years to elude the vigilance of his foes; and in all probability would for the time have escaped the doom that overtook him, had not the sudden clearing-up of a fog shown him to be within short range shot of the ship that captured him.

With this bold and hardy character, Ralph Rogers and Peter Crasler made several voyages; and from his instruction and ample practice, became initiated into all the secrets and mysteries of smuggling. Whatever of repugnance they had entertained for depravity and vicious action; whatever of reverence they had felt for moral and religious duties, was completely annihilated whilst associating with Will Watch and his outlawed companions. An almost continual state of intoxication, aided by the terrors they naturally felt of being, sooner or later, overtaken by the strong arm of justice, kept their minds in a fearful state of excitement, and rendered them desperate in the extreme, and ever ready to partici-pate in deeds of danger and violence. At length, however, the image of Jane began to soften their artificial ferocity, and create better and more natural feelings in the breast of Ralph. On these occasions he would brood over the sad necessity which compelled him to remain separated from the only object that linked him to humanity, and pour forth his thoughts into the ear of his old companion and friend. Peter, too, though not under the fascinating control of female witchery, found, after a time, a restlessness and impatience for which he could not account, and always lent a ready and willing attention to Ralph's complainings. Love, and the desire of change, at last prevailed; the "Susan" was left to her fate; and the friends, with pockets well replenished by the gains she had made, once more visited the scenes of their infancy and the seat of their early home. Here a different reception awaited them than what they had formerly experienced; Goodman Pitt's favourable report of their good qualities, and the knowledge that they had been engaged in a calling which many of the inhabitants of the Island actively followed, produced a marked and sensible

3

change in their favour; and they now found a hearty and cheerful welcome, where, on the former occasion, they had experienced nothing but harshness and rude incivility.

Soon after their arrival, Ralph rewarded the affection of Jane Pitt; and Peter, more out of compliment to them than for any other reason, also "changed his condition." For a time all was gaiety and pleasure; but when the novelty of living on shore had somewhat abated, and they began to feel the cares and wants attendant on their new situation, they found it necessary to look about them for employment. No great variety of choice awaited their decision; and even if there had, the little ability they possessed would not have allowed them to engage in any other than the one they had so lately followed. From necessity, therefore, more than choice, they once more resumed illicit trading, and very soon became known to all the neighbourhood as confirmed and established smugglers.

Success at first attended both their endeavours, but a twelvemonth had scarcely elapsed before the fickleness of fortune became painfully apparent to poor Peter. Loss after loss followed close upon each other, and a few months convinced him that he was ruined beyond redemption.

It was at this period that government discovered the inefficacy of her measures for the suppression of smuggling, and that her late offer of an amnesty to those smugglers who should enter into the naval service, had rather augmented the practice, than decreased it. As a last resource, therefore, the plan was adopted of offering a large reward and permanent employment, in a civil capacity, to such as should discover their lawless associates, and the means by which the system of smuggling was pursued with such unparalleled success.

Peter Crasler found himself a husband and a father, with no means of fulfilling these duties; without resources for his present support, or hope for the future; and incumbered by a heavy debt (incurred indeed for contraband articles, but which must be discharged before he could proceed further in his career) from which he never could hope, by fair means, to extricate himself. On the other hand, government had offered him the opportunity of retrieving his fortunes, a permanent and safe employment, and quick and efficient means of discharging the debt which oppressed him. His situation was without hope and friendless, and the temptation strong, besides, he himself had no security against the treachery of his accomplices, and surely, he thought, surrounded as he was by want and danger, there could be no harm in performing an act, which the law had made a duty, and his own distress a moral necessity. His decision was soon made, for his wants were powerful and pressing: his offer was as promptly accepted and immediate relief granted, accompanied by instructions to make all the observations he could, and to attend at the custom-house in London on a day named.

His absence was soon observed by his companions, for suspicion ever attaches itself to the poor and unfortunate as well as to the guilty; and his wife, being boisterously and roughly urged by Ralph Rogers and other smugglers, acknowledged her husband's apostacy. Consternation seized them all, for the knowledge Peter possessed forboded universal ruin. Ralph, in the bitterness of his rage, denounced him a villain, and swore eternal enmity against him, and prompt revenge. He renewed these threatening expressions in his cooler moments, and from the uncontrollable passion he evinced at the mention of Peter's name, and the reserve and gloomy silence he observed on other occasions, it was generally supposed that he meditated some signal act of vengeance. Poor Jane, who could in most matters soothe him into tameness and quietude, found her usual influence gone, and her endeavours to soften him met only by increased rage and vows of animosity; nothing daunted, however, by want of success, she resolved to renew her exertions upon every fitting occasion, and to keep a strict and guarded eye upon her husband's every action.

When the panic which had seized the smugglers upon the news of Peter's defection had somewhat subsided, they began to take measures for counteracting the effects which were naturally to be expected from it. With this view they emptied all the caverns on the south beach of the Island, and disposed of their commodities at as great a distance from home as safety would warrant. Having made everything secure, they suppressed their smuggling operations until the approaching storm was blown over, when they hoped to be enabled to resume them with greater safety.

Two months had now elapsed since Peter Crasler had left the Island, and the last quarter of an October moon warned the smugglers that the time of year best adapted for their pursuits was rapidly passing away unattended by the usual advantages. Peter knew the use made of the season likewise, and suddenly, in the dusk of the evening, made his appearance in the Island, attended by six dragoons. After giving his party directions to proceed onwards, and wait his arrival at that part of the road in the south parish where the two branches leading from the beach first meet, he hastily and alone sought his home; and in the embraces of his wife and chil derived a momentary and sincere delight. Tears, the constant companions of true affection, fell in copious streams from his eyes as he returned their caresses and thought of the character he had assumed to protect them: he devoutly blessed them in the fulness of his overflowing heart, and promising a speedy return, left them to join his companions; not, however, before his wife had informed him of the resentment of Ralph Rogers, and warned him to be careful of his presence.

The arrival of Peter and his dragoons was quickly spread through the Island, and their advance southward construed into a design to examine the caverns. Jane Rogers was one of the first made ac-quainted with this intelligence, and her mind became instantly oppressed by the most dreadful forebodings. Ralph had left home for Rowland's Castle, three miles to the north of Havant, early in the afternoon, and she began to hope that the sudden visit of Peter and the soldiers was unknown to him. She quickly, however, abandoned this hope when she thought how utterly impossible it was for such a body of men to advance through the heart of a smuggling country, with declared intentions of hostility, without tidings of their presence being instantaneously communicated over every part of it. She resolved, therefore, since she anticipated the most fatal consequences from a meeting between her husband and Peter, to do all in her power to prevent one; and as she knew not where to find the former, she determined to seek the latter, and to invoke him by the remembrance of their former friendship, and the obligations he was under to her and her parents in the hour of his distress, to avoid the sight of his former friend and companion, but now implacable enemy. With this view, poor Jane left the infant which smiled at her breast to the care of a neighbour, and sought her silent and solitary way to the shore, where from the information she had received, she was taught to believe that Peter had already arrived. As her dwelling stood in the north-east part of the Island, and no part of her way lay near the road, she had no opportunity of either making inquiry for her husband, or extending her informa-tion as to the advance of Peter and his party. Impelled forward, however, by her fears, she advanced at a rapid pace, and soon found herself at the caverns, the supposed object of search. Here all was silent, save when the hollow moaning of the night blast, and the sullen fury of the advancing wave, venting itself in surly murmurs on the shore, broke upon her attentive and listening ear. Should she remain, or proceed farther? Whilst she hesitated in agonizing uncertainty, the advance of lights from the westward determined her to stay beside the cavern belonging to her husband until their approach. There she stood, her eyeballs stretched to watch their motions, her mind totally absorbed by their fitful glare, and dead to every other object around.

Ralph Rogers had returned from Rowland's Castle earlier than was expected, and was "homewards wending his weary way" when Peter Craaler and his party passed him at a brisk trot, on the road between Havant and Langstone. Ralph soon guessed the purport of their visit, and, burning with revenge, internally vowed to wreak his vengeance, at all hazard, upon the apostate Peter. Arrived at Langstone, he found that the tide had for a time interrupted their progress. Here he endeavoured to procure a gun, but not being successful, he took boat and reached the Island ; where, under pre-tence of shooting wild fowl (for the season was remarkably severe), he borrowed, at the first house he came to, a heavy mud-stock, a species of musket capable of doing great execution at a long distance, which he amply loaded with heavy slugs. He had been here but a very short time before the heavy trampling of horses warned him of the approach of his foes: having ascertained the way they were advancing, he exerted his speed, and kept before them until they halted, at the meeting of the branch roads, for the arrival of Peter. Here he could restrain his impetuosity no longer; veiling himself under the darkness of the evening, he boldly advanced up to the mounted body of men, with the fixed determination of shooting Peter upon the spot. Happily for the latter he had not yet arrived. The surprise and intensity displayed by Ralph on discovering his absence, awakened the suspicions of the serjeant of the party, who, observing his agitated and threatening motions, and seeing him armed with a powerful and destructive engine, ordered two of his men to sieze and detain him. Ralph evaded the command, by clearing the adjoining hedge on the left, and escaping in the gloom over the neighbouring fields. He did not proceed, however, out of the sound of the horses, but after recovering himself from the sur-prise he at first naturally felt, on being so near an arrest, cautiously retraced his steps, and still remaining under cover of the darkness, anxiously and silently awaited the future operations of his enemies.

At this juncture the horsemen were joined by Peter, to whom, with an oath of admiration at Ralph's agility, they carelessly men-tioned his sudden and singular appearance as that of some mad smuggler. They now moved forward, taking the left-hand road, and soon arrived on the beach. As all was darkness, and no object presented itself to guide them along the shore, they halted for a moment and procured a light, from materials provided for the purpose, which they communicated to two flambeaux, and then slowly and heavily advanced over the shingle in the south-east direction.

Ralph, whose anger had been considerably increased by the attempt made to arrest him, had dogged them from the first moment of their advance. Keeping within the fields to the left of the road, he was enabled distinctly to hear their conversation; and having satisfied himself that Peter was now one of the party, and that their intention was to search the caverns, he diverged a little to the south-east and increased his speed, so as to arrive on the beach before them. Having cleared the last hedge, which divides the enclosures from the shore, he ran eastward, close besides the fields until he came parallel to his own subterraneous recess. Here he paused to observe their ulterior motions. He saw the lights moving slowly in a compact body along the strand; and his every faculty at once became overpowered with a keen and burning desire of vengeance. He advances to take them in flank, and sees the object of his bitter revenge in advance, on foot, shrouded in the shades of night, near the mouth of his cavern, apparently pointing it out to his followers ! Now is the moment of vengeance ! he can accomplish his purpose and escape pursuit ! Full of these blood-thirsty emotions, he raised the deadly weapon to his shoulder, and, taking unerring aim, with savage joy, pulls the fatal trigger ! Oh, God— a loud and teriffic shriek conveys to his horror-stricken and bewildered ear the dreadful truth—the life blood of poor Jane Rogers is poured out by the hands of her infuriated husband—and frail mortality is once again taught the often repeated, and in this instance, fearful lesson, to beware of the influence of passion, and pause on the actions which its headlong impulses dictate.

HAYLING ISLAND.

AN ODE,

TO WILLIAM PADWICK, ESQ.

LORD OF THE MANOR.

Ocean! roll thy flood along,
  Gently rippling to the gale,
While, responsive to the song,
  Zephyrs murm'ring soft prevail;
And the harp's expressive thrill
Wakes each tuneful chord at will.

Lovely isle! bright gem of ocean!
  As the waters round thee glide,
How I love to trace the motion
  Of the never-slumb'ring tide;
Dash the billows now their spray,
Now in whispers sink away.

Glances hence, how pleas'd, the view
  In the soften'd ev'ning rays,
To the lofty hills and blue,
  Which fair *Vecta's* coast displays.
Long to fashion and to wealth,
Lov'd resort of ease and health.

Tho' far humbler rise thy beach,
  From the circling wave's embrace
And thy beauties may not reach
  All the charms of that fam'd place
Still within the grateful line,
Speak the claims so justly thine.

Softest sands the foot treads *here*,
  Gently sloping to the wave,
Where, without a parent's fear,
  E'en the infant child may lave;
While the tide, like chrystal stream,
Clear reflects each lucid beam.

Would the eye, by land or sea,
  O'er the varied prospect rove;
Hourly glide along by thee,
  Scenes the patriot bosoms love,
Britain's bulwarks—that proclaim
To the world, her matchless fame.

Far and wide, from plain or height,
  Trace the bright horizon round,
Richest landscapes here delight,
  With luxuriant harvests crown'd :
While the tiller's sun-burnt brow,
Prompts the pray'r—"God speed the plough."

Here, by gen'rous care design'd,
  (What will not such care supply?)
Pleasures to engage the mind,
  And each taste to gratify;
Never may ungrateful strain
Speak such care bestowed in vain.

Structures ev'ry grace that boast,
  Lo! beside yon terrace green,
Length'ning rang'd along the coast,
  Rise, in splendour, on the scene;
NORFOLK'S, STAUNTON'S, PADWICK'S shine
Central, in the *Crescent* line.

Hither, fair, who seek retreat
  When the sultry summers burn,
From the town's oppressive heat,
  Hither, fair, your footsteps turn.
Hebe breathing o'er the isle,
Renovates each fading smile.

Gem of England's southern sea!
  Thou deserv'st a brighter lay,
Who now strikes the harp to thee,
  Treads too oft in sorrow's way ;.
Yet along thy peaceful shore
  He delights the song to pour.

Still thy sandy beach along,
  Changing tides shall ebb and flow,
When the heart, now rous'd to song,
  Sleeps in wakeless silence low.
Life, receding from its shore,
Yields the welcome wave no more!

Ocean! ere I quit thy stream,
  Emblem of eternity!
Rise my thoughts to the Supreme,
  HIM, whose hand hath bounded thee,
He, when thou shalt cease to flow,
Shall, nor age, nor limit know.

The Manor of Havant.

———◆———

THE Hundred of Bosmere, from the Saxon "bos," sig-
nifying a wood, and "mere," a marsh, anciently called
the Hundred of Boseberg, comprises the manors of Havant,
Warblington, Lymbourne, and Hayling, bounded on the west
by the Hundred of Portsdown, on the north by the Hundred
of Finchdean, on the east by the Hundred of Bourne,
and on the south by the sea. The whole of the eastern
coast of Hampshire was originally peopled by the Belgæ,
a Germanic tribe who landed and settled on the southern
coast of Britain at some indefinite period, anterior to the
Roman invasion. There is every reason to believe that the
coasts of Hampshire and Sussex were selected for early
settlements from the facilities afforded for the pursuits of
hunting and fishing, and from their contiguity to the sea.
Upon the establishment of the Roman empire in Great
Britain, the invaders naturally occupied those localities which
had either been chosen by their conquered opponents, or
which seemed calculated to offer advantages in retaining
possession of their new acquirement. Clausentum, the
present Bitterne, Portus Magnus, the present Portchester,
and Regnum, the present Chichester, became their stations,
covering a space of thirty miles from west to east, each of
these being at such a distance from the shore as to obviate
the probability of an unexpected attack from a piratical
enemy. From Clausentum a road passed through Portus
Magnus to Regnum, following the course of the existing road
in many parts, and at intervals between these principal
stations, were smaller field encampments in the vicinity of
which, first villages and then towns sprang into existence,

under the shelter of the powerful conquerors. The Romans fully appreciated the importance of a good and available communication between their inland camps and the sea, and the road crossing the street of Havant at right angles from north to south, seems to have been one of the main approaches from their encampment on old Winchester through Rowland's castle to the harbour and island of Hayling. In confirmation of this, various remains of pottery and many coins have from time to time been found in the vicinity of the line, as well as in the town of Havant, but not to such an extent as would enable one to form any very accurate idea of the size or importance of the place prior to the Norman conquest.

The present name, corrupted from Hauehunte, or Havonte, is Saxon in its derivation; similar to that of Boarhunt, which lay in the centre of the forest of Portchester, and it may therefore be concluded that the Roman settlement was adopted by the new invaders more particularly as many of the existing local names bear undeniable evidence of their Saxon origin. Within a few years after the Norman Conquest, the celebrated survey called Domesday was compiled by order of the Conqueror, and the entry in reference to Havant follows in these words; "The monks of the diocese of Winchester hold "Hauehunte; they always held it. It was assessed in the "time of King Edward at ten hides. It is now assessed at "seven hides. Here are four ploughlands; twenty villagers "employ six ploughs. Here are two mills which pay fifteen "shillings, and three salterns which pay fifteen pence; also "woods which furnish ten hogs. It was and is now worth "eight pounds. Brockmaton was and is now worth one "hundred shillings."

The Manors on the southern sea coast were not so highly assessed as those inland, from the circumstance of their being exposed to the depredations of the Norse and Danish pirates, and this reason is specially assigned in reference to the valuation of Fareham in Domesday; but it is nevertheless evident that even at this early period Havant was a place of some importance, and that the lands within the manor were in a higher state of cultivation than those in the immediate neighbourhood. The tythings comprised within the manor were those of Havant, Brockhampton, Leigh, Langstone, and Hayling North. One of the mills mentioned in the survey is still subsisting on its original site at Brockhampton, and is now held by the Messrs. Snook, on lease for lives, from the Bishop of Winchester, and the other stood on the site of that now occupied by the town mill, which was rebuilt by the late Mr. John Crasweller, in the year 1822. To these have been added the mill erected some years since by the late Mr. John Smith Lane, below the site of Battine's ancient mill, and the two now standing in the village of Langstone. Mills in former days belonged almost exclusively to the lords of manors, the tenants and inhabitants being constrained to grind only at the lord's mill, and upon payment of the accustomed toll in kind. This will, in some measure account, not merely for the great number of mills enumerated in early records as objects of profit to the landholders, but for the large sums which they are constantly stated to yield; the rent being sometimes in kind, sometimes in money, sometimes in grain, and sometimes from the fishery in the mill stream. At Lolingeston, in the county of Kent, a mill rendered fifteen shillings and 150 eels. At Wichendone, in the county of Buckingham, a mill rendered twenty shillings and four score eels. At Wasmertone, in the county of Warwick, a mill rendered twenty shillings, four measures of salt, and one thousand eels. At Arundel Castle a mill rendered ten measures of corn and ten measures of provisions, besides four other measures. Mills are not mentioned subsequently to Domesday, until the statutes 31 Henry III, and 13 Edward I, by which the toll is directed to be taken according to the custom of the land, and according to the strength of the water-course, either to the twentieth or twenty-fourth corn.

Of the three salterns here enumerated one remains on the north shore of Hayling, and two have ceased to exist. One of the latter was situate to the south of Wade Court, upon the northern part of the Langstone millpond: it was abandoned in the early part of the eighteenth century, and is shown upon a map among the Wade muniments, dated in

the year 1725 as the property of Mr. Thomas Jervoise.
These Salterns as originally used were unquestionably ponds
and pans for procuring marine salt by the process of evapo-
ration; and Saint Augustin, in his work *De civitate Dei*,
speaks highly of the salt made in this locality, and states that
it is superior to every other made on the British coasts.
Inland salterns were what are now called the refineries of
brine or salt springs.   At the time of the survey, rock
or fossil-salt was unknown in England; the first pits of it
were accidentally discovered in Cheshire, on the very spot
where Domesday mentions brine springs, so late as the year
1670.   From the rent paid, these saltworks of Havant
do not appear to have been very extensive, or of any great
value.

It will be observed that there is no mention made of
any church at Havant in the general survey, but this
circumstance by no means proves that there was no church
in existence at the date of the return.   The Inquisitors,
it appears, were to inquire upon the oaths of the sheriffs,
the lords of every manor, the presbyters of every church, the
reves of every hundred, the bailiffs and six villains of every
village, into the name of the place, who held it in the time of
Edward the Confessor, who was the then possessor, how many
hides the manor contained, how many carucates in demesne,
how many homagers, how many villains, how many cottars,
how many serving-men, what free-men, how many tenants in
socage, what quantity of wood, how much meadow and
pasture, what mills and fish-ponds, how much added or taken
away, what the gross value in the time of King Edward, what
the then value, and how much each free-man or sock-man
had.   The Jurors were moreover to state when any advance
could be made in the value.   By this it will be seen that
churches *per se*, formed no part of the subject matter for
inquiry, and that if entered at all it was not as of course
but incidentally only where there had been an early endowment by donation of glebe lands or otherwise.   There
was doubtless a church at Havant at the date of the survey,
although the precise time of its erection cannot now perhaps

be clearly ascertained, and the following facts will be found to strengthen, if not to establish the conclusion.

In the year 678, Wilfred, bishop of Northumberland, having been expelled from his province, went to Rome, and returning thence, came into the kingdom of the South Saxons, which then contained seven thousand households or families, and which had not as yet been converted to the Christian faith. He there preached the gospel with the license of King Edilwalke, who gave him the Isle of Wight, with the province of the people, anciently called Meanuari, which he had won from the West Saxons. The bishop baptised the chief lords and the priests, the residue of the inhabitants being baptised shortly afterwards. The King also gave Wilfred, Sealsea, then containing eighty-seven households, where he built an abbey, and having baptised all his tenants there, to the number of two hundred and fifty, he enfranchised them from all bodily servitude and bondage. In the year 959, Athelwald was made bishop of Winchester, and by his zeal and unaffected piety acquired great power over the mind of his royal master, King Edgar. The chronicles inform us that the latter "was so beneficial to the church, namelie to monkes, the advancement of whome he greatlie sought, both in building Abbeies, newe from the ground, in repayring those that were decaied, also by enriching them with great revenues, and in converting collegiat churches into monasteries, renouncing secular priests and bringing in monks in their places. There passed no one yeare of his reigne wherein he founded not one Abbeie or other. The Abbeie of Glastenburie which his father had begun, he finished. The Abbeie of Abingdon also he accomplished and set in good order. The Abbeie of Peterborough and Thornie he established. The Nunrie of Wilton he founded and richly endowed, where his daughter Editha professed, and where also she at length became Abbess. To be briefe, he builded to the number of forty abbeies and monasteries, in some of which he placed monks and in some nuns. By his example in those daies other nobles, as also prelates and some of the laitie, did begin the foundation of sundrie abbeies and monasteries; as Adelwold, bishop of Winchester, builded the abbeie of Elie, and (as some say) Peterborough and 'Thornie, although they were established by the King. Also Earl Ailewin, at the exhortation of the same bishop Adelwold, builded the Abbeie of Ramsay, though some attribute the doing thereof unto Oswald the archbishop of Yorke, and some to King Edward the elder." From the Register of the Priory of Edyndon, in Wiltshire, we learn that in 967, Edgar also granted a charter to the Benedictine abbey and nunnery of Romsey, in this county, dedicated to the Virgin Mary and Saint Elfleda, the first abbess on record being Merwenna.

In the year 979, Ethelred the brother of Edward the Martyr, King of England, gave the manor of Havant to the monastery at Winchester. Alfreda, the mother of Edward the Martyr, after the murder of her son, and in expiation of her crime, founded the monastery of Wherwell, in this county. The capitals of the columns supporting the tower of Havant church are identical with those at Wherwell; the latter are admitted to be Anglo-Saxon. It is not therefore improbable to suppose that Havant and Wherwell churches were built by the same architect. It was a practice at that time almost universal, upon the gift of a manor to a religious house, like that dedicated to Saint Peter at Winchester, for the abbot to build a church on his newly-acquired property for the convenience of his tenants and freemen, and we know from Domesday and other early records, that most of the manors which were then held by the monastery were so provided. It would be unreasonable to conclude that Havant was without a church when Warblington had two, Bedhampton one, and Hayling another. Havant is the chief place of the hundred, and the size of its church, coupled with local tradition, appear to indicate that it was then, as now, the mother church of the district, standing upon the site once occupied by some Roman edifice. It has been called a quarter cathedral, and the site of the ancient rectory, coupled with the bishop's arms, and the retention of the name of " Pallant" in the adjoining street, would seem to indicate that in early times it must have possessed a bishop's palace for occasional residence on episcopal progress through the diocese. Beside this, Havant is a peculiar of the Bishop of Winchester, and as such was exempt from the ordinary ecclesiastical jurisdiction. The possession of a peculiar was formerly much coveted, and although at the present day little value is attached to it, yet in a time when the church was differently constituted, and arbitrary power not unfrequently exercised, it was a highly-valued privilege. In the beginning of the thirteenth century the extortions of the papal power were exorbitant to a degree, insomuch that Pope Honorius demanded a tenth of all personal property in England, Ireland, and Wales, from all classes, laity as well as clergy, to enable him to carry on the war against the Emperor Frederick, and this, under the fear of excommunication, was granted and eventually paid. As it was to the manifest interest of the pope to place in the offices of the church those who would comply with the unceasing demands made upon them, it was not an unusual thing for him upon the consecration or re-erection of a church, where the bishop or abbot accommodated himself to the papal views, to create the district appertaining to the church a peculiar of the bishop or abbot, giving them power to grant probate of wills, to administer the effects of deceased persons within the peculiar jurisdiction, and rendering them wholly independent of, and exempt from the power and correction of their metropolitan ; by this means compelling all parties in the event of any disagreement to appeal to himself as the supreme governor in all matters relating to the peculiar.

It appears that this system of exemption was attended with great evils, and there is a letter upon record of King Edward III to the pope, complaining of the conduct of the Bishop of Winchester, who had, in consequence of special and peculiar exemption, appealed from his metropolitan to the apostolic see, A. D. 1337. The letter exposes the demoralizing tendency of the system, "for," says the monarch, "it "would be of most pernicious example, if by such false sug- "gestions as these, suffragans could escape the correction of "their metropolitan, and oppress their subjects *ad libitum*,

"without any fear of a speedy remedy; and also that they
"should be able to compel them to be continually going to
"the Roman court to obtain redress."

The church of Havant is dedicated to Saint Faith, and the
peculiar, from the dedication, has always been styled as that
of Saint Faith.   Among the numbers who suffered in the
persecution of Dioclesian were many females, whose constancy
has been the admiration of after ages.   Saint Faith was a
lady of the Pais de Gavre in France, of great beauty and
chastity of life, qualities in those days assuredly marking her
out for persecution.   Venerable Bede says that in one month
alone 17,000 persons suffered martyrdom; one of this number was Saint Faith, who was put to death after having endured the most cruel torments by order of Dacian the Præfect,
about the year 290 : her name is still retained in our calendar.
The crypt under Saint Paul's, built in the year 610, by
Ethelbert, King of Kent, is the first church that we find to
have been dedicated to the memory of the martyred virgin,
and the priory of Horsham, founded in 1075, by William de
Braiose, is the last.   In a grant of confirmation by King
Henry I to the alien priory of Jumieges, during the primacy
of Anselm, Archbishop of Canterbury, and about the year
1100, lands, then and still parcel of the manor of Hayling,
are there spoken of as situate "at Leigh, near Saint Faith's,"
confirming the existence of the church at that period, as the
parish unquestionably derived its name from the dedication
of the sacred edifice.

There is a general impression that there were but very
few churches in the country at the time of Domesday, but
the impression is not founded upon fact.   In Domesday
alone, which did not comprise all the counties, and as before
observed, only mentions churches incidentally, not less than
1700 are enumerated, and it is remarkable that while 222
churches are returned from Lincolnshire, 243 from Norfolk,
and 364 from Suffolk, only one can be found in the return for
Cambridgeshire, and none in Lancashire, Cornwall, or even
Middlesex, the seat of the metropolis.   Undoubted evidence
has been adduced of the existence of one church in Kent, and

of several others in Northamptonshire, which certainly are not noticed in the survey, and no notice whatever is taken of the church at Dorchester, although the seat of a bishopric had been removed from it but a short time before the commencement of the survey. The fourfold distinction of churches noticed in the third law of Canute in 1033, seems to import that in his time these sacred buildings might together amount to a large number, and it is manifest that in the reign of Edward the Confessor there must have been a very great increase of what was strictly·denominated parish churches, it being asserted in one of the laws ascribed to that king that in many places there were three or four churches where in former times there was not one. And if, as tradition and local remains testify, thirty-six churches were destroyed by the Conqueror in order to enlarge the New Forest, this of itself is an argument that they could not have been so few as the number entered in Domesday, and the general impression seem to imply.

It was not long before the monks took steps to improve the position of the town; for in the second year of the reign of King John, Godfrey de Lucy, bishop of Winchester, and son of Richard Lucy, Lord Chief Justice of England, obtained the grant of a market from that monarch in the following terms:—" John, by the grace of God, &c., to the " Archbishops, &c.: Know ye that we have granted, and " by this, our charter, have confirmed to the church of " Winchester, which is built in honour of the blessed apostles " Peter, Paul, and Saint Swithun, one market every week, to " be held in the town of Haueunte; so, nevertheless, that it " be not to the injury of the neighbouring market. " Wherefore it is our will, and we positively command, that " the aforesaid church and·monks serving in it, shall have " and hold the aforesaid market, well and in peace, freely and " quietly, wholly, fully and reasonably, with all liberties and " free customs to the same market belonging as is aforesaid. " Dated the 4th day of November, in the second year of our " reign." (*Rot. Chart.* 2 Joh. p. 1, m. 22).

In the 51 Henry III, proceedings were taken to determine

2

if the prior of Saint Swithun of Winchester, brother Geoffrey
le Noreys, and William de la Berton had unjustly disseized
Reginald Oysen of his free tenement in Hafont; whereupon, as
the pleadings state, " brother Geoffrey and William come and
" the prior does not appear, but the aforesaid brother Geoffrey
" and William say that if any disseizin has been made it was
" not done by them nor even by the prior, but that it was
" done by Ralph Russel, a former prior of Saint Swythun, a
" predecessor of the now prior, who thereof died seized as of
" right of his church aforesaid : And Reginald cannot gainsay
" this ; Therefore the aforesaid Geoffrey and William are with-
" out day, and Reginald takes nothing, &c., and is in mercy
" for his false claim." (Ab. plac. Rot. 17.)

In the thirteenth century various disturbances arose between the bishop of Winchester and the monks of St. Swythun
in reference to the vacancies which occurred in the monastery
upon the death of the prior.   During the vacancies of abbeys
and monasteries, unless the right were purchased or relin-
quished, they escheated to the patrons, who, according to their
respective claims, placed a man and horse at the gate of the
monastery, presented the superior or reserved only the grant
of the congé d'elire, with confirmation, fealty, and homage of
the elect.   Where the king was patron, the clerks in custody
committed great depredations for themselves and their master.
In houses possessing the right of election, that right, where
the number of monks or canons was not sufficient, was resigned to the bishop, and this appears to have been the case
with the monastery of Saint Swythun.   In the year 1284
however, and during the prelacy of John de Pontissera, the
differences between the bishop and the monastery were
finally settled, and a composition was arranged by which the
prior and his convent granted the manors of Drokensford,
Alwarestok with Gosport, and Havontre with their tenants of
Heling and the hamlet of Cnoel, to the bishop and his successors, to hold the same for ever.   In return, and as an
equivalent for this, the bishop for himself and his successors
granted and released all the right that he had in the temporalities of the priory of Saint Swythun during the period of

any vacancy, and in all the manors and lands belonging to the priory, saving only to the bishop and his successors, the advowson or patronage of the same, so nevertheless that he should have the power of placing one serving-man in the priory in the name of a recognition of his patronage, who during a vacancy should be maintained by the chapter. (*Annales Ecclesiæ Wint.* tom i, p. 315).

By the Pipe Rolls of the Bishopric for this period, which are still preserved, it appears that Simon de la Bere, as bailiff, rendered an account of 112*s.* 9½ ¼*d.* for the whole rents of assize at the term of Saint James the Apostle, and the term of Saint Peter ad Vincula; and he also at the same time paid over 10*s.* 8*d.* for two quarters of wheat sold for toll of the mill at Brockhampton, of which one quarter sold for six shillings and the other for 4*s.* 8*d.*; also 2*s.* 4*d.* received for four bushels of corn sold, arising from toll of the mill of Esmill; and 10*s.* 8*d.* which he had received for three quarters of wheat, with various other smaller sums for corn and allowances. (*Pipe Rolls*, 12 Edw. I). In the 24th Henry VI, Henry Beaufort, bishop of Winchester, then lord of Havant and Cardinal of England, granted to William Marche his valet, in fee, two tenements in the town of Havonte, lying near to Hamwell, for the annual rent of two shillings and other services, and the grant was duly confirmed by the Crown. (*Rot. Pat.* 24 Hen. VI, mem. 4).

In the 39th year of the same reign William Waynfleet, then bishop of Winchester and lord of Havant, obtained from the crown a confirmation of the existing market, and an additional charter of a two days' fair, to be held on the vigil of Saint Faith, the patron saint of the parish, in the words following: " The King to the Archbishops, Bishops, &c. Know " ye that of our special grace and of our knowledge we have " granted, and by this our charter have confirmed, to the " venerable in Christ, William, bishop of Winchester, that he " and his successors shall have for ever one market to be held " each week on the Sabbath-day at his town of Havont, in the " county of Southampton, and one fair there each year of two " days' duration, that is to say, in the vigil and feast of Saint

" Faith the virgin, with all liberties and free customs to the
" same market and fair belonging, so nevertheless that that
" market and that fair be not to the damage of neighbouring
" markets and neighbouring fairs, &c.   Given under our hand
" at Westminster the thirtieth day of January."

By the account of John Paynter, bailiff, in the 24th Edw. IV,
it appears that the rents of the manor from the grants of
parcels of the waste had increased very considerably.   This
account contains the payment of a rent of twenty pence, " for
" the fee farm of a certain parcel of land in the waste soil of
" the lord, in the market-place of Havant, below and near the
" burial-ground, containing in length one hundred and twenty
" feet, leased to John Hall, Richard Bell, Stephen Parker,
" Thomas Couse, Robert Morseley, Richard Arnald, their
" heirs and assigns for ever ;" and for six pounds for the farm
of the mill leased to John Paynter by indenture under a
lesser rent than it was accustomed to be rented for, twenty
shillings, so that the said John should support all repairs at
his own costs during the term aforesaid.

By the account of John Golde, steward, by William
Aylmer his deputy, from the feast of Saint Michael the
Archangel in the 11th year of the reign of King Henry VII,
unto the same feast in the 12th year of the same king, and in
the year of the translation of the Lord Thomas Langton,
bishop of Winchester the 4th, the new rents are found to be
still increasing.   Among the ancient rents occurs, " And for
" twenty pence for the fee farm of a certain parcel of land of
" the waste soil of the lord in the market of Havonte below
" and near the burial ground there, containing in length one
" hundred and twenty feet, and in breadth eight feet, in
" South-street, for erecting a butcher's and fishmonger's stalls,
" there leased to Richard Hall and others," &c.   The steward
accounts for 6s. 8d. for the price of one heifer, arising as a
heriot ; for the farm of the mill at Brockhampton nothing
here in charge because not at farm, but he answers for five
shillings for the farm of South mill, leased this year.   And
for 28s. 4d. for eight quarters of corn arising from the issues
of the mill there this year by oath of the accountant, price the

quarter 3s. 4d. &c. Heriots in money nothing this year, but he answers for 16s. 7d. for the perquisites of the turns of Saint Martin, and for 19s. for the perquisites of the turns of Hoke-day; and for 8s. 9d. for the perquisites of courts there held by the bailiff this year. Sum total of the receipts of court arrears, £51. 6s. 2d. Under necessary expenses he charges the lord with a stipend to one labourer to make one hedge around the lord's meadow at 3s. 8d.; and for a stipend to one miller to turn the mill stones 3s.; and for wages to mow and carry the hay in the lord's meadow with a cart, 2s.; and for wages to one carpenter to repair the old wheel of the corn mill, with nails purchased for the same, sixpence, &c. (*Pipe Roll*, 211.)

In the 18th year of the same king's reign a general survey of all the manors, castles, lordships, lands, and·tenements belonging to the see of Winchester was taken, and among the surveys is the following return for the manor of Havant.

	£	s.	d.
Havont is worth, viz., in acknowledgments of all the tenants of the lord there at the first taking of seizin ...	6	13	4
Rents of assize, and at the will of the lord there yearly, as in a preceding account	34	5	9½
The farm of one messuage with a garden adjoining, in the tenure of Geoffrey Harryst yearly, as in a preceding account	0	6	8
Farm of the lands, meadows, and pastures of the lordship there yearly, as in the preceding.	0	61	6
Issues of the manor there this year ...	0	10	9½
Farm of the mills there yearly, as in the preceding	7	0	0
And in the sale of stock arising from heriots, and estrays there this year ..	0	39	8
Fines of lands there this year ...	0	69	2

	£	s.	d.
Perquisites of courts there this year. . .	0	46	4

Sum of the value £60. 2s. 4½d. whereof in divers allowances worth in—

	£	s.	d.
Allowed or decreased rents there this year	0	61	3
Fee of John Gold, bailiff there yearly	0	60	10
Expenses of the steward and surveyor there this year	0	27	7
Amerciaments there this year ...	0	9	11

Sum allowed, £7. 19s. 7d.

And worth beyond, £52. 2s. 9d.

And so worth clear beyond reprises yearly £6. 13s. 4d. for recognitions £51. 17s.   (*Pipe Roll*, No. 215.)

The Manor of Havant continued uninterruptedly in the possession of the bishops of Winchester, as lords, until the year 1553, when it was leased out, for three lives, to Sir Richard Cotton, knight, then Comptroller of the Household to Edward VI. On the 20th December, 30th Elizabeth, it was in lease to Henry Cotton, clerk. On the 9th November, 33d Elizabeth, Jane Cotton, the widow of Henry, held the manor as a part of her widow's bench, and in the 42d Elizabeth it was in lease to Henry Cotton, clerk, then bishop of Salisbury. (*Court Rolls.*) From an account of the sale of church lands belonging to the see at Winchester during the Civil Wars, preserved in the Bodleian Library at Oxford, it appears that the manor of Havant had, with various other lordships, been seized by the commissioners, and that the manor was, on the 21st February 1647, sold by them to William Woolgar for the sum of £1162. 5s. 4d. (*Row B. 236.*)

Upon the restoration of Charles II, when all these grants were resumed, the then Bishop of Winchester confirmed Wolgar's possession to some extent by a lease for three lives. William Wolgar departed this life in the year 1680, unmarried, and without issue; and upon his decease Ann and

Dorothy, his two sisters, claimed to be entitled to the manor of Havant as his co-heiresses, and entered into possession accordingly. They both, some time previous to the year 1689, with their respective husbands, surrendered up the old lease, by which William Wolgar had held the manor, to the then Bishop of Winchester, who soon afterwards granted a new lease to the same Ann and Dorothy and their respective husbands and their respective heirs, during the lives of William Baldwyn, Henry Peckham, and Francis Woodden, and the life of the longest liver of them. Upon the death of the survivor of these three, Ann and Dorothy and their husbands, or those claiming under them, having neglected to renew, the lease fell into the hands of the Bishop about the year 1710. Upon payment of a fine the forfeited manor was shortly afterwards granted to Isaac Moody, esquire, of Havant, with all and singular the rights, members, and appurtenances for the three lives of John Carter, John Moody, and William Moody, and the life of the longest liver.

This gentleman was descended from the ancient house of Moody of Garsden, county Wilts; of this family Sir Henry Moody, knight, was created a baronet in 1621. On his death in 1631, letters of administration were granted to Sir Henry his son, who sold his Wiltshire estates and went to New England. He died, as is supposed, without issue, and the baronetcy upon his death became extinct. Isaac Moody married, in the year 1698, Rebecca, daughter of William Pannell of Havant, and upon his death on the 13th October 1726, he married Hannah, widow of Robert Mason, of Portsea. By his marriage with the latter, under settlement, he became lord of the manors of Copner, Portsea, and Frodington, and owner of estates in the parishes of Portsea, Widley, and Wymering. He had previously purchased the Bedhampton Park and other estates, and remained lord of Havant up to the time of his death on the 9th November 1728. On the 12th November in that year, he was buried in the chancel of Havant church, where a monument, with the arms of Moody, Vert a Fesse engrailed Argent, surmounted of another Gules, between three Harpies of the second crined Or; crest, a Wolf's head erased Gules, and bearing the following inscription, was erected to the memory of himself and his first wife:

> "*Near this lyeth Isaac Moody, gent., of this place, who*
> "*departed this life, November the 9th, Anno Domini*
> "*1728, in the 55th year of his age.*
> "*Also near this lyeth Rebecca, wife of the above Isaac*
> "*Moody, who departed this life October the 13th, Anno*
> "*Domini 1726, in the 48th year of her age.*"

By his will, dated 14th December 1727, which was proved in the Court of Chancery, he devised the Manor of Havant and other valuable estates to his younger son,—

John Moody, esq., of Havant, who was baptized in the parish church on the 14th November 1701. On the 6th May 1742, he married at Saint Mary's, Portsea, Mary, the only surviving daughter of · Mr. Thomas Longcroft of Portsmouth. She died without issue, and was buried at Havant on the 22d July 1752. Under the settlement made upon her marriage, bearing date the 30th April 1742, her husband acquired upon her death considerable real and personal property at Copner, Baffins, and elsewhere, in the town of Portsmouth and island of Portsea. On the 25th June 1740, a fresh lease of the manor was granted to John Moody by the then Bishop of Winchester, to hold the same to him and his heirs during the lives of William Moody the grantee, John Moody and Daniel Bartlett, and the life of the longest liver of them, under the yearly rent of £42. 1s. 4d. payable half yearly. The description contained in the lease was—" All " that the manor of Havant, in the county of Southampton, " with all the lands, tenements, reversions, services, meadows, " pastures, and other hereditaments in Havant, Lee, Hayling, " and Brockhampton, in the said county of Southampton, to " the said manor belonging, or in anywise appertaining or " therewith, or with any part or parcel thereof used, occupied, " enjoyed, or letten, or which at any time before this hath " been accepted, reputed, taken or known as part, parcel, or " member thereof: and all Courts Leet, views of frankpledge

"and all that to view of frankpledge doth belong or apper-
"tain, wards, marriages, reliefs, escheats, goods, and chattels
"of felons and fugitives, goods, waifs, estrays, perquisites of
"courts, liberties, franchises, mills, waters, and fishings, with
"all and singular other hereditaments, commodities, profits,
"and advantages to the said manor belonging or appertain-
"ing" (except as therein was excepted.)—(*Chan. Proceed.*,
Halsey *v.* Moody.) A great deal of litigation took place
during the lordship of John Moody, partly in consequence of
William Woolgar, or his representatives, having sold off various
portions of what was claimed to be demesne land of the
bishop, which portions had, on the renewal of the lease in
the year 1710, been entered upon by Isaac Moody, and partly
in reference to an agreement and purchase made by the latter
of one Evans, who conceived that certain copyhold lands of
which William Woolgar died seized had descended to him as
his customary heir. It is stated in the bill, and admitted by
the answer, that no deeds or documents setting out and de-
scribing such demesne lands had ever been furnished by the
bishop, and that Isaac Moody had experienced the greatest
difficulty in identifying the lands upon which he had entered
as demesne, and the title to which was then in dispute. The
transaction with Evans was conducted on his part by John
Evans, then Bishop of Meath, a relation of the vendor, and
there are some curious and interesting letters from the Bishop
Evans to Isaac Moody on the nature and particulars of the .
vendor's claim, and also of the claim of the bishop himself
to be reimbursed monies which he had paid for the advancement in life of Dorothy, one of the coheiresses of William
Woolgar, who went to Bengal "for the bettering of her for-
"tune," and there married King, an Indian merchant. King
died some few years after his marriage, and Dorothy, his
widow, died shortly afterwards. A will, purporting to be that
of Dorothy King, was produced upon her decease, and upon
the validity of this Isaac Moody's title in a measure rested.
The suit however was by mutual arrangement at last brought
to a close. John Moody died suddenly at the Manor-house
without issue, and was buried at Havant on the 6th July,

1764.   By his will bearing date the 17th November 1763,
he devised "his manor of Havant, in the county of South-
"ampton, with the rights, members, and appurtenances thereto
"belonging," unto Samuel Leeke and Thomas Holloway, in
trust, for the payment of his debts, for the purpose of raising
a sum for the liquidation of certain legacies, and subject
thereto to convey and assure the manor of Havant, with its
rights, members, and appurtenances unto his great nephew
James Newland of Havant, his heirs and assigns for ever.
This will was proved in Chancery ; on the 19th September
1755, a fresh lease of the manor for three lives was granted
to Samuel Leeke and Thomas Holloway, which, upon Leeke's
death in 1775, was on the 6th April, in the same year, surrendered by Holloway.   On that day a fresh lease for the
lives of William Moody, Richard Prior, and Richard Bingham
Newland, was granted by the bishop to Thomas Holloway
upon the trusts of John Moody's will, of the manor of Havant,
by the description contained in the lease of the 25th June
1740, "Except and always reserved unto the Lord Bishop,
"his successors and assigns, all great timber and trees, oak,
"ash, elm and beech now standing, growing, or being, or
"which at any time hereafter during all the continuance of
"the term shall stand, grow, increase, and be in and upon the
"said demised lands and premises, or any part or parcel
"thereof, with free liberty of ingress and egress to and for
"the said Lord Bishop and his successors to fell, cut down,
"take and carry away the said timber and trees at all conve-
"nient and seasonable times in the year.   And also except
"and reserved the free purlieu of hunting, chasing, taking, and
"custody of deer, in a parcel of ground called the Thicket,
"—parcel of the premises.   And also the advowson, gift, free
"disposition and patronage of the church of Havant."
    The rent reserved under this lease was £42. 1s. 4d., and
Thomas Holloway covenanted for the maintenance and repair
of the demised premises upon having from the bishop's
woodward upon the demised premises a sufficient allowance of
rough timber on the stem for repairs, and twelve cords of
firewood, "with all other convenient and necessary botes."
(*Proceedings*, Franklin and Bishop of Winchester).

James Newland, the devisee under the will of John Moody, died under age, and the manor of Havant passed upon his decease to his brother, Richard Bingham Newland esquire. By indenture bearing date the 24th October 1775, Thomas Holloway, as surviving trustee of the will of John Moody, conveyed the manor by a general description to hold to the said Richard Bingham Newland, his heirs and assigns, during the lives of William Moody, Richard Prior, and Richard Bingham Newland the grantee, subject to the rent and covenants contained in the lease of the 6th April 1775. The latter lease was surrendered on the 14th April 1784, and on the same day a new lease of the manor of Havant, by a similar description to that contained in the surrendered lease, and subject to the same exceptions, rent, and covenants, was granted by Brownlow, lord bishop of Winchester, to Richard Bingham Newland, to hold the same with the appurtenances (except as excepted) to the said Richard Bingham Newland, his heirs and assigns, for the lives of Richard Prior, Richard Bingham Newland the grantee, and Richard Bingham Newland the younger, and the life of the longest liver of them. (*Bishoprick Records*). By indentures of the 22d and 23d December 1800, Richard Bingham Newland conveyed the demesne mill of Brockhampton, with various closes then occupied with it, to Richard Power of Havant, gentleman, to hold the same during the term granted to himself, and he covenanted to obtain, if possible, upon renewal, a separate lease for the lives of such persons as each party should respectively nominate. By other indentures of the same date he conveyed the Red Hill brick-kiln and yard to William Pearson of Rowlands Castle, brickburner, to hold the same during the term granted to himself, with a similar covenant to the last in case of renewal, and by other subsequent indentures he conveyed the manor of Havant, with its rights, members, and appurtenances, to William Garrett esquire, subject to the rent, covenants, and exceptions, and for the same term as granted to himself.

William Garrett remained lord up to the year 1820, when he sold the manor to the present owner, Sir George Thomas

Staunton. There had been a previous contract for sale to John Julius Angerstein esquire, but it was abandoned in consequence of some objections which were raised by the latter to the completion of the purchase. By indentures bearing date the 31st December 1819, and 1st January 1820, William Garrett conveyed the manor with its rights, members, and appurtenances (except the premises conveyed to Richard Power and William Pearson), to hold the same to the said Sir George Thomas Staunton, his heirs and assigns, during the lives of Richard Prior, Richard Bingham Newland the elder, and Richard Bingham Newland the younger, and the life of the longest liver of them, subject to the rent, covenants, and exceptions contained in the lease of the 14th April 1784.

On the 21st June 1826, the bishop renewed the lease of the manor to Sir George, and upon the 12th December in that year, in consideration of the surrender of the then existing lease, a fresh lease was granted by the bishop (subject to the former exceptions, and to the exception of Brockhampton mill and the Red Hill brick-kilns) to hold to Sir George, his heirs and assigns, for the lives of the Princess Victoria, Edward Billis, and William Hoare, and the life of the longest liver of them, at the apportioned rent of £30, and under the ancient and accustomed covenants.

In the year 1827, arrangements were made for an enfranchisement of the manor, and by indenture of bargain and sale enrolled in the Court of Chancery, and bearing date the second day of February in that year, the bishop, under the powers of various Acts then in force for the redemption and sale of the land-tax, and enabling bodies corporate to sell portions of their manors and estates, in consideration of the sum of £2075. 1s. 9d. and with the consent of the Commissioners specially appointed under the Redemption Acts, conveyed the manor with its rights, members, and appurtenances to Sir George, his heirs and assigns, for ever discharged from all incumbrances, except tithes. The deed contained an exception of Brockhampton mill, which had become the subject of a separate lease; the Red Hill brick-kilns, which had been conveyed in fee by the bishop to William Pearson; the timber upon Havant Thicket, and the other manorial wastes, and the advowson and patronage of the church of Havant. (*Barg. and Sale* reciting lease inrolled 21st Mar. 1827.)

Within the chief manor of Havant, and held under it, are the mesne Manors of Hall Place, Brockhampton, and Leigh. On the 8th November, in the twenty-second year of the reign of King Henry VI, Lord Henry Beaufort, Cardinal of England and Bishop of Winchester, by deed indented and confirmed by the Chapter of the Monastery of Saint Swythun, granted to John Barbour and his assigns for ever, by service and the rent of 44*s*. 4*d*. " one messuage with a curtilage " called Hall Place, four yardlands of land, and one water mill " in Havont, in the county of Southampton, and one mes- " suage with a curtilage and one yardland of land in Brock- " hampton, in the same county." The crown confirmed this grant in the same year. (*Pipe Rolls*, tem. Hen. VI, and *Cal. Rot. Pat.* 22 Hen. VI, sec. 1. mem. 17.) At the turn of Saint Martin, 33 Hen. VIII, the jury of the manor presented that John Tawke, who held freely of the lord four yardlands of free land by the yearly rent of 44*s*. 4*d*. and other services, had died since the last court, whereupon there happened to the lord for a relief 44*s*. 4*d*. and that John Tawke his son, then of the age of four years, was his next heir. In the year 1699, Francis Woodder was owner of this estate, and by. his will bearing date the 1st December in that year, he devised it in fee to his half-sister, Dorothy Evans. The latter intermarried with Arthur King, a merchant connected with the East India Company's service, and by her will bearing date the 25th December 1711, she devised the estate to her sister Elizabeth, the wife of Nathaniel Halsey. Upon the death of Halsey, Elizabeth his widow married Josiah Chitty, and upon Chitty's death she became the wife of Ascanius Christopher Lockman of Richmond, esquire, who died in the year 1741. The property, after being the subject of litiga- tion and a Chancery suit, eventually descended to Elizabeth the only child of John Halsey, who was the son and heir of Elizabeth by Nathaniel Halsey her first husband. By indentures bearing date the 3d and 4th October 1777, Elizabeth Halsey conveyed the estate to Thomas Jeudwine of Havant, brewer. By indentures bearing date the 19th and 20th March 1792, Thomas Jeudwine conveyed to John Butler, and by indentures bearing date the 14th and 15th January 1803, John Butler conveyed to John Crassweller, who by his will bearing date the 28th October 1825, devised the estate to Jane the wife of Charles Beare Longcroft, for life, and upon her decease to her elder son Charles John Longcroft, in fee. (*Hall Place Title Deeds*).

This manor comprised various tenements in the town of Havant, held by payment of quit rent and relief upon death or alienation. The list of all these tenements will be found entered upon the court rolls of the manor of Havant at fo. 68 of book 3. The old manor-house, which was built in the year 1640, with materials taken from Warblington Castle after it had been dismantled was pulled down in the year 1795, when the present house was erected by the late Mr. John Butler.

The mesne manor of Brockhampton includes about fifteen or sixteen copyhold estates, situate in the tything of Brockhampton, and the title to the manor follows the possession of "one messuage and one yardland of bondland" within the same tything, held by copy of Court Roll, under the chief manor of Havant. Quit rents are payable from these estates to the mesne lord and heriots in the case of death. There are no separate rolls, but the copyholds are all entered upon the Court Rolls of the manor of Havant. In the year 1748 Thomas Shepherd was lord; in 1764 Thomas Land became lord; he devised the estate by will to the late Francis Foster, who by will devised it to his son Thomas Land Foster, the present lord. The title of the Lord of Brockhampton to the quit rents and heriots has, upon several occasions, been disputed by the Lord of Havant, but the seizure of the heriots has always been enforced by the mesne lord, and immemorial usage has (whatever may have been the origin of the right) conferred upon him a title which nothing at the present day can resist with any reasonable chance of success.

In the muniment room of his Grace the Duke of Norfolk,

there is a Feodary Book of the time of Henry VI., compiled
from very ancient and then existing documents, some of which
were antecedent to the Norman conquest. This book contains an account of the various manors and lands then forming parcel of the honour of Arundel, which extended as far
as Rowland's Castle, and among the outlying lands are mentioned those at "Riderslond." Adjoining Havant Thicket,
and leading from the latter to Stockheath, is a lane still called
" Ryder's Lane," and there is little doubt but that the lands
mentioned in the Arundel feodary book were situate in this
part of the manor of Havant. About the year 1550, John
Lord Lumley married the Lady Jane, eldest daughter of
Henry Fitzalan, last Earl of Arundel of that stock, and a
settlement was made by the Earl of the Stanstead property,
then parcel of the Honour, and of Ryderslond, then called
Mengehams, probably from the name of some previous
tenant, upon Lord and Lady Lumley, and the issue of their
marriage. This was effected by a demise for the term of one
hundred years, and, subsequently, by a settlement of the
reversion. In the 7th Elizabeth, a licence was obtained from
the crown for alienation of one hundred and twenty-six acres
at Leigh, to William Aylmer, and by an indenture bearing date
the 10th November in that year, Henry Earl of Arundel, Lord
John Lumley, and the Lady Jane his wife, conveyed the same
as then or late parcel of the manor or lordship of Hayling in
the county of Southampton, to William Aylmer, in pursuance
of the licence reserving fealty, and one red rose yearly to be
paid at Midsummer, if it were demanded, for all manner of
services and demands. The conveyance contained a grant of
such deeds, court rolls, rent rolls, &c. as related to the parcels
conveyed. Upon the death of William Aylmer, Mengehams
descended to his son William Aylmer, and upon the death of
the latter, in the reign of James I, the crown seized Mengehams as an escheat; but on the petition of Francis Aylmer, an
inquisition was taken, by which it was found that William
Aylmer, the first purchaser, had died seized of the premises
in his demesne as of fee tail with remainder over, and having
issue of his body lawfully begotten one son William, who,

the first purchaser after the decease of William Aylmer, entered into possession, and was seized thereof in his demesne as of fee tail until the time of his death; that Francis Aylmer was the son' and next heir of the said William Aylmer, the son of William Aylmer the first purchaser, and that Francis, at the death of his father, was of the age of twenty-five years and upwards, and that the lands were held of the King *in capite* by knight's service, but for what part of a knight's fee was unknown.   King James I, therefore, by a general livery under value under the great seal bearing date the 23d November, in the 20th year of his reign, commanded the premises to be restored to the said Francis Aylmer, which was accordingly done, and Francis, by a recovery suffered in the reign of Charles the First, barred the entail.

Upon the death of Francis Aylmer the lands passed to his heir, George Aylmer, who married Thomasin the eldest daughter of Thomas Franklin, clerk, rector of the parish of Chalton in this county.   A settlement bearing date the 20th and 21st September 1697, was made upon this marriage by which the lands were limited to the heirs male of George Aylmer, and in default to the heirs female.   The property ultimately vested in Thomas Aylmer, the only surviving son of George, who suffered a recovery to bar the entail.   By indentures of lease and release bearing date the 29th and 30th days of June 1781, Thomas Aylmer, in consideration of £3422, conveyed the property to Joseph Franklin esquire, of Catherington in this county, to hold the same unto the said Joseph Franklin, his heirs and assigns for ever.

The Aylmers in succession and Joseph Franklin after them conceived that by the purchase of Mengehams at Leigh, they had become lords of a manor of Hayling North, and this impression led them ultimately into difficulty and litigation. It is hardly necessary to say that there never was such a manor as that of Hayling North, and that the only manor of which the Aylmers and Joseph Franklin were lords, was the mesne manor of Leigh, within the manor of Havant, comprising a few parcels of land near Mengehams and some tenements held of the mesne lord, like those of Brockhampton, by payment of quit rents and heriots upon death. The mistake I imagine arose from the fact that within the manor of Hayling there was a tything of Mengeham ; and the lands at Leigh bearing the same name, the latter were conveyed by the Earl of Arundel and Lord and Lady Lumley to William Aylmer, as parcel of their manor of Hayling instead of as parcel of the honour of Arundel.

At the time of Aylmer's purchase a quit rent roll seems to have been handed over, these rents were undoubtedly paid in the 12th of Elizabeth, and irregularly collected down to the year 1793. In pursuance of their imagined rights, the Aylmers and Joseph Franklin, appointed gamekeepers and cut bushes and young heirs on the wastes of the manor of Havant. Every year they drove the thicket, and the estrays were taken into the gate-room of Mengehams. These estrays were either sold, or in the case of forest horses of a certain size killed in order to prevent the commons and waste lands being stocked with useless cattle. Joseph Franklin kept a pack of hounds, and hunted throughout the parishes of Havant and Hayling North, he shot game and killed deer there, and in short acted as lord of the supposed manor and exercised his rights almost without interruption. He assumed also to be as lord owner of the soil of Havant Thicket, which he claimed as appurtenant to his supposed manor, and upon various occasions he cut timber there which he used upon the Mengehams. In the year 1794, the Bishop of Winchester having cut a quantity of timber in Havant Thicket, Joseph Franklin thought proper to draw it away and cut more. Upon this the bishop brought his action of trespass, wherein Franklin justified the trespass complained of, alleging the freehold to be in himself. On the trial of the cause the bishop proving by several persons that they had cut timber in Havant Thicket by his order, sixty years before the trespass, and Franklin not being able to prove the cutting beyond fifty-three years when Thomas Aylmer had exercised the assumed right, the bishop gained a verdict with 40s. damages. Some time after the trial, it was discovered that the witnesses who had proved the cutting by the bishop sixty years before

4

the trespass had made a considerable stretch in point of time none of them having worked in the Thicket until thirty-eight years before the trespass was committed, whilst the oak tree cut by Aylmer fifty-three years before the trespass was then in existence and served as a well curb at the Leigh farmhouse. The opinion of the late Vice-Chancellor Sir Launcelot Shadwell was taken in reference to the case, but the matter was subsequently dropped, and no further proceedings were ever instituted.

Joseph Franklin conveyed the lands called Mengehams to William Garret esquire, then lord of Havant, and the mesne manor merged in the chief manor. The present lord purchased Mengehams with the Manor of Havant.

The Manor of Flood lies wholly within the ambit of the manor of Havant, but is separate and distinct from it, and consists of various estates, copyhold at the will of the lord, which are subject to a heriot on death or alienation, to quit rents, and an uncertain fine upon admission. The eldest son is the customary heir, and upon the death of a copyhold tenant, his widow is entitled to her free bench. The tenants have the same rights of common as those of the manor of Havant. This manor appears to have been created after the manor of Havant had been leased out in 1553, the lands were probably the private property of the then lord, and were granted out by him at will, in order to raise an income by the fines paid on the original grant, and upon subsequent alienations. These copyholds lie dispersedly over the manor of Havant at Durrants on the eastern borders of the Thicket; some are to be found at the eastern extremity of the town, and some in Homewell; they are not however very numerous. There are separate court rolls, the earliest of which bears date in 1646. At this time William Woolgar was lord; upon his death the manor passed, like that of Hall Place, under his will to Dorothy Evans; eventually by purchase to Isaac Moody; from him under his will to his son John Moody; from him under his will to Richard Bingham Newland; from him in 1815 to William Garret; and from him in 1820 to the present lord.

The Manor of Havant rectory lies also within the manor of Havant, but is separate and distinct from it, passing with the living to each succeeding rector. It consists of some few houses and gardens running from the corner up to the bridge crossing the north street, which are held by copy of court roll, and are subject to a fine upon admission, a heriot upon death or alienation, and an annual quit rent. The eldest son is the customary heir. The present copyholds were doubtless part of the parish glebe, and the estates were granted out by rectors in the troubled times to raise an income. The Court Rolls are separate from those of Havant, and the earliest bears date in the year 1657.

The Thicket, Stockheath, and Leigh Green are the common wastes of the Manor of Havant. The former is a large tract of land containing about 800 statute acres, was formerly a chace or privileged place for deer and beasts of the forest, and till within the last thirty years a herd of fallow-deer ranged freely over its uncultivated space. These were preserved by the Bishops of Winchester, who appointed keepers and took every care to keep up the stock. There being however no park or inclosure the deer strayed away into the neighbouring lands and were gradually killed down. The copyhold tenants are entitled to herbage for their cattle and pannage for their swine, the summer pasturage of the cattle being stinted to the number that the tenant can fodder on his copyhold estate during the winter. The tenants have also a right to cut bushes for the repair of their fences and the usual botes.

Stockheath contains 17 statute acres, and has from time immemorial been the cricket-ground of the town of Havant.

The boundaries of the Manor of Havant are described in the perambulation of the 29th September 1820, as beginning in west marsh at the rails which part the two marshes adjoining the sea, proceeding northward on the east side of the rails towards Mill meadow, keeping the west side of the fence of Mill meadow half way along Mr. James Hewett's meadow, then over into Mill meadow, along the east side of the fence into the lane leading to Brockhampton Mill at an ash tree, proceeding along the west side of the land to the corner of the Rev. John Webster's meadows crossing over into Mr. Webster's meadow on the north side of the hedge, then into the arable field under the east and south hedges into the second arable field of Mr. Webster, through the gateway along under the east hedge on the west side over the stile, along under the south hedge on the south side following the direction of the hedge to Mr. John Midlane's Mill meadow, crossing into the field again along under the west hedge to the river going along the middle of the river to the north end of Hermitage croft, crossing the river into Long meadow, proceeding along the south hedge of Long meadow half-way then over into Hermitage croft again, and into the road from Stockheath under the east hedge of Hermitage croft southward into the turnpike road; proceeding along the turnpike eastward along under the north hedge to the corner of Mr. John Hammond's orchard, then over into Mr. James Hewett's field continuing about three rods under the south hedge, then over into the orchard again, proceeding under the west and north hedges of the orchard to the corner of the Rev. Thomas Frank's field, proceeding up the field northward on the west side of the hedge into Miss M. Marshall's field, along up the west hedge on the east side, and on the north hedge on the south side into Mr. Arthur Atherly's twelve acres, along the north hedge over the stile into Mr. James Platt's two fields, proceeding along the east hedge on the south side to Mr. White's Stockheath barn-field, turning round the south hedge to Stockheath lane, crossing the lane leading from Stockheath on the opposite side, proceeding to the parish cottages and other cottages, taking in Mr. Samuel Sharp's meadow, over into Stockheath again along under the west hedge on the east side by other cottages to Stockheath barn croft, up to Welche's cottages under the west hedge, taking in the lowermost of Welche's houses and land to the top of Ryder's lane into Havant Thicket, thence proceeding along under the east side of the hedge which divides Bedhampton Park from Havant Thicket up to the place where the ancient bound tree stood, called Lady Oak (now occupied by a stone inscribed G. T. S. 1820), proceeding along the east side of Blendworth inclosure bank, crossing the road to Horndean and the road to Rowland's Castle, thence up to Rowland's hills and following the direction of the fence belonging to Rowland's hills southward to Whicher's gate, keeping at a distance of eighteen feet from the fence of Rowland's hills as a drift road belonging to Rowland's hills, crossing the road at Whicher's gate excluding the cottage and garden, and proceeding along the east side of the hedge over Comley bottom now inclosed, and the hedge which bounds Mr. Joseph Holloway's land from Emsworth common also inclosed, up to Pollington's corner, thence crossing the road into another field of Mr. Joseph Holloway's, down to the south-west corner of the same field, then turning to the east into a field of Mr. Charles Earwaker, continuing along the hedge southward through a meadow of the said Charles Earwaker and a small field of Mr. John Todd through Mr. Joseph Holloway's barn-yard and gate-room into an oven of the cottage at East Leigh belonging to Mr. Joseph Holloway, in the occupation of Thomas Prior (into which oven crept a boy), and proceeding along Leigh lane southward under the west hedge to little Denfield, keeping under the north hedge and proceeding westward into the twenty-two acre field belonging to Mr. John Butler to the north-west corner thereof, turning round and following the west hedge of the same field and through the remaining land of the said John Butler down to Gravel-pit barn into the turnpike road, crossing the same and proceeding along the old lane lying between east Townsend field and a field of Mr. John Knight, and following the direction of Lymbourne stream through Langstone mill-pond to the great sluice there, leaving the mill-pond and following the direction of the stream as it runs through the mud to the channel in the harbour at low-water mark, thence into Hayling North in the island of Hayling. And be it remembered that the farms, lands, and hereditaments belonging to John Bannister, Stephen Rogers the elder, and Stephen Rogers, the younger, Jesse Crassweller, John Hellyer, Thomas Rogers, George Rogers, John Quinnell, Sarah Rogers, Mary Ann Rogers, Elizabeth Whitley and Joseph Lane, in Hayling North, are lying in the Manor of Havant, and are copyholds of

inheritance and subject to the same fines, heriots, customs, and
services as the other copyhold estates held under the Manor
of Havant, then proceeding along the channel in a boat
westward, keeping on the north side of the channel as far as
Brockhampton Mill Rythe, then up the Rythe into West
Marsh where the perambulation begun.

The Court Rolls of the Manor of Havant in the possession
of the present lord, reach back to the year 1611, and, with
the exception of intervals during the first twenty years, are
reasonably perfect. They contain the entries of the Court
Baron, partaking generally of the nature of customary courts,
for surrender and admittance and the settlement of disputes
relating to property among the tenants, and those of the Court
Leet, which extended to all crimes, offences, and misde-
meanors at the common law, as well as to others, which have
been subjected to it by Act of Parliament. These are
still inquired of by a body of the suitors elected, sworn,
and charged for that purpose, who must not be less than
twelve nor more than twenty-three, and who in some
manors continue in office for a whole year, whilst in others
they are sworn and discharged in the course of the day.
The customs of the manor, both with regard to descent and
with regard to the rights of the lord and those of the tenants,
are very full and explicit. They were first presented, and
were probably first reduced into writing in the year 1393,
and run as follows :

The son and eldest daughter are to inherite lands. There
are within the said mannor tennants in meane and tennants in
base, and the tennant in base doth hold with or of the meane
tennant, and the meane tennant doth hold of lord, and shall
make ffine with the lord for the whole.

If the tennant in base doe dye seized of lands, the tennant
in meane shall have herriott and releife of him.

If the tennant in base or in meane doe committ wast, the
lord shall have lands by escheate, viz., if he be convicted of
ffelony, if the tennant in base doe not maintaine his houses,
or if he be not resident, the tennant in meane shall have a
paine against him to amend the same by a day (that is to say)

a money paine or penalty, and the second paine fforfeiture of the tenement on which the paine is sett downe.

A yard of bondland and half a yard of bondland shall pay for herriott the best beast.

If the tennant in base doe alienate lands, the lord shall have herriott and ffine.

If many yards lands or half yards lands are holden under one fine, there shall be but one herriott paid for all, viz. the best beast; and for want of beast the best good or implement of houshold.

If a cottager being resiant upon his cottage doe decease, he shall pay his best beast for herriott, and if he shall have noe cattell he shall pay then for herriott his best garment or other his best good, and if he be not resiant upon his cottage he shall pay for herriott xij*d*.

The wife may hold the lands for terme of her widowhood if she will without ffine, but if she marry before she ffine, she looseth the land, and the next heir shall be admitted to ffine, and if she doe ffine in her widdowhood, as she may if she will, then she shall holde for terme of her life, and shall pay at her death for herriott her best beast if she have any cattell, but if she have a husband at the time of her decease then she shall pay noe herriott, neither hath she any goods or cattell of her own dureing the life of her husband.

The wife is next to fine after the death of her husband if she will, and the husband ought to fine for the wife with the lord, and soe for the woman heire with the land; and the woman shall give half the ffine aforesaid after the decease of her husband.

If any man doe marry a woman, whether he be heire or bond, he shall pay to the lord one-half of the ffine of his wife, and yett he shall only have the estate dureing the life of his wife.

It is to be noted that a certaine man holding in the right of his wife, one messuage and toft and iiij acres of bondland, did pay for a herriott his best beast, as that appeareth in the one-and-twentieth year of Henry Beaweford, and in the second year of Henry the Sixth, in the court rolls of the tything of Leigh.

Herriott shall be paid as well upon surrender as after the death of the tennaut.

No tennant may surrender his land if he be not of the lordship, but only before the steward or clark of the bishop-rick. The bayliffe or clark of the bayliwick may take sur-render of lands lying within the bayliwick, soe that the surrender be made in the bayliwick and not without.

The tythingman or warden may take surrender within the mannor of a tennant being in health, in the presence of two or three of the tennants, soe that the same surrender be not made upon condicon, for if it be conditionall then it cannot be taken but by the officers of the lord, except the condition be that he or his wife shall enjoy the land for the term of their lives. The tythingman or warden, or one of the lords, tennants of the mannor, may take surrender in sickness, or in point of death within the mannor, soe that the same surren-der be made in the presence of one witness, whether he be any of the lord's tennants or some other person whatsoever. If any surrender be made to any other person of any lands, and the same be not presented at the lawday or court within one year next after the making of the said surrender shall be void, and the year and day being past before presentment thereof be made, the lord shall have the land by escheat. A tennant lying in extremity of sickness may surrender his lands if he will, under condition that if he recover that sick-ness and doe live that then the surrender shall be void.

The tennant may surrender his land in mortgage, soe that the surrender be made before the steward or clark of the court or bayliffe of the bishoprick, and be written in the court rolls.

The tennants may take and sell the woods and under-woods growing upon their finable lands, soe that they make noe waste or destruction in the coppices. Also they may take the timber growing upon their finable land for the repaireing of their tenements from time to time without any assignment, soe they make noe wast. And if the lord doe assign timber for repaireing of any tenement of the mannor upon any lands, the tennant upon the same lands shall have the lopps of the said timber. And if any timber be taken up for the king the tennant shall have the lopps and alsoe the price of the said timber.

If any tennant in meane have not timber growing upon his tenement for the repairing thereof, the lord shall allow half the timber for the repairing thereof out of the comon wood, but not for the new-building of every house.

The meane tennant shall allow timber to the base tennant of the tenement if there be any, or else he shall be allowed timber out of the comon wood or elsewhere by the lord, only for repairations, and further, the lord shall allow timber for the repairations of the other tenements and cottages in the town of Havant which are holden by ffine.

A tennant may ffine for his land at the first or second proclamation if he will, but if he will not he shall be amerced; and if the tennant or some other for him doe not come and make ffine at the third proclamation he looseth his land, and if he doe dye before he make ffine with the lord his heire shall pay the ffine of his predecessor and also his own ffine.

If he to whom surrender is made doe decease before he hath fined for his lands, and soe that there be one proclamacōn between the surrender and his decease, the lands shall come into the hands of the lord by escheat. If not then the heire shall fine for the land as before, paying his two ffines, viz. his predecessor's and his own.

A tennant cannot demise his lands above a year, if he doe he forfeits his estate.

If any doe voluntarily permitt his tenement to fall or be pulled down without license he forfeits his estate.

If any tennant doe implead another of the lord's tennants of the said manor out of the court without license, he forfeiteth his estate.

The meane tennant shall have two paines in money sett downe on him to repaire his tenement, and if he will not at the third paine he forfeiteth his estate.

The tennants doe give for pawnedge of their hogs yearly at the ffeast of St. Martin, for every hog above a year old ij*d.*, of three-quarters j*d.*, of half-a-year old a penny, and for piggs

5

weened from their dams a oᵬ. whether there be any mast or noe mast in the lord's woods.

These customs have been somewhat changed with regard to the heriots, the cutting of timber on the lands of the copy-hold tenants, and the allowance of timber to the tenants for the repair of their buildings ; and as these heriot and timber customs are become of considerable importance at the present day, it is desirable as far as possible to see in what way the alterations have taken place, and the encroach-ments made upon the rights of the tenants. On reference to the Custom·Roll it will be seen that the heriot due upon many yardlands or half-yardlands holden under one fine is " one heriot paid for all, viz. the best beast, and for want " of a beast the best good or implement of household stuff." In cases too numerous to mention these best beast heriots have been changed upon the Court Rolls into best good heriots, which has materially depreciated the value of the copyholders' estates, inasmuch as under the proper custom, the best beast must first be seized, and in default of a best beast then the best good. The custom of a best beast heriot enabled a tenant to provide against the contingency, because so long as a beast was found to answer the lord's claim, the latter was confined to the object of his seizure, whereas under the best good heriot it was impossible to know what might be taken—a picture for instance of far greater value than the estate in respect of which it was seized, and in addition to this, the lord, supposing him to be entitled to a best good heriot, would be authorised to go into another county in order to make his election, if the tenant lived there, in preference to the seizure upon the copyhold tenement itself. These alterations are not the work of late years, but arose during the period when the manor was leased out by the bishops, antecedent to the present century. In the evidence taken before the Commissioners in the suits of Halsey v. Moody, and Halsey v. Moody and Brooke, I find it deposed upon the oath of Edward Bayly, M.D., then a copyhold tenant, and whose ancestors to the fifth generation had likewise been copyhold tenants since the year 1609, "that "he had seen many copies of admittance of persons to copy- "hold lands and tenements held of the manor of Havant, and "in the margin of such copies he found the words *heriot* "*optimum bonum* written and inserted on account of the "heriots claimed by the lord of the said manor," and that he, having occasion to compare such copies with divers other copies prior in time to them and relating to the same lands, found that the heriots had been changed into *optimum bonum.* This fraudulent alteration of the heriots was further confirmed by the evidence of Robert Andrews of Hayling, taken in the same suits. The heriot question eventually became the subject of an action at law. Upon the death of Thomas Longcroft the brother-in-law of John Moody, James Newland the steward of Moody's trustees seized a valuable cow as a heriot, stated to be due in respect of a copyhold estate of which Thomas Longcroft had died seized. An action was at once brought by George Moody Longcroft, as the executor of his father, against the lords; the case was tried at the Winchester Assizes, and upon holding the Court Rolls up to the light the ancient entries of *unum solidum* were clearly seen to have been erased, and the words *optimum bonum* inserted in their place. The verdict was of course adverse to the lords, and the copyholders of the manor presented Mr. Longcroft upon the occasion, with a silver urn in the shape of a cow, bearing an inscription commemorative of the trial.

By reference to the Custom Roll it will also be seen, that the mesne tenant, if he have no timber upon his estate, is to be allowed half by the lord for repairs out of the common wood; that the base tenant is to be allowed timber out of the common wood for repairs, and that timber shall be allowed by the lord for the repairs of the other tenements and cottages in Havant, holden by fine. Upon a recent occasion a copyhold tenant in want of timber for repairs, was refused an allowance, and it was stated in answer to the application, that no exercise of the right of allowance had been maintained in latter years, and that the timber was not the property of the

lord but of the bishop, being excepted out of the conveyance
of the manor. As there are very many entries upon the rolls
confirming the ancient custom, some of those occurring since
the manor has been leased out have been carefully extracted,
and are here subjoined.

25th March, 42 Elizabeth.—The homage further present
that the barn of Jane Latthew is dilapidated for want of
timber (marrenn.), therefore timber is allowed, and a day is
given to the aforesaid Jane to repair the aforesaid barn before
the feast of Saint Michael the Archangel next, under a pain.

4th June, 2 James.—The homage further present that the
several tenements of Edward Leake gentleman, John Kent,
and Henry Cosen are dilapidated for want of timber, viz. the
tenement of the aforesaid Edward Leake *pro duobus caricatibus*
(*Anglicè* two tunns), the aforesaid John Kent for one tunn,
and the aforesaid Henry Cosen for one tunn; therefore the
aforesaid separate quantities of timber are allowed.

6th May, 4 James.—The homage further present that
the tenement of Gregory Hall and the cottage of Thomas
Courtier in the south street of Havant are out of repair
for want of timber. Book ii, p. 21, 1612.—The homage
further present that the mansion house belonging to four
yardlands of land the property of Mary Vachell, widow, lying
in Hayling within the manor aforesaid, had been burnt and
accidentally consumed by misfortune of fire happening to
it. Therefore the aforesaid Mary Vachell is commanded that
she erect and substantially build a house upon the tenement
aforesaid before the feast of the Annunciation of the blessed
Virgin Mary now next ensuing, under the pain to be levied
of £3. 6s. 8d. And since there is not sufficient timber growing upon the lands aforesaid to build the house aforesaid,
therefore timber for the erection of the same is to be assigned
from the woods and coppices of the lord according to the
custom of the Manor aforesaid. Book ii, p. 46, 1615.—The
homage further present that the tenement of Jane Bellson,
widow, is dilapidated and falling down for want of repair, and
that two tuns of timber are required for the repair of the

tenement aforesaid in the judgment of the carpenter. Book ii, p. 68, 1614.—Inhabitants of Leigh tything ordered to repair Aylmers bridge. At p. 71, the homage further present that the bridge called Aylmers bridge had not been repaired in pursuance of the pain laid upon the inhabitants of Leigh at the last Tourn because they had not timber assigned them. Book iii, p. 3.—The homage further present that the several tenements of Zachary Roman, Ann Jones widow, John Wingham, John Bowler, Robert Leaper, and Richard Wood, parcel of the manor, are out of repair, and that each one of them requires timber for the repair of his tenement aforesaid. Book iii, p. 10.—The homage further present that the tene-ment upon the copyhold lands of Zachary Roman in Hayling is out of repair, and that he is in need of one load and a half of timber to repair his tenement aforesaid. Book iii, p. 18.— The homage further present that the tenement and barn upon the customary lands of Zachary Roman in Hayling are out of repair, and that he requires two loads of timber to repair the tenement and barn aforesaid. Book iii, p. 33.—The homage further present that the tenement of Bartholemew Sone is very dilapidated and out of repair, and that he requires three loads of timber for the repair of the tenement aforesaid. Book iii, p. 35.—The homage further present that the several tenements and barns upon the customary lands of John Chatfield gentleman, and Clement Roman are out of repair, and that each one of them requires two loads of timber for the repair of the tenement aforesaid. Book v, p. 66.—The homage also present that the buildings of John Sopp require repair, and that there is need of three loads of timber to repair the same. They also present that the build-ings of William Bayley require repair, and that there is need of six loads of timber to repair the same. They also present that the customary tenants of this manor are entitled to have timber allowed from the common wood for their necessary repairs where there is none growing upon the premises. Book v, p. 75.—The homage further present that the build-ings of John Biggs knight, one of the customary tenants of this manor, require repair, and that there is need of three tuns of timber to repair the same, to be had from the common wood for the repair of the same according to the custom of the manor aforesaid. They also present that the buildings of William Bayley, one of the customary tenants of this manor, stand in need of repair, and that six tuns of timber are required to repair the same to be had from the common wood for the repair of the same according to the custom of the manor aforesaid.

The Leet Rolls, in which most of the foregoing present-ments are found, are irregular from about the year 1745 to about the year 1796. The entries adduced, show that the custom was clearly recognized and acted upon at the time they were made. The position of the lord and his copyhold tenants is the same as in former days; the heriots, fines, and quit rents then payable are still due, and because the bishop and the lord may have entered into an arrangement to which the copyholders were in no way parties, but under which it is said the former acquired the exclusive property in the timber, and because in later years the allowances have not been required or demanded to the same extent as formerly, is it to be contended that the copyholders are to be deprived of a permanent and valuable privilege? It is true that the timber was excepted out of the conveyance to the present lord, but the Thicket or common wood is still parcel of the Manor of Havant, timber is still growing there, and it may fairly be asked why the ancient allowance should where needed be withheld.

The ancient presentments of the Courts Leet and Baron may be conveniently classed under the following heads :—

Firstly,—Those which relate to general offences within the Liberty.

Secondly,—Those which relate to weights and measures.

Thirdly,—Those which relate to the repair of public build-ings and public highways.

1st. GENERAL OFFENCES.—The homage present that Elena Barram, the wife of Humphrey Barram of Havant, barber, is a common scold among her neighbours, therefore she is adjudged to the tumbrell. A paine that noe butcher within this liberty doe sell any bull flesh within the toune of Havant until the same be bayted in the market place uppon paine of every of them 6s. 8d. They present that there is a Book that concerns their custome now remayeninge in the handes of John Hannam bayliff of the said manor. It is ordered that Stephen Bellson, William Woods, William Aylmer gent. Richard Langrishe, Thomas Hipkin, Alexander Higgen, and William Stonard, shall meet before Whitsontide next and shall tax indifferently the inhabitants of this liberty for a contribution towards an amerciament of 40s. set on them for want of a cucking stool, and that the tythingmen of the several tythings, shall presently after the taxation, levye suche somes of money as shal be bye the said parties taxed, and shall paye the same to the lord's bayliff. Book i, commencing in 1566. —They present that Robert Dudman made an affray and drew blood from Humphry Barram with a stick, and fine him 3s. 4d. They also present that Alice Toms the wife of Robert Thoms is a common scold and she is adjudged to the tumbrell. They also present that Richard Townsend, during the feast of the purification of the Virgin, made an affray upon Robert Norrys and drew blood with a dagger, and they fine him 3s. 4d. They present that William Woolgar, Philip Mitchell, Nicholas Wyngham, and others, permit, and each one of them permits, unlawful games in each one of their houses, therefore they are each fined 2s. 6d. We present Robert Woods and Nicholas Godfrey for playing at cards in the house of Arthur Woolgar, and we pain them 12d. each. It is ordered that no inhabitant receive into his house any unknown or strange person to inhabit with him unless they shall first find sufficient sureties to exonerate the town under the penalty in each case of 20s. William Stonard is fined 5s. for disturbing the Court. They present that Robert Dudman is an habitual drunkard, and he is fined 3s. 4d. They present that Eleanora Barron is a common scold and a disturber of her neighbours, and she is adjudged to the tumbrell. William Stone is commanded to provide a remedy that the smoke which comes out of his kiln which he lately erected, should not be injurious to John Talke under a penalty of 40*s.* It is ordered that Thomas Heather shall not scald any porkers in the street, or lay any soile thereafter there upon pain to forfeit 5*s.* It is ordered that W. Geldernet, J. Goodchild, and other inhabitants of Havant, remove glandered and diseased horses from the commons of Havant, within ten days, under a pain of 10*s.* Book iii.—We take a pain against Thomas Lambe that he take away the window of his shop that offends Mr. Streete in taking away the light of Mr. Streete's hall window to the west end of it, between this day and the first day of November next ensuing, upon the pain of 20*s.* The homage present John Baylie for a common anoyance of the inhabitants of this manor, for not buringe of his murrin beast for which they amerce him 13*s.* 4*d.* Wee present Francis Aylinge, Richard Woods, Widow Monck, William Reed, William Bagshall, and Ann Bayly for keeping of geese and ducks which doth much anoy the fresh watter or water course that they keepe them upp after the 21st day of December next, uppon paine of 3*s.* 4*d.* each of them. We present Joseph Barkett for alowing hys wife to wash children's clouts and other things in the head of Homewell spring, also Sarah Bratton for washing of linen, tubs, dishes, and other things in the head of the said spring, and that they forbear doing the same again under the penalty of 40*s.* each person for every such offence. Book iv.—A pain set against Thomas Green, Thomas Heather, and Harry Heather, butchers, that they remove their tressels and planks on which they lay their meat on the market days under Mr. Battine's window and in the highway, that they remove them always on the Saturday nights, on the pain of 3*s.* 4*d.* a piece for every time so offending. A pain set against every inhabitant of the parish that they keep their chimnies clean and well swept, that they fire not to flame out, on the pain of 3*s.* 4*d.* for every time so offending. A paine of 3*s.* 4*d.* was formerly taken against the inhabitants of the parish of Havant that they keep their chimnies clean swept, and do present that the chimney at Mr. Street's house in the East Street was on fire, and that it did flame out at top. A paine is set against John Russell for keeping of an unlawful shovelboard table and to play unlawful games, and that he forbear the same in time to come under the pain of 6*s.* 8*d.* The Jury do present as a common nuisance, many do tie their horses in the streets on the market days to the great danger of children passing by. It is therefore ordered by this Court that the crier after publication made thereof, the next market day shall from time to time put all such horses into the common pound, and the offender shall pay for every time so offending, 12*d.* a horse. A pain is set against any butcher that shall kill or stick a sheep in the open street not having wherewith to receive the blood, upon the pain of 3*s.* 4*d.* for each time so offending. A pain is set against Robert Childs that he take down his flue, newly built at the east end of his house, because for fear of danger of firing his house and the town which houses do adjoin his house, we pain him that he take it down between this and the last day of November next coming, or build it higher so as no danger come thereof, under £5 pain. Book iv.—We present Thomas Cook, Richard Browman, Francis Higgins as persons unqualified for selling beer being Papists and not having licénces. We present the carrion in the garden of John Betsworth at the Bell, as a nuisance to Mr. Edward Holton. We present the dung in Hamwell lane belonging to Mr. James Andrews, as it entirely stops up the kennel and hinders people from passing, and we adjudge that unless it be removed by the said Mr. James Andrews within ten days from the date hereof, it shall belong to any person who shall think proper to take it up. We present, for so we are informed, that William Harris, one of the present tythingmen of this liberty, being called out of his bed on Tuesday the 13th of October (1757), about 11 o'clock of the same evening to quash a riot at the house of Moses Smith, bearing the sign of the Old Starr in Havant, he was there insulted by Serjeant Cornall who drew his sword and threatened his life, and took from him by violence the staff of his office. We present the post and seats that is fixed on and projecting from any house to be a nuisance and to be removed in ten days, under penalty of 40*s.* to be paid to the overseers of this parish for the benefit of the poor. We present the posts adjoining to the house of John Lellyett to be a nuisance, and that the same be taken up or removed by the said John Lellyett within two days next after notice given him for that purpose under the forfeiture or penalty of £5, to be levied on him the said John Lellyett. We present that if any person shall permit or suffer any waggon, cart, roller, or any implement of husbandry to be left in any of the streets of Havant after it is dark, every such person shall forfeit and pay the sum of twenty shillings for every such offence. We present that all vagrants and beggars, gypsies, and such others as are found within this liberty particularly mentioned and described in the Act of Parliament of the 39 Elizabeth and the 17 George II, are a nuisance, and that they ought to be taken up in future and dealt with by the future officers as is directed by the same statutes (1731 to 1775).·

2d. WEIGHTS AND MEASURES.—We present Robert Smith the miller for taking excessive toll and we pain him 3s. 4d. (tem. Eliz.) We represent that Reuben Hart sells by unlawful measures, therefore he is fined 8d. (Book ii, 1612). We present that John Burton, Thomas Palmer, John Hammond, John Russell, John Kempe, Arthur Jenkinson, Johanna Monck widow, and William Reed commonly sell drink by unlawful measures against the form of the statute, each fined 12d. Edward Searl, Vincent Merriot, Agnes Boundy, Richard Long, J. Kempe and J. Cock commanded not to sell bread for the future except by the assize according to the form of the statute, pen. 12d. We present that Richard Hobbs, fish salesman, exposed to sale and sold unwholesome fish and we pain him 12d. (Book iii.) We present that John Sones for selling unsufficient tanned leather and for selling of ten sole hides to Thomas Martin not tanned. We present the said Thomas Martin for buying of untanned leather. Francis Sapp the elder is amerced 3s. 4d. for being a forestaller and regrator of the market. The widow Boundy, Richard Long, the wife of Michael White, and J. Pink are amerced 2s. 6d. a piece for selling of bread not of lawful assize. Mathew Streete, John Upham,

John Russell, and Richard Stempe are amerced 4*d*. a piece for selling beer by unlawful measures. We present Thomas Heather for buying of provisions in the market before the proper time as altered, one side of beef, and selling it again, we amerce him 6*d*. We present the constables to provide weights and scales to weigh bread and butter in with all other things by the 20th day of May (1646), and we pain them 20*s*. if they do not provide the same. (Book iii). We present that if at any time hereafter any lead weights short of weight shall be found in the custody of any person or persons by the coroners of this liberty, upon a view such coroners shall make the same full weight by driving stubs therein, and that the owner or owners of such weights, shall forfeit and pay the sum of one penny for each and every stub driven therein to make the same full weight; and that if any person or persons within the jurisdiction of this Leet, shall have in his, her, or their custody, any brass or iron weight, short of weight, such person or persons shall for each and every such weight, forfeit and pay the sum of one shilling to the coroner; and that if any person or persons keeping a public house within the jurisdiction of the Leet shall be detected or have in his, her or their custody, any measure short of the standard measure of this kingdom, such person or persons shall for each and every such measure forfeit and pay the sum of one shilling for each and every such measure to the coroner of the jurisdiction of this Leet, on his discovering the same (1769).

3d. PUBLIC BUILDINGS, HIGHWAYS &c.—It is ordered that the inhabitants of the Parish of Havant shall amend the highway leading from Havant to Langstone, and also so much of the wadeway as lieth within the parish of Havant before the feast day of St. James the Apostle upon paine of twenty shillings. (27 Nov. 1 James). We present that the pound and the fish shambles are in dilapidation, and that the Lord of this Manor ought of ancient right to repair and amend them. (4 April 1611). We present that Sarah Pystor the wife of Ròbert Pystor clerk with other women, they account about the time of Hocktide 1609, collected in certain sums ten shillings, and detains the same which ought to be applied to the reparing and amending of the bridge called Hamwell now in ruins. It is ordered that the constable of Havant repair the stocks and make good the tumbrel and pillory, before the next court upon pain of 20s. They present that the market bushel belonging to the town of Havant is too small, and that a half bushel is wanted to measure the corn, the inhabitants are therefore desired to make for themselves a bushel and half bushel according to the standard, before the feast of St. Philip and James next ensuing, if it appear in the Court Rolls that they ought to make the same, under a penalty of 20s. (1612). It is ordered by the tourn with the assent of the haywards of the town, that the haywards make or cause to be placed a pump in the well called the Town well before the feast of St. Michael the Archangel, under the penalty of £5. We present the Lord of the Manor for not repairing the market house sufficient both in scaling, walling and other fencing belonging to the market house, that it may be sufficient to keep those dry which come to market. We pain him five pounds to be paid to the poor of the parish of Havant, if it be not repaired between this and the first day of December next coming (1645). Item, whereas the market house is not sufficiently repaired according to the former presentment being presented the last court to be repaired by the first day of December last, it not being as yet done we finding it to be a very great disabling to all the inhabitants by reason of the market being not so well served in corn, and also provision to the undoing of the tradesmen, we presenting it formerly five pounds, and finding it not done do pain the said Lord of the Manor ten pounds to the poor of the town of Havant. (1646). We present Mr. Woolgar (the then lord) to fence up the pound between this and the 20th day of May next 1647. We present the common pound to be in repair, and to be repaired by the Lord of the Manor of Havant (1656). We present the constable of this town of Havant, and Liberty to make a new pair of stocks and repair the whipping post between this and the first day of July next coming, upon pain of 20*s*. We present the market house fallen down, and that the same be rebuilt again. (1710, 4 May.) We present the market house being down being an impoverishment to the whole inhabitants of the town, particular to poor people and all tradesmen for want of a market, and we desire that it may be built by Midsummer next, the inhabitants being very willing to build their part. (Oct. 1710). We present the cage of Havant being entirely down. (1737). We present Pallant lane as choked up with straw and dung. (1768). We present that the constables and surveyors of the highways for the time being be requested to survey the pitching before the doors of the several inhabitants of the said Liberty, and where they find the same out of repair to give notice to the occupier of the house, whose right it is to repair the same within fifteen days after such notice be given, and in case such person or persons shall neglect to repair the same in pursuance of such notice the person or persons so neglecting shall forfeit and pay twenty shillings. (1774).

The business of the Court Leet has in a great measure long since passed to the Quarter Sessions. It was formerly held twice a year, but is now held annually only in the month of October, when nuisances are presented and the following officers elected, viz. two constables for the Liberty of Havant, Leigh, Hayling North, and Brockhampton; a coroner of the market, leather-sealer, ale-taster, and haywards.

THE CHURCH of Havant is in the form of a Latin cross, and stands surrounded by the churchyard. The custom of building churches in the form of a Latin cross, that is with the nave longer than the chancel, was first introduced into this country about the reign of Edward the Confessor. It consists of a chancel, nave, side aisles, and transepts, with a square embattled tower, having a massive buttress at the east angle to counteract an original settlement, and a turret staircase at the north-east angle. The pillars which support the tower and were continued through the nave, form the most ancient portion of the edifice. The centre pillar is of white stone and the two side shafts are of black Sussex marble, the beauties of which are concealed beneath successive coats of whitewash. Upon cleaning away a part of the wood-work round the base of the pillars in 1832 when the building was under repair, the workmen discovered that the existing structure stood upon the foundation of one still more ancient, and that the basement of the pillars rested upon a solid concrete of Roman brick and cement, so close in texture and quality that it resembled lava, and resisted all the ordinary processes of decay. Between the basement and the original foundation a coin of Antoninus Pius was found struck about the year 140 A. C., with a copper coin of Magnus Maximus and Flavius Victor. The capitals of the pillars are of Anglo-Saxon architecture, and are rude in design and detail; from these spring four pointed arches of very early English date, massive but devoid of that ornament usually the characteristic feature of prominent arches. They are all plainly chamfered with the exception of that upon the western side facing the nave, which is moulded to correspond probably with the style of that part of the building. At about four feet above the spring of the chancel arch there is a projection which has always been called a piscina, but inasmuch as it does not con-tain a drain for the water, and as it could only be used by persons in the roodloft which was taken down at the Reformation, I am inclined to think that it was a stand for an hourglass rather than a piscina. In all churches previous to the Reformation the pulpit faced the west, that the faces of the congregation in acts of devotion might look towards the east according to the custom of primitive times, and the minister measured the length of his sermon by the turn of the glass. The tower is fifty-four feet high with embattled pinnacles, and is ascended by the turret newel staircase which is of stone, entered by a long, round-headed doorway. A few paces above this there is a doorway with a triangular arch which led formerly into the roodloft and belfry, but is now closed up. Above this, two doors each with a triangular Romanesque arch lead into the belfry, and above the belfry a third triangular arched doorway leads into the bell-loft which contains a peal of six bells with chimes, the machinery of which is at the present moment out of order. In the bell-loft there are four windows of Anglo-Norman or Early English architecture, the stonework of which is large and wide jointed, and the masonry very good.

The walls of the tower are four feet thick, and are composed of stone, for the most part hammer dressed, and a rubble concrete of mortar and flint, with a large quantity of small Roman brick. At the south-west angle of the cornice is a gurgoyle head much disfigured. Somewhat below the cornice about the centre of the west side is another head, which, with the exception of the mouth, is still perfect. It is cut out of a single large stone between four and five feet in length, hewn evidently for the express purpose, which running from the outside carving through the wall projects about a foot into the interior of the bell-loft. The sculpture represents the full face of a man with dilated eyes, long hair parted in the centre, and features expressive of cruelty and ignorance. A similar stone faced the eastern side of the tower; the inside projection into the bell-loft still remains, but the face on the outside has been cut away to make room for the dial of the clock, and the subject of the carving has passed away from remembrance. There have been various conjectures as to the object and explanation of the western head, some calling it a gurgoyle, and some supposing it to be a corbel stone; the better idea however is that it is an indication stone, sometimes also called a perpent stone, similar to those found at Bosham in Sussex, at Aldborough and Kirkdale in Yorkshire, at Postling in Kent, and Great Bookham in Surrey, and that it is commemorative of the foundation and dedication of the structure either as a temple or church subsequent to the Roman era. It has no opening at the mouth, therefore cannot be a gurgoyle, and if it had been intended for a corbel it would not have been its present size or length as the corbel table round the tower is plain, and each corbel very much smaller. It much resembles that found some years since at Bosham, which is

generally considered to have been a representation of the
Saxon god Woden, and it is possible that this stone may be
contemporary with some edifice which in Anglo-Saxon times
before the conversion of the inhabitants may have been a
heathen temple dedicated to that god whose sacrifices were
offered on the fourth day of the week, and from which we
derive our present name of Wednesday. It is clear that Anglo-
Saxon temples were adopted for Christian worship, for in Pope
Gregory's epistle to Melito the abbot, A. D. 601, the following
order occurs : " The idol temples ought not to be destroyed,
" but let the idols which are in them be destroyed. Let holy
" water be consecrated and sprinkled in these temples, let
" altars be built and relics be deposited, and because they are
" in the habit of slaying many oxen in sacrificing to dæmons,
" on the anniversary day of the dedication or the birthdays of
" the holy martyrs (i. e. the day of their martyrdom), let booths
" be constructed of the branches of trees around those churches
" which were formerly temples, and let them celebrate the
" solemnity with religious festivity." (*Spel. Concilia*, i, p. 89).
In the Ecclesiastical laws of king Edward, A. D. 967, can. 28,
these solemnities are called *"encænia ecclesiarum,"* or church
wakes, and great abuses having arisen out of this practice, laws
were at various times made to control them.   Any one who
visited a church upon the anniversary of its dedication was
supposed to be entitled to an indulgence of forty days, but
this custom was much curtailed by Othobon the legate in
1268, when he forbade the holding of a fair or market within
the walls of churches, it having been the usage previous to
that time to sell cakes and ale within the sacred building
itself.

    Now the fairs of the Manor of Havant are held on the 17th
of October, and the 22d of June.   By the Act 24 George II,
1752, it was provided, that the natural day next immediately following the 2d of September 1752 should be
called and accounted to be the 14th of September, omit-
ting for that time only the eleven intermediate nominal days
of the common calendar ; and by the fourth section it was
enacted that the holding of all markets, fairs, and marts

affixed to certain nominal days of the month, should be thereafter kept eleven days later. Applying therefore this rule to
the fairs of Havant, we find the former held eleven days later
than the feast of Saint Faith, the time mentioned in both the
charters, and the latter, eleven days later than the eleventh of
June, which falls on the feast of Saint Barnabas. The Saint
Faith fair is held in the Fair-field, the occupants of the various
booths paying stallage for their standings, while the Saint
Barnabas fair is held in the streets and around the walls of
the church. There is no grant of the Saint Barnabas fair in
existence ; tradition is altogether silent as to its origin, and to
what are we therefore to attribute it ? Saint Barnabas who was
a native of Cyprus, preached at Salamis, Paphos, and travelled
through Asia Minor in company with Saint Paul. He preached
at Rome, and it is said that he visited Britain. At Glaston-
bury formerly grew a walnut tree, which never budded until
the Saint's day, and in reference to his festival, the old adage
is still preserved in Somersetshire of

> " Barnaby bright, Barnaby bright,
> The longest day and the shortest night,"

marking the commencement of Midsummer or nightless days,
continuing until the 2d of July. The Midsummer daisy,
or *Chrysanthemum leucanthemum*, was also called Barnabas
daisy. Presuming the fair of Saint Barnabas to have been
first celebrated as an *encænium* or church-wake,—and the site
of the holding, and the absence of a special charter strengthen
the supposition,—it may well be that the dedication, on the
conversion of the Saxon temple to a Christian church, took
place in the seventh century under Bishop Wilfred to Saint
Barnabas ; and that, upon the rebuilding of the church in the
tenth century, upon the donation of the manor by King
Ethelred to the monastery of Winchester, the sacred edifice
was re-dedicated to Saint Faith, the more ancient festival of
Saint Barnabas being still retained as the church-wake of the
inhabitants, in accordance with primitive custom.

The Chancel, built in the early part of the fifteenth century,

7

was originally very elegant in design and execution; it has five windows, one of which is now stopped up, in the Perpendicular style, with a vaulted roof, ribbed mouldings, and brackets to correspond. The bosses in the roof are very curious, of a date long antecedent to the fifteenth century, and probably formed part of the chancel which stood on the site of the present one. The beauty of the work is entirely concealed by whitewash; the groove in the main arch, used for the screen and hangings which separated the body of the church from the altar, is still visible. On the south side of the altar the fretted tracery of the sedilia is to be seen, but the piscina and ambrey have been plastered over. The sedilia were for the officiating ministers, for by a constitution of Henry Woodlocke, bishop of Winchester A.D. 1308, it was specially ordered that in all churches commonly valued at fifty marks and upwards, there should be one deacon and one sub-deacon continually ministering. (*Wilk. Concilia*, ii, p. 295). The munificent William of Wykeham doubtless supplied the funds for the rebuilding of the chancel and the repair of the tower, for upon an examination of the beams in the belfrey in 1832, when the whole was surveyed, several Nurenberg tokens were discovered in the bonding of the timbers, which were of the date of 1400, and upon the corbels of the south-west window of the chancel are still to be seen a head, apparently of the bishop, and a crowned head, which is certainly that of Henry IV, his royal patron. The vestry has been added subsequently; it contains nothing worthy of notice with the exception of the parish chest, hewn out of a solid log, bound with iron, secured with three locks, and very similar to those of the twelfth century. The ancient Anglo-Saxon font which stood in the nave was, for some unexplained reason, destroyed in 1832.

The Orientation of the Church is not strictly in accordance with the cardinal points of the compass; but this is explained by the custom of our forefathers, who, when a church was about to be built, watched and prayed on the vigil of the dedication, and took that point of the horizon where the sun rose for the east. (*Ant. Rep.* i, p. 72). The grant of indulgences was a great encouragement to those who felt disposed to contribute to the erection of a church, and an interesting account of the building of Crowland Abbey in 1112, is preserved in the narrative of Peter Blesensis, vice-chancellor to Henry II. "Prayers being said and "anthems sung, the Abbot himself laid the first corner stone "on the east side. After him every man according to his "degree laid his stone: some laid money, others writings "by which they offered their lands, advowsons of livings, "tenths of sheep and other church tithes, certain measures "of wheat, a certain number of workmen and masons. On "the other side, the common people, as officious with emu- "lation and great devotion, offered, some money, some one "day's work in every month until it should be finished, some "to build whole pillars, others pedestals, and others certain "parts of the wall."

The first register book of Baptisms preserved in the vestry begins the 18th December 1653, and ends the 13th August 1731. The second book begins the 15th August 1731, and ends the 27th December 1812, from which time the new register commences.

The first register book of Marriages begins the 24th January 1653, and from this time to the 24th June 1657, there are thirty-four entries of marriages before justices of the peace at Portsmouth. There is no marriage registered from the 26th January 1659 to 29th July 1661, from the 27th October 1664 to the 12th May 1667, from the 12th May 1667 to the 29th June 1669, or from the 29th June 1669 to the 4th May 1673. This book ends on the 9th May 1729. The second book begins the 19th September 1731; there is no entry of marriage from the 9th May 1729 to the 19th September 1731, and it ends on the 10th February 1754. The third book begins the 16th August 1754, and ends on the 10th November 1793. The fourth book begins 26th November 1793, and ends the 25th December 1812, from which time the new register commences.

The first register book of Burials begins the 8th January

1653—no burial is entered from a blank date immediately following 22d May 1660 to 1662, none in 1669, and ends on the 15th April 1697. The second book begins 7th August 1698, and ends the 10th September 1730 ; but in this as well as in the preceding book, the names of the persons buried are so much obliterated by damp as to be nearly illegible. The third book begins the 14th October 1730, and after a burial on the 21st May 1758 the following memorandum is entered in the register : "The register from this time to "the 20th June 1761, was destroyed by accident." This book ends on the 29th November 1812, from which time the new register commences.

An organ was added to the church in 1779, but this being out of order was removed in 1832, and the present organ by Lincoln was substituted and paid for by sub-scription. The churchyard covers an acre of ground, and, like Dereham and other ancient sites, has a well to the east of the chancel. There was usually in the early ages a fountain near the principal entrance where the people used to wash themselves before they entered the sacred edifice. It was termed Cantharus Phiala, and by modern writers Leontarium. One is found adjoining the churchyard of Havant, still called Homewell, a corruption of Hamwell, sig-nifying the well of the town.

Thomas Aylward, the first rector upon record, was con-temporary with William of Wykeham, was employed by him as his private secretary, and shared his patron's confidence. Tradition has handed down that Aylward had the honour of entertaining the bishop as his guest at the rectory, and that he wrote the life of Wykeham, which was bequeathed to Winchester College, and became specifically entrusted to the care of the warden for the time being. It seems that the MS. descended in successive charges to the wardens, until Chaundler, warden, deposited it in the custody of Waynfleete bishop of Winchester, by whom it was lost. Wykeham appointed Aylward one of his executors, and left him a considerable legacy. He also committed to him the

pious charge of completing a tomb over the remains of his
father and mother, who were buried at Southwick, and placed
in his hands a sum sufficient to defray the necessary expenses.
Aylward died on the 6th April 1413, and was buried in the
north transept of the church, where a brass plate represented
hm in his clerical vestments in the attitude of prayer, with
the following inscription :

> " *Dne. in tua misericordia confido.*
> *Hic jacet Dnus. Thomas Aileward,*
> *quondm. Rector, istius Ecclie, qui obijt*
> *vj. die mensis Aprilis,*
> *Anno Dni. Millo ccccxiij.*
> *Cui aie. ppicietur Deus, Amen.*
> *Sis testis Xte, quodnon iacet hic lapis iste,*
> *Corpus ut ornet, sed mors ut pmediet.*"

This tomb was in the centre of the transept, and in 1797,
on an alteration of the seats, the brass slab, which stood about
a foot above the level of the floor, was removed and placed in
an upright position against the north wall.   Over the inscription it bears the arms of Aylward : a chevron between three
garbs, two in chief and one in base.   Upon the occasion
of the removal, the workmen who were employed having an
idea that the tomb itself contained treasure, cleared away the
soil, and opened the stone sarcophagus where the body had
been deposited.   There was no appearance of previous
disturbance, but not a vestige of humanity remained to indicate the tenant of its narrow cell.

William Ramsey appears to have been rector in 1543,
Lawrence Stone in 1558, and Robert Pystor in 1610.
(*Court Rolls, H. M.*)   Francis Ringsted is mentioned by
Walker, in his *Sufferings of the Clergy*, as rector of Havant, and
he also states that during Cromwell's usurpation his property
was sequestered, for which the commissioners brought him to
a composition of £40. Ringsted obtained thirty several orders
for fifths, but could not get one of them obeyed, insomuch
that it is said to have broken his heart. (*Walker*, p. 347;
Butler, p. 20.)

John Bellchamber was rector in 1658. Upon his death
William Browne was inducted on the 13th June 1668,
and John Reade was inducted on the 9th December 1669.
(*Havant Register.*) Dr. George Hooper, an eminent and
learned English divine, was inducted as rector on the 4th
March 1670. He greatly distinguished himself by his
acquirements in philosophy, mathematics, Greek, and Roman
antiquities, and by his study of the Oriental languages. He
was chaplain to Morley bishop of Winchester, and afterwards
to archbishop Sheldon. He passed through many important
offices, and eventually died bishop of Bath and Wells in 1727.
(*Gen. Bio. Dic.*)

John Lardner A.M. was inducted on the 22d November
1672, and was buried at Havant on the 6th June 1699.
Peter Edge was inducted on the 14th June 1699, and
Alexander Forbes D. D. prebendary of Winchester, was
inducted on the 16th December 1702. (*Havant Register.*)

Joseph Bingham A.M. was inducted into the living of
Havant on the 6th December 1712, and was born at Wakefield in the county of York in the month of September 1668.
He learned the first rudiments of grammar at a school in that
town under Mr. Edward Clarke. In 1683 he was admitted
into University College Oxford, where he behaved in a very .
sober and studious manner. He took the degree of Bachelor
of Arts in 1687, and soon after was chosen fellow of the same
college; he obtained his master's degree in 1690, and was
presented by Dr. Radcliffe to the rectory of Headbourn
Worthy near Winchester, then of the annual value of £100,
without any personal application. In this country retirement,
and with all the disadvantages under which he laboured for
want of useful and necessary books, he undertook a learned
and laborious work, the first volume of which he published in
1708 under the title of *Origines Ecclesiasticæ* or the Antiquities of the Christian Church, in octavo, which he afterwards
completed in nine volumes more, containing twenty-three
books. He discovers in this work a prodigious fund of reading
especially in the Fathers; as likewise a great deal of judgment, sincerity, and candour; and shows what industry and

diligent application are capable of doing. He published several other works; but, notwithstanding his great learning, merit, and other excellent qualifications, he continued only rector of Headbourn Worthy till the 6th December 1712, when he was collated to the rectory of Havant by Sir Jonathan Trelawney, bishop of Winchester. He died rector of Havant on the 17th August 1723, in the fifty-fifth year of his age, and was buried in the churchyard of Headbourn Worthy. Though he had not the strongest constitution, he was a person of untiring energy and indefatigable research. He expressed in his will a dislike to a monument, and none was ever erected over his grave. (*Biog. Brit.*)

Ralph Baddeley A.M. was, on the 7th November 1723, presented by the Crown to this living in trust for the son of Joseph Bingham the late rector, and upon the 10th December 1727, Richard Bingham A.B. student of Christ Church Oxford, was inducted as rector. He died upon his birthday, the 28th August 1764, and was buried in the chancel, with a mural tablet bearing the following inscription:

"Juxta sepulti sunt Richardus Bingham, per 37 annos hujus ecclesiæ Rector dignissimus. Et Maria, ejusdem conjux egregia. Obierunt hic, annis 61 jam completis, Natali die 28 Augusti 1764. Illa, cum annum ageret 78, Die 13 Septembris 1780."

The Rev. John Mitchell B.D. was inducted on the 1st February 1765. He was distinguished as an acute mathematician, and was appointed one of the commissioners for ascertaining the correctness of Harrison's timepiece. As rector he was in every respect a worthy character and was much esteemed by his parishioners. The next rector David Renaud A.M. was born at Whitchurch in the county of Hereford, on the 1st August 1730. He was educated at a large grammar school in Hereford, and removed from thence to Brazen Nose College Oxford, where he obtained a scholarship; he was presented to the rectory of Lewcombe near Bristol, and afterwards, by the governors of Guy's Hospital, to the vicarage of Dewsall in Herefordshire. Dr. Thomas, bishop of Winchester, presented him first to the rectory of Hannington in this county, and afterwards to the rectory of Havant, into which he was inducted on the 17th February 1776, and where he continued to reside during the remainder of his life, greatly beloved by all his parishioners for his kind and benignant disposition. He died on the 28th August 1807, and was buried in the chancel of Havant church, with the following inscription upon a mural tablet :

> " *Hic infra conditur quod mori potuit viri vere Reverendi* *Davidis Renaud A.M. per annos* XXXI. *hujus ecclesiæ* *Rectoris dignissimi, qui flebilis occubuit die Aug.* XXVIII. A. D. MDCCCVII. *annis* LXXVII *modo completis.* *Necnon Annæ, ejusdem conjugis eximiæ, quæ e vita decessit* *die Decembris* XVIII. A.D. MDCCCXIII. *Ætatis suæ* LXXIX. *Etiam Annæ horum filiæ dilectæ quæ ætate* *florente morte correpta fuit, nata die Oct.* XI. A.D. MDCCLXVIII. *Mortua die Maii* XVI. A.D. MDCCLXXXIX."

The Rev. Charles Augustus North succeeded Mr. Renaud, and was inducted on the 12th August 1809. He held the living of Alverstoke as well as that of Havant, and the former being the more lucrative of the two, he resided there exclusively, keeping only a curate at Havant. He died in 1825, and on the 24th September 1825, the Rev. George Robert Mountain, son of the late bishop Mountain, was inducted into the living. In his time and by his exertions the church was repewed, the tower repaired, and the nave rebuilt. The parish and infant schools were built and subscriptions raised for their maintenance; the church at Red Hill was built and endowed, the organ at Havant was purchased, and the weekly services increased. Clothing clubs and other parochial institutions were established under his immediate care, and he contributed to every good work alike by his personal influence and attendance. No man ever lived more respected or died more beloved, and the font which stands in the centre of the church bears the following inscription to his memory :—

"*The Font placed in this church in the year of our Lord*
MDCCCXLVII, and dedicated to the service of Almighty
God, was erected by a contribution of the inhabitants of
this parish, as a memorial of their affection, esteem, and
veneration for the Reverend George Robert Mountain,
Rector of Havant, who having for a period of xx years,
with zeal, with kindness, and untiring diligence,
ministered to the temporal and spiritual necessities of
those committed to his pastoral charge, died on the xxv
day of June A.D. MDCCCXLVI, in the fifty-seventh year
of his age."

Upon the death of Mr. Mountain, the Reverend Thomas
Goodwin Hatchard was presented to the living, and inducted
on the 15th of July 1846.

In the chancel and south transept the following, among
many other inscriptions, will be found—

"*Near this place are deposited the remains of Elizabeth*
Mildred Wale Mountain, formerly of Little Bardfield
Hall in the county of Essex, and widow of the late
Lord Bishop of Quebec, first Protestant prelate of that
see, whom she accompanied to Canada in 1793. Having
returned to her native country in 1825, she departed
this life on the 13th April 1836, in the 78th year of
her age."

"*Juxta Thomas Longcroft arm. natus 24 Oct. 1723,*
mortuus 1 Junii 1776, et conjux fidelissima Susannah
Longcroft, nata 16 Sept. 1733, mortua 1 Nov. 1777.
Spe lætæ Resurrectionis placide quiescunt."

The south transept contains the following inscriptions :—

"*In an adjacent vault lie the remains of Christopher*
Stevens, gentleman; for many years an inhabitant of
this place. Born 1st April 1779; died 17th of
December 1843, aged 64 years."

8

" *Near this place lie the remains of Mary Blackman, late of
the city of Chichester, and daughter of William Symonds
gent. and Elizabeth his wife, of this town, who departed this life July 20th* 1759, *aged* 40 *years.*"
Arms,—Az, a Chevron between three Trefoils Or.

" *To the memory of Charles Marshall, Esq. near forty-five
years Lieutenant in the Royal Navy. He was a
dutiful and loyal subject, a brave and experienced
officer, a skilful and intrepid seaman, an affectionate
relation, a faithful friend, and an honest man. He
died on the* 28th *day of December* 1803, *aged* 65 *years.*"
Arms,—Barry of six sa. and ar. a Canton ermine.

The windows of the north transept were originally of painted
glass, and it might possibly have been at one time an oratory.
At the extremity of the south transept under a handsome
niche (now removed) would appear to have been deposited
the remains of the founder of the chantrey.   Not many years
since there was a tomb with a mutilated sculpture, but all
trace of it has now wholly disappeared.   The four chancel
windows are of painted glass ; that to the east bears no
inscription. The south-east window represents Saint Peter and
Saint Paul, and bears—

"*Deo optimo maximo et memoriæ Georgii Roberti Mountain per viginti annos hujus parochiæ pastoris fidis-
simi mærentes ejus amici Richardus Grant eques et
Georgius Augustus Shawe armiger hanc fenestram
voverunt* A.D. 1847. ' *Qui bene præsunt presbyteri,
duplici honore digni habeantur : maxime qui laborant
in verbo et doctrina.*' (1 Tim. v. 17.)"

The south-west window represents Faith, Hope, and Charity,
and bears in three compartments :

FAITH.—" *Omnipotens æterne Deus da nobis Fidei, Spei et
Charitatis incrementa; atque ut ea quæ promittis*

*assequi valeamus, fac ea nos amare quæ præcipis per
Jesum Christum Dominum nostrum. Amen."*

HOPE.—*" Nonnulli hujus parochiæ Incolæ Deum miseri-
cordem honorandi et hanc ædem Sanctæ Fidei dicatam
exornandi causá hanc fenestram posuerunt* A.D. 1848."

CHARITY.—*" Induti loricam Fidei et Charitatis et galeam
spem salutis."*

The northern window represents the Virgin Mary, the
Saviour, and Saint John, and bears :

*" In honorem Dei et in memoriam viri admodum reveren-
dissimi Michaelis Solomonis Alexander D.D. primi
Episcopi Anglicani Hierosolymis Thomas Goodwin
Hatchard M.A. hujus Ecclesiæ Rector hanc fenestram
posuit* A.D. 1847."

The living of Havant is in the deanery of Droxford, and
remaining in charge ; having peculiar and exempt jurisdiction,
which it exercised so lately as the years 1813 and 1817, in
the probate of Wills. In the valuation of Pope Nicholas
taken in 1291, it is rated as follows :

	TAXATIO.	DECIMA.
Ecclia de Havehunte. . .	26 13 4	2 13 4
Et est in pensionar. . .	2 0 0	0 4 0

In the Nonæ Rolls, 15 Edward III, Henry Hamond,
Matthew Bacon, John Jugeler, and John Blakewyne,
parishioners of Havant, say upon their oath, " that the tithes
" of corn, wool, and lambs of the parish of Havant were of
" the value of twelve pounds in the 14th year of the reign.
" And they say that the aforesaid tithes did not amount to
" the tax of the aforesaid church by reason that the aforesaid
" church is endowed with one messuage, twelve acres of
" land, jurisdictions, and franchises, with the appurtenances,
" which are of the yearly value of seventy-four shillings and
" eightpence. And they say that the tithe of hay and other

"small tithe, with the oblations and mortuaries, are of the "yearly value of £16. 18s. 8d." (*Inq. Non. co. Suth.*)

In the Valuation of 33 Hen. VIII, preserved in the Augmentation Office, it is again rated,

	£.	s.	d.
Penc'ones Ecclia de Havent. . . .	2	0	0
In the King's Books.	24	6	0¼
Yearly tenths.	2	8	7¼
Easter Dues but not regularly gathered.	0	0	4

In the year 1840, in pursuance of the recent Commutation Act, the tithes of the parish were commuted into a fixed rent charge of £674, which is subject to deduction for poor-rate, highway-rate, health-of-towns-rate, ecclesiastical payments, and the usual allowance for collection.

Havant is not rich in gifts either to the parish or to the poor ; but William of Wykeham by his will bequeathed to the "church, *Unum vestimentum integrum, viz. pro sacerdote, diacono, et subdiacono, cum capa etiam, et uno chalice.*" (*Lowth*, p. xi. Ap.) The only land within the parish appropriated to charitable purposes was the Church-acre, originally part of a common field called Long Close, more extensive than the inclosure still bearing that name, the private rights in which were purchased up many years since. It was an original allotment, and lay to the west of the road leading from Havant to Leigh. It is described as the "Church-"acre," the boundaries being shown upon a map made for John Moody, about the year 1756. The rent was paid in the year 1755, by Moody to the parish officers of Havant, and the following receipt will be found entered in the Havant vestry book of that date,

"Received of Mr. John Moody by the hands of John "Wacket the sum of thirteen pound for twenty-six years' "rent due at Michaelmas last for the Church-acre this 1st of "April 1755, by us

"WILL. ROMAN ⎫
"DANL. VEAL ⎬ *Churchwardens.*
　　　　　　　　 ⎭

"The above is a true copy, DD. RENAUD."

Persons born within the parish of Havant are included among the natives of ten different localities, in favour of whom six scholarships were founded in Brazenose College Oxford, in the year 1537 by Dr. John Claymond, President of Corpus Christi College in that university. The endowment of each, as settled by a reference in accordance with an order of the Court of Chancery, the date of which does not appear, is £1 per quarter, with other small emoluments; but the practice of late years has been to divide the annual income between three persons instead of six. The nomination to these scholarships is in the President and certain Fellows of Corpus Christi College, but they are so little known, and have been so little in request, that no appointment has taken place since 1811.

In the year 1837-8, a small Church dedicated to Saint John the Baptist, to which a parsonage house and school have since been added, was built at Red Hill by the late rector of Havant, assisted by the Rev. William Norris rector of Warblington: the two contributed an annual endowment of twenty-five pounds each, and a portion of each parish was assigned to Red Hill in order to constitute it a separate district. By an order in council dated the 15th June 1840, this district was defined. The outline commencing at the northern extremity of the parish of Havant, follows the boundary of the parish eastward, inclining to the south, to its junction with the parish of Warblington; it then runs along the boundary of the latter parish in a north-easterly direction to the extreme north point, and from thence in a south-easterly direction till it comes to a road passing through the lords allotment of Emsworth Common, from Two Stone Bottom to Pollington's Corner, and following the said road towards the south-west to the latter point, at which the road falls into another road called Leigh-lane; at the second junction of the two parishes it runs along Leigh-lane in the parish of Havant to its termination in the road leading from the town of Havant to Horndean : the outline of the district then follows the road from Havant to Horndean northward, till it reaches the entrance to a lane on the left of that road

called Thicket-lane, and then descending that lane to the
lower extremity, passes from thence along the paling of
Leigh Park, by which the park is separated from Havant
Thicket, to a place called Bondfields, where it strikes again
upon the boundary of the parish of Havant, which boundary
also becomes the outline of the district for the remainder
of its length, as far as to the northern extremity of the
parish.

The presentation is alternately in the rector of Havant
and the rector of Warblington: the first incumbent, the
Rev. Henry Blyth, was presented by the rector of Havant,
and upon his decease the Rev. Thomas Yard was presented
by the rector of Warblington, and continued incumbent until
the month of March 1850, when he resigned on his presentation to the rectory of Ashwell in the county of Rutland.
The Rev. John Hawker who succeeded him, is the present
incumbent. At the foot of Red Hill on the 24th day of
April 1850, Charles Dixon Esq. of Stansted laid the first
stone of a building in the Elizabethan style of architecture,
called "Stansted College," founded and endowed, as the
inscription states, by Charles Dixon Esq. of Stansted, late
a Merchant of London, for six of his less fortunate brethren.
Each of the brethren receives £50 per annum, a separate
apartment, with spiritual and medical attendance and other
requisites; £50 per annum is secured for another decayed
merchant and his wife as superintendents of the establishment; £50 for repairs and taxes; £50 for wages of
domestics; £20 for the incumbent of Red Hill Church as
chaplain; £20 for the services of a medical practitioner, and
£10 for books and garden expenses. The grounds comprise
about five acres, the college is surrounded by a terrace
walk, and contains a vestibule for indoor exercise, and a common dining hall. It was opened for the reception of inmates
on the 1st May 1852.

There is a Roman Catholic Chapel at Brockhampton
attached to the residence of the priest, which was built in
the year 1752. Previous to this the cottages at the corner

of Brockhampton-lane, lately occupied by Mr. West, deceased,
served the purpose of a chapel, and service was also performed
at the houses of the Roman Catholic families in the neighbourhood. There being no chapel at Chichester the district
was one of some extent; for some reason the old religion
seemed to linger here among many of the yeomanry and
lower classes with greater tenacity than in other parts of
England, and in after times James II had adherents who,
possibly from accident, but more probably perhaps from
motives of prudence, adopted this locality as their residence
whilst he held his court in France, in order to be in communication with his emissaries. Colonel Andrew Heron, said
to have been a natural son of the monarch, and to whom
he gave a ruby brooch of great value until lately preserved
by his descendants, was living for some time at Leigh;
Lord Dormer was living at Idsworth, the upper part of the
old house being used as a chapel; the Fordes were the
owners of Up Park; the daughter and sole heir of Sir
Edward Ford intermarried with Ralph Lord Grey of Werk,
whose son, Forde Lord Grey, was created Earl of Tankerville;
his only daughter intermarried with Charles Bennett Lord
Ossulston, who was created Earl of Tankerville. The
Carylls also, whose history is one of peculiar interest, were
the Lords of Harting and Lady Holt. Their descent is
traced by Berry and Dallaway to Sir John Caryll who lived
in the reign of Henry VII, to whose son, Sir John Caryll,
there is extant a grant, from Henry VIII, wherein he is
described as armiger and attorney-general of the Duchy of
Lancaster, of the Manor of Bexington, and the advowson of
Sompting, then late parcel of the possessions of the Priory of
St. John of Jerusalem; but I find in the 19th Henry VI
1461, a feoffment from John Gatere and William Cooke of
Warneham in Sussex to John Caryll of lands in Horseham,
and as the Carylls are found residing in Warneham, and
lords of that manor at the time of Henry VIII's grant, I
conclude that they must have been of ancient settlement
there. In the 4th Elizabeth 1563, John Caryll was residing
at Warneham, and in 1608, his son Sir John Caryll was

settled at Angmering. Sir John Caryll, the grandson of the attorney-general, married Mary the daughter of Lord Dormer of Idsworth, and on the death of Sir Philip Sidney in 1610, he obtained a grant of the hundred of Dumford, and the manor of Harting. His son John Caryll of Harting married Catherine daughter of Lord Petre; his daughter Anne married Sir Charles Smith, afterwards Viscount Carrington, after whose decease her life estates were on the 3d May 1721 conveyed in trust for payment of her debts amounting to no less than £21,300.

There were great disturbances as to the rights of free warren, fishing, and common of pasture, claimed by the Carylls in Harting Combe and Fyning Wood, part of the wastes of the Manor of Harting; and the various points were submitted to Sir William Forde and Richard Lewknor, who, by an award dated 12th January 1630, ordered that Sir John Caryll and John Caryll his son and heir apparent, should put down and destroy the warren of conies and the decoy and fish-ponds in Harting Combe and Fyning Wood. John Caryll by will dated 17th October 1680, left rings of the value of forty shillings a piece to his wife, four sons, and two daughters-in-law, with the motto "Death, Judgment, Hell, Heaven;" £50 among the priests of Sussex, Hants, Wilts, and Dorset; £60 to the poor Catholics in those counties; and £25 among the poor of Harting, West Grinstead, Washington, and Shipley, in which parishes his property lay. John Caryll, grandson of Sir John, a staunch loyalist, was in 1643 obliged to compound for his estates, and paid a fine of £2795. Under pressure of attainder he, on the 3d August 1652, conveyed all his property to his friend Sir John Kempe upon special trust and confidence. The attainder appears to have been waived; but he became involved in his circumstances, and on the 6th May 1670, in consideration of £3500, he conveyed to Sir John Bennett the manor-house and lands of Dawley in Middlesex, and other lands in Hartington, Harmansworth, and Fekenham. Richard Caryll, who married Johanna the daughter of Sir Henry Bedingfield, supported the cause of

King James II, and followed his fortunes to his court at St. Germains, where James created him Baron Caryll.

At some time before 1679, John Caryll, the eldest son of Richard, known as "the friend of Pope," moved from East Harting, the ancient residence of the lords of Harting, to Lady Holt; for on the 7th January in that year, an agreement was entered into between Richard Caryll on the part of John Caryll his son, described as of Holt, whereby "All that " newly inclosed and impaled Park, lately part of Holt Farm " in the parish of Harting, with the stock of deer, and the new " mansion-house of the said John Caryll in the said parish," were with certain farm lands let to one Edward Roper of Eltham in Kent, for eleven years at £75 a year. There were then 240 deer in the park, including ten brace of bucks, and seventeen brace of sores, and it was agreed that the same number should be left at the end of the term; and that in the event of any difference between the parties, the matter in dispute should be left to the arbitration of Richard Norton of Southwick, and Richard Cotton of Watergate. John Caryll, the son of him of Lady Holt, married Mary the daughter of the Earl of Seaforth, and died in the lifetime of his father, leaving two sons, John Baptist Caryll who died unmarried, and John Caryll who married Frances the daughter of William Viscount Molyneux, and resided at Maison sur Seine near Paris, styling himself Lord Caryll. The fortunes of the family did not improve notwithstanding their brilliant alliances, for having, on the 9th December 1740, borrowed £10,000 of Mrs. Whetham, and being unable to pay £1500 the arrear of interest, on the 29th December 1744, the Baron was obliged to execute a power to Richard Chorley to receive the rents of a part of his property and to pay the interest on the mortgage. The deer were sold and the park was neglected, and on the 10th October 1758, he, as John Caryll of Lady Holt, and Dorothy his wife, (his first wife the Lady Frances Molyneux having died without issue), mortgaged " the Home Farm and the disparked park " in the Manor of Harting, containing, as it is stated, 630 acres, and then in the occupation of John Higgens, to John Joliffe of Petersfield for £6050. His position was beyond redemption, for, in the 32 Geo. II, 1760, Dorothy his second wife having also died without issue, "An Act for the sale of the inheritance of part "of the settled estates of John Caryll, Esquire, in the county "of Sussex, to discharge incumbrances affecting the same," was passed, and on the 15th April 1763, in consideration of £2000, he conveyed Huckholt Farm and other lands to Sir Matthew Featherston-haugh. Lady Holt, in which he still resided at intervals, was soon afterwards sold to the Duke of Richmond, and he, the last of his family, was left utterly destitute. In his distress he took refuge in the Roman Catholic Mission at Brockampton, and lived there, making it his home up to the time of his death, which took place in 1780. The Carylls lie buried in the Mortuary Chapel attached to the Church of Harting. Their arms were Argent, three Bars Sable; in chief, as many Mullets of the last. To their family the Mission of Brockhampton is generally supposed to owe its origin.

The Rev. David Morgan, otherwise Pelagius, was the first established minister, and he may be said to have founded the mission. Upon his death, on the 14th November 1758, he was succeeded by the Honourable and Reverend Thomas Talbot, who became a bishop, and died 24th April 1795. Lord Dormer of Idsworth married the sister of Bishop Talbot, and the latter left the premises and adjoining lands to the mission, which has since been endowed by the Sone and other families to the extent of about £1600. Bishop Talbot was succeeded by the Reverend Richard Cornthwaite, the Reverend James Appleton, the Reverend John Earle, and the Reverend Richard Southworth. The latter was professor in the English College of Douay in Flanders, and resigned his chair on his appointment to Brockhampton in 1786. He was universally respected by all who had the pleasure of his acquaintance, and laboured for thirty years in the cure entrusted to his charge. He died on the 19th November 1817, and was buried in the churchyard of Warblington : his gravestone bears the following inscription :—

" Here lie the mortal remains of the Reverend Richard Southworth, late pastor of the Catholic Chapel of Brockhampton, having fulfilled all the duties of his station during thirty years, with zeal, prudence, and charity, truly admirable. He departed this life on the 19th day of November 1817, in the 75th year of his age, regretted by all who knew him, but particularly by his surviving congregation, who, as a small token of their gratitude, have raised this stone to his memory. Requiescat in pace. ' Have pity on me, at least you, my friends.'—Job."

Upon the death of Mr. Southworth, the Reverend Mr. Kemble succeeded to the cure, and upon his removal to Moorfields Chapel, the Reverend John Kearns was appointed. He has recently been removed, and has been succeeded by the Reverend Daniel Donovan. On the 28th December 1848, the chapel became a licensed building for the solemnization of marriages under the recent Registration Act.

LANGSTONE, which lies about a mile south of Havant on the road to Hayling, was an acknowledged port in former times, being one of the members of the port of Southampton (*Hale, de jure maris*); and upon occasions of general levy and the issuing of ship orders, the town of Havant furnished from its port of Langstone one ship of war properly equipped for the defence of the realm. (*Rym. fœd.* v. 9, p. i, p. 4.) The hamlet stands at the confluence of the waters forming the harbours of Langstone and Chichester, and vessels of from three to four hundred tons can discharge their cargoes at the quay on either side of the causeway leading to the bridge. With greater accommodation, the harbour might and probably will recover its former trade and importance, especially as the approaches are good and the dues so light in comparison with Portsmouth and other surrounding ports. After the fatal battle of Worcester and the defeat of the royal arms, King Charles, with Lord Wilmot his only attendant, fled for concealment to Heale near Salisbury, and from thence, having made his way over Old Winchester to Hambledon, and eventually to Colonel Gounter's at Racton Park, he was under the necessity of waiting there several days before a passage could be provided for him to the continent. In the interval, Lord Wilmot and Colonel Gounter visited Langstone, in the hope of obtaining a boat there, but none could be had; and in a manuscript account some time since discovered in an escrutoire of the Colonel's, it is stated, that the noble lord and the Colonel eat oysters at Langstone, and much enjoyed their frugal fare. They returned from Langstone to Racton, and, after enquiry at Brighton, a vessel was found, on board of which they embarked, and in a few hours they were out of the reach of their enemies and in safety on the opposite shore. The Windmill at Langstone is built upon a piece of land formerly waste, but granted out by John Moody when lord of the manor. It is still copyhold, and subject to the rent, fine, and heriot, reserved under the original grant.

The parish of Havant, under the provisions of the Poor Law Amendment Act, became in the year 1835 the centre of the union called the Havant Union, comprising the parishes of Havant, Bedhampton, Farlington, Hayling North, Hayling South, and Warblington. The union workhouse, of which the Rev. Charles Hardy, vicar of Hayling, is the present chaplain, is situate in the West street, and the board meetings are held there on every Tuesday. Havant returns three guardians, Warblington three, Bedhampton one, Hayling North one, Hayling South one, and Farlington one. The population of the parish of Havant in the year 1811 consisted of 1824 souls, including 357 inhabited houses. By the census of 1841 it had increased to 2019, and in 1851 to 2416, being an increase of 592 in the course of forty years. In 1800 the poor-rate amounted to £996; in 1813 to £1525. 5s. 6d.; and in 1851 the exact actual expenditure, including the establishment charges, amounted to £1222.13s.11d.

The neighbourhood is abundantly supplied with water of the finest quality, the average of the land is good and well cultivated, the locality extremely healthy, and it has hitherto entirely escaped the visitations of the cholera. The streets were first paved in 1786, during the waywardenship of the late Mr. John Butler, and were again partially repaved about five years since by voluntary subscription. For the greater convenience of the district, a bench, auxiliary to that of Fareham, was established at Havant in the year 1831, and the town has recently been made a polling-place for the election of members within the southern division of the county.

A Friendly Society was organised in the year 1750, and in its most flourishing state consisted of 137 members, its funds in the strong box amounting to £200. At one period it maintained seven superannuated persons at 4s. per week, besides paying the bounty-money for several of its members who were drawn for the militia; but, notwithstanding the assistance it afforded to the parish at large, the longer the society continued to exist the poorer it became. Some of the younger members withdrew their names and formed a society of their own, not being disposed to contribute to the relief of age or indigence without considering that they might become old or indigent themselves. The strong box was closed in the expectation of a dissolution, as there were no younger members to maintain the required succession. At length the survivors dwindled down to the number of twenty-eight, their funds to £131; and, as there seemed to be no probability of reviving the institution on a basis of mutual security, the society, after an existence of sixty-four years, dissolved itself, and each member received for his share the sum of £4. 11s. 4d.

In the year 1776, several of the inhabitants formed themselves into a Viduarian Society for the better support of their widows; and articles were framed for their mutual benefit. The society continued to flourish a few years, and would have answered the end of its institution, providing a source of comfort to many distressed families, had not the fund been too soon anticipated, and the principal expended before any interest had been allowed to accumulate. (*Butler*, p. 53.)

The present Friendly Society was re-established in the year 1829, and bids fair to answer the purpose for which it was formed. It numbers seventy-four members, and has a gradually increasing fund, amounting, on the 7th June 1854, to the sum of £336. It is in every respect well conducted, and receives the patronage and support of the rector and principal inhabitants of the town.

On the 25th October 1734, between three and four o'clock in the morning, an earthquake was felt here; the shock being so great as to have been observed by one or more persons in most houses of the place. There was a quick tremulous motion, which continued about two or three minutes, then ceased, and after a very short interval was repeated in the same manner, and lasted about the same space of time. The shaking of the beds was perceived, and the houses were sensibly felt to rock; the progressive motion being from east to west. There had previously been more rain and wind than usual for several months, especially from the beginning to the middle of October, about which time it cleared up, the weather becoming very cold with frost, the wind blowing hard from the north-west. On the 24th it was calm, with rain in the afternoon, the mercury standing at $30\frac{2}{10}$. After the earthquake there was a gale of wind which lasted for several hours. (*Phil. Trans.* No. 444, p. 362). On the 30th November 1811, at a quarter before three in the morning, another shock was distinctly felt: the concussion was so violent that it awoke many from their sleep, and caused considerable alarm. It was accompanied by a loud rumbling noise; the sentinels on duty at Portsmouth confirmed the fact; at Fratton it was so severe that they got up and left their beds, and it was also very strongly felt at Gosport and the surrounding neighbourhood.

Various Coins have at intervals been found in the removal of ancient buildings, and in gardens surrounding the town. Most of these have been lost, but some are still in the possession of the persons who discovered them, and among them the following may be mentioned:—

About sixty Nuremberg tokens, on altering an old house in the North street, the property of the Holton family.

A considerable number of silver coins of the reigns of Henry VII, Henry VIII, and Edward VI, found in a house which stood at the corner of the North street.

At Rowlands Castle.—A head of Dioclesian with a radiated crown, and a sceptre with a ball bearing an eagle displayed : on the reverse, a naked figure with a spear in his left hand and Jupiter's thunder in his right; on the ground in front an eagle, and in the space behind the figure the letter A. A head of Flavius Valens with a band of pearls : on the reverse, a Roman soldier, his right hand pressing down a bound captive, his left supporting a military ensign, which the Romans called Labarum. A head of Licinius Galienus bearded, with a radiated crown : on the reverse, a stag passant. A laureated head of Flavius Valerius Constantinus : on the reverse, Ceres with a cornucopia. And a head of Flavius Valentinianus crowned with a band of pearls : on the reverse, a female figure winged, in her right hand a chaplet, in her left a branch of palm.

There is no ancient site of a Manor House, as the lords were never resident within their manor prior to the year 1553, the rents being previously, and for some time subsequently, to that period paid by the farmers or lessees at the Episcopal Palace of Wolvesey at Winchester. The present Manor House, occupied by Mr. Evans, was built by Isaac Moody, who made it his residence; John Moody and Bingham Newland also lived there, but upon the death of the latter it was sold. The oldest house in the town is that in Homewell the property of the Holton family for nearly two centuries, which, from evidence gleaned from the title-deeds, was no doubt built not less than 360 years ago. It has been tiled and partly modernized, but the exterior still retains its original features. The upper floors project as usual ; a considerable portion of the framework is of timber, the intervening spaces being filled in with rubble and masonry. At the time when this house was built, and up to a comparatively recent period, one third of the buildings consisted of woodwork, and this, when the property was of copyhold tenure, was obtained from the Havant Thicket. From all that I can learn, it seems that the bishops never cut timber in the thicket at all for their own purposes until about the year 1756, from which time the practice increased until they claimed the whole; admitting however, by the terms of their leases, the existence of some allowance of timber for the purposes of manorial repairs, and the usual botes. About fifty years ago, there was a yard which had existed from time immemorial, to the north of the railway on the west side of the Leigh road, the site of which is now occupied by the cottage and garden lately belonging to the Russells. It was wholly appropriated to what was then called ' " the parish allowance." This allowance of timber was brought down from the thicket, stripped, and was deposited in the yard, where from forty to fifty sticks might generally have been seen. The waywardens of the parish took what they required, and one Linney a sawyer, long since dead, was employed by them for many years to cut out posts and rails for parish purposes. These were used at short intervals on the road from Havant to Langstone, and from the Dog Kennel barn to the Flood gates at Leigh; for the gate and piles at Dog Kennel, for the bridges at Stockheath, for Aylmer's bridge, for the fencing round Homewell, and for the wadeway between Langstone and Hayling Island. At a somewhat earlier period, the owners of copyhold houses claimed what was needed for the repair of their houses, out of the common allowance yard, and having paid for the sawing, removed and applied it to their necessary repairs. A portion of the allowance yard was granted out by the lord as parcel of his waste, and some of the timber was in consequence placed on the opposite side of the road. Encroachments were gradually made upon the yard, the waywardens for a time compelled the allowance, but delays were created, obstacles were multiplied by the bishop, and eventually the rightful and accustomed allowance both to the copyholders and the parish entirely ceased.

The ancient Rectory of Havant stood upon the site of a house now the property of Mr. Clarke, to the south of the

present butcher's shop in the North street; it was of the
age of Edward III, and was distinguished by the arms of
William of Wykeham carved on the outside. In this house,
which was pulled down in the year 1822, tradition reports
that Aylward entertained the noble prelate on his progress
through the parishes of his diocese. For some unexplained
reason, the rectors of Havant discontinued residing in this
house, and until about one hundred years ago occupied a
a small thatched dwelling, which stood on the glebe, within
a few yards of the cottage in which the late Mr. William
Kennett resided up to the time of his death. The Rev.
Richard Bingham abandoned the old rectory, and built the
present one, which was enlarged and repaired by the late
Mr. Mountain, and is pleasantly situate about a quarter
of a mile from the church, on the road from Havant to
Langstone.

About ninety-five years since, a fire broke out which
consumed almost the whole of the West street, and portions
of the North and East streets of Havant. The houses were
all at that time partly timber-built and roofed with thatch
or shingle. Upon reference to the court minutes of that
period, presentments are found to guard against the recurrence
of such a disaster; but I have not been able to discover any
written account of the origin and extent of the fire which
so changed the general appearance of the town. In the
year 1780, there were two fires in one night, and upon this
occasion the house, now the property of the Robins family,
formerly called the Sun Inn was burnt to the ground: the
opposite house was built by Mr. Newland on the site of an
ancient blacksmith's shop. In the year 1755, John Morey
and a fellow-bricklayer were at work in a house which had
formerly belonged to the Woolgar family, but then the
property of the Venthams, occupied by James Andrews, at
the corner of the South street, and in removing the hearth-
stone of a fireplace they discovered three jars covered over with
slate, which upon examination were found to contain Gold
coin of the reign of Charles I, but to what amount no one

except those who stumbled upon the treasure and the occupier of the house could gain any satisfactory intelligence. Fifty-four pieces of gold coin weighing twenty-seven guineas and a half were, as stated in a memorandum, paid to John Moody then lord of the manor, but there is every reason to believe that a very much larger sum was discovered and applied by the occupier to his own purposes, for immediately upon the discovery, the latter took a post conveyance and started for London : upon his return, he purchased various houses in the place, among the number the yard and premises in the West street adjoining the Star bridge, lately belonging to the Hammond family. This was at that time a tan-yard ; Andrews pulled down the old premises, and built a brewhouse with malthouse and other necessary outbuildings. In the original tanpits, which stood in a line running from north to south, he planted a row of chesnut trees, some of which have recently been cut down, but two are still standing. It was supposed that the money had been con-cealed by some of the Woolgars, and that at the time of the great plague, those to whose keeping the secret had been entrusted had died without the opportunity of revealing the depository of the secreted treasure.

The ancient Market-house which is believed to have been erected on the confirmation of the grant of King John in the reign of Henry VI, and which stood adjoining the churchyard on the eastern side, became dilapidated in the year 1645, and eventually fell down in 1710. (*Leet Rolls*). At the latter period it was rebuilt on its former site, and consisted of an open arched passage, and an inner inclosure, where fifty persons might conveniently stand, fitted up with stalls and the usual requisites for market purposes. Ad-joining there was a cage, and over the whole a room let as a school-room, but used by the lord of the manor for holding his courts, and transacting the manorial business whenever occasion required. There was barely room for a wagon to pass between the market-house and the buildings on the opposite side, and timber carriages on their way to Langstone took a road by Homewell through the stream passing the old manor house of Hall place, and entering Langstone lane about a hundred yards above the present rectory. At this time also, there was a row of elm trees on the western side of Langstone lane of the same age as those lately standing in the meadow, but they were cut down by Mr. Butler on his purchase of the property. The second market-house was pulled down about sixty years ago, and a new one was built upon its site, which stood until the year 1828, when it was complained of as a nuisance, and was taken down. The butchers shambles, and fish-stalls for which the lease was granted to John Hall, and others in the reign of Edward IV, extended from the market-house southward under the church wall to the house lately belonging to Woods; meat was supplied from the surrounding neighbourhood to the great benefit of the inhabitants, but they were suffered to go to decay for want of common repair, and ceased to exist many years ago. There were within the time of memory, shops running from the market-house to the north-west corner of the churchyard, and on the west side of the north entrance stood the Church House, founded in former years for the use of the poor, where spits, crocks, and utensils for dressing provisions were provided by the parish free of charge. Here says Silas Taylor, speaking of rural parishes, "the "housekeepers met, were merry, and gave their charity. "The young people also met there, and had dancing, bowling, "shooting at the butt and other rural sports." This church house was afterwards converted into an almshouse, the last occupants being two aged paupers of the names of Bishop and Carpenter: the whole was pulled down some years since.

Prior to the year 1762, the road through the town was wholly paved with stones, from the centre of the highway up to the houses on either side, which were furnished with posts and seats before the doors, on which the inhabitants sat for purposes of business or ease, protected from the weather by the overhanging floor called the "pentice." It does not appear

at what time the Star, Ruttle, and Hermitage bridges were
built, but it is probable that they were made at this time,
when an Act of Parliament " For repairing and widening the
" road from Cosham, in the county of Southampton, to the
" city of Chichester," was obtained.   The preamble recites
" That the road leading from Cosham in the county of South-
" ampton through the parishes of Widley, Wymering, Farling-
"ton, Bedhampton, Havant and Warblington in the said county
"and through the parishes of Westbourne, Chidham, Bosham,
"New Fishbourne and Saint Bartholomew, in the county of
" Sussex, to the city of Chichester in the said county of Sussex,
" was in many parts thereof so very ruinous and deep in the
" winter season that carriages could not pass without great
" danger and difficulty, and was in many parts thereof very
" narrow and incommodious."   These certainly were very
sufficient reasons for the passing of the act, and of the truth
of the recitals contained in the preamble there can be very
little doubt.   As a confirmation of this, at the October
Sessions held at Winchester in the year 1751, that part of
the high road which lay within the parish of Bedhampton
was indicted "for that the same was and yet is very ruinous,
"miry, deep, broken, and in such decay for want of due repa-
" ration and amendment of the same, so that the liege subjects
"of our lord the King through the same way with their horses,
"coaches, carts and carriages, could not, nor can go, return, pass,
" ride, and labour, without great danger of their lives and the
" loss of their goods, to the great damage and common nuisance
" of all the liege subjects of our lord the King."
    From the papers and evidence in this case, it appears that
at the time of the indictment, the great road from the West
country into Sussex, was nothing more than a lane, deep in
ruts, with breaks as they were called, at a distance of two
hundred and fifty yards apart, to enable two vehicles when
they met, to pass each other; and as the road was only of the
width of one carriage, except at the breaks, it followed as a
matter of course, that no travelling could take place after dark
with any degree of safety.   There was then but little traffic
with Portsmouth; the principal witness examined on the

occasion being only able to prove that he went from Havant to Portsmouth once and sometimes twice a week, with flour in a cart, drawn by two horses, and that his average load was about sixteen cwt. The only public conveyance then between Chichester and Portsmouth was a stage wagon, which performed two journies each way during the week. It may be inferred that the road was barely passable, as James Bold, then the owner of Wade Court, on behalf of the defendants, could only state that he had upon one occasion driven his mother from Havant to Portsmouth in a one horse chaise, and that she did not express her alarm or fear of being thrown out of the chaise ; and John Moody's coachman was obliged to admit that after frost and rain the chalk was very slippery, and that it required considerable care to prevent an overset. The indictment was afterwards arranged, the parish undertaking to repair the highway.

This being the case with the highways, it may easily be conceived that the byeways were next to impassable for any description of carriage. The road from Havant to Leigh was generally covered with water during the winter months, and foot passengers used a path to the east of the road hedge the whole distance. There was a similar footpath to the south of the road hedge, between Havant and Emsworth. Even so late as 1800, the road from Whichers gate to Horndean and that over Stockheath were indicted at the same sessions. In the brief for the defence it states that these roads had never been repaired by the parish of Havant or any private individuals, and that from want of proper materials, the common roads of the parish (which were full ten miles in extent) could not be kept in a decent state of repair. The road from Havant to Horndean then passed through Rowlands Castle and Blendworth, there being no direct causeway as at present, between Whichers gate and Horndean ; there was no causeway at all over Stockheath, so that no carriage could pass on either line of road, except in the height of summer when the turf of the commons was hard and dry. These indictments were however afterwards respited, and an arrangement was entered into by which the parish took upon itself the burden of the repairs.

When the Turnpike Act was carried into effect, there stood at the eastern entrance of the town, a public-house called the " Royal Oak," the site of which comprised an ancient gravel-pit, and had been granted out by John Moody when lord of the manor. It became necessary to remove this house, and it was accordingly done : some bones were found in exca-vating for the road, and it was currently believed that some one had been murdered and buried there, but nothing was discovered which could give a clue to the circumstances under which the body had been interred. In digging a foundation under the west path of the South street some years since, the labourers found a coffin containing human remains, and several coffins were also found in digging out a cellar under the corner house belonging to Mr. Bulbeck. There was every appearance of the bodies having received Christian burial, and it was generally supposed that the churchyard had originally included the site on which the house stood.

The burial-yard attached to the Church of Saint Faith has been probably used for sepulture from the seventh or tenth century. If 1000 years are assumed to have been the term of its existence as a place of interment, and twenty burials annually are taken as the average for that period (the present rate being from thirty-three to fifty-two), we shall have as the result, no less than 20,000 bodies mixed with the subsoil of less than one statute acre of ground. It is difficult to realize to the imagination such a mass of human remains heaped together in the midst of the living, and it is now impossible to calculate the extent to which disease may have been generated from so much corruption. The Jews never open a grave a second time—the earth which receives a body remains for ever unclean ; the Egyptians embalmed their dead ; the Romans either burned the body, or buried it without the city walls ; Christians have alone heaped up their dead to such a fearful extent in the midst of the living, the surface of the yard being several feet above the level of the adjoining streets.

In order to remedy so crying an evil, a new Cemetery has been formed to the north of the line of railway at some distance from the town. The site was presented to the parish by Sir George Staunton, and the subsoil is flint gravel. The Mortuary Chapel and necessary walling have been erected by subscription. One statute acre has been inclosed for the members of the Church of England, and one quarter of a statute acre for the Dissenters. The inclosure walls are formed of flint and brick. The entrance gateway and the chapel are built of flint, with Caen-stone dressings. The style of the work is Gothic, and the chapel will accommodate about fifty persons. The windows are of stained glass, the floor of red and black tiles six inches square, and there is an outer iron gate which is closed during the day, the inner door being left open to secure a proper ventilation. A small turret and bell complete the whole, and the total sum expended did not exceed £416, of which the chapel cost about £200.

On the 30th July 1851, a petition, signed by more than one tenth of the rated inhabitants of the town and parish, was presented to the General Board of Health, requesting an inspection of the town in order that the provisions of the public health act, might, if necessary, be applied to the place. Robert Rawlinson, Esquire, a superintending inspector, attended at the Bear Inn, Havant, on the 2d of October following, when an inquiry into the sanatory state of the town, its water supply, its drainage, and its sewerage, took place, and the result was, that the inspector recommended the General Board to apply the provisions of the act to the parish and town of Havant. This was accordingly done, and the local board are now charged with the very necessary improvement of the town.

By permission of the local board, a Gas Company to whom the board have delegated their powers, has been formed, with a capital of two thousand five hundred pounds, the whole of which was subscribed for in the town, and the plan of

Mr. Hedley (who was the successful competitor for the premium offered by the company) in the construction of the necessary works has as far as possible been adopted by Mr. Child the contractor, and the work has recently been completed, and the town lighted, under the superintendence of Mr. Dickson, the company's engineer.

The formation upon which the town of Havant stands, is alluvium, resting upon the London clay. Like most alluviums, it is of varying character; gravel, sand, clay, and mixtures of these, alternating and changing at short intervals of space apart. Within the area of the county there are;—lower members of the tertiaries, London clay, plastic clay consisting of variegated sands, clays and lignite; portions of the cretaceous system, chalk, and green sand. London clay crops out along the beach line generally to the south, and chalk forms the northern portions of the district. • The higher or chalk and sand portion of the locality, is absorbent, the rain-fall sinking into the porous shala, and is there stored up as in a vast reservoir, to be gradually given out by numerous springs in the lower belt of land near Havant and Bedhampton. Above 100,000,000 gallons of spring water rise to the surface daily, within an area of a few square miles; and there are springs of fresh water between high and low water-mark on the beach. From one so situated, a considerable portion of the poor inhabitants of Emsworth supply themselves with water. The varying and uncertain character of the alluvium is shown in the fact, that within about one hundred yards of a large spring, yielding some 2,000,000 or 3,000,000 of gallons daily, a well had to be sunk at the workhouse seventy feet deep before water could be reached; and there are other similar instances, where one hundred and seventy feet have been bored without finding water, although a large spring poured forth a continuous stream not a quarter of a mile distant. The average temperature of the springs rising to the surface at Havant is 50·0. This steadiness in the temperature of the water indicates that their source is deep, probably not less than one thousand feet.

There is a feature in some measure peculiar to the stratifi.
cation of this district connected with the meteorology, namely,
"the Lavant springs." The Lavant is an intermittent
outburst of water in the lower valleys commencing at
Idsworth and Week, which occurs after long continued and
heavy rain, on the chalk and sand formations of the high
lands and downs. The torrent of water finds its way by
Finchdean, Rowlands Castle, Maize Coppice, and Aylmers
bridge to Havant, and from thence into the sea. The Lavant
of the year 1852 was heavier than for forty years past.
For some time the ordinary channels sufficed to carry off the
increasing waters, but at last the rush was so great, that the
fields to the north of the town presented the appearance of a
lake, and the hedges were in many places completely covered.
On the 27th November, the flood was at its highest; there
was a deep stream from the station to the church corner, and
on that and the following day a boat plied in the North street.
Carts conveyed passengers over the river which ran across
the West street at the Star bridge; the cellars were filled to
the extent of three and four feet deep, and for some time
the greatest possible inconvenience prevailed, from the mass
of waters pouring through the town. Near Epsom, there
are occasional outbursts of a character similar to that of
our own locality, the intermittent spring bearing the appropriate name of the Earth-bourne.

On the 15th March 1847, the Chichester and Portsmouth
branch of the London, Brighton, and South Coast Railway
was opened for traffic, and the trade of the town has since
that period been steadily on the increase. On the 8th Aug.
1853, the first sod of the line of railway from Godalming
to Havant was turned at Buriton, and the work is now in
progress of completion. The advantages of a rapid and
easy communication with neighbouring towns, and the great
metropolis, have materially tended to cheapen the necessaries
of life; carriage is not so expensive as in former days, and
produce can be supplied and received within the space of a
few hours. There are now nine malthouses, and four

11

breweries at work, three coalyards, and three fellmongers' yards, the parchment dressed at Havant being superior to any carried into the London market. The roads are excellent in every direction, the tolls light, and houses for occupation much sought after. There is no want of employment among the poor, and although without any staple article of trade or manufacture since the decrease of the wool trade, the business and prospects of the town are certainly as good as those of any place of a similar size in its immediate neighbourhood.

The Manor of Warblington.

—◆—

THE early history of Warblington is involved in considerable obscurity; and the strides which have taken place
in the development of topographical inquiry at Southwick,
Portchester, and elsewhere in the immediate neighbourhood,
have done but little for this particular locality.   There are
numberless manors scattered throughout the country, with
perhaps the merest remains of buildings which have long
since passed away and crumbled into dust; and yet attached
to these remains there are charters to be found, conferring
extensive and valuable privileges; records affording all the
information which could be desired by the historian or the
antiquary; with tradition filling up the more minute details of
remote antiquity, so that the fragments not unfrequently
create an interest which the edifice itself failed wholly to
produce.   The discovery of coins, whether from a British,
a Roman, or a Saxon mint, often throws a light on the people
whose footsteps we are endeavouring to trace; and by the
position of an earthwork, the material of a foundation, or the
groining of an arch, we are enabled to gather with some
degree of confidence, a history of the purposes for which the
shattered columns were originally raised.   But it happens
occasionally, from the absence of some, and the mutilation of
others of these vestiges, that the inquirer is baffled, and then,
as in the case of Warblington, conjecture is of necessity compelled to supply the place of accurate and historic narrative;
and however pleasing it may be to the antiquary to collect
the incidents which are to be met with, and to weave them
into the shape of a chronicle of the past, it must sometimes
happen that the evidence which to him is more than con-

clusive, fails to satisfy the sober and dispassionate reader. It is therefore peculiarly the province of the writer, to select with care the information he details, and to avoid a conclusion on any point, however trifling, which may not be warranted by a show, if not a reality, of fair and satisfactory proof. And as it is the province of the writer to be cautious in advancing any proposition without authority, so is it on the other hand the province of the reader to accept the information as the best that can be obtained, and to give the writer credit for the labour and research which may have thrown a gleam of sunshine, however faint, upon the passages of departed centuries.

The parish of Warblington lies at the south-eastern extremity of Hampshire. On the west it is bounded by the parish of Havant, on the north and east by the county of Sussex, and on the south by Langstone harbour, which separates it from the Island of Hayling. There are undoubted indications of very early settlement within its ambit. The word itself is apparently Saxon, and it possesses a Church at the southern extremity, with a Castle there, and one at Rowlands Castle, both of which have for very many years been in a state of ruin and desolation, and of the history of which, comparatively speaking, nothing is known. At the present day but little, I fear, can be done in arriving at any very satisfactory conclusion on the subject; still there are documents, hitherto unnoticed, which tend to throw some little light on the character of the buildings and of the objects for which they were originally founded. Without stopping to speculate on the condition of the country previous to the Roman Conquest, we may assume Domesday to be the starting point of authentic information, and under the head of the Hundred of Ghidenetroi in the county of Sussex, we find the following entry :—

"The Earl Roger de Montgomery holds Borne in demesne; Earl Godwin held it. There are there thirty-six hides, but then and now it is assessed for twelve hides. The land consists of thirty carucates. There are two carucates in

demesne and twenty-seven vilains, and thirty-one borderers
with fifteen ploughs. There are seven servants and four mills
of the value of forty shillings, and a fishery of sixteen pence,
and wood for three hogs.

"There are in Chichester six houses of the value of thirty
pence. To this manor appertains Warblitetone in Hantescire.
In the time of King Edward it was assessed for twelve hides,
now at four hides. The land consists of   [*sic* in
original]; there are two carucates in demesne, and seventeen
villagers, and twelve borderers with five ploughs. There are
two churches (or religious houses) there, and six servants, and
one mill of the value of ten shillings.

"Of this land Pagan holds four hides. Alric held it for the
benefit of the monastery. There is one carucate in demesne
and eight vilains, and five borderers with two ploughs, and
one mill of the value of ten shillings, and two acres of
meadow. In Chichester there is one house worth twelve
pence. The whole manor in the time of King Edward was
valued at thirty pounds, and afterwards at ten pounds. Now,
what the Earl holds is valued at forty pounds, and yet it pays
fifty pounds. What Pagan holds is and was valued at sixty
shillings." (*Domesday*, fo. 23 b.)

Roger de Montgomery was the favourite soldier and companion in arms of William the Conqueror. He was one of
those who contributed largely to the success of the expedition; and there is a very curious account still extant in the
form of a manuscript, evidently of the eleventh century, in
the Bodleian Library, numbered 3632, bearing the title of
"De Navibus per magnates Normanniæ provisis pro pas-
"sagio Ducis Willielmi in Angliam," and which runs as
follows :—

"Willelmus Dux Normannorum veniens in Angliam ob
adquirendum regnum jure sibi debitum, habuit a Willelmo
dapifero filio Osberni sexaginta naves. Ab Hugone postea
comite de Cestria totidem. Ab Hugone de Munfurt quin-
quaginta naves et sexaginta milites. A Remo elemosinario

Fescanori postea episcopo Lincoliensi unam navem cum xx
militibus. A Nicholao Abbate de Sancto Audoeno xv naves
cum c militibus. A Roberto comite Augi sexaginta naves.
A Fulcone Dauno xl naves. A Geroldo dapifero totidem.
A Will' comite Deurons octaginta naves. A Rogero de
Mungumeri sexaginta naves. A Rogero de Baumont lx
naves. Ab Odone episcopo de Baios c naves. A Roberto
de Moretein c et xx. A Waltero Giffard xxx cum c militibus. Extra has naves que computate simul м. efficiunt
habuit Dux a quibusdam suis hominibus secundum possi-
bilitatem unius cujusque multas alias naves. Matildis postea
regina ejusdem ducis uxor' ad honorem ducis fecit effici
navem que vocabatur Mora in qua ipse dux vectus est.
In prora ejusdem navis fecit fieri eadem Matildes infantulum
de auro, dextro indice monstrantem Angliam et sinistra
manu imprimentem cornu eburneum ori. Pro quo facto dux
concessit eidem Matildi comitatum Cantie."

All those who contributed ships were afterwards rewarded
accordingly; and Arundel (comprising Borne), Chichester, and
Shropshire, we are told, fell to the share of Roger de Montgomery.

For a very long period subsequent to Domesday, there is no
direct evidence to show by whom, or under what tenure, the
Manor of Warblington was held. Much therefore must be
left to inference, and it will perhaps be desirable in the first
instance to trace the descent of the manor so far as it can be
ascertained from existing legal records, giving afterwards such
scanty information as can be gleaned in reference to the family
of De Warblington, which undoubtedly derived its name
from the immediate locality.

Whatever may have been the tenure of the Manor of Warblington or by whom held subsequent to Domesday, it was at
all events an escheat of the Crown in the early part of the reign
of King Henry III, for in the *Testa de Nevil*, compiled partly in
that reign and partly in the time of Edward I, under the head
of the Hundred of Boseberg, it is stated that "The Manor of
"Warblington is an escheat of the lord the King, as the land

"of the Normans, and it is worth fifteen pounds, and thereof
"Matthew the son of Herbert has ten pounds, and William de
"Angulum one hundred shillings." (B. 65, m. 169). It was
not held by the Crown for any great length of time, as it
appears to have been granted by Henry III, together with
the hamlets of Empsworth, Eastney, and Watlington, to
Matthew Fitzherbert, one of the barons who had strenuously
supported the cause of King John, and who was sheriff
of Sussex from the twelfth to the seventeenth of John, and
from the first to the thirteenth (except the third) of Henry III.
The grant to which there is no date but which must have
taken place between 1216 and 1230, ran as follows:

"King Henry III gave the Manor of Warblington with
"the hamlets of Empsworth, Estney, and Watlington, to
"a certain Matthew, son of Herbert, and to his heirs in fee,
"within the liberty of the rape of Hastings," (*Fines,* 7
Edw. II, m, 1)

This Matthew Fitzherbert was a very distinguished person-
age in the reigns of King John and King Henry III, and was
descended from the same ancestor as the Herberts, Earls of
Pembroke, namely, Henry Fitzherbert, chamberlain to Henry I.
He was himself the youngest son of Herbert Fitzherbert, who
held the same office under King Stephen and Henry II, and
from his posterity, the Finches, Earls of Winchelsea, trace their
pedigree, the name of Finch being first assumed by his grandson in the reign of Edward I. There is some difficulty in
determining the date of Matthew Fitzherbert's death, but it
is believed to have taken place prior to 1230, when the Manor
of Warblington descended to his son and heir Herbert, who
conducted himself with great bravery in France against the
Dauphin, particularly in the battle of Xantoigne in the year
1242, and for his services to Henry, was honoured with many
privileges and emoluments.

In the 15 Henry III, 1231, that monarch by his charter
granted to Herbert, free warren in the manors of Barton and
Warblington, in the county of Southampton (*Rot. Chart.* m. 7),
and in the twenty-third year of the same reign, 1239, he
granted to him a market and fair at Emelesworth, and con-

firmed the prior grant of free warren in the Manor of Warblington, and in various other Knight's, fees then held by Herbert.
(*Rot. Chart.* m. 4). In the *Testa de Nevil* there is a confirmation of the tenure of Herbert in the following entry:
" William Angulum holds one hundred shillings worth of
" land of the lord the King in capite in Warblington, of the
" fee of Robert de Curcy; which land contains four hides of
" land rendering to the lord the King annually one pair of
" spurs. Herbert the son of Matthew holds the remainder of
" the aforesaid manor by the same service as Robert de Curcy
" held it of the lord the King." (Fo. 168.)

There was something peculiar in the original grant to
Herbert, and by a charter preserved in the *Formulare Angli-
canum* of Madox, form 531, it appears that even during the
life of Herbert, some doubt about his title was entertained.
The record of the donation was a grant of six does annually
from Herbert, the son of Peter, out of his park at Bethameton,
to Herbert the son of Matthew, and ran in these words : " To
" all the faithful in Christ to whom this present writing shall
" come, Herbert the son of Peter greeting in the Lord. Know
" ye, that I Herbert, have given and granted for me and my
" heirs, to the Lord Herbert the son of Matthew, and his heirs
" lawfully begotten, on account of the friendship as well as
" the bond of consanguinity between us, three does in the
" falling season from my park of Bethameton, and three does
" in the doe season, without any hindrance on the view of my
" bailiffs. And if it should so happen that the said Lord
" Herbert, the son of Matthew, should have no heir law-
" fully begotten, I have granted for me and my heirs the said
" donation in the park aforesaid to Peter, the son of Matthew
" his brother, only during the life of the aforesaid Peter. But
" if it should so happen that the lord the King should give an
" exchange to the aforesaid Herbert the son of Mathew, for the
" Manor of Warblington, or that the land of the Normans and
" the land of the English should become common, and on
" account of that community, or from any other cause, the
" aforesaid manor should pass from the said lord Herbert the

"son of Matthew or his heirs, the before named lord, Herbert
"the son of Peter and his heirs are released from the said
"donation. And in testimony whereof to this present writing
"made in the form of a Chirograph, I the said Herbert the
"son of Peter and Herbert the son of Matthew have inter-
"changeably affixed our seals. These being witnesses : Lord
"Baldwin, Earl of Devon, Lord Bassed, Lord John Bassed,
"Lord William de Bretinoll, Lord Henry de Borhunth, Lord
"Matthew Crocket, Lord Manasses the son of Matthew,
"Reginald the son of Peter and many others."

The seal attached to this deed was of yellow wax and bore
the representation of a mounted knight. No date is found
upon it, but as the Baldwin Earl of Devon was without doubt
the grandson of William de Redvers Earl of Devon, and was
by King Henry III invested with the Earldom of the Isle of
Wight in 1240, the deed was executed at that time.

In the 53 Henry III, 1268 Peter the son of Matthew died
seized of lands within the Manor of Warblington, as appears
by the Inquisition taken upon his decease. The William
Aguillon mentioned in the *Testa de Nevil* was sheriff of
Sussex during a part of the year 46 Henry III, 1261 ; and
upon his death that part of the Manor which he held descended to his son Robert Aguillon who was sheriff of the
county of Sussex from the 45 to the 51 Henry III. He was,
about the 8 Edward I, 1279, summoned " to show to the lord
"the King by what warrant he took the fines of the assize of
"bread and beer in Warblington which belong to the Crown
"of the lord the King without his leave and will. And
"Robert says that his tenements which he now hath in
"Warblington are escheats of the Normans, and that at the
"time when the aforesaid tenements were in the hands of the
"Normans they always had and took the aforesaid fines of the
"assize of bread and beer. Moreover he says that the lord
"the King Henry the father of the lord the now King, gave
"to the ancestors of him Robert the tenements aforesaid with
"the privileges aforesaid, as freely as the Normans held them,
"and by that title he claims to have the fines aforesaid. And

12

" William de Giselham who prosecutes &c. says that the lord
" King Henry the father of the now King was seized of the
" aforesaid fines to be taken for the assize of bread and beer
" and also of the view of frankpledge until the aforesaid
" Robert took possession of them to the personal injury of
" the lord the King. Whereupon a Jury was ordered to be
" summoned at Wilton." (*Plac. de quo War. com. Suth.* fo.
771; *Rot.* 39.) The Jury was summoned, and the judgment
as to the claim of Robert Aguillon was postponed; but, as I
do not find any further entry in reference to the matter, it is
probable that the point was conceded on the part of the
Crown.

In the 15 Edward I 1286, Matthew the son of John
acknowledged in the court of the King, that the town and
castle of Devizes and the Manors of Rudes and Erlestok and
Hakleston in the county of Wilts, the Manors of Stok in
Hammes, Ylampton, Hocford and la Sturce and Piworthi in
the county of Devon, and the Manors of Warblington and
Hunton in the county of Southampton with the appurtenances
were the right of the King and Queen.   And in consideration
of this acknowledgment, the King and Queen granted to the
aforesaid Matthew the aforesaid town and castle and the
manors with their appurtenances as in demesne, with the
homages, services of freemen, wards of the castle, advowsons
to the before named tenements belonging without any
reservation, to be holden by the same Matthew of the King and
Queen and the heirs of the King, all the life of the aforesaid
Matthew, rendering therefore yearly £40 for all service,
custom and exaction.   (*Rot. orig.* 15 Edw. I; *Rot.* 20.)

Upon the death of Geoffrey de Lisle in the 22d Edward I,
1293, he was by inquisition found to have died seized of
the Manor of Warblington as mesne lord of Matthew the son
of John and Alionora his wife (*Inq. p. mort.* 32. 22 Edw. I),
who died in the 3 Edward II, 1301, and was found by inquisition to have died seized of large possessions, and among
them of the Manor and fee of the Church of Warblington.
(*Inq. p. mort.* No. 49, 3 Edw. II.)

The manor on the termination of Matthew's life estate reverted again to the Crown, and in the 6 Edward II, 1312, another Matthew Fitzherbert, probably the son of the late tenant for life, was in possession of the Manor of Warblington, Empnesworth, the Manor of Estney, and the hamlet of Middleton. An inquisition *ad quod damnum* was taken in that year, apparently with a view to contemplated alienation. (*Inq. ad quod dam.* No. 124, 6 Edw. II). The latter could only however have affected the mesne estate, as the manor had previously been granted for life to Robert le Ewer. I do not after this find with any degree of certainty that the Fitzherberts held either the Manor of Warblington or lands within it, but for a considerable period subsequently to the reign of Edward I, the family of Fitzherbert possessed lands within the rape of Hastings, and Vincent Herbert otherwise Finch, who lived in the reigns of Richard II and Henry IV, married Isabel daughter and heiress of Robert Cralle of Cralle in the parish of Warblington.

In the 7 Edward II, 1313, " It was commanded to John " Abel Esquire, on this side Trent, that he seize into the " hands of the King the Manor of Warblington, with the " hamlets of Empnesworth, Estneye and Middleton, which " Isabella Bardolf and Phillis de Estneye having usurped " obtained seisin of and detained." (*Rot. Orig.* 7 Edw. II, *Ro.* 1). This was done without doubt, for in the 10 Edward II, 1316, we find by an inquisition *ad quod damnum*, that Robert le Ewer (*Inq. ad quod dam.* No. 104, 10 Edw. II) was in possession of the Manor of Warblington under his grant for life.

In the 4 Edward II, 1310, the reversion of the Manor of Warblington was granted by the Crown to Ralph de Monthermer (*Pat.* 4 Edw. II, p. 1. m. 3, in *Turr. Lond.*) who attended Edward I in his wars with Scotland, and behaved so valiantly in 1296, that Edward bestowed upon him the castle and honour of Tonebrugge with other lands in the county of Kent, together with various manors in the counties of Surrey and Sussex. This nobleman married for his first wife Joan of Acres daughter of Edward I, and widow of Gilbert de Clare Earl of Gloucester, from which circumstance he lost the King's favour, being only a retainer of her husband, and was imprisoned; but by the intercession of Anthony Bec bishop of Durham, they were reconciled in the following year, and his wife's lands with others in addition were restored to him. He was taken prisoner at the battle of Bannockburn in 1314, but had his ransom remitted, and sat in Parliament from the 27 Edward I to the 18 Edward II. The royal grant ran in these words. " The King to all to " whom &c. greeting; Know ye that we have granted for us " and our heirs to our beloved and faithful Ralph de Monther- " mer, and Thomas and Edward his sons our nephews, that " the Manor of Warblyngton with its appurtenances, which " Robert le Ewer holds for the term of his life of our grant, " and which after the death of the same Robert reverts to " us and our heirs after the decease of the same Robert; " shall remain to the before named Ralph, Thomas and " Edward, and the heirs of the body of same Thomas to be " begotten if there be any, to be held of us and our heirs " by the services therefore due and accustomed for ever. " And if after this sort he should not have an heir, then after " the death of the same Robert and of the aforesaid Ralph, " Thomas and Edward, the aforesaid manor with its appur- " tenances shall go to the heirs of the body of the same " Edward to be begotten, to be held of us and our heirs by " the aforesaid services for ever. And if the same Edward " should die without heir of his body begotten, then the " manor aforesaid with the appurtenances after the death " of the same Robert, and of the aforesaid Ralph, Thomas " and Edward shall revert entirely to us and our heirs. In " testimony &c."

This charter was granted by the king at Berwick-on-Tweed the 29th December 1310, and indorsed was a precept to Robert le Ewer, that he should do fealty to Ralph, Thomas, and Edward Monthermer as grantees of the reversion, and inasmuch as the donation could not take effect immediately,

the king on account of the laudable service which Ralph
Monthermer had rendered him, willingly and of his special
grace granted to him in recompence for the Manor of
Warblington, the Royal Manor of Westcuderlye to hold as
long as Robert le Ewer should live. (*Pat.* 4 Edw. II, p. 1,
m. 3, in *turr. Lond.*)

Thomas de Monthermer succeeded to his father's estates,
and was slain in a naval engagement between the French
and English in the year 1340.   An inquisition *post mortem*
was taken upon his death in the following year.   His only
daughter and heiress Margaret, married Sir John de Montacute
or Montagu son of William first Earl of Salisbury, to which
title his elder brother succeeded.   He served in the wars
in France under Edward III, and was at the battle of Crecy
in 1346.   In 1372, he is mentioned as in the king's fleet
at sea in the retinue of his brother the Earl of Salisbury.
He was present in the expedition into Scotland undertaken
by Richard II in 1385.   He was then a Knight Banneret,
and was retained to serve the king in person attended by
another banneret, five knights and their esquires, sixty men
at arms, and sixty archers.   As steward of the royal household
he was sent to conduct into England Ann of Bohemia, with
whom Richard the Second had contracted marriage.   He
was summoned to Parliament as a Baron of the realm from
the 31st Edward III, to the 13 Richard II, 1389, in which
year he died.   His will was dated the 20th March 1388,
and directed that he should be buried in the Cathedral
Church of Salisbury, between two pillars, or in case he should
die in London in the Cathedral Church of Saint Paul, where
he was baptized.   He ordered that a black woollen cloth
should be laid over his body, covering it and the hearse on
which it rested; the ground underneath to be spread with
cloth of russet and white of which every poor man attending
his funeral should have enough to make himself a coat and
a hood.   That on the day of his funeral the lights should
consist of five tapers, each weighing twenty pounds, four
mortaries each of ten pounds weight, and twenty-four torches

to be borne by as many poor men in russet and white. That
the emblazonments about his hearse should consist only of
one banner of the arms of England, two of the arms of
Montacute, and two of Monthermer; by the last, the five
tapers were to be placed. That there should be a plain
tomb made for him with the effigy of a knight thereon,
bearing the arms of Montacute, and having a helmet under
his head. (*Stod. Mon. Eff.* No. 72). He was interred
in the Lady Chapel of Salisbury Cathedral, and his tomb,
still remaining, shows that the directions of his will were
pretty closely followed. Under his head is his helmet,
bearing a griffin for his crest. His surcoat quarters, Argent,
three Lozenges in fess Gules for Montacute; Or, an Eagle
displayed Vert for Monthermer.

Sir John de Lisle of Gatcomb, who died 23 Edward III,
1349, held the Manor of Warblington as the mesne tenant
of Sir John de Montacute (*Inq. p. mort.* 23 Edw. III, No.
155), and William de Wintershull, who died 35 Edward III,
1360, appears to have done so subsequently. (*Inq. p. mort.*
35 Edw. III, No. 82). Lady Margaret Montague died
18 Richard II, 1394, and by inquisition taken upon her death,
was found to have died seized of the Manor of Warblington,
and of the advowson of the church there. (*Inq. p. mort.*
18 Ric. II, No. 30).

Sir John de Montacute, who was found by Inquisition to be
the heir of his father, succeeded to the family estates upon the
death of his mother the Lady Margaret. He distinguished
himself much at the siege of Bourdeilles in France, and enobled
his high descent. He was the chief leader of the Lollards,
and in the heighth of his zeal caused all the images in the
Chapel of Sheen to be thrown down. He married Maud the
daughter of Sir Adam Francis, and, by the death of his uncle
without issue, became third Earl of Salisbury. Upon the
deposition of Richard he joined a conspiracy for his restoration, but the plot being discovered he was surprised and
taken prisoner. He was almost the only nobleman who

remained staunch to Richard on the invasion of Bolingbroke, and was beheaded by the townsman of Cirencester on the 5th January 1400, when his estates became forfeited to the Crown.

Thomas Montacute his eldest son was the greatest hero of his age: by the attainder of his father for high treason he was deprived of his paternal property ; but Henry IV, compassionating his situation, restored Warblington to him, together with the Earldom of Salisbury, in the tenth year of his reign. He acquired great renown as a military commander during the reigns of Henry V and VI, and in addition to his own Earldom had that of Perche bestowed upon him, and was appointed Seneschal of the Duchy of Normandy. He was struck by a cannon shot at the siege of Orleans in 1428, and died at Mehun on the 3d November in that year, whence his body was carried to England and buried with great pomp at Bisham in Berkshire. An inquisition was taken upon his death in the following year, when he was found to have died seized of the manor and advowson of Warblington. (*Inq.* p. *mort.* 7 Hen. VI, *no.* 57.)

There is a curious episode in the history of the Earldom of Perche which may not be uninteresting in connexion with the account of Thomas Montacute. Upon the death of John, the French Dauphin attempted to place himself upon the throne of England. The barons in general were as averse to Henry III as they had been to his father, and with this view they countenanced the Dauphin Louis, who thus supported, and having received the homage of the Londoners, marched with the Count de Perche, and a large body of French troops to Lincoln. Randle Earl of Chester convened the northern barons, and taking young Henry with him, an interview took place in the Cathedral. The Count insulted Randle, calling him a dwarf ; Randle retorted vowing to God and our lady, that before the morrow he would be stronger, and greater, and taller, than the steeple of the Cathedral. They met on the morrow at the head of their respective followers, and the Earl with a fury which swept all before him, bore down upon the Count, and slew him with very many of his followers.

Randle returned, rushed into the Cathedral, and having seized upon Louis, made him swear by the Evangelists, and by the relics of saints then upon the altar, to evacuate England immediately with the whole of his army. According to Holinshed, the Count de Perche was killed in the churchyard of Lincoln Cathedral, and a general engagement having taken place, the French were routed with very great slaughter; a peace was subsequently agreed upon, and the Dauphin returned to France.

Thomas Montacute left an only daughter Alice. She married Richard Neville son of the Earl of Westmoreland, who in right of his wife became Earl of Salisbury. In the 23 Henry VI, 1445, the Manor of Warblington was with other property leased to this Richard Neville, and Alice his wife; "To have and to hold to the same Earl, and "Alice, and the heirs of the same Alice for the term of "twelve years next ensuing fully to be completed, rendering "therefore annually to us one red rose only at the feast of "Saint John the Baptist." The sad fate of Neville is so well known to every historical reader, and to the admirer of Shakespeare, that it would be superfluous to enlarge upon his life. He joined the York faction, became Lord Chancellor, was attainted of high treason at the parliament held at Coventry on the 20th Sept. 1460, was taken prisoner at the battle of Wakefield in 1461, and was subsequently beheaded at Pomfret. His corpse and that of his wife were interred at Bisham 16th February 2, Edward II, 1463-4.

Warblington once more devolved upon the Crown, and a long interval takes place before we can again trace its history. The next possessor on record, is Sir Richard Cotton, Knight, privy councillor to King Edward VI, who resided on the estate, and in the year 1552, entertained that monarch on his journey to the sea coast for the recovery of his health. Edward, in a letter written from Christchurch, speaks of his tour, and says, "We have been occupied with killing wild "beasts, in pleasant journeys, in good fare, in viewing of fair

" countries, and rather have sought how to fortify our own,
" than to spoil another man's. And being thus determined
" came to Guildford, from thence to Petworth, and so to
" Cowdrey a goodly house of Sir Anthony Browne's, where
" we were marvellously yea rather excessively banquetted;
" from thence we went to Halvenaker a pretty house besides
" Chichester, and from thence we went to Warblington a
" fair house of Sir Richard Cottons. And so to Whaltan a
" fair great old house, in times past the Bishop of Winchester's,
" and now my Lord Treasurer's house. In all these places,
" we had both good hunting and good cheer &c." Sir
Richard was a great favourite of that prince, and in Strype's
Memorials a letter from Edward is still extant, recommending
Sir Richard to represent the County in the Parliament
convened that year. In the next year 1553, after the King's
death, we find him among the number of those who wrote
to Queen Mary in favour of the unfortunate Lady Jane
Grey, and on that account being involved in disgrace on
Mary's accession to the throne, he retired to Warblington,
where he probably died, leaving it to his eldest son George
Cotton, who, in a subsidy granted to Queen Elizabeth in
1578, was rated at £50 for his lands. Henry Cotton a
younger son of Sir Richard was born here, and Queen (then
Lady) Elizabeth stood for his godmother. He was educated at
Magdalen College Oxford, and consecrated Bishop of Salisbury
on the 12th November 1598. He died on the 7th May 1615.

In the 10th James, 1612, the Manor of Warblington was in
lease from Richard Cotton, (whom I take to have been the son
of George Cotton,) to George Cotton heir apparent of Richard
Francis Clarke and Edward Wakeman. In the 20th James,
1622, it was in lease from Richard Cotton to George Cotton,
Thomas Lord Kelley, and George Symonds; and in 1627, when
a survey of the manor took place, he was still lord. In 1666
Richard Cotton of Warblington and Bedhampton, son of John
Cotton, married Elizabeth Lumley daughter of the Honourable
John Lumley of Stansted, and dying in 1695 was buried in
the chancel of Warblington with the following inscription :—

13

" Here lyeth interred the body of Richard Cotton of Bed-hampton and Warblington Esquire, son of George Cotton Esquire, and Elizabeth daughter of Sir George Symonds and husband to Elizabeth daughter of the Hon. John Lumley, Esquire, and sister to the Right Hon. Richard Lord Viscount Lumley of Stansted, now Earl of Scarburg, who piously departed this life the 28th of March, A. D. 1695.

" Maritum amantissimus, fratrum generosissimus, omnium justissimus."

By his Will dated in 1692, he devised all his estates to William Cotton his only surviving son, who died unmarried in 1736. William Cotton who resided at and is described as of Watergate in the county of Sussex, by his Will dated the 25th July, 1728, proved on the 5th August 1736, in the Prerogative Court of Canterbury, devised the manors of Warblington and Emsworth to his nephew Thomas Panton absolutely. By settlement of the 5th and 6th January 1767, made on the marriage of Thomas Panton the younger with Elizabeth the daughter of Elias Bird of Roehampton, the Warblington and Emsworth manors and estates were conveyed to Brownlow Earl of Exeter and Lord William Manners, to the use of Thomas Panton the younger and his issue in tail male, and in default of issue male or female, upon trust to pay the rents of the manors and estates to Mary Duchess of Ancaster for life, with remainder to the use of Robert Bertie Marquis of Lindsey, his heirs and assigns for ever. Robert Duke of Ancaster and Kesteven died on the 8th July 1779, and under his will dated the 29th May 1779, proved in the Prerogative Court of Canterbury, on the 23d July in the same year, the Warblington and Emsworth manors and estates passed to his sister the Baroness Willoughby of Eresby and her issue in tail male. The baroness married Sir Peter Burrill of Beckenham in the county of Kent, Baronet, deputy Great Chamberlain of England. Thomas Panton the younger had no issue, and sold his life interest to Richard Barwell Esquire, of Stansted, who took a demise of the estates for one hundred years; and by indentures of the 14th and 15th September 1792, in consideration of £6420 then paid, and of £15,000 to be afterwards paid as provided by the deed, Sir Peter Burrill covenanted that if Thomas Panton should die without issue the Lady Willoughby d'Eresby and her eldest son by Sir Peter if living, would, after the decease of Panton and such failure of his issue, convey the property to him absolutely.

Richard Barwell died on the 2d September, 1804, and was buried in Westbourne in the chancel of which church there is a monument to his memory by the celebrated sculptor Nollekens. By his will dated the 25th July 1804, proved in the Prerogative Court of Canterbury on the 12th October in the same year, he devised all his manors and estates to his widow Catherine Barwell, Edward Daun, and John Butler upon general trust for sale. In Trinity term 49 George III, a recovery was suffered by Sir Peter Burrill, who had become Peter Lord Gwydir, the Baroness Willoughby d'Eresby, the Honourable Peter Robert Drummond Burrill and Clementina Sarah his wife, whereby the entail was barred, and under indentures of the 3d and 4th July 1809 they conveyed the Warblington and Emsworth manors and estates to Mr. Barwell's trustees their heirs and assigns for ever. The trustees subsequently in the year 1825 sold the property to Messrs. Brown and Fenwick; both are since dead, and the estates are now held by the trustees of the latter for the benefit of his family.

This comprises all the chief lords, or lords who held the Manor of Warblington *in capite* of the Crown, and it will be seen that de Warblington does not occur amongst them. There is no such name on the Roll of Battle Abbey, and it was evidently local in its origin. The family attained considerable influence in the thirteenth and fourteenth centuries, several of them having served the office of Sheriff of Hants, but at the present moment, as far as I can ascertain, it has become extinct. Their history and connexion with the Manor of Warblington will be best gathered from the following extracts, obtained from the authentic and still existing records.

In the Catalogue of the Serjeanties entered in the Red Book during the reign of Henry II, 1154-1189 (*Lib. Rub.* fo. 126 a), it is said that Robert de Venuz held by the service of the Marshalsea, and William de Warblington by the service of the Marshalsea in the King's house.

In the reign of Henry III, 1216-72, the *Testa de Nevill* records, in reference to the Hundred of Sunburne: "The "land of William de Montellis in the Ville of Cu'pton, be-"longing to the Marshalsea of the Lord the King, and " William de Warblington answers for £10. In the Hundred " of Odiham William de Warblington holds Silefield of the " Lord the King by the serjeanty of the Marshalsea of the " Lord the King, and it is worth £10, and he holds it ·by "inheritance; and that Thomas de Warblington held of the " Countess Alice two knights' fees and a half, parcel of the " honour of Hastings held of the King *in capite*."

In the 29 Henry III, 1244, William de Warblington acknowledged a knight's fee and a quarter in Hantshire (*Mad. exch.* i, 494), and upon an aid being granted to Henry III in that same year, the *Great Pipe Roll* records that William de Warblington was rated at two marks and a half for one knight's fee, and the fourth part of one fee of ancient feoff. ment. *Vetus feoffamentum* was the feoff granted by the Crown to barons or knights prior to the death of Henry I; *novum feoffa- mentum* was the feoff granted after the accession of Henry II.

Thomas de Warblington was Sheriff of the county of Hants in the 20th, 21st and 22d, and from the 26th to the 33d of Edward I, except the 30th, and from the 1st to the 5th Edward II. He also held the Manor of Shirefield *in capite* of the King, by the service of being Marshal of the King's *meretrices,* and of dismembering malefactors and measuring the gallons and bushels in the Royal household. (*Pas. Comms.* 24 & 25 Edw. I.) In the 24th and 25th Edward I, the county of Southampton with the castle of Winchester, was committed to this Thomas de Warblington during pleasure of the Crown, he rendering a stipulated rent to the Exchequer.

In early and feudal times the Crown exacted fines for licenses of various kinds. For example, fines were often made by tenants *in capite* for licence to marry, or that they might not be compelled to marry, and in the fines of Michaelmas Term, 26th and 27th Edward I (*Rot.* 63 a), we find the name of Thomas de Warblington occurring in the record of a fine paid by Margaret Camoys to marry whom she pleased. The entry is in these words :—" Sussex, Margaret Camoys, " who was the wife of John de Camoys deceased, who held of " the King *in capite*, made a fine of one hundred marks with " the King that she might have the licence of the King to " marry whom she would, and by that fine leave is granted to " her that she marry whom she please, so that he bear fealty " to the King.   And because the King by his letters patent " inrolled in Hilary term then last past, granted to Edmund " Earl of Kent, his kinsman, that he should have and receive " such fines until the Earl should be satisfied in respect of " debts owing by the King, neither have such debts been " paid.   The Treasurer and Barons are forthwith to assign " the aforesaid Margaret that she make satisfaction to the " said Earl in respect of the aforesaid one hundred marks, in " part payment of the aforesaid debts, that is to say that she " pay him fifty marks at Easter next, and fifty marks at the " feast of Saint Michael next following.

"And William Paynel, Knight of the County of Sussex, " Walter de Pavelin (Pavilly), Knight of the County of Wilts, " Robert de Glamorgan, and Thomas de Warblington, Knight " of the County of Southampton, being present in court, " undertook, each one by himself and for himself, to be bound " to pay the said Earl the aforesaid hundred marks, at the " terms above mentioned, unless the said Margaret then paid " them.   And they covenanted for themselves, their heirs " and executors, that the Barons of the Exchequer concerning " the lands and chattels to whose hands soever &c., would " cause the aforesaid hundred marks to be placed to the " account of the aforesaid Earl, in the form aforesaid.   And " the before named Margaret has letters and the aforesaid " Licence, dated the second day of October, under the hand

" of the Treasurer &c." "And after that came Walter de
" Eylesbury, the executor of the will of the aforesaid Earl in
" full parliament at Lincoln, and acknowledged that the said
" Earl received the hundred marks, as William de Carleton
" and Roger de Heyham, Barons of the Exchequer, testify,
" and so they are quit."

When debts due to the King had in former days been put
in charge in the Revenue Rolls, they were sent out from the
Exchequer in process to be levied. The person principally
entrusted with the levying and collection of them was the
sheriff of each county, whose authority was much greater
then than at the present moment. The most ancient process
that was used for this purpose was called the summonce of
the Exchequer, which issued twice in the year into all the
counties of England, and was returnable against the times
of holding the *Duo Scaccaria*. The summonce was more
generally known under the name of the summonce of the
Great Roll or of the Pipe. In the 32d Henry III the summonce of the Great Roll for Northamptonshire was delivered
to the sheriff of that county by the hand of John le Franceis
a Baron of the Exchequer. (*Trin. Com.* 32 Hen. III., *Rot.*
96.) In the 49th year of that reign the summonce of the
Great Roll for Lancashire was delivered to Alexander de
Elleswik the clerk of the sheriff. Afterwards we find that
another sort of summonce is mentioned, called the summonce
of the Green Wax or of the foreign escheats, but the summonce of the Great Roll still continued in use, as it does to
this day. In the 27th Edward I, Thomas de Warblington,
sheriff of Hantshire, sat rendering his account at the
Exchequer. He was opposed before Peter de Leicester, one
of the barons, upon certain summonces of the Exchequer,
sent to him under Green Wax by four rolls, the particulars
of which were given in evidence. Thomas de Warblington
asserted that the summonces in four rolls had never come
to the hands of himself or his clerks, and that for that reason
he ought not to be charged with them. It appeared in evidence that the four rolls were indorsed in the ordinary form,

as delivered on the 6th July in the 25th year of the reign, 1296, and the officers stated that the rolls were sent to the sheriff by the messengers of the Exchequer, but that they were ignorant as to whether the same had been received by the sheriff, nor did they recollect the names of the messengers. The result of the proceedings was that Thomas de Warblington was acquitted of blame, and the rolls were directed to be re-issued. (*Pas. Com.* 26 c, 27 Edw. I, *Rot.* 25.)

In the 30th Edward I, the towns of Seford, Shoreham, Portesmuth, Suthampton, Lymeton, Ermme, Pole, Warham, Lym, Teygnemue, Plymmuth, Fouy and Briggwater, neglected to furnish the requisite number of men and ships commanded by the Crown for the maintenance of the war with Scotland, and an order issued to Thomas de Verblynton and Peter de Donewych to punish the offending towns, in whatever manner they should deem expedient. (*Abb. Rot. orig., Rot.* 12.) This was probably effected by tallage or fine, which was the usual course with contumacious towns or baronies in early times.

In the Hundred Rolls a sort of second general survey of lands held of the Crown, I find that in the county of Kent Thomas de Warblington held of the lord the King *in capite*, sixteen virgates and eight acres of land in Thevesham by serjeanty, one Walrafrus de Mariteus holding a moiety of the same land of the aforesaid Thomas, which tenement Thomas de Peferel then held, but by what service, the jurors of the inquisition were unable to decide. That William de Warblington held another moiety of the aforesaid land of the aforesaid Thomas de Warblington by the service of sixpence or one pair of spurs annually for all services. That Alice de Bodegisham held of the said Thomas de Warblington and William de Warblington, three acres and a half of land by homage and the payment of two shillings and sixpence annually in lieu of all services. That William Maschet held of William de Warblington thirty acres of land by homage and the rent of nine shillings annually. That Margaret the daughter of

Roger de Warblington held of William de Warblington twenty-six acres of land by homage and the rent of three shillings annually. That Milicensia de Leycester held of the said William nine acres of land by homage and the rent of sixpence annually. That Robert de Romely held of the said William twelve acres of land by homage and the rent of two shillings annually. That John de Venella held of the said William twelve acres of land by homage, and by the rent of six shillings annually, and suit of court. That Robert the son of William Macefry held of the said William one acre and a half by homage and the rent of sixteen pence annually. That Alice de Bodegisham and Katherine de Frating held of the said William three acres and a half of land by the rent of three shillings annually. That William de Swaffham held of the said William two acres of land by homage and the rent of one penny annually. That Alice de Warblington held of the said William one half acre of land by homage and the rent of one halfpenny annually, and that William de Warblington had in that ville seven vilains and four crofts of land. (*Rot. Hundred Com. Cant*, m. 2.)

King Edward I, on his return from the Holy Land, in the second year of his reign 1274, discovered that during the reign of his father King Henry III, the revenues of the Crown had been considerably diminished, by tenants *in capite* alienating without licence, and by ecclesiastics as well as laymen withholding from the crown under various pretexts its just rights and usurping the right of holding Courts and other Jura Regalia, and that numerous exactions and oppressions of the people had been committed by the nobility and gentry claiming rights of free chase, free warren, and fishery, and demanding unreasonable tolls in fairs and markets. One of the first acts of his administration after his arrival was to correct these abuses; before, however, any specific remedy could be provided for the correction of them, some evidence was required of their peculiar nature and extent. The King, therefore, on the 11th of October in the second year of his reign, appointed special commissioners for the whole kingdom, to whom were delivered certain articles of inquiry applicable to the abuses above mentioned. The inquisitions taken in pursuance of these commissions were entered on the Rolls called the Hundred Rolls, which were returned for the most part into the Exchequer. From thence the crown was furnished among other things with evidence on oath of a Jury of each hundred and town in every county of manors and lands formerly in the hands of the crown, the persons holding the same, the authority and how alienated, together with presentments upon every royal right usurped to the prejudice of the subject.

The Statute of Gloucester was enacted in the sixth year of this king's reign, and the first chapter relating to liberties, franchises, and *quo warranto*, was founded upon the previous inquiries under this commission. A comparison of the Hundred Rolls and the Rolls of pleadings in *quo warranto*, fully justifies this conclusion. Immediately after the passing of the Statute of Gloucester the stated period of the Circuit in Eyre returned, and on the justices going their iter, writs of right and of *quo warranto* issued very generally against such persons as claimed manors, liberties, &c. where the jurors had previously said before the inquisitors 3 Edward I, 1275, "*Nesciunt quo warranto*," the parties held or claimed, and again, where they said the party held or claimed "*sine warranto;*" in such case a writ sometimes issued, but the party usually came in upon the general proclamation directed by the statute without any special writ of *quo warranto*, the entry in the former case being "A.B. summonibus fuit ad respon- "dendum Domino Regi quo warranto," and in the other "presentatum fuit Inquisitoribus Domini Regis quod A. B. "clamat," and *sine warranto*.

Previously to the departure of the Justices in Eyre on their circuit immediately following the enactment of the statute of Gloucester, these identical Inquisitions or Hundred Rolls were delivered to them for the purpose of holding pleas upon the claims stated therein. The judgments do not apppear in all cases, the same being sometimes adjourned *coram Rege*, and at other times *coram Rege in parliamento*, and frequently no judgment whatever was given, the king's attorney not choosing further to prosecute his writ.

These rolls contain an entry showing that the master of the military order of the Temple in England was summoned to answer the lord the king concerning a plea by what warrant he held six oxgangs of land with the appurtenances in War-blington, which was of the ancient demesne of the crown. The master by his attorney appeared and pleaded, that he held two out of the six oxgangs of the gift of William the son of Roger de Warblington, granted by his deed, which he produced in proof of the fact; and that he held four oxgangs of the gift of Simon Saginarius, by virtue of his deed of gift, which he also produced in confirmation of his plea. And he stated that the lord Henry the king, the father of the lord the then king, granted and confirmed to the brethren of the military order of the Temple in England all donations of men, alms, and lands, to them and their predecessors, whether con-ferred by others, or acquired, or obtained by any other means. And upon being asked whether he had any other special warrant from the crown he said he had not.

Alanus, the attorney of the king, applied for judgment on the part of the crown, inasmuch as the gift as pleaded by the master of the templars was not specified by the royal charter of confirmation. (*Plac. de quo war.*) The judgment in the cause was deferred to a future day, and as I do not find any further notice taken of the matter, I conclude that the crown withdrew its claim and suffered the Templars to retain pos-session of the lands which had been so bestowed upon them.

By the forty-second roll of the pleas of *quo warranto*, it appears that the parson of the church of Warblington was summoned to show by what right he took the fines of the assize of bread and beer in Warblington which pertained to the crown. The parson appeared and pleaded, that he did not claim the fines of the assize of bread, therefore it was adjudged to be in the lord the king. And as to the fines of beer, he pleaded that he and his predecessors, rectors of the church aforesaid, from time whereof the memory of man had run not to the contrary, had taken in manner claimed, the fines of beer appertaining to the church. The matter was put in issue by William de Gyselham, who prosecuted on the part of the crown, and the sheriff was commanded to summon a jury at Wylton. Afterwards at Marlborough in the octave of Saint Michael, the jurors upon oath returned a verdict that the parson and his predecessors, rectors of the church of Warblington, from time whereof the memory of man had run not to the contrary, had after the manner claimed taken the fines of beer, that is to say, from their tenants and persons convicted of offences against the assize of beer, and that he, the parson, had himself taken penalties for transgressions of this kind.

Thomas de Warblington lived in the reign of Edward II, held various manors about the year 1313, and by the inquisition taken upon his death 10 Edward II, 1317, he was found to have died seized of several manors in the county of Surrey, and of those of Shirefield, Odiham, and Warblington in the county of Southampton. (*Inq. p. mort.* 10 Edw. II, 55.)

In the 19th Edward II, 1326, Thomas de Coudray paid a fine of one hundred shillings to enfeoff William de Warblington, parson of the church of Warblington. (*Ab. Rot. or.*) Edward confirmed Shirefield to John de Warblington, son and heir of Thomas de Warblington, subject to the tenure before mentioned. John died in the 6th Edward III, and by the inquisition taken upon his decease was found to have died seized, among many other manors, of those of Shirefield and Warblington, the latter held as of the Barony of Hastings. (*Inq. p. mort.* 6 Edw. III, 54.) His wife's name was Margaret. His son John de Warblington, who married Alice, succeeded him, and upon his death, in the 25th Edward III, 1351, was also found by inquisition to have died seized of many manors, and among them of the manor of Warblington, held as of the Barony of Hastynges. (*Inq. p. mort.* 25 Edw. III, 54.)

Margaret de Warblington died in the 40th Edward III, 1365-6, having held the fees of Roffeld and Doyle in Oxfordshire, for her dower. John de Warblington, who succeeded his father, obtained in the 42d Edward III, 1367-8, a grant of free warren in the Manors of Shirefield, Bishopstoke, Stratfield, Tourgis, Bromle, Botteler, Candeversden, Tamidge and Warbelton. (*Rot. chart.* 42 Edw. III, 10.) That King also committed to him the office of Coroner of the Marshalsea and the office of clerk of the markets of the royal household, to be held during the royal pleasure. (44 Edw. III, *ter. par. pat. Rot.* m. I4.) This John de Warblington dying in the 49th Edward III, was found to have died seized of the manors above mentioned, subject, as far as Shirefield was concerned, to the original tenure, which continued until after the death of his widow Katherine. (*Inq. p. mort.* 49 Edw. III, 57.) In the 8th Richard II, 1384, Alice Warblington, widow of John de Warblington, died, and was found by inquisition to have been seized, amongst other lands, of the Manor of Warblington, with the advowson of the church there, held as before of the ancient Barony of Hastynges. (*Inq. p. mort.* 8 Ric. II, 40.)

William de Warblington was sheriff of the county of Southampton 12th Henry IV, 1410. William Warbelton is mentioned in the list of the gentry in Hampshire returned by the commissioners 12th Henry VI, 1433, and in the 29th year of the same reign Thomas Warbelton was sheriff of the county. In the 35th Henry VI, 1456, that King granted to William Warbelton in fee (*Pat. Rolls*, m. 13) the office of constable of the Castle of Odiham, together with the custody of the park of Odiham, in the county of Southampton. In the 8th Edward IV, 1467-8, William Warbelton, Arm., died, and upon the inquisition taken upon his death it appears that he held the Manors of Shirefield, Odyham, Chynham, Basynge, Bishopstoke, Butlers Candover, Preston Candover, Flexland, Kingsclere, Wodelande and Echemswelle (*Inq. p. mort.* 8 Edw. IV, 44), and upon the death of his widow Margaret, 2d Richard III, 1484, she was found by inquisition to have died seized of the same manors. (*Inq. p. mort.* 2 Ric. III.)

The tenure by which the de Warblingtons held their Manor of Shirefield was analogous to pimp tenure, an explanation of which will be found in Selden. The Mare-schall was a great officer of the king's court, and the office was anciently, and is at this day, hereditary. It is now vested in the most noble the Duke of Norfolk. Mareschall was also a general name for several officers who were employed about the royal horses, game, &c. For example, ten marks were allowed to Hugh the mareschall and his fellows for tending twenty of the King's palfreys, in the reign of Richard I. The sum of £132 was allowed at the Exchequer to John Palmer, for himself and twenty-one grooms, and for hay, oats, and farriery (*marescalcia*) for fifty horses of the King's stable. There was also a marescalcia of the Royal birds, and in Ireland a "*Marescalcia mensuræ Regis.*" (*Pat.* 10 Edw. II, m. 8, pars 2.) In the 11th Henry II, a charter, made between Robert Abbot of St. Alban and others of the one part, and Laurence Abbot of Westminster of the other part, was executed at the Exchequer, before several of the justices, and before the King's chamberlains and his mare-schalls. (*Mad. form. Ang. in Differt.*, p. 19.) In the 14th year of the same reign William Fitz-Aldelin is styled mare-schall, and certified to the King, that of the land which the King gave to William Fitz-Aldelin, his mareschall, with Juliana, daughter of Robert Dorsnell, Baldwin Wischard held one knight's fee of the old feoffment in Essex, John Gernun the fourth part of a knight's fee, and that he himself held the rest in demesne by his service or serjeanty of the King's Marshalsea. (*Liber ruber.*, fo. 86 a.) Beside this there was an office styled Magister Marescallus, which Sir Henry Spelman thinks was introduced at the time of the Conquest. William Fitz-Osbern and the Grentemaisnels first bore it in England; afterwards it was held by the family of the Marescalli, and subsequently, on failure of their male issue, it passed to the Bygods, from whom the Dukes of Norfolk derive their title as one of inheritance.

The de Warblingtons, who were evidently of consideration prior to the year 1278, when their grant was pleaded in answer to the *quo warranto* by the Templars, were probably an offshoot from the stock of the Montgomeries or of the d'Albinis who succeeded them, and held the manor as mesne lords from the grantees of the crown. Whether they ever resided at the Castle is uncertain, but as they had grants of Odiham, and more important fees in the northern part of the county, the inference is that they lived there rather than at Warblington. No arms are assigned to them in the lists of the sheriffs, although Thomas de Warblington served the office on no less than twelve different occasions. As far as can be learnt they never held the Manor of Warblington as chief lords, and although the name is returned in the list of the gentry in the reign of Henry VI, yet as it does not occur subsequently in the Visitations preserved in the Heralds' College and at the British Museum, we may fairly conclude that the male branch of the family ceased to exist shortly after the reign of Edward IV.

THE CHURCH.—About half a mile south of the turnpike road, and lying midway between Havant and Emsworth, stands the Parish Church of Warblington. To the north and north-east are the remains of Warblington Castle, now occupied as the Castle Farm. The present appearance of the Church dedicated to Saint Thomas à Becket, is not in keeping with the original design, windows having been added at a com-paratively recent period without reference to the style of the architecture, or to the restoration of an edifice possessing great peculiarities and considerable beauty. Its extreme length of nave is fifty feet by forty feet in breadth, with side aisles sepa-rated by a row of drop arches supported by piers of two different characters. Those on the south are of a style peculiar to the period when the Early English merged into the Decorated, in the first part of the fourteenth century, each comprising a centre octagonal pillar, surrounded by four shafts of black Sussex marble, with ornamented capitals placed at right angles, giving great elegance and lightness to the elevation. On the north the columns are circular, unadorned, and of greater solidity, being only eight feet in height, including bases and capitals, and two feet in diameter. This distinction has been

Worthington Church and Castle?

AND
EN FOUNDATIONS

conjectured to refer to the share which each of the supposed foundresses had in building the Church; but other churches, Titchfield for example, present a similar anomaly. Each aisle is terminated by a small chauntry, or sacellum, about eight feet square; these have been called oratories, and as such served other beside mortuary purposes; because it must be borne in mind that the laity, in former times, were not admitted into the chancel, which was reserved exclusively for ecclesiastics, and that the sacrament was administered, as in Arundel Church, in the chauntry of the side aisles. In the windows of that on the south side a quantity of stained glass was some time since visible, but at present six barbed roses only remain, irregularly placed, and of a yellow colour. It is difficult to make out whether they were intended to form part of an escutcheon or not, but it is probable that they were merely ornamental, without reference to heraldic bearing.

The Chancel is of great length as compared with the nave; adjoining it at the north-east corner there is a chapel, now used as a vestry, which contains a beautiful piscina, surmounted by a trefoil canopy with crocket and finial, having on either side a small pinnacle with triangular heads. Within the chancel itself on the northern side, the hagioscope, commanding a view of the altar, as at Chipping Norton in Oxfordshire, for the use of the attendant who, in former days, rang the sanctus bell at the time of the elevation of the host, is still in perfect preservation: there is another piscina on the southern side of the chancel, under a trefoil head, and arched canopy; at one time made use of as a font. A slab of black marble inserted in the wall close to the door of the vestry bears the following inscription:

> *" Before this monument lyeth buryed the*
> *Bodye of Raffe Smalpage, late Chaplè*
> *To the righte honorable the Erle of*
> *Soothampton, Lord Chancelor of*
> *Englande and parson of this churche.*
> *Obiit 6 die May, aº Domini, 1558."*

It represents him kneeling, in his robes, before an altar, with a book upon it, and a label proceeding from his mouth on which are the words—" O prayes the Lord."　Behind him are his arms.　An escutcheon within an orle of martlets.

Another slab is inscribed :

> *"Here lyeth Francis Cotton, son unto Richard Cotton*
> *of Warblington, and unto Elizabeth his wife, who*
> *was daughter unto John Lumley, son unto the Lord*
> *Lumley of Stansted, who departed this life the 25th*
> *of September* 1687, *ætatis suæ* 12."

The Chancel also contains monuments to the memory of the late Charles Short, Esquire, of Woodlands ; the Reverend Robert Stopford ; the Reverend William Norris ; John Mc. Arthur, Esquire ; and other persons having vaults within the Chancel.

The chancel pavement consists of the red and yellow glazed tiles so frequent in churches of monastic foundation, and was entirely relaid with lozenges of Portland stone during the last reparation of the building.　These tiles were used at a very early period, and the patterns on them were not confined to a particular foundation, for similar ones are found in Saint Cross, Winchester Cathedral, Romsey Abbey, and Titchfield, it being generally believed that they were made by the monks for the ornament of their churches, and that the knowledge of the art was brought by them, in the first instance, from the Continent.　They were usually about six inches square, ornamented with figures of birds, beasts, grotesque patterns of leaves or flowers, short sentences as at Saint Cross, armorial bearings, and rarely knights on horseback, as in the chancel of Romsey Abbey Church.　Sometimes they are singly complete, but at others four of them combine to form a pattern, and from the singularity of these decorations they have become an object of interesting inquiry to the antiquary.　Those at Warblington are tolerably perfect, and exhibit ten different patterns, of which the most remarkable are a *fleur-de-lis* within a bordure checky, two castles party per pale, two lions rampant regardant addorsed; an escutcheon bearing three *fleur-de-lis*, having two birds like falcons for supporters, and an eagle with two heads displayed, carrying on its breast an escutcheon on which is a lion rampant.

There is a door in the chancel, one at the west end of the nave, and one at the north, beneath a porch of massive timber, coeval with the building, and ornamented with ogee trefoils and lattice-work.

The Church is surrounded by a churchyard of some size, which, on the 19th of October, 1809, was enlarged, the whole containing about an acre and a half. The elm trees which once adorned it are gone, but there is still a yew of very great age, measuring twenty-six feet in circumference, which serves in some measure to protect the building from the south-west gales, which in the winter time sweep up the harbour. The situation is quiet in the extreme and whether in ages past the population at Warblington was greater than at the present moment we cannot tell, but the locality certainly presents no indications or traces of the fact; tradition is altogether silent on the point, and we may therefore conclude that there was some other reason for the foundation of a church where, from the general appearance of the locality, the population must ever have been scanty. It is no doubt difficult to arrive at any thing like a satisfactory conclusion on the history of the edifice, its first erection and after maintenance; and conjecture must, therefore, in the present instance, supply the place of fact where the latter is wanting.

The existing Church stands undoubtedly on the site of one more ancient, and of this there is recorded and internal evidence. Doomsday speaks of II *æcclæ*, and at the time when that survey was compiled in the year 1088, Emsworth was not in existence. There are no remains of a church elsewhere in the parish, and it must therefore have stood where the present church now stands. In the Bishoprick register, during the episcopate of John de Pontissera, William de Ulburigge appears as having been presented to the living of Warblington in 1282; and the entries which have before been quoted both from the Hundred Rolls, and those of *quo warranto*, confirm the existence of a church long antecedent to the present edifice. Upon an examination of the nave, there seems to be little doubt but that it was built, in accordance with the generally received opinion, in the first half of the fourteenth century. The arches and original windows are of that date, and the porch at the northern entrance, engraved in the *Glossary of Architecture*, (Pl. 117) similar to those at Aldham in Essex, Horsemonden and Brookland in Kent, Hascombe in Surrey, and Northfield in Worcestershire, is of the same period.

The walls of the Chancel are very ancient: they are constructed of undressed stone, and, as far as one can judge, are those of the original church. At all events, they are not coeval with those of the nave, and if that be so why should they not be those of the church which was standing at the time of Doomsday. The windows are insertions of the date and style of the nave, the piscina the same; but the remains of the arches which are still to be seen on the south side are without mouldings, and the general character of the masonry seems to indicate that the walls are those of the ancient church, repaired, and somewhat altered perhaps on its re-erection in the fourteenth century. On the right side of the chancel door is the original consecration stone of the church, containing the figure of a circle in the centre with a line drawn to each side, and probably intended as an emblem of eternity. There is a stone of precisely the same description at Warnford, and one at Corhampton: both of these are undoubtedly Anglo-Saxon, and we may therefore reasonably presume that of Warblington to be of the same antiquity. The chancel contains very many stone coffins, solid, hollowed out to receive the body with receptacles for the head, shoulders, arms, legs and feet, of various lengths from five to seven feet, and generally about two feet in width at the head, whence they gradually lessen to the feet where they only measure twelve inches. These are all plain with the exception of two, which bear the figure of a cross of eight points degraded at the base. These ornamented coffins were originally within the communion rails, but were removed to their present situation during the alterations in 1800.

In the northern oratory or sacellum, is an ancient stone coffin, which was opened in 1800, and then contained the imperfect remains of four skeletons. Within the south sacellum may be seen the effigy of a lady in stone, with a hound at her feet, very much mutilated, and reclining under a decorated canopy. There is no inscription whatever, but the figure is supposed to represent one of the foundresses; and this supposition has been confirmed by the discovery of a stone coffin placed immediately without the sacellum, in a line with the tomb. The lid was perfectly plain, but on removing it, a skeleton believed to be that of a female, was discovered, which measured six feet in length; the right thigh had been once broken, and had healed before the decease of the person. On the seats being removed in the north aisle, a niche appeared in the outside wall containing another coffin of similar material, on the top of which lay the figure of a female in grey marble, more ornamented than the former one, and presenting a fine specimen of the period when it was executed. On raising it, the remains of a second female skeleton were found, much decayed by damp, but having its teeth and hair in beautiful preservation. From this circumstance, the late Mr. Butler who witnessed these discoveries, and whose account of them I have here followed, concluded that this was the tomb of the other foundress, both of whom had lain there upwards of 450 years.

In the month of October 1852, the nave of the church underwent repair. The workmen stripped the walls on either side, and found under the plastering, a fine oak roof in perfect preservation. They also found the remains of encaustic painting, which at one time had evidently covered the walls separating the nave from the side aisles. It was very difficult to make out what the paintings had originally been intended to represent, but by patiently watching the gleams of sunshine which fell on the southern wall, a drawing of one portion was obtained with considerable accuracy. It would seem that the paintings comprised a series of the miracles of our Lord ; each compartment was separated from the other by the stem of a tree or vine, with branches, and leaves over the heads of the figures. The whole was studded with crimson stars. One compartment represented two women with pitchers, the adjoining compartment containing our Saviour bearing a cross ; the woman nearest the Saviour had a halo round her head, and the two might have been intended for the marriage of Cana in Galilee, or for the wise and foolish virgins. The third compartment represented the Saviour carrying his cross, and in the distance four men in a furnace, the flames being clearly distinguishable, and the subject evidently that of the burning fiery furnace of King Nebuchadnezzar. At the back of the pulpit a coat of arms was visible, but the bearing was so utterly lost, that it could not be made out ; no means were taken to bring out the colours of the paintings, or of the coat of arms, and the whole having been plastered over, it is to be feared no further information can be gleaned from the discovery. It is more than possible, from the position of the coat of arms, that it had reference to the restorers of the church in the fourteenth century.

Near the church and in former days communicating with it, stand the ruins of what was once the Castle of Warblington. A single turreted tower, and a single gateway, formerly defended with a drawbridge, a portcullis, and a moat, the latter of which still remains, are all that have come down to us to speak of the size or character of an edifice which must at some time have been one of great beauty and considerable pretension. A portion of the turret angle has been converted into a stable, the tower is tenanted by pigeons, and another portion of the interior apartments has been converted into the present farm-house. The walls are stone and of great thickness, but those of the tower and gateway are faced only with stone, the inside being of brick. A deep moat and corresponding fosse surround the ancient site on three sides, but on the fourth the earth has been levelled. Ivy clings to and mantles the shattered turret, and the arches of the porch are festooned with it. The foliage of the elm and of the ash is to be seen through the ruined casements, and though desolation has completed her work, yet the hand of nature has been busy to compensate for the wanton destruction apparent at every step. The building originally formed a quadrangle, surrounded on every side by a moat thirty feet wide and ten feet deep, fronting the west, with an entrance under an arched gateway flanked by turrets, a porter's lodge to the south, and an armory to the north. The southern quadrangle comprised the chapel, forty-two feet by thirty-two feet, the great hall fifty-eight feet by thirty-two feet, communicating at one end with a small cellar, and at the other with the buttery, kitchen, and brewery. The state apartments occupied the northern quadrangle, with a gallery and sleeping rooms above. The interior was of brick faced with stone, brought from the Isle of Wight, or Caen in Normandy. A very particular description of the building when perfect, is to be found in a survey of the Manor of Warblington, taken in the 8 Charles I, 1632, by William Luffe, general surveyor to the right worshipful Richard Cotton Esquire, the lord of the manor, and by his command :

" The site of the principal Manor House of Warblington is
" a very fair place, well moated about, built all with bricks
" and stones, and is of great receipt, built square, in length
" 200 feet and in breadth 200 feet, with a fair green court
" within, and buildings round the said court, with a fair
" gallery and divers chambers of great count, and four towers
" covered with lead, with a very great and spacious hall,
" parlour, and great chamber, and all other houses of office
" whatsoever, necessary for such a house, with a very fair
" chapel within the said house, and the place covered all with
" tiles and stones ; and there is a fair green court before the
" gate of the said house, containing two acres of land, and
" there is a very spacious garden with pleasant walks adjoin-
" ing, containing two acres of land, and near to the said
" place, groves of trees containing two acres of land, two
" orchards and two little meadow plots containing eight

" acres, and a fair fishpond near the said place, with a gate
" for wood and two barns, one of five bays the other of four
" bays, with stables and other outhouses."

As the Cottons were staunch royalists, and adhered to the
cause of Charles, they became obnoxious to Cromwell's party,
and at length drew upon themselves the destruction so
liberally dealt out during the civil wars to all who did not
favour the forces of the Parliament.   History is silent on
the demolition of the Castle, but the vulgar tradition assigns
it to Cromwell, and there is every reason to believe it in
this instance to be correct.   A detachment of troopers was
probably sent by Sir William Waller to dismantle it, either
when proceeding to besiege Portsmouth, or after having
recovered Chichester from the hands of the King's partizans,
both which events took place in 1642.

After the building was reduced to a heap of ruins, its
materials were dispersed over the country, and may be traced
in various old houses in Emsworth, Havant, and the neighbourhood.   Even Portsmouth is said to have shared in the
spoliation, and to this cause is ascribed the title of Warbling-
ton-street, which had previously been called Hogmarket-
street.   It is perhaps to these depredations as much as to the
violence of Waller's troops, that we owe the Castle's present
state of desolation. (*Lit. reg.*)

The architecture cannot, I think, be ascribed to an earlier
date than that of the church, in or about the first half of the
fourteenth century, and in order to understand the relation
in which the castle and church stood to each other, some
opinion must be hazarded on the first foundation.   Now the
Conqueror's survey speaks of "II *æclæ*," and that they were
within the Manor of Warblington.   One, as I have before
endeavoured to prove, was on the site of the existing Church,
and I take it that the other occupied the site of the Castle.
The word *ecclesia* signified in early times not only a church,
but any place in which Almighty God was served, including
in that definition a religious house or monastery, and if we

look to the latter part of the entry in reference to Warblington, it will be seen that *"monaster"* is used in speaking of one of the *"duæ ecclesiæ,"* and that being so, I can only look upon the Castle as the site of the Monastery, to which four hides of land were attached, as it is said, *" ad usum monasterii."* It is generally believed that the Castle was of Roman foundation; was in fact a Roman station in communication with Portchester and Chichester, the *Portus magnus* and *Regnum* of the Itinerary, but I cannot see on what authority such a conclusion is founded. Not a coin of the empire has ever been found near to or within the Castle, not a particle of Roman masonry meets the eye, not a single brick of Roman workmanship, not an article of pottery of Roman manufacture can be produced, and there is not, as far as one can learn, any good reason for supposing that a Roman station ever existed at Warblington.

The Monastery and Church were probably founded by the same persons in connexion with each other, and as Edgar, in conjunction with Athelwold, manifested such zeal for religion, it is very possible that the two may have been built and endowed by them. There are various little circumstances tending to prove the existence of a monastery; the chancel of the Church, for instance, being so long in comparison with the nave, indicates that it was attached to a religious house, in which the brethren were admitted to the exclusion of lay members, who were placed in the nave. Bosham, Arundel, Titchfield, Hayling South, and many others, are especial examples of this peculiarity. Again, the crosses engraved on the stone coffins in the chancel, are very similar to those in the Abbey Church of Romsey, which are admitted to have been religious insignia, and to have accompanied the sepulture of priors, abbots, and ecclesiastics of rank; and there being several of them, it follows that it was not an accidental circumstance, but that a series of such individuals have at some early period been buried here, the crosses and coffins being of no later date than that of the twelfth century. The glazed tiles are also considered to have been manufactured

in the monastic establishments, and being similar to those at
Saint Cross, Winchester Cathedral, Romsey and Titchfield,
where such institutions are known to have existed during the
period of which we are speaking, we may, I think, fairly
assume that those in Warblington Church were made at the
same time and under similar circumstances.

Into whose hands the manor passed after the death of Roger
de Montgomery we know not, but it would certainly seem that
it was held by some noble resident in Normandy, most likely by
Hugh de Montgomery, and afterwards by Robert de Belesme,
his heir, attainted of high treason, under the tenure of
England, as the Abbot of Jumièges held Hayling in right of
the grant to his alien Norman abbey. This is confirmed by
the entry in the Book of Escheats before cited, where it is
said that the manor is an escheat "*sicut terra Normannor,*"
and the tenure is also alluded to in the claim of Robert
Aquillon, and in the grant by Herbert the son of Peter to
Herbert the son of Matthew. When Normandy (which had
for a long time been annexed to the Crown of England) was
seized by the King of France, a great number of lands became vested in the crown of England by way of escheat or
forfeiture. Whilst England and Normandy were united
under the power of the King of England, the lands of the
English and Norman were common, that is, the English held
lands in Normandy by hereditary right, and the Normans
held lands in England in the same manner. But when upon
the separation of Normandy from England the King of
France seized the lands which the English held in Normandy,
the King of England seized the lands which the Normans held
in England. By this means the lands in England holden
by Normans, became vested in the King of England as
escheats, under the name of *Terræ Normannorum,* and then
the King of England at his pleasure granted them out to
Englishmen, under condition, until the lands of the English
and Normans should be common again, but the community
of lands between the English and Normans was never
afterwards restored.

The Castle farm containing two hundred statute acres is and

has been from time immemorial tithe free, subject only to a small modus by way of recognition. The three orders which enjoyed in right of such order exemption from the payment of tithes, were those of the Cistercians (discharged by the Council of Lateran), the Templars, and the Hospitallers. In the *Quo warranto Rolls* the Master of the Temple claimed to hold six oxgangs of land. The oxgang measure is not a very defined quantity in itself being originally as much as an oxteam could plough in a year. Agard considered it of the same dimensions as the ferding or fourth part of a hide; taking the hide at one hundred and twenty acres, makes the oxgang thirty acres: six of these would therefore be one hundred and eighty acres, not very wide of the quantity of the Castle farm. The Templars very probably, on the dissolution of the alien monastery, obtained a grant of a part of the four hides attached to the house at the time of Domesday, and upon the general confiscation of the lands of their order in 1307, these six oxgangs were no doubt granted as the demesnes of the manor to the family of Fitzherbert, still, as before, retaining their exemption from the payment of tithes.

If therefore we come to the conclusion that the Castle occupies the site of a monastery instead of a Roman entrenchment, it is at once understood why the Church was so built, and why we are not to look for the traces of a population in its immediate vicinity.

The tradition runs, that the last male possessor of the name and Castle of Warblington left two coheiresses, who built the Church in the early part of the fourteenth century, and were buried one on either side of the nave. The effigies to which allusion has been made, are evidence in favour of the tradition; but upon examination of the descents of that period, I do not find that any De Warblington had, at that time, been resident at the Castle, or that any one of them left two coheiresses; but it certainly is remarkable, that about the year 1312, Matthew Fitzherbert ceased to hold, but whether by death or otherwise does not appear; that after that date none of the name of Fitzherbert ever held the manor or lands within the Manor of

Warblington, and that in the year 1313 a warrant should issue to the Escheator of Southampton, commanding him to disseize Isabella Bardolf and Phillis de Estneye, which was accordingly done before the expiration of 1316. The tenure of the Fitzherberts was probably one in fee tail, and, under the circumstances above stated, it seems not at all unlikely but that Isabella and Phillis were his daughters and co-heiresses, particularly as Phillis is described as of Estneye, an appendant to the Manor of Warblington, and that as such co-heiresses they claimed to be entitled to the Manor, on the decease of their father. There was ample time for them to have built the Church during the period that they held possession, and therefore, substituting the name of Fitzherbert for that of De Warblington, the tradition is not only possible, but from the coincidence of the date and the possession of those who then held the Manor, exceedingly probable.

The most congenial idea to the minds of those who take an interest in antiquarian research, is to believe that the lords of Warblington resided at the Castle of Warblington in the days of yore, but I am not aware of any evidence to warrant this assumption; and if we look at the state of things existing at that period, we shall find them somewhat incompatible with the maintenance of a feudal Castle at Warblington down to the middle of the fourteenth century.

At the northern extremity of the Manor adjoining to the forest of Stanstead, once stood a Castle, the history of which is nearly as obscure as that of Warblington, but there are some notices of it which enable us to ascertain something, although but little, of its origin and decay. The only remains of Rowland's Castle now to be seen, are two large masses of wall composed of flint, undressed stone, chalk and mortar. The walls are about ten feet thick, the mortar apparently not Roman, and powdering to dust when rubbed. At one time a double vallum surrounded the Castle, with a fosse of considerable depth. The outer vallum is about 700 yards in circumference, and the fosse appears to have been filled partly from a spring to the south of the outer vallum. It was circular in shape, with outworks extending to the west, defended by a second vallum and fosse to about the distance of 600 yards. There is a postern entrance to the South still perfect. No Roman work is to be seen, the workmanship being like that of the Anglo-Saxons, and the shape corresponding with other forts of their construction. There are evidently works extending to the south and to the south-east, near the bed of what seems to have formed an ancient Roman road. Coins have been found in great abundance in and around the site of Rowland's Castle, and only about five years since a crock was dug up full of Roman coins, principally copper, which were disposed of at Portsmouth before any person of intelligence was aware of the discovery ; the situation was on the line of a supposed Roman route from Old Winchester to the coast and Chichester, and there are the remains of Roman work and pottery in the immediate vicinity.

To the south, on the verge of Mayze Coppice, at a short distance from the ruins of the Castle, were some years since discovered, the remains of a Roman building, which stood on an eminence, rising with a gentle ascent from the little valley beneath. An apartment could be traced, eighteen feet by fourteen feet, with the pavement entire, consisting of red brick tessera, two inches square, the plaster on the side walls still perfect, composed of lime, tempered with powdered brick, a cement much used by the Romans, and with which they composed their pavements. This apartment appeared to have been the principal one in the whole building, and was considerably ornamented, as pieces of stucco painted in fresco were found among the rubbish. Adjoining to this was one of smaller dimensions, supposed to have been the sudatory or sweating bath, from the circumstance of finding an entire earthen flue with several broken fragments, a portion of lead pipe, and various tiles with thin edges turned up, to serve as tunnels or flues, placed under the floor to convey heat. Near the supposed entrance was another building twenty feet square ; this might have been the cold bath, as the Romans made it a common practice to use the cold bath immediately after the sudatory. To the eastward was a third building of large dimensions, the site plentifully strewed with charcoal and fragments of pottery. Amongst others, there was part of an earthen vessel capable of holding twelve gallons, impressed on the inside with the marks of fingers.

From these buildings a causeway, with a fosse on either side, extended in a southernly direction towards the sea coast, and several other earth-works now levelled with the plough. Near the farm-house was a small barrow, which was opened; nothing was found but a quantity of charred wood, and a small fragment of pottery marked with crescents. On other parts of Mayze Coppice are still to be seen black earth with traces of burning, and innumerable fragments of pottery, a proof that a manufactory of earthenware was carried on here.

The buildings which once stood at Mayze Coppice and on Rowland's Hill were, no doubt, in possession of the same proprietor, and formed a Roman station of some importance. It is conjectured that a track-way ran from hence to Chichester, passing south of Stansted House, through Lisle Wood, by the Old Pack Horse Inn, and following the lane south of the park fence to Lord Halifax's Tower, crossed the Westbourne road between Racton House and the park; but as no traces of it can be seen on Hambrook Common, the present road from Racton Park to Funtington has been supposed to occupy its original line, trending through Lavant to Chichester. (*Butler.*)

Rowland's Castle had, by tradition, a subterranean communication from its keep or donjon (which was twenty feet square and of great strength), with Warblington Castle and Church, and it was believed, some years since, that the northern entrance to the passage had been opened, but no search was made to see the direction it took. These passages were not unfrequent in former times, when life was not so secure as at the present moment, between fortresses and religious houses, and many of those which were said to have existed have recently been brought to light. Among many others the most interesting is that from Windsor Castle to Burnham Abbey, a distance of four miles, passing under the bed of the Thames, presumed to have been discovered in April, 1853.

In Lyttleton's *History of Henry II*, he states that Rowland's Villa, after the departure of the Romans, fell into the hands of the Saxon invaders, who converted it into a fortress, and that its castle, towers, and battlements were in a perfect state of repair when Henry II, who was fond of the chase, passed several days there in hunting and amusements. Henry II began to reign in 1154, and, as the Castle was perfect in his time, it seems probable that it had become an escheat of the crown before the 17th Stephen, 1142, because in that year all the castles improperly erected by noblemen and lords, without licence, were ordered to be razed, according to Matthew Paris, who says—"That all those castles, which contrary to good "reason and good order, had been made and builded by any "manner of person in the days of King Stephen, should be "overthrown and cast down, which were found to be 1115." If therefore Rowland's Castle within and parcel of the Manor of Warblington, were perfect and in a habitable state, so late as at some period between 1154 and 1189, what good reason can there be for supposing that there existed another Castle at Warblington at one and the same time, particularly as there is no information on the destruction of the Monastery, which in all likelihood was used as a place of residence until it was pulled down to make way for the Castle. It seems to me that Rowland's Castle was occupied down to about the middle of the fourteenth century, when it fell into a state of decay, up to which time there was no Castle whatever at Warblington, but that upon the accession of Sir John de Montacute who married Margaret, daughter and heiress of Thomas de Monthermer, he built the present Castle of Warblington, and that from that time it was occasionally occupied by the various lords until the grant to Sir Richard Cotton, who held the Manor of the King *in capite* by the fortieth part of a knight's fee, after which he and his descendants resided there permanently up to the period when the Castle was besieged and demolished in 1642.

In the will of Thomas Jervoise, Esquire, of Herriard, made in the year 1739, and in the early title deeds of the property, there is mention made of Rowland's Castle and of the purlieu there. This purlieu comprised Rowland's Hills, which had been added, as I conceive, to the ancient forest of Stansted, parcel of the Honour of Arundel, prior to the *Charta de Foresta*, but having by the provisions of that Act been disafforested and severed from the forest of Stansted, it became purlieu, or pure and free from the laws and ordinances of the forest. It was bounded on the west and north-west by Havant Thicket, and the ancient driftway or deer-leap of sixteen feet from the standard surrounding the purlieu as against the thicket, is still preserved to the owners of Rowland's Hills.

The advowson of the rectory and perpetual presentation to the Church, was appendant to the manor, and remained in the Cotton family from the time of Edward VI, until 7th December 1764, when it was sold off by Thomas Panton to John Unwin of Took's Court, who in the same year presented the Rev. Samuel Torrent, M. A. to the rectory. On the the 17th May 1777, John Unwin conveyed the advowson to the Rev. John Ramsay, rector of Stanford, Dingley, Berks. On the 15th November 1786, it was conveyed to Ann Norris, who presented the Rev. William Norris on the 15th April 1789. On the 1st January 1794, Mrs. Norris conveyed the advowson to Richard Barwell, Esquire, who afterwards conveyed it to the late Rev. William Norris, who, at his death, was succeeded by his son the present rector, the Rev. William Norris. (*Butler.*)

The Parsonage-house stands pleasantly situated in the midst of the glebe, at a short distance from the Castle and Church, looking out over the terrace and lawn, upon Langstone harbour, and sheltered on the north and east by oak and elm timber. Scarcely any traces of its former antiquity remain; its gothic doors and windows having long since been removed. The rector is entitled to the great and small tithes of the parish, which, under the Commutation Act, were assessed at £740, in addition to which there is a glebe of thirty acres. The Castle farm being the ancient demesne land of the manor, is covered by a modus as before stated in lieu of tithe.

William de Vleburigge was presented to the living of Warblington in 1282. Ralph Smallpage died rector of Warblington on the 6th May 1558. Mr. Payne was rector during the civil war, and a great sufferer when Cromwell drove the regular clergy from their livings. He was succeeded by John Harrison in 1644, on the presentation of George Cotton, and in 1667, Sebastian Pitfield was rector. In 1690, Richard Brereton was presented by Richard Cotton. He was also rector of Westbourne, where he died, and was buried in the chancel of that church. He was succeeded in 1721 by Vincent Bradstone, presented by William Cotton, who was buried at Warblington on the 6th March 1739-40.

This gentleman left three daughters, one of whom died unmarried in 1757, another married James Wingham and died s. p. in 1784, and the other married John Phipps, and died s. p. in 1799. In 1740, Samuel Dugard, A. M. was presented by Mr. Thomas Panton to hold during the minority of Mr. Slaughter, at whose request he subsequently resigned the living, became afterwards incumbent of the Chapel at Gosport, and subsequently vicar of Westbourne, where he was buried in the middle aisle of the church with the following inscription :—

The Reverend Samuel Dugard, Vicar of this parish, departed this life, February 17, 1776, aged 72 years.

In 1752, John Slaughter was rector in the nomination of Thomas Panton, and was buried on the 17th June 1764, on the north side of the communion table. Samuel Torrent succeeded him on the same presentation. He was the son of the Rev. Mr. Torrent, rector of St. Giles, Reading ; was educated at Merton College, Oxford, of which he became

fellow, was pepetual curate of Edgeware, presented by Lord
Coventry,who was related to his first wife,his second wife being
Frances, daughter of Mr. Briscoe, and widow of Mr. Child,
banker, of Temple-bar, London.   He died at Bath, and was
buried in the Church of St. Giles, at Reading.   On the 14th
May 1789, the Rev. William Norris, A.M. was inducted on
the presentation of Anne Norris, and upon his decease in
1827, the present rector, the Rev. William Norris, A.M,
succeeded to the living.

	£	s.	d.
Warblington is a living remaining in charge, rated in the King's books	19	9	4½
Yearly Tenths	1	18	11¼

In the Taxation of Pope Nicholas, 20 Edward I, 1292, it
stands :—

	TAXATION.			DECIMA.		
Ecclia de Warblington ..	25	6	8	2	10	8
Et est pensionar ...	0	10	0	0	1	0
Vicar ejusdem ., .	4	6	8	0	8	8

The *Nonæ Rolls*, 15 Edward III, 1340-1, contain the following
entry in reference to the church of Warblington :—

> Deanery of Drokenesforde.
> Parish of Warblyngton.

Some of the men of this parish, Johnatte Crouch, Richard
Wymond, William Coterel, William Bailiff, sworn, say upon
their oaths, that the ninth of corn, wool, and lambs of the
aforesaid parish of Warblyngton, were worth in the 14th
year aforesaid 1339-40, £11 2s. 4d.   And they say that the
aforesaid ninth could not amount to the tax of the aforesaid
church in the year aforesaid, because that the said church is
endowed with one messuage, one garden, one dovecote, ten
acres of land, one acre of meadow, pasture for sheep
and hogs, rents and services, the assize of bread and beer,
a court and perquisites of court which are worth per annum

£6 6*s.* And they say that the tithe of hay and other small tithes, with oblations and mortuaries, are worth per annum, £12 15*s.*

In the 8th Charles 1632, when a general survey of the manor was taken, it was said under the head of the rectory.

" The parsonage of the said Manor of Warblington is of " the lord's gift, nomination and presentation when it hap- " peneth to fall void ; the site of the rectory is a fair mansion " house, with a barn and out-houses, and there is 44 acres of " glebe lands, and John Payne, Clerk, is parson there, and it " is valued in the King's books at ——"

BAPTISMS.—The oldest register of baptisms appears to have been about 1660, the time of the Restoration, and contains the entry of several baptisms as far back as 1631, and continued to 1660, fairly written in the same hand, from which it is conjectured that the old registers were lost during the civil war, and that this register was begun by inserting such names as could be collected of persons baptised during the interval : this remark applies equally to the registers of marriages and burials, which are bound up in the same book and commence in the same manner. When Mr. Harrison came to the living, he endeavoured to supply the loss of the register for a few years preceding his induction, and he re-covered as many entries as the memories of his parishioners could furnish. There is no register in the handwriting of Mr. Payne, and it is therefore probable that he took the register books with him when driven from his living. In 1660 the entries of baptisms proceed with tolerable regu-larity to the 25th January 1734-5. The next register commences the 2d May 1736, after an interval of fifteen months, and is continued to the 6th January 1760, with the following chasms from July to December 1744, and from October 1745 to March 1746. The next register commences in January 1760, and is continued to the 18th October 1787, regularly and correctly kept. The next book commences on the 8th November 1787, and is regularly kept until December

17

2

1808. The next book commences in January 1809, and is continued to the end of the year 1812, when the new register books, as directed by the Act of 52 Geo. III, take place.

MARRIAGES.—The most ancient register of marriages commences with the entry of several from 1644 to 1660, which being in the same handwriting and apparently written at the same time, are presumed to have been recorded from the best information that could be procured of such marriages having been solemnized during that period, and afterwards continued to March 1735-6. The next book on paper commences in April 1736, and is continued to February 1754. The leaves of this book are so much damaged and injured by damp that some of the entries are not legible. The next book commences in May 1754, in pursuance of the Act 26 Geo. II, c. 33, and is regularly kept until October 1792, in a good state of preservation. The next book begins in January 1793, and continues down to the end of the year 1812.

BURIALS.—The entries of burials commence in 1647, and are continued in the same handwriting until 1660, from which time the entries appear to have been made as occasion required, to the end of the book, which concludes the 9th March 1735-6, no omission appearing. The entries of burials in 1658, 1663, 1666, 1667, 1668, 1669, 1670, 1671, 1672, and 1673, are unusually frequent, and mark a high degree of mortality in those years. The next book commences on the 14th April 1736, and is continued with apparent accuracy and without interruption till December 1759. The next book commences on the 8th February 1760, and is kept regularly to its conclusion 11th July 1787. The next book commences on the 27th July 1787, and is regularly kept till the end of the year 1808. The next commences in 1808, and concludes with 1812. (*Butler.*)

In 1789, a Chapel dedicated to St. Peter, was erected at Emsworth for the performance of divine worship, the rector of the parish laying the first stone, inscribed D. O. M., on the 10th July in that year. The funds were supplied by voluntary subscription of the inhabitants, the distance of Emsworth from the parish church being the principal induce. ment to the undertaking. The officiating minister is maintained by a stipend arising from the income of the pew rents. The Rev. Daniel Davies, B. D. was for very many years the minister; upon his death the Rev. Mr. Allen was appointed, and by a recent arrangement among the proprietors, the nomination was ceded to the incumbent of St. James, who appointed the Rev. Mr. Bibby, and subsequently the Rev. Mr. Morse, to the charge. In digging the foundation the workmen found a small brass cross about three inches in length and opening with a joint as if intended for the reception of some costly relic.

A Church dedicated to Saint James has recently been built in Emsworth, and by an Order in Council of the 4th June 1841, a separate district parcel of the parish of Warblington has been assigned to it. The boundaries commence at the boundary post on the road going by the Wadeway to the Island of Thorney at the south-east angle of the parish of Warblington, and follow the bounds of the parish of Warblington, between it and the adjoining parish of Westbourne northward, till they arrive at the Mill-stream opposite Lumley Mill; there they turn to the south-west down the mill-stream till they come to the corner of the hedge of the garden belonging to Hurst's Row, which hedge in a few yards bounds a footpath leading over meadows from Westbourne; the boundaries of the district follow this path westward till they arrive at a large parish road leading from Emsworth to Westbourne and Horndean respectively, which road they follow northward, leaving Flint Cottage in the angle where the two roads separate to the right, till they come to a bridge which crosses the Horndean road; here they turn to the south and follow a small stream which rises in Emsworth Common, and flows through Cold Harbour Farm, till it reaches the bridge on the turnpike road leading from Emsworth to Havant; the boundaries pass under this bridge through the middle of the mill-pond, through the mill sluice, and thence to the boundary post again.

The endowment consists of £50 per annum charged on the rectory of Warblington; £15. 19s. 6d., the interest of money in the hands of the governors of Queen Anne's bounty; and about £56 made up from the pew rents, fees, and the value of the glebe and parsonage house. The duty was at first performed by the Rev. Morgan Davies as a licensed curate, he was succeeded temporarily by the Rev. Charles Baring. The first incumbent was the Rev. S. P. Field, the second was the Rev. H. H. Victor, and the third and present incumbent is the Rev. Henry W. Sheppard.

The inland boundaries of the manor of Warblington are co-extensive with those of the parish, except that to the south of the turnpike road, they do not include the manor of Lymbourne within their ambit. By the survey of the 3d Charles 1627, taken under a royal commission, the seaward bounds of the Manor of Warblington were set out as " begin-" ning at a certain lake called Swathe Lake, and so unto the " channel of the sea beyond the grounds called the Pewitt " Grounds, and so directly along the said channel over to a " lane called Pooke Lane, near to Langstone, and all the sea " on the north part of the said channel within the said bound " is belonging and appertaining to the Manor of Warblington, " containing by estimation one thousand acres of land flowed " with the sea at every full sea."

Under the same survey it was found that the grounds called the Pewit Grounds, containing by estimation four acres, or thereabouts, produced yearly for the use of the lord of the manor three hundred dozen of pewits, some years more and some years less, commonly sold at ten shillings a dozen, and that the lord was entitled to wreck of sea and fish, of warrant, namely porpoise, sturgeon, and such like.

By another survey of the 8th Charles 1632, it was found that there was then belonging to the manor one wheat mill and a malt mill, both under one roof, then let at a rent of £20. This was, I presume, the mill at Emsworth; the mill attached to the monastery is not noticed as being part of the castle appurtenances. It stood until within the memory of man at the southern point of the castle pond, and the original arch spanning the little brook is still to be seen. It was found that there was belonging to the manor a park, "wherein were " lately game of deare, but now disparked and converted " into arables and pastures;" that the sum total of the demesne rents amounted to £245, and that there were various free and customary tenants who held estates under the manor by free charter and copy of court roll, at the rents, reliefs, heriots, and fines there particularly set forth.

The Manor of Emsworth, comprising the village of Emsworth and its vicinity, is entirely within the ambit of the Manor of Warblington, and the two formed, correctly, but one manor; the customs of the former are identical with those of the latter. The Manor of Warblington rectory extends over a few cottages, gardens, and closes of land, granted out to several tenants by the lords, rectors for the time being, each tenement being granted to three persons to be held for life in succession one after the other; on death, surrender, or forfeiture, subject to a fine on admission, and an annual quit rent. These copyholds are supposed to have been formerly part of the glebe, and to have been granted out like those of Havant, by the rectors during the rebellion. The whole have recently been enfranchised by the rector under the voluntary Copyhold Enfranchisement Act.

The earliest Court Rolls that I have seen of the Manor, then called the Manor of Warblington and Emsworth, bear date the 16 James I, 1618, and contain the Rolls of the Courts Baron and Leet. The entries which relate to the Customs of the Manor are as follow: all being within the period from the 16 James I, 1618, to 15 Charles I, 1639.

At this Court, the tenants of this manor by a general consent and agreement between themselves, and the approbation of the lords of the said manor, have appointed Roger Kettell to be hayward of the common and common fields, and do agree to allow him for his pains eight pounds per annum, to be paid quarterly, and to be levied by equal and rateable taxation of every tenant according to his land.

The Homage further present, that by the custom of the manor from time whereof the memory of man runneth not to the contrary, all the tenants of the said manor by licence and agreement of the lords of the manor or their stewards, and not otherwise, could cut and have necessary and fit timber, for the repair of their tenements, parcel of the same manor, and timber called stake timber, and bushes for the repair of their inclosures with like licence and assignment.

Upon view had and taken by the lords of this manor, and the tenants of the same, of certain lands called Dawe's Marsh, and other lands thereto adjoining, being the customary lands of John Coldam, and of the great danger of overflowing that, as well the said lands, as the demesnes of his manor are subject and liable unto by the decay of the sea beach and banks there, it is thought fit and ordered that the said John Coldam shall sufficiently repair the sea beach or bank on the south side of the said lands called Dawe's Marsh, adjoining to his arable lands there, before the feast day of Saint James the Apostle, next coming, upon pain of 40s.

The Homage present, that the custom of the said manor from time whereof the memory of man runneth not to the contrary, has been exercised and approved for the customary tenants of the manor to have by assignment of the lords of the manor, or by the assignment of their officers, timber for the repair of their tenements, parcel of the said manor, being out of repair; also bushes and stake timber for the mending of their fences when dilapidated.

They further present, that the tenement and barn upon the customary lands of Richard Burgis are in decay for want of timber, and that he requires half a load of timber for the same, which is allotted to him, and the same Richard is commanded to repair the tenement and barn aforesaid, this side of the feast of All Saints, next ensuing, under a penalty of 40s.

It is at this Court condescended and agreed unto by the lord of the said manor, and all the freeholders and copyholders of the same, that the said tenants may inclose and sever the commons and wastes of this manor from the commons of the manors and lordships adjoining, and forasmuch as upon consideration thereof the present charge of making of mounds and fences for the inclosure thereof, the said tenants do conceive that the charge thereof will amount to twenty pounds, or thereabouts, and upon examination they also find that there are forty yardlands within the said manor which have benefit by the said inclosure, and are therefore liable to an equal charge of the said work, after the rate of ten shillings for every yardland, and so rateably for more or less quantity according to their several quantities of land holden of the said manor, which rate the said tenants have now assented unto, to be levied of them by way of taxation for the finishing of the said intended inclosure, and so therefore desire that it may be ordered to be paid accordingly. It is therefore at this court ordered, by and with the consent of the said tenants, as well freeholders as copyholders, that the said commons shall be forthwith severed and inclosed, and that every one of them shall pay towards the charge of the said inclosures so to be made for every yardland which any of them holdeth, part of the said manor the sum of ten shillings, and so rateably for more or less quantity according to their several quantities of land holden, and that every one making default of payment shall forfeit to the lord of the said manor the sum of forty shillings, in the name of a pain to be levied on the goods or chattels of him or them that shall make default.

6 April, 6 Char. I.—Since the lord of the Manor of Havant and his tenants have recently claimed part of the commons of the Manor of Warblington, in a certain place called Comewell Bottom, under colour of perambulation by the same made by the highway, from the gate called Wood-yers gate, as far as Pays Cross, the Homage upon their oaths present, that to their knowledge by the space of forty and eight years by continual perambulations, there made the metes and bounds of the manor aforesaid extend, and are

as follow. That is to say, from Pays Cross under the hedge to Hollowgate, and so under Banisters rails to Woodyers lane end, and that the lords of the manor aforesaid through the whole of the time above mentioned, also from time whereof the memory of man runneth not to the contrary have been in the habit of, and accustomed to cut down and carry away to their use, underwood and trees growing within the bounds aforesaid, without any interruption or impediment whatsoever.

1 April 7, Chas. I.—Whereas by virtue of a former agreement in that behalf made as appeareth 24 September, 4 Charles. The common of this manor hath been, and is severed and inclosed from other commons, and waste grounds thereunto adjoining, towards which inclosure the lord of the said manor hath given an allowance of timber for gatès and posts, as also stake timber, and bushes in lieu and recompense whereof, the said tenants as well freeholders as copy and leaseholders, for them, their heirs, assigns, and successors, have consented and agreed, and do consent and agree, that the lord of the said manor and his heirs and assigns shall and may from henceforth depasture, and feed upon the said common, eight beasts, and all the said tenants have nominated and appointed John Wingham to be bayward to drive the said inclosed common from time to time as occasion shall require, to prevent all incroachments, and overcharging thereof, and to keepe and make the fences and gates, and to present all offences at the courts of this manor, and they are contented to allow him for his pains herein to be taken yearly, six pounds to be levied by equal and rateable taxation after the rate of three shillings for every yardland, and according to that proportion for more or less quantity, and that every tenant refusing to pay shall forfeit to the lord ten shillings in the name of a pain, the same forfeiture to be levied by distress.

18 April, 9 Charles.—The Homage present, that the tenement upon the customary lands of Thomas Holmes was casually burnt down. Therefore he is commanded to rebuild the tenement aforesaid, before the next court, under pain of ten pounds.

21 October 15, Charles I. The Homage at a court of this date held before William Brown seneschal, under a commission from the crown, issuing out of the court of Wards, present, that through all the time of their memory the customary tenement of the manor have descended to the younger son, daughter, and nephew respectively of a tenant dying seized; and be it to a less near relation, to a collateral, from an uncle or aunt, and from a kinsman or kinswoman, the heir is to pay a reasonable fine. Nevertheless upon a question of title to a tenement called Wymonds, two copies were produced, one whereof in the twenty-second year of the late Queen Elizabeth, and one in the twenty-eighth of the same reign, by which the same tenement was twice granted for the term of life only, but Richard Hedger pro_ duced a copy dated in the fifth year of the late lord King James, containing a grant made to his wife by the words "*sibi et suis*," and no older copy of grant thereof to any one to hold "*sibi et suis*" appears, but the estate of the aforesaid wife during his life is valid—afterwards to be inquired of. But in the next court it was affirmed by the whole homage, that all and singular the customary tenements of the manor aforesaid are hereditary in form aforesaid, although they say sometimes indeed ignorant stewards omit those words "*sibi et suis*," nor make those estates hereditary, which by the custom of the manor ought to be made of inheritance, and where the right of the heir is an admission for life, it is an admission of inheritance.

And they present that the lord of this manor by himself and his customary tenants through all time of their memory, have been accustomed to have common of pasture with their cattle levant and couchant, upon the lands and tenements of the manor aforesaid at all times of the year upon the waste called the Heath of the manor of Warblington, as pertaining to the manor and the tenements aforesaid, yet they are to inquire whether it was otherwise on account of vicinage.

And they present that the custom of the manor is, that the customary tenants should cut, by assignment of the lord or his bailiff in the waste of this manor, certain bushes in which there is no growth, some young oaks or ash towards the repairs of the fences of the tenants of the manor aforesaid.

And they further present that once in every year, when the court is held within the manor aforesaid, the tenants of the said manor are bound to provide at their own proper charge, a dinner for the lord and his steward and for their requisite servants, at the price of fourteen shillings, towards which each tenant pays twelve pence, under a penalty of five shillings for every one not paying it.

Bartholomew Sone asks for two tuns of timber towards the repair of his customary tenement, and John Huyt asks for one tun, therefore let the bailiff do according to the custom.

For many years past the Court Leet of Warblington and Emsworth has fallen into disuse, but in former days when local justices were less frequent than at the present moment, the court exercised a wholesome power in checking offences against the peace and against morality. Among the many entries to be found in corroboration of this, the following have been extracted as they are found upon the Rolls of the Leet.

13 April, 17 Jas. The homage present that the Butts within the view of frankpledge are in decay, the inhabitants there are therefore commanded to repair the same Butts before the feast of Penticost next ensuing, under a penalty of twenty shillings.

They present also that the Whipping-post is in ruin ; therefore the inhabitants there are commanded to repair the aforesaid post before the feast of Penticost next ensuing under a penalty of five shillings.

2 January, 18 Jas. The homage present that John Foster on the fourth day of November last, broke open the common pound within the view of frankpledge, and took from thence his hogs there impounded, and he is in mercy 6s. 8d.

9 April, 20 James. The homage present that the Stocks within the tything of Emsworth are out of repair; therefore it is commanded the inhabitants there that they sufficiently repair the Stocks aforesaid, on this side of the feast of Philip and James next ensuing, under the penalty of 6s. 8d.

24 Sept. 20 James. The homage present that the inhabitants of Emsworth have not repaired the Stocks within the tything aforesaid, in accordance with the order at the last court; therefore they are in mercy according to the order made, 6s. 8d., and the inhabitants are commanded sufficiently to repair the aforesaid Stocks, on this side of the feast of All Saints next ensuing, under a penalty of 13s. 4d.

19 March, 21 James. The homage present that John Asted and Nicholas Asted are strangers, and are now lodging in the house of John Golden, therefore each one of them is commanded to find sureties for his good behaviour, or to remove from his lodging aforesaid before the next view of frankpledge, under the penalty in each case of 40s.

They also present that Thomas Downe took a certain Seed into his tenement to dwell there as an inmate, against the form of the statute, and that he has continued there by the space of six months, therefore he is in mercy 6s.

24 April, 2 Charles. The homage present that Kittle, widow, on the twentieth day of March last past, sold bread not being of proper weight, therefore she is in mercy 6d.

11 April, 3 Charles. The homage present that William Hunte, before the last view of frankpledge, took certain strangers into his house to inhabit there as inmates, against the form of the statute in such case made, therefore the said William Hunt is commanded to remove the said strangers before the feast of Penticost now next ensuing, under a penalty of 20s.

9 October, 3 Charles. The homage present that John Smyth incroached upon the highway in Emsworth, therefore he is in mercy 3s. 4d., and he is commanded to level the incroachment aforesaid before the feast of All Saints next ensuing, under the penalty of 10s.

They also present that the wife of the said John Smyth is a common scold, therefore she is adjudged to punishment by the Tumbrell.

12 October, 5 Charles. The homage present that Richard Sone and Alice Dance, widow, are common bakers, within the village of Emsworth, and that they have broken the assize of bread. Therefore both are in mercy 3s. 4d. each.

. 11 October, 7 Charles. It is ordered that the inhabitants of Emsworth shall not place any sea ore in the street of Emsworth, under a penalty in every case of 6*s*. 8*d*.

21 October, 15 Charles. The homage present that the Common Pound of this tything is out of order for want of timber, which it is the duty of the lord to allow, and for the customary tenants and freemen to pay for the repair of the same; therefore it is ordered that the woodward assign timber at the proper time to be taken. And it is ordered that each one of the tenants aforesaid, after such assignment, contribute rateably to the repair of the pound aforesaid, under a penalty of 10*s*. on each defaulter.

The Parish of Warblington originally comprised the tythings of Emsworth, East Leigh, and Nytimber; the latter has merged into Warblington, and the name is now obsolete. Emsworth Common, to which the entries before quoted relate, was at the northern part of the parish, and contained about six hundred and fifty acres, the greater part of which was covered with oak timber, and the lower part with bushes and furze. In 1805, an inclosure of this common was first agitated between the lord and his copyhold tenants, and in the year 1810, an Act of Parliament was obtained for that purpose. 371 acres covered with fine growing timber, were allotted to the lord in lieu of all his claims to the remainder of the common, amounting to 280 acres, which were allotted as freehold to the copyholders in proportion to their claims, every proprietor of a copyhold house rated in the poor rate at £5, received one share, and every proprietor of copyhold land rated at 40*s*, was entitled to the same. The Commissioners in pursuance of the Act, dated the 20th December 1810, made and set out the different allotments, and the whole of the allotments, with the exception of that made to the lord, have been brought into cultivation. By a clause in this Act, Cold Harbour Green containing 6a. 3r. 19p. was reserved to the inhabitants of the parish of Warblington, " that the same shall and may, from " time to time, and for ever hereafter, be used by the inhabit- " ants of the said parish as and for a place of amusement, " without interruption." (*Butler*).

At the eastern extremity of the parish on the stream called the Ems, which takes its rise at the foot of the South Down hills, and divides the counties of Southampton and Sussex, stands the village of Emsworth. The main channel of the east passage of Langstone harbour runs up to it, and affords great natural accommodation for the colliers and coasting vessels which trade to the port. Not very many years ago it contained but a few straggling houses, principally occupied by fishermen, and now it is become a place of considerable traffic. The Smyth family were shipwrights and builders here, and several vessels of considerable tonnage have been launched from the yards, the largest being that of four hundred and seven tons burthen, built in the year 1848, by Mr. David Palmer Walker. The principal business carried on is that in the coal, timber, and seafaring line, there being no heavy harbour dues as at the regular ports.

The fishery of Emsworth was, in the reign of King Henry II, valued at 8s. 8d. per annum, and the harbour was from a very early date, celebrated for the quality of its oysters, which are larger than those called natives, and less than those which are caught off the coast of France and around the Channel Islands. The fishermen have ever looked upon every stranger dredging in the harbours of Langstone or Chichester as an intruder upon their private rights, and every effort was for many years past used both by local regulation of a resident committee, and by application to Parliament, to obtain, on the part of the fishermen, a recognised legal and absolute exclusion of all persons using smacks of a large size, and not resident on the shores of the harbours. A great cry was made of the injustice done to the fishermen by permitting the Eastern smacks of heavy tonnage and more powerful gear, to come into the harbours and carry away all that came within the reach of their dredges, and the matter was generally looked upon as a hardship, except by those who thought that the dredging in deep water ought not to be confined to those who lived in the immediate neighbourhood of the sea; that the waters were open to all, and it was at all events notorious, that even when the so-called monopoly existed, and before the intrusion

prevailed, there was no more prudence among those who
earned large sums of money; there was no saving, no improvement of the family, no increase of education or intelligence;
nay, on the contrary, it tended to limit the efforts of the
fishermen themselves to a range within the harbours, beyond
which they rarely ventured; it tended to demoralization, and
the tavern was often full, when the children were in actual
want.   It is a fact well ascertained by those who have turned
their attention to the matter, that the deep sea fishermen are
as a mass far more industrious, far more sober, and far more
saving, than the harbour fishermen.   The prudence which
dictates the husbanding of the earnings to purchase a larger
boat and better gear, becomes a habit productive of the best
possible results to themselves, their families, and those with
whom they are brought into contact; while on the contrary,
the little energy required for harbour fishing, is content to put
up with things as it finds them, to follow the narrow course
which generations have before trodden, and to see strangers
derive a large profit from that to which, from their local
position, they naturally look as a principal means of .
support.

At first, the Eastern fishermen hove overboard the spat or
young oysters, reserving to themselves those only of a larger
size, which they carried away with them for sale or deposit;
but by degrees it became a question whether the spat might
not be turned to some more profitable account in the way of
deposit, and they found that the result answered their ex-
pectations.   They then carried away oyster and spat together
without regard to the remonstrances of the fishermen.   The
case became desperate; it was said that the fishermen were
ruined; that in a short time there would not be an oyster
left in the harbours, and that the fishermen and their families
would be compelled to ask for bread and a home in the union
poorhouse.   To crown the whole, as the demand for oyster-
beds within the harbours increased, the lords of the Manors
of Hayling, Farlington, Portsea, and Milton, granted out
portions of the mud lands in the channels within their
respective boundaries, to persons who cleared and converted

them into layings or deposits; and in pursuance of the statute, gave notice of the fact by the erection of boards, with printed intimations warning all persons to abstain from dredging within the limits of the boundaries defined.

In these oyster-layings, not only harbour oysters, but Jersey, Falmouth, Channel and other produce, were deposited for growth, and ultimate sale to the London merchants; but the course adopted by the more industrious portion of the community, was felt by the Emsworth and Bosham fishermen to be a grievance that could not be borne, and they resolved upon seizure of the oysters and destruction of the beds. They asked advice of some who thought like themselves; they applied for pecuniary assistance to others, who might at least have considered the equities of the question before yielding their adhesion to such a cause; sympathy was, as it ever is, remarkably cheap where it costs but little, and the result was, that they attacked in a body the various oyster-layings, beginning with that belonging to the Russells in Crastick Lake. Hard words and still harder blows were exchanged, the worst possible feeling was excited in the fishermen, and they only discovered when the case was ultimately disposed of at the assizes, that they had no right whatever to disturb the soil of the oyster-layings, the fee of which was vested in other parties.

Time wore on, the oyster-beds increased in size and in number; large quantities of spat were laid down; the Eastern boats came as before, carried away oysters and spat without regard to the fishermen, and it might naturally be supposed that the race of dredging fishermen had long before this become extinct; but what is the fact? The fact is this, that the Eastern boats so scarify and disturb the sides and bottom of the channels, that the growth and development of the oyster are increased manyfold; the spat is moved and distributed, and every successive year sees an improvement in the quantity bred. The oyster-layings contribute largely to this result, inasmuch as the spat from the layings travels down the channels with the ebb of the tide, and by this means the laying becomes as it were a depôt for the propa-

gation of oysters, in spots where, before the beds were made,
no oysters existed ; and if anything were wanting to corro-
borate the fact of the increase, it may be found in the number
of boats now employed at Emsworth and Bosham exclusively
engaged in this particular trade. Beds of considerable size
have lately been made under manorial grants from the lords
of Bosham, Thorney, Nutbourne, and Prinstead. The lessees
of these are men of capital and energy, and all that are willing
to work can obtain employment at remunerative wages. The
trade, which was some years since confined to the winter
months, now ranges throughout the entire year, and as the
demand is regular, the supply must of course correspond.
Jersey, France, Falmouth, and the Channel contribute to the
stock required, and all that can be caught meet with a ready
sale. The best interest of Emsworth and its vicinity, is by
every means to encourage and foster these depôts, which
bring labour, money, and example to the industrious fishermen, without calling upon the neighbourhood to share in the
risk or in the regulation of the employment.

There is a Custom-house at Emsworth, and the Griper is
stationed at the mouth of the harbour to prevent smuggling.
In former days, and up to a comparatively recent period, the
running of contraband goods from the French coast, particularly brandy, was of very common occurrence. Whether
from the natural propensity to purchase that which was
forbidden by the laws, or from sympathy with the courage
and daring which characterised the exploits of the smugglers,
certain it is that the practice met with pretty general approval
among the middle and even the better classes of society ; and
I believe that there were few in those times who did not
wink at circumstances of which notice should have been
taken, and who were not surprised occasionally to find a keg
of spirits in their barn or their stable. Many such instances
are within the recollection of the older inhabitants, but the
profits are now less, the risk multiplied, and the thing has
become of much less frequency. Fatal affrays often occurred
between the smugglers, who were usually well mounted and

armed, and the revenue officers, and a frightful tragedy which took place in the year 1747, and for which the perpetrators suffered the extreme sentence of the law, created a great sensation in the immediate neighbourhood.

In the month of September 1747, John Diamond with other smugglers went over to Guernsey and purchased a quantity of tea; on their return they were taken by a revenue cutter, and the tea was lodged in the custom-house of Poole.

Sixty of the gang, well armed, met in Charlton forest, and on the night of the 6th October, leaving thirty on the road to act as scouts, the remaining thirty proceeded to Poole, broke open the custom-house there, and carried away the tea. The next morning they returned with their booty through Fording-bridge, where crowds of people assembled to see the caval-cade. Among the spectators was Daniel Chater, a shoemaker, known to John Diamond, who threw him a bag of tea as he passed along. Soon after, a proclamation of reward was issued for the apprehension of those concerned in the burglary; and Diamond being in custody at Chichester on suspicion, Chater, in conversation with his neighbours, admitted that he knew Diamond. The collector of the customs at Southampton sent William Galley, a tidewaiter, and Daniel Chater with a letter to Mr. Battine, a magistrate for Sussex residing at East Marden, and surveyor-general of the customs, desiring him to take the examination of Chater in reference to the affair and the identity of Diamond.

In their way to Rowlands Castle they called at the New Inn at Leigh, and inquired the road to East Marden; they saw George Austen, John Austen, and Garnet, who said they were going that way and would show them. About noon they arrived at the White Hart, Rowlands Castle, kept by Elizabeth Payne, who had two sons, both of them reputed smugglers. Mrs. Payne took George Austen aside, and told him she was afraid the two strangers intended to injure the smugglers; he said they were merely carrying a letter to Mr. Battine on common business. This increased her suspicion, and she sent one of her sons for William Jackson and

William Carter.   In the meantime Chater and Galley wished
to go, and asked for their horses, but Mrs. Payne told them
that the man was gone out with the key of the stable, and
would soon return.   As soon as Jackson and Carter came in
she communicated her suspicions to them, and advised George
Austen to go away, telling him that as she respected him he
had better go home lest he should get into difficulty.   Mrs.
Payne's other son brought in Steel, Downer, Richards and
Sheerman, all belonging to the same gang.   After having
drunk together, Jackson took Chater into the yard and inquired after Diamond.   Chater said he was in custody, and
that, much against his will, he was going to appear against
him.   Galley soon after came into the yard for his companion, when Jackson abused him and struck him in the
face.   Upon their return into the house Galley and Chater
became uneasy and wished to go, but they were persuaded to
stay and drink till they became intoxicated : whilst they were
asleep in another room, the letter was taken from them and
read in the kitchen, the contents of it showing a design to
promote an information against some of their gang.   At this
instant John Raiss, another confederate, made his appearance,
and Steel proposed to throw them into a well adjoining the
house ; another proposed to ship them over to France.   A
third, that they should be kept in some place of confinement
till the fate of Diamond was known, and that the same
punishment should be inflicted upon them.

   While Galley and Chater were asleep, Jackson spurred
their foreheads, and whipping them, forced them into the
kitchen, their faces covered with blood.   They then put
Galley and Chater on the same horse and tied their legs under
his belly.   Steel led the horse, and the rest of the smugglers,
except Raiss, who had left them, whipped them over the head,
eyes, face, shoulders, and back, and continued this frightful
punishment until the sufferers, unable to bear the anguish of
the torment, rolled from side to side, and at last fell together
with their heads under the horse's belly, and at every step the
horse's feet struck one or other of their heads.   They set
them upright again, and continued the same cruelty as far as

Dean, when they once more fell: they were then separated. Galley was placed behind Steel and Chater behind Downer, and whipped as before. It was then agreed to carry them to the well in Lady Holt Park, and murder Galley, upon which they took him off the horse and threatened to throw him into the well, when the unhappy man desired them to dispatch him at once, instead of which they put him upon a horse again, and whipped him over the downs till he fell off; he was then laid across the saddle before Downer, who tortured him until they arrived at the public-house at Rake. Carter took a candle and lantern, borrowed a spade, and Downer, assisted by the landlord, dug a hole in Harting Combe, and there buried poor Galley.

Chater had been conveyed to the house of Mills for greater security. During the remainder of the night and the whole of the next day, the gang continued at Rake, drinking and in consultation: they determined at length to return to their houses during the night, that their neighbours' suspicions might not be excited, and on the Wednesday evening following they met at Rake by appointment. John Cobby, William Hammond, Benjamin Tapner, Thomas Stringer, Daniel Perryer, John Miles, Thomas Willis, and Richard Mills were there in addition to those who murdered Galley, and as soon as they were all assembled, they renewed their consultation at midnight as to the best mode of dispatching Chater.

Richard Mills proposed to chain Chater to a post, to load a gun with two or three bullets, to lay it upon a stand with the muzzle levelled at his head, and having tied a string to the trigger, that they should all pull together and share in his murder. This proposal was, however, considered far too humane, and they determined at last to take Chater from the custody of Mills, and to throw him into the well at Lady Holt, as the most effectual mode of concealing the transaction from the world. The gang accordingly proceeded to the Turf House occupied by Mills; Tapner, Cobby, and some others, with oaths and imprecations, pulled out large clasp knives, and bid Chater go down on his knees and say his prayers. Chater knelt as he was directed, and having offered up a fervent prayer, ventured to inquire what they had done with Galley. Tapner instantly drew his knife aslant over his eyes and nose, with such violence as almost to cut both his eyes out and his nose quite through; with a second blow he gashed his forehead to the bone. They then proceeded towards the well, Tapner, more cruel than the rest, striking him across the face with his whip, and swearing that if Chater blooded his saddle, he would send his soul to hell. They arrived at the well, which was surrounded by paling and thirty feet deep, about midnight; they dismounted Chater, and Tapner, taking a cord out of his pocket, made a noose, fastened it round his neck, and bade him get over the pales, which he did with great difficulty. Tapner then tied the rope to the pales, and all of them forced him into the well, but expecting from his struggles that death would not soon release him, they pulled his legs out of the well, untied the cord, and his body fell head foremost into it. They stood by the well for some time, and hearing him groan, they borrowed a ladder for the purpose of going down and dispatching him at once; in their confusion they could not however raise the ladder over the pales, and scarcely knowing what to do, they threw in logs of wood and large stones, until the groaning finally ceased. To prevent suspicion, they next destroyed the horse which Galley had ridden and cut his hide into small pieces, but Chater's escaped and returned to its owner's home.

The transaction was soon discovered, and a large reward being offered by the Government, an anonymous letter was sent to a person of distinction, intimating that the body of one of the unfortunate men was buried in the lands near Rake. Upon this search was made, and the body of Galley was found standing almost upright with his hands covering his eyes.

A second letter was received stating that Steel was concerned in the murder; he was at once apprehended, when he turned king's evidence and made a full disclosure of all the circumstances. The well at Lady Holt was searched, when the body of Chater was found in a mangled state, his eyes starting out of his head, and Tapner's rope around his neck.

Several of the gang were taken; Raiss voluntarily surrendered himself, and confirmed the statement made by Steel. A special commission was issued for an assize which was held at Chichester on the 16th January, 1748-9, the prisoners were found guilty of murder, and five of the principals were hung in chains. Jackson died soon after his condemnation from the terror of a public execution.

The fair originally granted to Herbert the son of Matthew, in 1239, is still held at Emsworth on the eve of Saint Thomas à Becket, the patron saint of the parish, and another on the Monday in Easter week. Two fairs are also held at Rowlands Castle, one on the 12th of May, for horses, toys, and pedlary, and from the pleasant time of the year when it takes place, and the beauty of the surrounding country, in times past a large concourse of people was drawn together, but at this day it is comparatively deserted: the other falls on the 12th of November, for the sale of horses and pigs. There is no charter that I can discover applicable to the origin of these fairs at Rowlands Castle, and it is therefore probable that they existed for the sale of merchandize and cattle before the Conquest, and that they were protected by the lords of the Castle, who were, by custom, entitled to tolls and the fines arising from the Court incident to fairs for the redress of all grievances happening. while they lasted. I find no trace of the market granted to the same Herbert, and conclude therefore that it must have been found on the return of the writ of "*ad quod damnum*," which issued on the establishment of a market or fair to the injury of that at Havant of prior creation, and therefore abandoned.

By the census taken in 1811, the population of the entire parish was 2066; by that taken in 1831, it was 2118; and by that of 1851, it was 2302. The expenses of maintaining the poor in 1783 amounted to £453. 4s. 7d. and in the year 1851, to £1276. 18s. 8d. The parish is included within the Havant

Union, and three guardians are annually elected to attend the
weekly meetings at Havant. Emsworth is deficient in springs
and badly supplied with water, although the well-springs on
Emsworth Common yield an unlimited quantity at an elevation of a hundred feet above the level of the sea, and pipes
might be laid at a very trifling expense from thence into the
place. There is no description of manufacture carried on here;
but rope, net, and sack-making keep a considerable number
of hands in constant employment.

The South Coast Railway passes at a convenient distance;
there is a station with every accommodation for the transit of
goods and passengers, and the roads in the immediate
neighbourhood are excellent. House-rent is reasonable, and
the supply of meat, poultry, and fish, abundant.

There are two friendly societies—one holding its annual
feast at the King's Arms, the other at the Dolphin—and a
company has recently been formed to supply a district of the
parish with gas, under the management of inspectors appointed
under the Act for Watching and Lighting Parishes.

Within the parish of Warblington, but not within the
manor, and possessing a separate boundary of its own, is
the Manor of Lymbourne, comprising the Wade Court estate,
and having jurisdiction over various freehold tenements held
under the Manor, the quit-rents, for which however have
not for many years past been collected. On the west and
south-west it is bounded by the manor and parish of Havant;
on the east and south-east, by Pook-lane and the seaward
bounds of the Manor of Warblington; on the north, by the
turnpike-road extending southward to the channel of Langstone harbour.

It is not mentioned *eo nomine* in Domesday, and as it lay
within the parish of Warblington, it is probable that it was
held by Roger de Montgomery as parcel of the Manor of
Warblington, and that, like that manor and the lands in
Hayling, it descended to Hugh de Montgomery, afterwards
to Robert de Belesme, and that on the attainder of the latter
it became an escheat of the Crown in the reign of Henry I.

Whether in ancient times the wadeway from the main land
to Hayling ran from Pook-lane across to the opposite shore
we know not; but the lane and the remains of a hard, or land-
ing-place, seem to justify the supposition in connection with
the fact that Lymbourne was called La Wade at a very early
period, which could hardly have been the case if the wadeway
had not crossed to the island from some part of its southern
boundary.

The first entry that is found in reference to Wade, is contained in the Close Rolls in the reign of King John, under the
head of " *de terris Normannis datis*" (*Rot. Claus.* 6 John, m.
21), by which it appears that the king had granted to the Earl
of Arundel the lands of Wade in the county of Southampton,
then lately belonging to Juliana de Wade. This evidently
points to the attainder of Robert de Belesme and to the donations to the Earl of Arundel mentioned elsewhere. The
estate remained in the hands of the Earls of Arundel and
their mesne tenants for some considerable period, and Henry
de la Wade, a mesne tenant, in the 50 Henry III (*Pat.*
50 Hen. III, m. 30), 1266, was keeper of the silver vessels to
that monarch. Upon the death of John le Fauconer de la
Wade in the 33 Edward I, 1303, he was found by inquisition to have died seized of the Manor of Lymbourne (*Inq.
p. mort.* No. 44) in the county of Southampton. William de
Fauconer de la Wade obtained for his services grants of wreck
and free warren in the hundred of Bosebergh, which will be
more particularly noticed hereafter. In the 35 Edward III,
1361-2, William de Wintershall died seized of lands at Wade
(*Inq. p. mort.* No. 8, vol. ii, p. 243), and in the 38th year of
the same reign Henry Fauconer of Fawkenhurst died seized
of the Manor of Lymbourne (*Inq. p. mort.* No. 17, vol ii,
p. 266), which he held by the service of keeping a falcon.
In the 50 Edward III, 1376, Robert Cantel of Warblington gave forty shillings for a licence granted to John
Botiller of Lymbourne, that he might be enfeoffed of the
Manor of Lokerle in the county of Southampton (*Abb. Rot.
orig. Ro.* 46, p. 348). In the 12 Richard II, 1389, William

Upton, who held a carucate of land at La Wade in the Manor
of Lymbourne, was found by inquisition a felon, and his
property was confiscated (*Inq. p. mort.* No. 136).   In the
same year, Isabella the wife of Geoffrey Roukele, the sister
and heiress of John Botiller, was found to have died seized of
lands at Lokerle and Tuderlee, and of the Manor of Lymbourne
(*Ibid.* No. 46).   In the 21st of the same reign, 1398, Richard
Earl of Arundel died seized of seventeen acres of land at
Helsey, of the Manor of Lymbourne near Havant, of Benithe
within the parish of Hameldon, and of Lompesland in the
parish of Eastney (*Inq. p. mort.* 9, 10 Edw. IV, No. 48).   In
the 7 Edward IV, Thomas Pounde died seized of the Manor of
Lymbourne, the Manor of Drayton, and the Manor and lands
of Bere (*Inq. p. mort.* 7 Edw. IV, No. 72).   In the 9th and
10th of the same reign, Richard Dalyngrigge, Armiger, died
seized of the Manor of Lymbourne, and of lands in la Wade
and Warblington (*Inq. p. mort.* 9, 10 Edw. IV, No. 48).   In
after times Lord Chadwick Paulet, third son of Lord Paulet
of Basing, and governor of Portsmouth in the reigns of Queen
Mary and Queen Elizabeth, was lord of Lymbourne.   In
1645, Arthur Hyde of Hinton Daubeny was lord (*Court
Rolls*), and on his death in 1654, it passed to Lawrence Hyde.
It subsequently became the property of Thomas Jervoise
Esquire, of Herriard, who, by will dated 2d May 1739,
devised this estate, with Rowlands Castle and purlieu, to
trustees, to be sold for the payment of debts and legacies.
On the 18th March 1752, the Manor of Lymbourne, with
Wade Court, was sold under a decree of the Court of
Chancery to Mr. Robert Bold.   By indentures dated 21st and
22d September 1752, Robert Bold settled this manor and
estate on his son James Bold, who died intestate and without
issue.   Mr. John Knight purchased the whole from the
representatives of James Bold's coheiresses, and by will, dated
23d February 1808, he devised it to his two sons, the late
Mr. John Knight and the late Mr. William Knight.   The
latter, by indentures dated 1st and 2d November 1812, sold
his moiety to his brother for £4,500.   John Knight, by his
will dated 6th March 1824, devised the manor and estate to

trustees for sale, and on the 26th December 1843, the property was sold to Messrs. Knight and Moore, who, by indenture dated 27th September 1846, conveyed it to Mr. Charles John Longcroft, the present lord.

In a field called Lymbourne, derived from the Saxon *lyn* a field, and *bourne* a brook, there are the remains of an ancient encampment. The works, parts of which have been levelled, covered originally a space of about four statute acres, and consisted of an outer and an inner camp, the approaches to which could be flooded on all sides except the northern. No coins have been found either in the field or moats, and looking at the name and the situation so near the harbour, the probability is, that the works were thrown up by our Saxon forefathers on their landing from the Continent.

Hayling Island.

—◆—

THE Island of Hayling lies to the south of the parish of
Havant, having Cumberland Fort and Portsea on the
west, and West Wittering, the Manhood, and Thorney on the
east, the tidal waters which surround it on the west, north,
and east, forming the estuary, called Langstone and Chichester
Harbour. It is about six miles in length by four in breadth;
and comprises the parishes of Hayling North and Hayling
South. It is approached by a ferry at Eastoke on the eastern
extremity, by a ferry at Sinah on the western extremity, and
in former times by a ferry and wadeway on the northern
extremity communicating with Langstone, and passable for
carriages and passengers at low water; this has recently been
superseded by a bridge and causeway.

The surface of the Island is flat, presenting the ordinary
features of an agricultural locality, and along the entire breadth
of the southern shore there is a large tract of uncultivated
land known as Sinah Common, Beach Common, and Eastoke
Common. The shore commands an uninterrupted view of the
Isle of Wight, Spithead, and Portsmouth to the west, while
to the north Portsdown and a range of the Southdown hills
carry the eye as far as Chichester, the cathedral spire of
which may be seen towering in the far distance. At what
particular period the island became first inhabited we have no
means of ascertaining, but it was certainly in some state of
occupation at the time when Saint Ambrose wrote, because he
says in reference to this part of England. "Let us consider
"those things which are common to many and expressive of the
"divine favour, how water is turned into salt of such substance
"as frequently to be cut with a knife. This is not uncommon

" in the British salts, which have both the solidity and glossy
" whiteness of marble, and are very wholesome." This
manufacture of salt spoken of by Saint Ambrose, is still
carried on during the summer months, but depends in a great
measure upon the state of the weather. The Saxons landed
at Christchurch and Porchester, and at West Wittering,
where Ella is said to have disembarked the spot still retains
the name of " Ellanore;" it is therefore probable that Hayling
was visited about the same time, and colonized by the same
invaders, although no buildings of Saxon foundation are found
in the island. Leland notices the place, but his account
contains nothing more than a passing observation, " I saw
" Havant, a small market town, and near. it Warblington,
" formerly belonging to the Earls of Salisbury, but now to the
" knightly family of the Cottons. Opposite to it the two
" islands, the larger called Haling, the lesser Thorney, from the
" thorns growing in it ; each has its parish church."

In the *Annales Ecclesiæ Wintoniensis*, cited in Wharton's
Anglia Sacra, Hayling is stated to have come into the possession of the Church of Saint Swythun, at Winchester, partly
by the gift of Queen Emma, the wife of Ethelred, and of Canute,
and partly by the gift of Alwyn, bishop of that see. Emma
probably held it as dowry from Ethelred, who bestowed many
manors upon her, which were confirmed by Canute and her son
Hardicanute. King Ethelred the Unready, began to reign in
979. After the death of his first wife, he married in 1002
Emma, surnamed the Flower of Normandy (*Rob. of Glouc.*
v. i, p. 205), who was the daughter of Richard, second Duke
of Normandy, and sister of Richard third Duke, and of
Duke Robert, father of William the Conqueror. Edward and
Alfred were the issue of this marriage, and the circumstances
under which Hayling was granted to the Church of Saint
Swythun are so interwoven with the history of Queen Emma,
and so peculiarly illustrative of the period, that it will not be
uninstructive to narrate them in somewhat greater detail than
the mere fact of the gift would seem to require.

Ethelred dying in 1016, was succeeded by Edmund
Ironside his son, by Elgiva. Canute, who had ravaged the

country in the lifetime of his father, used every exertion to dethrone Edmund, till at length it was agreed between them to share the kingdom. Edmund was treacherously put to death in 1017; Canute laid claim to and obtained the crown, and by this means became the first Danish King of England. He sought to strengthen his throne by compassing the death of the sons of Ethelred, and the removal of those of Edmund Ironside. Edwin, the only surviving son of Ethelred by his first wife, was banished, but subsequently recalled and murdered. The two sons of Edmund were sent into Sweden, and Emma was under the necessity of placing her own sons, Edward and Alfred, under the care of their uncle Richard, third Duke of Normandy, in order to provide for their safety during the struggles between Edmund and Canute. The latter sought the alliance of the Norman Duke by marrying Emma, and as he had no male issue, she consented to the match upon the understanding that upon failure of his issue male by her, her sons by King Ethelred should succeed to the throne (*Ibid.* p. 317, *Polydor*). The marriage took place in July 1017, and in 1035, she was again left a widow in his decease, having had by him one son Hardicanute.

In the absence of Hardicanute in Denmark, Harold Harefoot his elder, but base-born brother, persuaded the nobility to proclaim him king, and he was crowned in the year 1036. The powerful and unscrupulous Godwin Earl of Kent, at first opposed the claims of Harold, being as he pretended the guardian of the late King's children, and urging that Canute had disposed of the kingdom by will in favour of Hardicanute. Harold, however, succeeded in conciliating the earl, and measures were adopted to secure the former in his seat. The first attempt was directed against Emma, whose destruction was determined upon. But as she was greatly beloved, they dared not practice openly against her, and it was resolved to obtain possession of her sons, Edward and Alfred. In order to effect this, a letter in their mother's name was written to them urging them to attempt the recovery of the throne which had been usurped by Harold (*Encomium Emmæ*). This letter ran as follows :—

" Emma, Queen only in name, to Edward and Alfred her
" son, sendeth motherly greeting. Whilst severally we bewail
" the death of our sovereign my lord and your father, and your-
" selves (dear sons) still more and more dispossessed of the
" kingdom your lawful inheritance, I greatly marvel what you
" determine to do since you know that the delay of attempts
" gives the usurper more leisure to lay his foundation, and more
" safely to set thereon his intended buildings ; for incessantly he
" posteth from town to town, and from city to city, to make the
" lords and rulers thereof, either by threats, prayers, or present
" rewards. But this in private they signify that they had rather
" one of you their natives should reign over them than this
" usurper and Danish stranger. Wherefore my desire is that
" either of you secretly, and with all speed, come unto me,
" whereby we may advise together what is to done in this so
" great an enterprise, than whose good success I desire nothing
" more. Fail not, therefore, to send word by this my messenger
" how you mean to proceed, and so fare ye well, my dearest
" bowels, and very inwards of my heart."

To this letter a reply was sent to the effect that Alfred
would shortly come over to comply with the wishes of his
mother. He came accordingly, and being met by Godwin on
landing, the Earl swore fealty to them, and promised to
conduct him to the Queen. But so far from doing this, on
arriving at Guildford, the whole party were made prisoners,
his men were slain except the tenth (reserved for sale or
service), and the unfortunate prince was sent to the Isle of
Ely, where his eyes were put out, and where he shortly after
died in great misery (*Langloft's Chr.* vol. i, p. 52). Emma
was at once banished the realm, her property was confiscated
(*Simon Dun.*), and in this distress she was kindly received by
Baldwin Earl of Flanders, with whom she resided, until the
death of Harold in 1040, which restored Hardicanute, who
recalled her to her former position (*Polydor*).

Upon this, Earl Godwin propitiated the favour of the King
by the present of a ship of most costly material and workmanship (*Hol. Chron.* vol. i, p. 737), and having cleared
himself by oath of the suspicious part which he had played

in reference to the death of Alfred, he is with Emma again found in the administration of the state. Hardicanute reigned but two years, and was succeeded in the throne by Edward, surnamed the Confessor, the only surviving son of Queen Emma by Ethelred the Unready, which event took place in 1042 (*Matth. Westmtr.*).

In three years after the accession of this monarch he married Egitha the daughter of Earl Godwin, described as being a very beautiful damsel (*Ingulph*, p. 905), well grounded in letters and, moreover, a most chaste virgin and of a most holy life, having in no respect the barbarism of her father or brother. Godwin, however, gave the king mortal offence by refusing to punish the inhabitants of Canterbury, who, in revenge for the slaughter of a fellow-citizen, by a retainer of Eustace de Bulloigne (married to Edward's half sister) had fallen upon and killed several of his retinue; Earl Godwin and his sons were banished, but eventually the quarrel was arranged, the Earl and his sons came to London and besought pardon of the king, which was granted, and his estates restored to him. (*Wm. Malmesbury. Dig. Leg.* p. 82).

Pending and for some time prior to these events, Earl Godwin, in conjunction with Robert, Archbishop of Canterbury, had endeavoured to accomplish the destruction of Queen Emma, who stood in the way of their schemes of ambition. This Robert had originally been a monk of the Abbey of Jumiéges, in Normandy, and having there befriended Edward and his brother during their exile from this country, he accompanied the King, who was attended by William, Duke of Normandy, and a small retinue of Norman nobility, on his accession to the throne, and, in return for the services which he had rendered, was created first Bishop of London, and was afterwards advanced to the primacy of all England. (*Hol. Chron.* vol. i, p. 741.) They poisoned the mind of the King against her, accusing her of consenting to the death of Alfred, of endeavouring to prevent the accession of Edward, and of criminal intimacy with Alwyn, Bishop of Winchester, who was consecrated in 1033. The king was greatly incensed, wrested from her all that she had to the value of a farthing, and sent her to the Abbey of Wherwell, founded by Elfrida in 978. Alwyn was despoiled of everything and forbidden to leave the city of Winchester on pain of death. The queen was permitted to write to the bishops, whom she considered faithful to her interest, and to express to them her grief and the poignancy of her feelings at the accusations which had been made against her. In her letters she stated that she was more hurt and vexed at the disgrace of the bishop than at her own, that she was prepared to prove by ordeal that the bishop was slandered in respect of improper communication with her; that neither of them had done or desired anything to the hurt of the king; that they should go to the king and intercede for their brother bishop, and should, by every means, persuade him to allow her to prove his and her own innocence; that a good conscience publicly accused of crime should be cleared only by a public trial, and that she preferred the ordeal of hot iron. They were to require that the king should cause the examination to be held in the Church of Saint Swythun at Winchester, that she felt assured of the assistance of the saint in testimony of her innocence, and that if they delayed to do this she should die. That if the king, her son, chose to punish his mother, neither confessing nor convicted of guilt, rather than admit her to the ordeal, he would be universally scorned.

The bishops to whom the queen had written consulted together, and addressed the king upon the subject of his mother's complaint. Edward would have pardoned without the trial by ordeal, and would even have asked forgiveness for his presumption, had not the Archbishop Robert opposed it. As the advocate of the stronger party, he strove to divert the endeavours of the bishops, and to turn the king against his mother by the language he held upon the occasion. " You " my brethren," said he, " have besought the king on behalf of " his mother, a beast, and not a woman, in order that I may " spare you, not by your own, but by her words you turn the " mother's crime against the son.

'En scelus, ecce Jovem placidum nimis, hanc nimis aulam
'Quæ scelius tractat, coram Jove de Jove causam.'

"That most impudent woman has dared to utter the injuries
"of defamation against the king, and designate the Lord's
"annointed to her partner in crime, who knows how to affect
"sanctity, so that she may make the King guilty of sacrilege.
"See the woman's malice.   For this reason only does she call
"Alwyn the Lord's annointed, that she may accuse the king
"of sacrilege because he has laid hands upon him, but let us
"hasten to the matter itself.   The woman wants to prove the
"bishop innocent, but who will prove her to be innocent, who
"is said to have consented to the death of her own son Alfred,
"and to have procured poison for Edward ?   But be it so !
"Let her have consideration beyond the condition of her sex,
"for she is a Queen. If ye will, I consent to an ordeal unheard
"of for ages.   And do you consent that I appoint the manner
"of it, so that if she come out of it wholly unhurt, ye shall
"condemn me to be deprived of my honors as guilty against
"God and the king, and shall restore them if proved innocent
"to their former honours. I take upon myself the whole blame
"(which is as I take it none) attached to the king.   I will
"detain you no longer ; that infamous woman for herself shall
"take four, for the bishop five, in all nine successive steps with
"naked feet, upon nine red hot ploughshares. If she shall
"flinch, if she shall not press each ploughshare with her whole
"foot, if she shall sustain the slightest possible injury, sentence
"shall be pronounced against the adulterer and adulteress.
"Let both be shut up in prison in the cloisters of the strictest
"religion.   You should know moreover that this sentence
"proceeds more from indulgence than rigour, which I will not
"say decrees, but permits that a capital crime shall be tried
"by examination of the feet."

The decree of the archbishop satisfied the King and the
bishops ; the sentence was announced to the Queen, and the
rumour of the coming ordeal spread rapidly through the
country. An immense concourse of people assembled at

Winchester. The King, the great nobles, and all the bishops, with the exception of the archbishop, were there to witness the ceremony. He feigned sickness at Dover, but the preparation for instant flight, should the proceedings terminate in the innocence of the accused, was the pressing reason for his absence.

The Queen, by command of the King, was brought from Wherwell to Winchester, and the whole of the night preceding her agony, she spent in watching at the tomb of Saint Swythun. Yet she slept a little, and according to Rudborne, saw the blessed Swythun strengthening her and saying thus, "Be of "good cheer, my daughter, I am Swythun upon whom thou "callest! Fear not the sentence of thy condemnation, when "thou passest over the fire it shall not hurt thee, but do thou "forgive this thy son's sin." The day being arrived, the clergy and people repair to the church, and the King sat as at a tribunal; the Queen is brought before her son, and is asked if she wished to fulfil that to which she is engaged. "My "lord and son," said she, "I that Emma who gave thee birth, "accused before thee of crime against thee and Alfred my "sons, and of consent to infamy and treason with the bishop "of this see; I call God to witness upon my body, that I may "perish if I have ever conceived in my heart the things of "which I am accused."

The ploughshares having been blessed, the Queen's shoes and hose taken off, her cloak and vest laid aside, she is led by two bishops to the torture. The bishops who conducted her wept, and they, who were much more terrified than she was, urged her not to be afraid. A great lamentation is made throughout the Church, and there was a voice as of one crying out, "Saint Swythun, Saint Swythun, keep her!" If the thunder had at that moment rolled, it could not have been heard for the peoples' cries, so urgently did they appeal to heaven, that Saint Swythun might then or never hasten to her assistance. God felt its power, and Saint Swythun is sent down by force as it were from Heaven. The queen, without any clamour, made this prayer before the commencement. "God who freedst Susannah from the wicked elders, who

" deliveredst thy three servants from the fiery furnace, deign
"to deliver me from the fiery trial prepared against me."
Behold the miracle! The bishops directing her steps, she
trod in succession upon the nine red hot (igne candentes)
ploughshares, pressing upon them with the whole weight of
her body, and felt neither the heat nor the naked iron! At
length she said to the bishops, " When shall I reach the object
"of my wishes? Why do you lead beyond the church, me
"who am to be examined within the church?" For she was
even proceeding further, and knew not that she had already
undergone the requisite ordeal. To whom the bishops made
answer as well as they could for sobbing: " Lady," said they,
"look behind thee, that which thou deemest unfinished is
" already finished." She looked back, and now her eyes were
opened, and then for the first time she saw the iron and
comprehended the miracle. " Lead me," said she, " to my
son, that he may see my feet, and know that I have sustained
no injury." The bishops having returned with the queen,
found her son Edward with head uncovered, prostrate on the
ground; words for pity sake had deserted him, so that his
tears flowed abundantly, and he could not restrain himself.
When he had risen and had become fully acquainted with the
matter, the holy man threw himself at the feet of his mother,
begging her pardon, and saying, " Mother, I have sinned
" before heaven and against thee, and am no more worthy to
" be called thy son." To whom his mother replied, " Let
"bishop Alwyn be called before you, and when you shall
" have satisfied him, you will the more readily obtain my
"forgiveness." The bishop, who had not sat in the ranks of
the prelates, was called to the king. The king solicits and
obtains his pardon, and after having been beaten with stripes
by his mother and each of the bishops, he received three
blows of a rod from the hand of his weeping parent, and then
kisses being given and returned, the king received them into
his favour, and they him to their love. And what had been
taken from the queen and the bishop was restored to them.
The manner and order of the miracle were proclaimed to the
people on the outside, by the king's command; and so suddenly

their tears were turned into joy, insomuch that you might have seen them laughing and weeping at the same moment.

There were then given on account of this miracle twenty-one manors to the church of Winchester, and the monks there serving God; three from the King, Portlond, Wyke-helewell, and Waymuthe; nine by the Queen (one for each ploughshare), Brandesbury, Bergefeld, Fyffhyde, Hoghton, Mychelmershe, Ivyngho, Wycombe, Weregrarys, and Hay-lynge; nine by the bishop, Horcham, Estmeone, Westmeone, Hentone, Wybneye, Yelinge, Millhoke, Polhampton, and Hadyngtone. The ploughshares were buried in the western part of the cathedral cloisters. (*Hist. Mag. Wynt.* p. 233; *Ann. Eccl. Wynt.* p. 291.)

This trial by ordeal arose in early times with the Saxon pagans, and continued as an ordinary mode of appeal in great crimes down to the year 750, when it was forbidden by the order of Stephen the Pope as being too severe. It was quite in consonance with the feelings of a people who determined all events by the casting of lots, and was performed with fire and water; the first being applicable to persons of high degree, the last to persons of inferior quality, and existed in this country so late even as the reign of King John. Bishop Alwyn did not long survive the acquittal of the Queen. He died in 1047, having held the see of Winchester fifteen years, and was buried in his own church. (*God. de Præsal. Aug.,* p. 212.) Queen Emma died in 1052, and was buried in the Church of Saint Swythun, near her second husband Canute. (*Rudó.* p. 289.)

Upon the conclusion of the ordeal, the archbishop fled into Normandy, and from thence to Rome, to lay his statement of grievances before the pope. On his way back bearing letters of exculpation from his Holiness, he was taken ill at Jumiéges, and dying there was buried in the church of the holy Virgin, which he had founded and built with great magnificence. (*Wm. Malmesbury, de gestis, regum,* p. 82.) Earl Godwin died in 1053, and was buried in the old monastery

at Winchester; his death was sudden, and it is thus related
in the Chronicles of Hardyng.

> " And as Kyng Edward in his palayce of pride,
> Duke Goodwyne then sittyng at his table,
> Sawe the butler on his one fote slyde
> And lyke to fall that other fote full stable ;
> As he was seruying the king at his table
> Then held hym vp that he fell not to grounde,
> Kyng Edward say'd to Gudwin in that stounde.
>
> As his one fote ye se helpe that other
> Full well and trewe I fynde it dayly nowe,
> Had ye ne bene thus had helpe me my brother ;
> Therle then to the kyng on side gan bowe
> And sayd, ' if I were cause I praye God nowe
> This breade passe not my throte, but dead I bee
> And straungled here anone that ye may see.'
>
> At his prayer anone with that he died,
> For with that breade straungled was he y^t stound,
> It might not passe his throte as men espied,
> Wherefore the kyng then bad drawe out y^t hounde
> Vnder the boorde as he that false was founde
> On whome God shewed an hasty judgment
> Approued well by good experiment." (p. 229.)

Edward the Confessor died in 1055, and was buried with
universal lamentation at the church of Westminster. (*Speed*,
b. 8, c. 6.) Upon his death Edgar Atheling, the grandson of
Edmund Ironside, laid claim to the throne, and William Duke
of Normandy surnamed the Bastard contended also for
the kingdom by gift of Edward and also by consanguinity.
Both of these, however, being abroad, Harold, the eldest
surviving son of Earl Godwin and brother-in-law of the late
king, obtained possession of the crown. After a brief
struggle between Harold and his brother Tosto, in which the
latter was slain, William duke of Normandy prepared to

assert his right to the crown by an invasion of the realm.   He
founded his pretensions upon an agreement said to have been
made between him and the Confessor, ratified and confirmed
by Harold himself, who had solemnly sworn to hold the
kingdom for William, and to marry Adeliza his daughter.
This had taken place as William asserted when Harold sailing
from his palace at Bosham had been driven upon the coast of
Normandy, and had been delivered up to William by the
Earl of Ponthieur : the history of the transaction from the
period of Harold's departure from Bosham down to
his oath to the duke, is still preserved in the interesting
tapestry of Bayeux sometime since engraved by the Society
of Antiquaries.

William sent ambassadors to Harold, reminding him of his
oath, which the latter declined to fulfil, upon which William
collected an army, and landed at Pevensey in Sussex.   He
justified this step on the refusal of Harold to give up the
throne and marry Adeliza in accordance with his engagement,
and in "revenge for the wrong unto Robert archbishop of
" Canterbury, who was exiled by the means and labour of
" Harold in the days of King Edward." (*Hen. Hunt.*) The
battle of Hastings followed, Harold was defeated and slain,
and William, thereafter surnamed the Conqueror, was
established upon the throne of England.

Harold appears to have been in possession of lands in
Hayling, acquired probably by force during his short reign.
Upon the conquest, William seized into his own hands the
vast possessions of those who had either borne arms or had
fallen at the battle of Hastings.   He also despoiled numerous
Abbies on the most trifling pretexts, among them that of
Saint Albans (*Baker's Chron.*), and confiscated the estates of
those who had assisted Harold, which in some instances he
remitted on payment of a fine proportioned to the means of
the owner.   Harold had an uncle named Godwin abbot of
the monastery of Hyde at Winchester, who led with him to
the battle of Hastings twelve monks of his house, and twenty
knights bound by tenure of their fees.   The knights were
killed, whilst the abbot and his monks were found with

arms in their hands dressed in the habiliments of their order. William in his anger seized upon the Abbey with its large possessions, and kept it in his own hands for nearly two years without a pastor.   In the third year of his reign he visited Normandy, and upon his return he imposed a forfeiture upon the Abbey of one barony in respect of the abbot, and one knight's fee in respect of each monk who had fought against him. (*Dugdale's Mon.* vol.i, p. 211.) These he distributed among his dependents, and partly from his own connexion with the house, partly from the great love he entertained for his mother who lay buried within its walls, and partly from the friend-ship he had ever borne to Robert archbishop of Canterbury, William endowed the Abbey of Gemeticum with very large possessions, and among others, with the church of Harenge and the tithes of the whole Island, except the tithes of pulse and oats in the land of the bishop of Winchester.   Deshayes, in his *Histoire de l'Abbaye Royale de Jumiéges*, tells us that Edward the Confessor was brought up in the Abbey, and that he there imbibed those principles of piety and austerity which in after life procured him such a reputation for sanctity; that William the Conqueror, after the example of his prede-cessors, had a great regard for the monastery, and that upon many occasions the monks were partakers of his bounty. Among other donations, he mentions particularly that of " the Isle of Helling," and states that the monks founded a priory there which returned them an annual income of eleven hundred golden crowns.   The Conqueror often visited Jumiéges, and appointed the Abbé Gouthard who had attained great skill in the art of medicine, his first physician.   (p. 51.) After William's fall from his horse at Mantes, he was carried to the monastery of St. Gervais at Rouen, and was placed under the charge of Gilbert bishop of Lisieux and the Abbé Gouthard, the two most celebrated physicians of the age. Gouthard foreseeing its fatal termination never quitted the king during his last illness, and upon his death, which happened on the 9th September 1087, his body was transported to Caen, and there buried by Gouthard and the Archbishop of Rouen. (*Ibid.* p. 54.)

At a subsequent period, and during the abbacy of Jean de la Chaussée, Margaret of Anjou visited Jumiéges ; she was received under a canopy and treated with the greatest possible respect. She remained some time an inmate of the Abbey, and agreed to restore to the monks the Island of Halling which had been taken from them by the crown.

The towers of the Abbey of Jumiéges, styled in Latin the Abbey of Gemeticum, are still to be seen looming upon the horizon in the centre of a peninsula, formed by the windings of the river Seine. They are in ruins, but of exceeding beauty, and attest the grandeur and magnificence of the house when in its zenith. In the first days of the monarchy it was a marshy wild covered with wood, which extended on the right bank of the Seine from Duclair to Caudebec, but the name was subsequently limited to a portion of the ground nearly four leagues in circumference. Such was the extensive site occupied by the monastery and its dependencies from the time of its foundation, but it ceases to be matter of surprise when we learn that before the death of the first abbot, there were at Jumiéges nine hundred monks and fifteen hundred lay brethren as inmates of the monastery.

The public library of Rouen possesses a manuscript of William of Jumiéges, in which the historian is represented in a miniature presenting his work to the Conqueror as the patron of the Abbey. He wrote a Latin history of the Dukes of Normandy, lived at Jumiéges in the eleventh century, and his work is one of great use and information. He gives two explanations of the word Gemeticum ; this place, says he, is so called, because those who are shut up in it lament their sins, or because it is comparable for beauty and richness to a precious stone (*gemma*). Saint Philibert founded the Abbey of Jumiéges in the year 654, on a site which he obtained as a gift from Clovis II and Queen Bathilde his wife ; but in 841, the Northmen plundered his pious retreat, and ten years afterwards it was utterly destroyed. The monks were either killed or dispersed, and their monastery was sacked by the

Vue orientale des ruines de l'abbaye des Jumièges.

prise du Logis Abbatial en 1823.

Arms of Jumiéges.

Initial Letter to a M.S. by William of Jumièges

Tombeau des Enervés, à Jumiéges.

Statue of Rollo in Rouen Cathedral.

Norman freebooters. There remained standing only the
principal walls of the Church of St. Peter, of the western
entrance of which some vestiges are still to be seen. In the
year 930, William Longsword, son of Rollo, rebuilt the
monastery and richly endowed it; the Church was rebuilt in
1040 by Abbot Robert II, Archbishop of Canterbury; the
work was continued at intervals over a period of some years,
and the abbey resumed its original splendour in 1067, when
Saint Maurille, Archbishop of Rouen, dedicated the church to
the Virgin Mary, in the presence of William the Conqueror.
The ruins of this edifice are still preserved to us. Its ancient
choir had been replaced probably during the reign of Saint
Louis; the church was 265 feet long by 63 feet wide, the
square tower in the middle rose to the height of 124 feet, and
was 41 feet square. This tower was surmounted by a
pyramid of timber work of admirable workmanship and
prodigious height, which was destroyed in 1573, through the
cupidity of the Abbot Gabriel le Veneur. The two existing
towers over the front entrance are each 155 feet high, they
serve as a beacon for navigators to enable them to avoid
several rocks in the Seine below Jumiéges, and particularly
the rocks called the Millstones. The revenues of the house at
one time amounted to 40,000 French livres per annum.

There stood formerly in the Church of Saint Peter of
Jumiéges a tomb, on which the statues of two young men
richly dressed were to be seen; it was called the Tomb of the
Enervated, the explanation of which is said to be as follows :
Clovis II, successor of Dagobert, had five sons, and having
gone to visit the holy sepulchre at Jerusalem, he left Bathilde
his wife regent of the kingdom, but the lords who accompanied
the king rebelled against the regent on the ground that a
foreigner (the queen being a Saxon) had no right to wield the
sceptre in France. Two of the elder sons of Clovis entered into
the conspiracy, but the king returned and punished the rebels.
The judges dared not condemn the sons of royalty, but the
queen Bathilde would not permit such excesses to go un-
punished, and preferring that her children should be punished

in this world rather than they should be reserved for punishment hereafter, declared them incapable of succeeding to the
crown, and as the strength and corporeal power which had
served them to rebel against their father lay in their sinews,
she ordered that those of their arms should be cut, and that
insomuch they should be rendered impotent. This was done
accordingly, and they were then put into a small boat with
provisions, on the river Seine, without rudder or oars, assisted
only by one servant to minister to their wants. Confiding to
the divine protection, the boat drifted down the Seine until it
reached Normandy, where it stopped at the monastery of
Jumiéges.   When Saint Philibert the first abbot was informed
of this event, he went to visit them accompanied by his monks ;
being told who they were and the cause of their misfortune,
and admiring at the same time their manners and appearance,
he received them into the house, where, as the chronicle states,
they regained their health, and were instructed in monastic
discipline.

   Connected with Jumiéges, there are many peculiar traditions
and customs, among the latter the most singular is that of
" *le loup vert,*" but it would be foreign to the purpose to do
more than allude to it here.   The abbey has other claims to
celebrity, for it was here that Charles VII came to enjoy a few
days of solitude so necessary after the storms of a troubled
life.   He built a country house here, which, not more than
sixty years since, the monks used as a dormitory, and which
was then called "Old Charles VII."   The celebrated Agnes
Sorrel inhabited Mesnil at this time, and possessed all the
confidence and affection of which Charles was capable.   In
the beginning of January 1451, the garrison of Honfleur
having surrendered to the king, he went to pass the remainder
of the winter at Jumiéges.   It was there he had the misfortune
to lose the beautiful Agnes.   In her last moments she showed
great devotion and repentance, and died beloved by many
who had shared her liberality and kindness of heart.   Her
heart was deposited in the Abbey, her body was carried to
Loches according to her wish and placed in the choir of the

collegiate church. A monument was erected to her memory in both places. That at Loches was of black marble ornamented with the statue of Agnes in white marble, two angels supporting a pillar on which her head rested, with two lambs lying at her feet. On the monument was the following inscription in golden letters :—

> " *Cy gist noble damoiselle Agnes de Sorel, en son vivant dame de Beauté, Rocherie, etc. piteuse envers toutes gens, et qui largement donnoit de son bien aux Eglises et aux pauvres ; laquelle trépassa le neuvième jour de Février* 1449.
> *Priez Dieu pour le repos de l'ame d'elle. Amen."* (Deshayes).

The Prebendaries conceded the erection of the monument in gratitude for a sum of two thousand gold crowns which she had given them to purchase the lands of Fromanteau and of Bigorre, as well as some superb tapestry, jewels, and paintings. They had received all those gifts without scruple, but after the death of Charles VII, they pointed out to Louis XI, when visiting their Church, the tomb of their benefactress ; and like blundering courtiers, who, thinking to flatter the Prince, by acting as if the hatred which he had borne to her during life extended to her ashes, they begged him to permit them to have the monument removed out of the choir, pretending that it created scandal, and was prejudicial to their ceremonies. I consent, replied the monarch, indignant at their ingratitude ; but, you must first give up all that you have received from her. The royal answer effectually obviated every scruple, whether real or pretended, on the part of the cavilling priests, and the monument became an object of honour.

The tomb erected at Jumiéges was placed in the great church in the centre of the chapel of the Virgin ; it was of black marble and raised about three feet above the pavement. Formerly it was surmounted by a statue of white marble which represented Agnes on her knees holding a heart in her hands which she offered to the virgin, but this statue was destroyed by the Calvinists in the sixteenth century. The tomb of the Enervated was not more respected than that of Agnes Sorel. A number of statues raised in honour of the founders and benefactors of the Abbey, those for instance of Clovis II, Bathilde, Saint Philibert, Saint Hugh, Rollo Longsword, Charles VII, and Dagobert, were wantonly destroyed at the same time. The splendid roof was battered down for the sake of the lead to make bullets, the pews, altar, and ironwork were converted for purposes of warfare, and the great bell of the Abbey was sold to the proprietor of a cannon foundry at Rouen. To add to the sacrilege, the abbot took part with the revolutionary mob and actually joined in the work of destruction. (*Dibdin, Pic. tour.* vol. i, p. 112).

With this once famous Abbey, the Island of Hayling was long connected, and the abbots of Jumiéges were no ungentle masters. The grant by the Conqueror took place prior to the compilation of Domesday, as we shall find from the following entries, by which it will also be seen that William at that time held in his own hands the lands which had formed part of the estate of Harold.

· Hantescire the land of the king.
In Boseberg Hundred.

The king himself holds in Halingei two hides and a half. Leman held it of King Edward in parage. Harold took it from him, when he seized upon the kingdom and put it into his farm and it is yet there. It was then assessed at two hides and a half, now for nothing. The land there is one carucate and a half. In demesne there is one carucate and one villain and eight borderers, with half a carucate and one acre and a half of meadow. In the time of King Edward it was worth forty shillings, and afterwards twenty shillings, now seventy shillings. (*Domesday*, vol. i, fo. 38).

Hantescire, the Abbey of Saint Peter, of Winchester.
In Boseberg Hundred.

The monks of the bishopric of Winchester hold Helinghei,

1 Sᵗ Philbert. 2.3. Sᵗᵉ Austreberthe.

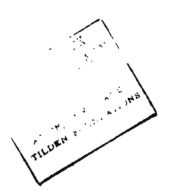

they always held it. In the time of King Edward it was taxed at five hides and now for four hides. The land is two carucates. There are there eleven villains with three carucates and a half and one acre of meadow ; there is wood for one hog. In the time of King Edward it was worth one hundred shillings, and afterwards four pounds, and now it is worth four pounds and ten shillings. (*Ibid.* fo. 43).

Hantescire, the land of Saint Peter of Jumiéges.
In Boseberg Hundred.

The Abbey of Jumiéges holds Helingey. Ulward held it allodially of Queen Eddid (Emma). It was then taxed for twelve hides, now for seven hides; the land is fourteen carucates. There are in demesne two carucates and twenty-three villains and twenty-seven borderers, with seventeen ploughs. There are three servants and a saltern of the value of six shillings and eight pence, and two fisheries of twenty pence and one acre of meadow. There is wood for the pannage of twenty hogs. In the time of King Edward, it was worth fifteen pounds, and afterwards ten pounds, now twelve pounds, and yet it renders fifteen pounds at farm.

The monks of the bishoprick of Winchester claim this manor because Queen Imma (Emma) gave the same to the church of Saint Peter and Saint Swythun, and then put the monks in possession of a moiety, the other moiety she demised to Ulward for his life, only so that after his death and burial the manor should revert to the monastery. And so Ulward held part of the manor of the monks until he died in the time of King William. This is so attested by Elsi, abbot of Ramsey, and by the whole hundred. (*Ibid.* fo. 43 b).

The saltern here mentioned is still in existence at Menge-ham, and the two fisheries are presumed to have been those of the eastern and western harbours, producing oysters, mullet, whiting, base, and other fish. Elsi here alluded to was appointed Abbot of Ramsey in 1080, and held it eight years, and to him a revelation was made at sea that the feast of the Conception of the Virgin should be celebrated. (*Rudborne,* p. 240). "Ramsey the rich," was a proverb in Huntingdon-

shire.   According to Fuller it was the Crœsus of all English
Abbies, for having but sixty monks to maintain therein, the
revenue amounted to £7000 a year or to £100 a year for
each monk, and £1000 a year for the abbot. (*Fuller's
Worthies, Huntingdon.*)

From Domesday we learn that three distinct portions of
Hayling are mentioned.   The king's land being that seized
by Harold and appropriated as part of that monarch's patri-
mony by the Conqueror.   The land of the monks of
Winchester, comprising that part of Havant manor granted to
them by Ethelred, and the land originally granted by Queen
Emma, being the larger part of the Island seized by William, and
granted after the conquest to the Norman Abbey of Jumiéges.

Very soon after the Abbey of Jumiéges had been established in its newly-acquired manor, and probably with a view
of obtaining a recognition of the original grant, a charter of
confirmation was sought from Henry I, and that king, mindful
of the dying injunction of William the Conqueror to favour
the religious houses of England and Normandy, yielded to
the wish and confirmed it in the following terms—

"Henry King of England to Anselm archbishop of Canter-
"bury, William bishop of Winchester, Henry de Port sheriff,
"and other his faithful men, French and English, of Hampshire,
"greeting: know ye that I grant to Saint Peter of Jumiéges,
"Haringey, and all things that pertain to it with sac and
"soc and thol and theam and infangenethef with all other
"customs, nor will I suffer that anyone take or diminish any-
"thing therefrom.   Witness, Robert Earl of Medelent, &c., at
"Winchester." (*Records of Court of Chan., Tower of London,
Anc. Chart.*, E. E. No. 8, 9.)

To this charter there is no date, but as Henry began to
reign in 1100, and Anselm, who was consecrated in 1093,
died in 1109, it was most likely granted soon after his acces-
ion.   Henry II ascended the throne in 1155, and confirmed
to Jumiéges the gifts which the Conqueror's munificence had
bestowed upon the Abbey.   He granted to the church of the
blessed Mary and Saint Peter of Jumiéges and the monks

there serving God, all the alms which were reasonably given to them in churches and lands and tithes and in all other things, to wit, of the gift of King William in England the greater part of the Island of Haringey, with the church and tithes of the whole island, except the tithes of pulse and oats in the land of the bishop of Winchester, and in the same island sac and soc and thol and theam and infangenethef with all other customs, and at Leuga near Saint Faiths half a hide, at Winterbornstoke the church and one carucate of land and five houses with the tithes of the whole parish. At Chiverton twenty-two houses and one carucate of land in demesne, and the church with the tithes of the whole parish and six chapels, to wit of Ammeleburg, and of Pelton and of Eston, and of the other Eston and of Feredon and of Wilton, and acquittance in all parts of England and of Normandy to the monks and their own servants, and things of the demesne of the church. Also to be quit of pannage in all their forests and acquittance in all England and Normandy of all things within and to the usage of the church appertaining. And he willed and commanded that the church of Jumiéges, and the monks of the same place, should have and hold all the before-named alms, with all their appurtenances in woods and plains, in meadows and pastures, in waters and mills, in vivaries and fisheries, in ways and paths, and in all other places and things to the same appertaining, well and in peace, freely and quickly, fully, entirely, and honorably, with all their liberties and free customs. This charter was witnessed by Rotrold archbishop of Rouen, and is dated from Rouen. (*Dug. Mon.*, vol. ii, p. 2, p. 1087.)

As we have seen that this Abbey had large possessions in the Island in the time of the Conqueror, the grants of Henry I and Henry II must have been charters of confirmation. The force of the words sac and soc, &c., in both grants is well known, but the terms in the last grant seem more particularly to demand consideration. It is evident that the king was aware that the Abbey was not owner of the lands of the whole Island, for he narrows his grant to the greater part of the Island in conformity with the return of its possessions in Domesday; but there is no such restriction in the words used to confer jurisdiction and manorial rights and franchises. This grant is also important as confirming to the Abbey without any larger words than those used to convey feudal jurisdiction the right of tithes throughout the Island. The exemption of the lands of the Bishop of Winchester from tithes, no longer exists, and probably was put an end to when the claim of every incumbent to the tithes of all lands within his parish was established.

I have mentioned in the account of Havant, the way in which the Bishop of Winchester had become possessed of the lands in Hayling held at Domesday by the monks of Saint Swythen at Winchester. Great disputes had occurred between the bishop and the monks in reference to the custody of the temporalities of the priory during a vacancy. By a composition mutually agreed upon, the prior and convent granted to the bishop and his successors for ever the manors of Droxford, Alverstoke, with Gosport and Havant, *with their tenants of Hayling* and the hamlet of Cnoel, and in return for this the bishop ceded all right during a vacancy, with the exception of the advowson of the priory, and subject to the maintenance of a servant by the priory, in recognition of the bishop's right of patronage. (*Annales eccl. Winton.*, p. 315.) This arrangement was confirmed by John de Pontissera in the year 1284, and stands recorded in the bishopric register of that year. These lands remained in the possession of the bishops of Winchester as forming part of the manor of Havant down to the year 1553, when they were with the manor let on lease, and were subsequently included in the enfranchisement made in the year 1827.

At some time in the early part of the reign of Henry III, and at all events previous to the year 1241 a priory was built in the Island, in order that the services of the church might be duly performed, and the revenues of the manor collected with regularity. The prior was appointed by, and dependent on the foreign house, and was removable at pleasure. In Rastall's entries, upon an aid being granted to the king, the prior of Hayling was summoned, and pleaded that the priory was alien and not conventual, and that all the priors of the same, from time whereof the memory of man ran not to the contrary, had been appointed (1 *Ed.* 1597, p. 28.) and removed at the motion and will of the Abbot of Saint Peter of Jumiéges in Normandy, and were not perpetual and not inducted. Of the priory itself no remains are at the present day to be found, but the site is well identified near Tourner Bury, on the south-eastern side of the high road leading to Mengeham and the beach by the traces of buildings which have from time time been discovered, and by the names of the closes in the vicinity, called Chappel park, Monk's and Abbot's land. Large stones have been ploughed up evidently part of a foundation, some hammer dressed, and some bedded in mortar, together with slabs of various sizes with the mortar still adhering to them. There were, not very many years since, two small buildings adjoining Tourner marsh, which were believed to have been used for stables, sloping pavements of smooth pebbles having been found in the course of making a garden there. The situation is quiet in the extreme, oaks which perhaps once sheltered the walls of the monastery are still to be seen, and there are artificial ponds at a convenient distance, which evidently served the purpose of fish stews for the religious inmates of the house, whilst a straight road communicates in something less than half a mile with the church of Hayling south.

From the *Notitia Monastica* we learn that the Priory became a cell of Benedictines to the foreign Abbey, the rule of which order was in substance as follows: The Abbot represented Christ; he called all his monks to council on important matters, and adopted afterwards the advice he thought best. Obedience, silence, humility, patience in all injuries, manifestation of all faults to the abbot, contentment with the meanest things, and employment were enjoined. No scurrility to be allowed, eyes to be inclined downwards, to rise to church two hours after midnight, to sleep clothed with their girdles on, the young and the old intermixed. Upon successless admonition and public reprehension, excommunication : and,

in failure of this, corporal punishment; the whole congregation
to pray for the incorrigible, and if successless, to proceed to
expulsion.   Children to be punished by fasting or whipping.
Habits and goods in the house to be in the hands of proper
officers, and the abbot to have an account of them.   No property.   Distribution according to the necessities of each.   The
monks to serve weekly and by turns at the kitchen and the
table.   At the end of their week, both he that left it and he
that began it, to wash the feet of the others, and on Saturday
to clean all the plates and linen.   Use of the baths, and flesh
for the sick ordered.   Rule mitigated to children and old
men who had to leave to anticipate the hours of eating.
Refectory in silence, and reading scripture during meals.
What was wanted, to be asked for by a sign.   Two different
dishes at dinner with fruit and one pound of bread a day for
both dinner and supper.   No meat but to the sick.   Three-
quarters of a pint of wine per day.   Immediate pardon to be
sought for a fault, breaking anything to be spontaneously
acknowledged before the Abbot and congregation.   Abbot
to give the signal for going to church, and nobody to sing or
read without his leave. Work from prime till near ten o'clock
from Easter till calends of October ; from ten to near twelve
reading.   After nones labour again till the evening ; from the
calends of October till Lent reading till eight A. M., then
tierce and afterwards labour till nones ; particular abstinence
in Lent from meat, drink, and sleep, and especial gravity.
Monks travelling to say the canonical hours wherever they
happen to be.   No other use than that of prayer to be made
of the church.   Strangers to be received with prayer, the
kiss of peace, prostration, and washing their feet as of Christ
whom they represented, then to be led to prayer, the scripture
read to them, after which the prior might break his fast.
Abbot's kitchen and the visitor's separate, that guests coming
at an unseasonable hour might not disturb the monks.   No
letters or presents to be received without the abbot's leave.
Novices to be tried by denials and hard usage before admission; a year of probation rule read to them in the interim
every fourth month admitted; by petition, laid upon the altar,

and prostration at the feet of all the monks. Parents to offer their children by wrapping their hands in the pall of the altar, promising to leave nothing to them, and if they gave any-thing with them, to reserve the use of it during their lives. When two monks met, the junior was to ask benediction from the senior, and when he passed by, the junior was to rise and give him his seat, nor to sit down till he bade him. The abbot to be elected by the whole society and plurality of votes, his life and prudence to be the qualifications. If pos-sible to prevent evagation, water, a mill, garden, oven, and mechanical shops to be within the house. Monks going on a journey to have the prayers of the house, and upon return pray for pardon for excesses on the way. No blows or excommunication without the permission of the abbot, mutual obedience, but no preference of a private person's command to that of a superior, prostration at the feet of the superiors as long as they were angry." (*Sanct. Patrum Reg. Monast.* Lom. 12mo, 1571, fo. 9, 51; *Concordia Regular.*)

As for the habits of the monks they were left to the dis-cretion of the abbot according to the nature of the country, as it happened to be hot or cold. In temperate climates a cowl and a tunic were sufficient, the cowl thicker for winter and thinner for summer, and a scapular to work in. The scapular was the upper garment during the time of labour which was put off, and the cowl worn during the rest of the day. Every one had two tunics and two cowls, either to change at night or to wash them. The stuff they were made of was to be the cheapest the country afforded. To the end that no man might have property of his own, the abbots found them with every thing that was necessary, that is beside the habit, a handkerchief, a knife, a needle, a steel pen and tables to write upon. Their beds were a mat, a straw bed, a piece of serge, a blanket and a pillow. Saint Benedict did not decide of what colour the habit should be, but it appears by ancient pictures that the garments worn by the first Benedic-tines were white, and the scapular black. (*Steevens.*)

Near the site of the ancient priory, evidently at some time connected with it and forming part of a wood, is a place called Tourner Bury, which has given rise to much dissertation, various suppositions having been entertained as to its origin, and the purposes for which it was originally made. It occupies a rising ground forming almost a circular vallum ; the diameter of its greatest width is 250 yards and of its narrowest 200 yards ; it is surrounded by a fosse, the vallum being about six feet high, the fosse the same ; but time has lessened the depth of the latter, the banks having washed into it and partially filled it up with leaves and decayed vegetable matter.   The interior space contains about three acres, and the furrows across it show that at one time it was under cultivation : there is timber upon it of recent growth, and upon the sides of the vallum are several oak and yew trees, perhaps coeval with the formation of the embankment.   No traces of any building, no bones or fragments of any kind have ever, that I am aware of, been found within its enceinte.

   Tourn signifies the sheriff's court, from attendance upon which only archbishops, bishops, abbots, priors, earls, barons, all religious men and women, and all such as had hundreds of their own, were exempt.   Bury signifies a town or inclosed place, from which the word Burgh is derived.   The tourn was the great court leet of the county of which the sheriff was the judge ; it took its name originally from the sheriff taking a tourn or circuit about his shire, and holding this court in each respective hundred.   By the statute of Magna Charta, chap. 35, it was enacted that no sheriff should make his tourn through a hundred but twice in a year, namely, once after Easter, and once after the feast of Saint Michael. His authority extended to treasons and felonies by the common law, as well as to the lowest offences against the king, as purprestures, seizure of treasure trove, of weights, estrays, wreck, &c. ; common nuisances, as selling victuals unfit for use, breaking the assize of bread and beer, keeping false weights and measures, and disturbances against the peace. By the universal common law of England, all men of the neighbourhood were bound to come up and be present upon every inquiry, whether of robbery or any other crime or offence.   The principle of local self-government through municipal action, was recognised and practised in every matter connected with the administration of justice, and every man (with the exceptions before mentioned) who did not attend was liable to a fine. About the reign however of Henry III, a sworn jury as a committee for the whole, began to be entrusted with the consideration of its offences, and its verdict to be accepted in the place and stead of the judgment of the whole. Previous to this time the duty of attendance being general, it followed that the assemblies were held in the open air, no building being large enough to hold the numbers who met together on these occasions. The parish church indeed was frequently used for the purpose, and so late as the reign of Henry III, a law suit was settled in Peter's church, Bristol, each party taking a solemn oath and agreeing to forfeit ten marks for every article of agreement which might be broken (*Smythe's Berkeley*, MSS. 119), but the order of Saint Benedict forbade the use of the church for any other purpose but for prayer. The Wittena-gemote or Saxon parliament so met upon Salisbury plain; on the creation of the Danish wapentakes, the chief of the wapentake whom we now call the high constable, as soon as he entered upon his office, appeared in the field on horseback with a pike in his hand; and all the chief men of the hundred met him there with their lances and touched his pike, which was the sign that they were firmly united to each other by the touching of their weapons. (*Fleta Liber.*) To a very late period the justices itinerant held their assize in the Strand of London, sitting on the stone steps by Somerset House, and to the present day there is a place in the Isle of Man called Tynewold Mount, to which the members of the Manx parliament go in procession to proclaim any new law or regulation to the people, who stand around with their heads uncovered while the edict is proclaimed in Manx and English. I am informed that Thornbury, on the banks of the Severn in Gloucestershire, was certainly used for the holding of the sheriff's tourn in former days, deriving its name from tourn, corrupted into Thourn or Thorn and bury, a town; and these circumstances coupled with the retention of the name, lead

one to think that after the place had served its original
purpose of defence, it was from its contiguity to the priory,
adopted for the gathering of the hundred on the tourn of the
Sheriff, which was held in Hayling down to the year 1781.

We have no account of Hayling in the *Hundred Rolls*,
which are very imperfect so far as relates to the county of
Southampton; but in the *Testa de Nevill* compiled in the latter
part of the reign of King Henry III and the commencement
of the reign of King Edward I it is stated, that the prior of
Hayling held the lands which he had in Helinge of ancient
feoffment, in pure alms of the lord the King in capite (*Com.
Suth*. No. 112), and that Ralph d' Anvers held two hides of
land in Helinge of ancient feoffment of the honour of
Gloucester, but by what service the jurors were ignorant
(*Suth*. No. 114). There is a further entry in reference to the
terra regis of Domsday, which it will be necessary to explain.

Upon Roger de Montgomery Earl of Shrewsbury and
Arundel, the Conqueror bestowed numerous manors and lands.
Bourne and Warblington were among the former, and the
latter included lands in Hayling. Like his royal master to
whom he was allied, he founded a monastery at Troarn in Normandy, and endowed it with considerable revenues. On the
death of William the Conqueror in 1087, and before the
celebration of the funeral solemnities, William Rufus his
second son came over into England, and by the assistance of
Lanfranke, a very powerful prelate, then archbishop of Canterbury, he obtained possession of the throne. The nobles were
rather disposed to have accepted Robert Duke of Normandy
the eldest son of the Conqueror, who was in Germany at the
decease of his father. Robert was in no way indisposed to
assert his title to the crown of England, and his designs were
furthered by his uncle Odo, Bishop of Baieux. The latter
fortified the castle of Rochester, and made forays throughout
the county of Kent. At his instigation Geoffrey, Bishop of
Constans and his nephew Geoffrey de Mowbray Earl of Northumberland sacked Bath, Berkeley, and a great part of
Wiltshire, and carried their spoil back to the castle of Bristol,
which they strongly fortified. Roger le Bygod ravaged the

county of Norfolk, retiring into Norwich; and Hugh de Grandesmel did the same in the county of Leicester.

Roger de Montgomery Earl of Shrewsbury assembled a large force at Shrewsbury from the borders of Wales, and in company with William, bishop of Durham, the King's household chaplain, Barnard of Hewmerch, Roger Lacie, and Rafe Mortimer, all of Norman or French extraction, invaded the country and made fearful havoc with fire and sword. They took and burnt the suburbs of Worcester, but the inhabitants with Bishop Wolstan at their head made a valiant defence, and sallying forth from the castle slew about five hundred men. A negociation was afterwards set on foot between William Rufus and Roger de Montgomery, and they were eventually reconciled in 1088 (*Hol.* vol. ii, p. 29). Upon the death of Roger de Montgomery he was succeeded by his second son Hugh, styled Earl of Shrewsbury and Arundel, who with Hugh Earl of Chester commanded the expedition against the island of Anglesey in 1098. They conquered the place, but the victory was stained with the prevailing cruelty of those days, Mathew Paris telling us that they put out the eyes of some, cut off the noses of others, and some they even mutilated (*Girald Cambr.*) It is also said that the Earl of Shrewsbury made a kennel for his hounds in the church of Saint Fridancus, but that in the morning they were all mad. Excited by the reports of the frightful atrocities which had been committed, a band of rovers from the Isle of Orkney under the command of one Magnus attacked the Earl of Shrewsbury; the latter was shot in the eye by an arrow from the bow of Magnus, which pierced his brain and his body fell overboard into the sea.

After the death of Hugh de Montgomery, Robert, according to some historians another son of Roger, and according to Simon Dunelm son of Hugh, who is said to have possessed the family property in Normandy, succeeded to the estates and honours of the Montgomeries in England. This Robert was generally called de Belesme or de Beliasmo, and in the following reign of Henry I in the year 1102, we find him conspiring against the crown, (*Hol.* vol. i, p. 50), fortifying the castles of Bridgnorth and Caircove in Wales, and placing the town of Shrewsbury with the castles of Arundel and Tickehill in a state of defence. He opened negociations with the Welshmen, but in the midst of his schemes he was by Henry proclaimed a traitor. Upon this Robert and his brother Arnold collected their Welsh and English forces, entered Staffordshire which they ravaged, and carried from thence into Wales as the place of the greatest security, a large body of prisoners, money, and cattle. In the mean time the king raised an army, and having besieged the castle of Arundel, left a force before the walls sufficient to reduce it. He then marched to Bridgnorth, sending the Bishop of Lincoln with a part of his army to Tickehill, and invested Bridgnorth in person with a very large force. Partly by threats and partly by solicitations, the Welshmen were induced to abandon the Earl and side with the royal army. Within thirty days after this, the king became master of all the castles held by the Earl, banished the latter for life and confined his brother Arnold in prison.

In the year 1104, Robert duke of Normandy being in England was, by fraudulent representations as it is generally believed, induced to give up the annual tribute of three thousand marks, agreed by Henry to be paid to him as the rightful heir to the crown of England. Upon the return of Robert to Normandy, an attempt was made, under colour of the fraud alleged to have been practised on him, to raise a quarrel between him and his brother Henry, and to seize Henry's Norman possessions. Robert was urged on by Robert de Belesme Earl of Shrewsbury and William Earl of Mortaigne, both of whom bore great personal hatred to Henry. The latter sent a large force over into Normandy and soon after followed them in person. He took Caen and Baieux and returned to England. Duke Robert followed him, and the brothers met at Northampton, but terms of arrangement not being agreed upon, Duke Robert returned to Normandy and prepared for the issue. King Henry followed him, and an engagement took place near the castle of Tenerchbray on the 27th September 1104. Duke Robert and the Earl of Mortaigne fought bravely, but were taken prisoners, together with William Crispine, William Ferries, Robert Estonhille the elder, four hundred men at arms and ten thousand footmen. (*Eadmerus.*) The Earl of Shrewsbury escaped by flight, but was afterwards taken prisoner. (*Will. Malm.*)

Robert Duke of Normandy was confined in Cardiff Castle until his death. No further mention is made of Robert de Belesme Earl of Shrewsbury, and it is generally supposed that he was imprisoned at Wareham in Dorsetshire, and that he died before the 22 Henry I, 1121, as in that year the title of Earl of Shrewsbury was borne by Warren, who held command of the marches, to prevent the incursions of the Welsh. (*Hol. Chron.* vol. ii. p. 11.)

Matthew Paris informs us, that Henry I gave the castle of Arundel in Sussex, and considerable possessions in that county, to Adeliza, his second queen, apparently for her dower, and this event happened no doubt soon after the attainder of Robert de Belesme. After the death of Henry, the Queen Adeliza married William de Albini, who, whilst residing at Arundel, had opportunities of affording protection to the Empress Maud, under circumstances of great difficulty; and it has been said that, in return for his services, he was by the empress created Earl of Arundel. This grant was, probably, confirmed by King Stephen, as the vicissitudes of fortune during the contest between Stephen and the Empress occasioned frequent changes in the disposition of their respective partisans, and compelled both the competitors for the throne to make extraordinary grants to their adherents. After the death of Stephen, Henry II succeeding to the crown, disputed many of the grants of Stephen; and there is extant a grant from that monarch to William de Albini, who is styled Earl of Arundel, of the castle and honour of Arundel, with other lands, to be held as his grandfather the king had held the same honour, making it in fact the subject of a re-grant after escheat.

At the time of the compilation of the *Testa de Nevill*, the

24

knights of the rape of Arundel, found by verdict that the rape of Arundel was held by the Earl of Arundel, nephew of the William Earl of Arundel above mentioned; and that the prior of Rungeton held four hides of land of ancient feoffment of the Earl of Arundel, and the earl of the king in the island of Heyling. (*Com. Suth.* No 102.) Rungeton or Runcton was a manor in Sussex, belonging to Roger de Montgomery, at the time of the general survey (*Dug. Mon. Ang.* vol. ii, p. 231), possessing a chapelry; and, upon the attainder of Robert de Belesme Earl of Shrewsbury, had passed to William de Albini, under the grant of Henry II. It would seem that the Earl of Arundel and the prior of Rungeton subsequently endowed the Abbey of Troarn, founded by Roger de Montgomery, with the lands in Hayling, and that this took place at some time previous to the 51st Henry III, 1266, because we find that William, described as abbot of the blessed monastery of Troarn and the convent of the same place, of the order of St. Benedict of the diocese of Bayeux in Normandy, granted and confirmed to John le Fauconer de la Wade all the lands and tenements which they had in the island of Heling, in the county of Southampton, to wit, whatsoever they had or should have there in demesnes, villenages, rents, tallages, aids, meadows, feedings and pastures, with villains, tenements and chattels, and with all escheats which could happen thereof without any reservation : to have and to hold to the same John, his heirs and assigns whomsoever, freely and quickly, well and in peace, in fee and inheritance for ever, with all commodities, liberties, and fee customs, and all other things to the aforesaid land and tenements appertaining, doing therefore to the chief lords of the same fee the service due and accustomed; and that the donation, grant, and confirmation of the charter might for ever remain firm, they caused the seal of the chapter and of the abbot to be affixed to it.

On the 4th January, 55 Henry III, 1270, that king inspected and confirmed the charter of the abbey of Troarn (*Tower Records, Chart. Rolls*, m. 9), having previously, in the 51st year of his reign, granted to John le Fauconer de la

Wade (*Chart. Rolls, Tower*, 51 Hen. III, m. 2) free warren in all his lands which he had within the island of Hayling; whilst to William Fauconer de la Wade he granted in the same year, that he and his heirs might for ever have wreck of the sea in the hundred of Boseberg, as well within as without the isle of Helingey, in the hundred aforesaid (*Chart. Rolls, Tower*, 51 Hen. III, m. 11); and also that he might carry away and make his advantage of the wreck, without the let or impediment of the crown, its sheriffs, bailiffs, or other ministers.   In the 33 Edward I, 1304, John le Fauconer died, and by inquisition taken in that year he was found to have died seized of five score acres of land, and of three hundred acres of land in the island of Heylinge (*Inq. p. mort. J. le Fauconer*, No. 44), the quantity (taking the hide at one hundred acres) exactly tallying with that held by the priory of Rungeton.

The grant of free warren to John le Fauconer contained no words of perpetuity, and consequently ceased at his death. The grant of wreck to William Fauconer, which bore date at Kenilworth, on the 5th December, was limited to him and his heirs; and, for some reason which does not appear, but most probably from the claim of the abbot of Jumiéges to the franchise as appurtenant to his manor, it does not seem to have been held valid; because I find that John le Botiller, who, under this title, assumed to be entitled to wreck in the 9 Edward II, 1315, impleaded John Oede and five others at Westminster, in the term of St. Michael (*Abb. plac. rot.* 18), for the seizure of five tuns of wine at Emsworth.   The grant to William Fauconer " of the wreck of sea in the hundred of " Boseburgh, as well within the island of Helingeye as without, " within the hundred aforesaid," was produced; but the jury found that the men were not guilty of any transgression, and it may therefore be presumed that the grant was invalid, or that there was a prior charter to some other grantee, particularly as the spot where the wine was found lay within the manor of Warblington, the lands of which were entitled to wreck, as declared in the return of the Inquisition of the 3 Charles, 1627.

There was some considerable litigation subsequently about the lands granted to John le Fauconer, arising partly from the fact that they were those very lands which had belonged to Harold, and were of the tenure of ancient demesne; for in the 9 Edward II, 1315, John le Botiler of Wymering and Joan his wife were attached, to answer William le Younge, Roger Gulderbrugg, Robert William, Robert le Hayward, William Thomas, Thomas Herbard, Robert Danyel, William de Istock, Richard Silvester, John le Ken, Walter Hamond, and William Cantelo, men of the said John and Joan of the · manor of Hayling, which was of the ancient demesne of the crown of England, as it was asserted, of a plea, wherefore they required from the said men other customs and other services than they ought to do, and than their ancestors, tenants of the same manor, had been accustomed to do in the times when the same manor was in the hands of the progenitors of the lord the king, formerly kings of England, against the king's prohibition. The tenants complained, that whereas they and their ancestors, holding the tenements which they then held in the time when the manor was in the hands of the progenitor of the king, held their tenements by certain services, every tenant in the time of King William the Conqueror being accustomed to hold one messuage and one virgate of land by the certain service of five shillings and eight pence farthing by the year, and by suit at the court of Hayling from three weeks to three weeks, that after the death of an ancestor they used to give half a mark for entry upon every acre of land, and after the death of a tenant the best beast for a heriot, and that they ought not to be tallaged; but when the lord the king tallaged his demesnes, by which services the tenements had been held until the said John le Botiler and Joan his wife required other customs and services not due from them, as from every one holding an acre of land after the death of an ancestor one mark ransom of flesh and blood at their will, tallaging them high and low at will with other services, grievously distraining them from day to day to do the same, in consequence of which a prohibition had been delivered to John and Joan, which the latter had disregarded in contempt of the king, of one thousand pounds, and damage of the tenants of five hundred pounds.

John and Joan justified their conduct, and prayed that the tenants might prove their tenure of ancient demesne. Whereupon the treasurer and chamberlains were commanded to examine the book of Domesday, which having been duly certified and read, proving the lands to have been those of Harold and of ancient demesne, John and Joan then urged that the lands were at one time in the hands of the abbot of Troarn, who enfeoffed John le Fauconer, after whose death they came into the hands of William le Fauconer, brother of John, from whom they descended to John le Fauconer, father of Joan the wife of John le Botiler; that in all former times, every one holding one virgate of land gave sixteen shillings by the year, with suit of court as often as they were warned the night before, and tallage four times a year at forty shillings, and after the death of a tenant the best beast in the name of a heriot; and upon the entry of the heir twenty shillings for every acre of land, of every tenant on marriage of his daughter two shillings, to come to the scotale of the lord every tenant for himself and his wife giving them two pence, and every one holding a habitation to be reeve and harvester.

The issue came on for trial, the tenants appeared by Richard de Wodecroft their Attorney; John le Botiler absented himself, but Joan appeared and maintained that the manor was of her inheritance, that John her husband had pleaded in disinherison of her, and she prayed leave to defend her right which was granted. Upon which she stated that where John le Botiler had claimed for a virgate of land sixteen shillings by the year, with suit of court tallage four times in the year at forty shillings, a best beast heriot upon death, and upon entry of the heir twenty shillings for every acre of land, on marriage of a tenant's daughter two shillings, attendance at the Scotale of the lord, payment of two pence by a tenant and his wife, and service as reeve and harvester from every inhabitant, he had not rightfully required from them the services stated, but in lieu of the same, she stated that every one holding one messuage and one virgate of land should pay

five shillings and eight pence farthing, with suit of court when
warned the previous night, on death of an ancestor upon entry
for every acre at the will of the lord, and the best beast for a
heriot, ransom of blood for marrying his sons and his
daughters at the will of the lord, tallage every year at the
will of the lord, every tenant, reeve, harvester, and wrecker
every year at the will of the lord, making carriage with his
horses of all victuals as corn, oats, &c. from the Manor of
Hayling to Andover, a distance of thirty miles, and elsewhere
within thirty miles as assigned on being warned the night
before; finding also for the lord throughout the autumn of
their sons and daughters to perform his work as much as he
would for two shillings and sixpence. She added that upon
the refusal of the tenants to do these services she had distrained upon them.

Upon a further hearing of the case the tenants absented
themselves, and a verdict confirming the services claimed by
Joan was recorded. John le Botiler died some time previous
to the 3d of Edward II, 1309, and John le Botiler his son
succeeded him, upon whose death in the 6th of Edward III,
1351, an inquisition was taken, and he was found to have
died seized of the lands in Hayling (*Inq. p. mort. J. le Botiler,
secd Nos.* Numb. 23) as trustee for the prior and Convent of
de Calceto, or the causeway near Arundel. In the 9th and
10th of Edward IV, 1468-9, Sir Richard Dalingrigge died
seized of the same estate, described as lands in Estoke, Northstoke, and Westhay, in Hayling, and was so found by
inquisition taken upon his decease (*Inq. p. mort. Ric. Dalingrigge,* No. 48), but whether as trustee for the convent of de
Calceto or not, does not appear. It is probable however that
this was the case. Sir Richard Dalingrigge left an only
daughter and heiress Philippa (*Sussex, Geneal. Berry*), who
married Sir Thomas Lewknor and carried Bodiam Castle in
Sussex, and other large possessions into his family. Sir
Thomas was attainted of high treason by Richard III, and
thereupon Bodiam Castle, the lands in Hayling and various
manors escheated into the hands of the crown. If not held
by Sir Thomas Lewknor at the time of his attainder, they
still formed part of the possessions of de Calceto.

In the year 1524, Cardinal Wolsey procured a Bull from Pope Clement the Seventh, and a licence from the king for the suppression of eighteen smaller monasteries, for the foundation of his college at Oxford (*Dall. West Sussex*, p. 295), among which were Beyham and de Calceto, in the county of Sussex. Upon the cardinal's disgrace they were seized into the hands of the crown, where they remained until the twenty-second year of the reign. The greater part was then granted to Lucy, fourth daughter of John Marquis of Montacute (*Ibid.*); but in the 6 Edward II, 1451, upon an inquisition taken after the death of William Pounde, a fine of the 34 Henry VIII, 1542, was recited between Wayte and Pounde, being a settlement of the lands in Estoke, Northstoke, and Westhay, in the island of Hayling, and in Southwood and Northwood there. (*Hayling Records.*) The name of the former occurs as lessee of the Bishop of Chichester, at Selsey in Sussex; and as the keeper of the park there in the reign of Henry VIII; and it also appears that Richard Pounde of Drayton, in the county of Hants, son of Anthony and grandson of William Pounde, married Elizabeth, daughter of William Wayte, and dying without issue left two sisters, Honora and Mary Pounde, his coheirs. (*Pounde Pedigree.*) The latter married Edward White, sheriff of Hants, eldest son of John White, of the body to King Henry VIII, grantee of the priory of Southwick, on departure of the canons, and the former married Henry Ratcliff Earl of Sussex. The lands in Hayling fell to the share of Honora; and in Hilary Term, 3 Elizabeth, 1560, a fine was levied between Sir Humphry Ratcliff, knight, and Sir John Ratcliff, knight, and Sir Henry Ratcliff, knight, Earl of Sussex and his wife Honora, of Northstoke, Eastoke, and Westhay in the county of Southampton. On the 1st November, 39 Elizabeth, 1597, a conveyance, by bargain and sale, was executed by Sir Robert Ratcliff, Earl of Sussex, to whom the lands had passed, in favour of Jonas Lattness, his servant and secretary, a fine accompanied it: the property being described as the capital messuage called Eastock, within the island of Hayling, containing by estimation two hundred acres, or thereabouts; and the manorial rights of Northstoke,

Eastoke, and Westhay, being reserved to the grantor. On the 20th November, 41 Elizabeth, 1599, a further conveyance was executed by the Right Honourable Robert Earl of Sussex, Viscount Fitzwalter, Lord Egremont, Thomas Kemp, and Thomas Kirby, to Jonas Lattness, of the manor seignory or lordship of Northstoke, Eastoke, and Westhay. This conveyance was enrolled in Chancery; and a further fine was levied between the Right Honourable Robert Ratcliff Earl of Sussex, Viscount Fitzwalter, Lord Egremont, Thomas Kemp, and Thomas Kirby of the one part, and Jonas Lattness of the other part. On the 17th of January 1630, a conveyance of the estate was executed by Harrison Lattness, son of Jonas Lattness, to Thomas Peckham, of London, in which the parcels were described as the manor-seignory or lordship of Northstoke, Eastoke, and Westhay, with the appurtenances in the island of Hayling; and Lattness covenanted against all incumbrances, "except the rents and services due to the chief lord of the fee." (*Report of Trial, Hellyer* v. *Miller.*)

Thomas Peckham, by indenture bearing date the 20th December 1665, in consideration of £1,100, enfeoffed and confirmed the estate described as the manor seignory or lordship of Northstoke, Eastoke, and Westhay, with the appurtenances in the island of Hayling, together with the farm of Eastoke, to John Peckham of Rumboldswyke, in the county of Sussex, his son, his heirs, and assigns for ever; "to be " holden of the chief lord or lords of the fee or fees of the " premises by the rents and services, therefore due and of " right accustomed." By lease, bearing date the 23d Jan. 1704, John Peckham demised half an acre of land in Westhay in the parish of Northwood, to one Edward Cooke of Havant, for a term of one thousand years. By lease, bearing date 6th July 1748, Peckham Williams, to whom the estate passed, demised to Thomas Miles and Robert Barber of Hayling, for the term of twenty-one years, a parcel of ground called Northside, otherwise the Small Mersh, containing, by estimation, five acres, then lately at the cost and charge of him Peckham Williams, converted into a saltern, and at that time used for making salt therein, situate on the south side of the island of Hayling, and the edifice then lately erected by him Peckham Williams, and used as a salthouse for the boiling, converting, and stowing of the salt there to be made, together with the implements and utensils for making the salt.

Peckham Williams, by his will bearing date the 11th April 1777, devised the property to John Williams his son-in-law, and by an act of Parliament, passed in the 42 George III, cap. 53, intituled "An Act for vesting part of the estates of "John Williams, Esquire, devised by the will of Peckham "Williams, Esquire, deceased, in trustees, to be sold for dis- "charging an incumbrance thereon," it was enacted, that the manor seignory or lordship of Northstoke, Eastoke, and Westhay, and the farm and lands called Eastock in the parish of Southwood, within the isle of Haling, then in the tenure of John Hellyer, at the rent of one hundred and five pounds per annum, and the salterns, then in the tenure of James Eyles, at the rent of fifteen pounds per annum, together with various other estates out of the island, should, after the passing of the Act, vest in George White Thomas and William Marsh, upon trust, with the consent in writing of John Williams, for the purposes of sale. (*Williams' Estate Act.*)

In pursuance of this power, and by indenture bearing date the 31st August 1804, and other indentures bearing date the 14th and 15th November 1821, the estate was conveyed to Elizabeth, the wife of Miles Poole Penfold (a daughter of Peckham Williams), for life, with remainder to the use of the appointee of Elizabeth Penfold, with remainder to the use of Elizabeth Penfold, her heirs and assigns for ever. (*Williams' Estate Act.*)

Miles Poole Penfold and his wife suffered a recovery in 1821; the former died, and was buried at Farnham, on the 20th October 1837: and Elizabeth Penfold, by her will bearing date the 23d January 1841, after disposing of a part of her property, devised her manors, or reputed manors, and the residue of her real and personal estate to her great nephew, John Leigh Hollest, absolutely. She died shortly afterwards. Hollest, in the month of July 1842, took the name of Williams, and by an indenture bearing date the 27th

April 1845, the so called manor of Northstoke, Eastoke, and Westhay, with the Eastoke farm and lands, and the saltern, were conveyed to Thomas Harris of Donnington, the present proprietor. This concludes the descent of the greater portion of the lands originally belonging to Harold, with the rest still paying the lady's silver ; and we will now return to speak of those which were held by the Abbey of Jumiéges.

In the 26 Henry III, 1241, there was a very grievous dispute between the prior of Hayling and the vicar of the parish, the whole island at this, and for a long time subsequently, forming only one parish,　In the pleas held at Westminster, in eight days of St. Michael, before Robert de Lexington and his fellows, in the 26th and in the beginning of the 27th year of the reign, Master Nicolas de Rye was attached to answer the prior of Helegey, proctor of the abbot, and convent of Gymeges of a plea, wherefore he prosecuted his plea in the Court Christian, concerning the church of Helegey, for the tithes of the whole island, which the abbot and convent claimed to have of the gift of the king's predecessors, and whereof the lord the king was patron. The prior complained, that whereas the abbot and convent had been seized of the church and the tithes from the conquest of England by the gift of King William, under his charter, and under the charter of King Henry I, which he then produced, and which testified to that effect, and had always theretofore been in peaceable possession of the same; Master Nicolas against the gift and charters of the crown, and against the prohibition of the lord the king, and in prejudice of his patronage, had prosecuted his plea in the Court Christian concerning the church and tithes of Hayling against the said abbot and convent.

The prior laid his damages at £100 ; Master Nicolas appeared, and denied that he had prosecuted any plea in the Court Christian, touching the church or tithes after the royal prohibition ; but he maintained that he was the rector of the church, instituted by the Bishop of Winchester, and that he was in possession of all the tithes as belonging to his church, of which Anketil his predecessor had also been seized. The prior contended that Nicolas was only entitled to the vicarage, and that the abbot and convent were the parsons, and had the church to their proper use of the gifts before mentioned. He also proffered the charter of Godfrey de Lucy, bishop of Winchester, during the reign of King John, which witnessed that he, by intuition of divine piety, had granted, and by his charter confirmed, in pure and perpetual alms, to the monks of Jumiéges the church of Ilelegeye, as they possessed the same of the gift of King William, with all things to the same appertaining; saving the authority and dignity of the church of Winchester and the episcopal rights. Pending the judgment of the court, Nicolas was prohibited from prosecution, and ordered to give absolution to those whom he had excommunicated, and it was also decreed that mutual restorations should be made by Nicolas and the prior.

Master Nicolas, however, was not disposed to acquiesce in the prohibition, and the prior was obliged to complain that Nicolas had not caused him to be absolved, nor done restitution for the trespass; that notwithstanding he acknowledged the prior to be the parson of the church, to have been instituted by the lord the pope, and to be entitled to the tithes as belonging to his church, yet that he had prosecuted the said plea after the prohibition of the lord the king, and that he had done so in prejudice of the lord the king, as the aforesaid priory was founded of the alms of the lord the King. Master Nicolas was put under restraint, and afterwards came and acknowledged that he had no right to demand the tithes of the church of Haylinge, for which he had contended against the prior and convent; that he would be contented with the portion possessed by Anketil his predecessor, that he would give up all the instruments in his possession within fifteen days of St. Martin, and that he would cause all excommunication on account of the cause to be absolved within the said term, and he confirmed his submission by a deed delivered to the prior.

It is evident from these proceedings that the prior had obtained his position by means of the privilege, claimed and exercised by the popes of Rome, who assumed the power of providing a successor to a benefice, or other ecclesiastical preferment, before a vacancy occurred.   By these provisions of the papal see, patrons of preferments were deprived of their patronage, and in all the best livings throughout England foreigners were introduced, so that by an inquisition taken in the year before this trial occurred, the ecclesiastical revenues of Italians in England amounted to 70,000 marks; whereas the royal income was barely 20,000 marks per annum.   The evils resulting from this state of things grew at last to an intolerable pitch in the reign of Edward III.; a statute was passed to prevent such provisions for the future, but it was found to be inoperative.   New statutes, each more stringent, were passed in various successive reigns; but the reformation in the time of Henry VIII. was alone sufficient to put a final stop to the practice.

About forty years before the date of these proceedings, Hubert, Archbishop of Canterbury, at a council held at Westminster, decreed, that priests should have power before autumn of excommunicating those who withheld the payment of their tithes, and also of absolving all such according to ecclesiastical form.   Master Nicolas imagined himself rector instead of vicar; and in the idea that the prior was defrauding him of his just dues, he thundered forth the censures of the church against his superior, and excommunicated him.   It was not a very usual step to take even in those days; and Master Nicolas must have had some confidence in his own powers to venture upon a quarrel where the odds were so much against him.   The priory of Hayling is first mentioned in this record; and there is little doubt but that it was built in this monarch's reign, as the prior pleads, that it was founded of the alms of the Lord the King—refering apparently to Henry III. the then ruling sovereign.

Whether the abbot and convent of Jumiéges had rightfully been seized of the whole of the tithes under the grant of Henry II, may admit of some doubt, as will be seen hereafter; but the question, which was one of considerable importance to Jumiéges, was soon afterwards set at rest by an application on the part of the abbot to the papal see for a grant of one-third part of the tithes which was conceded, and for a final termination of the disputes in reference to the amount of interest possessed by the abbey in the church and tithes of Hayling, which also received attention from his • holiness.

In the year 1253, Pope Innocent issued a Bull, addressed to the beloved sons the elect of Winchester, the dean and wardens of the Friars Minors, in reference to the church of Hayling. It recited, that the abbot and convent of Jumiéges, of the order of St. Benedict, in the diocese of Rouen, having alleged that they had, from time whereof the memory of man had run not to the contrary, received two parts of all the tithes in the church of Hayling, in the diocese of Winchester, in which they possessed the right of patronage, and that he the pope, at their petition, had granted to them, of his free grace, the same church with the other part, which Nicolas de Rye, the rector, then received, to retain to their own proper use after the cession or death of the same rector; so never-theless that in the same church a perpetual vicar should be appointed, to whom a fit portion of the profits of the same should be assigned for his maintenance, and for the support of the episcopal, archidiaconal, and other charges of the same church. And because dispute might arise in reference to the amount of such portion, he committed to the discretion of the dean and wardens, that upon considering the means of the church they were to tax the same portion by the authority of the pope, as according to the will of God it should seem fit to their circumspection to be done, restraining impugners by ecclesiastical censures, and setting aside all appeal. And if all could not be present at the execution of the mandate, two should be sufficient for the purpose.

This Bull was dated from Assessum, the seventeenth kalends of October, in the eleventh year of the pontificate. (*Appropriatio ecclesie de Hailinge.*)

By the authority, therefore, of the papal mandate, the dean and wardens attended personally at Hayling, and, after con-

sidering the means of the church, did, "with the counsel of
prudent men," tax and ordain the perpetual vicarage of the
church of Hayling, in the following manner, viz. That the
perpetual vicar for the time being should have the whole
• court, with the houses and appurtenances of the same court,
which Nicholas de Rye had formerly held, and had been
accustomed to have; and that he should also have all the
arable and uncultivated lands, with all their appurtenances,
which Nicolas de Rye then held (all the tenants with their
tenements which he had, excepted). And that he should have
all oblations and obventions, with other profits of the altar
and the small tithes of the whole island of Hayling; and
whatever appertained to the parochial right, whether it consisted in personal or real tithes, except the tithes of sheaves,
corn, and pulse, and the tithes arising from the court or
demesne of the abbot and convent of Jumiéges, and of the
prior of Hayling, which they decreed should be free from the
payment of tithes, unless they newly acquired any possessions
or anything were added to their demesne, whereof small tithe
had been accustomed to be given. That the abbot and convent of Jumiéges, or their proctors for the time being, should
have and freely receive all the great tithes of the whole island
of Hayling, which consisted in all kinds of corn and pulse,
except the tithes of the demesne lands of the vicar, which
they decreed should be free from the payment of tithes, and
that they should have all the tenants with their tenements
which Nicolas de Rye had formerly used. They also decreed
that the vicar for the time being, in the church of Hayling,
should bear the episcopal, archidiaconal, and all other charges
due, ordinary and accustomed; and that their taxation and
ordination might "obtain the force of perpetual stability,"
they thereto affixed their seals at Hayling on the Sunday next
after the Nativity of our Lord, in the year of grace, 1253.
(*Taxatio Vicarie de Hailing, apud Winton. quat.* 37.)

Under this appropriation, therefore, the vicarage of Hayling
was created and endowed. It is matter of observation, that
the bishop of the diocese is in no way mentioned or alluded
to in either of the documents; but the jurisdiction which is

now exercised by the ordinary of a diocese used at the period of which we are speaking, to be enjoyed by the pope, who, as supreme ordinary, claimed to himself a paramount jurisdiction under which he made visitations, corrections, dispensations, and tolerations within every diocese of the realm, and took from the bishops whatever he pleased. In consequence of this assumption of power he used to make appropriations, as in the present instance, wholly irrespective of the bishop, which were held to be valid. In a *quare impedit*, brought by the Earl of Salisbury against the prior of Montague, a case of the 29 Edward III was cited, where an appropriation was pleaded to have been made by the apostle, with the assent of the king, without mention of the ordinary; it was said that the pope was called by the name of "Apostle," and the appropriation was confirmed. And the pope used to make provisions until he was restrained by the statute of 25 Edw. III, 1350, which provision was a designation of the person who should be incumbent, and an admission, institution, and induction of him without application to the bishop, so that his authority became almost absolute, and bound the bishop as his inferior in all his acts. Such authority and jurisdiction as the pope used to exercise within this realm, was acknowledged by the parliament in the 25 Henry VIII, 1533, and in other subsequent statutes to be in King Henry VIII, so that he might lawfully exercise such jurisdiction as the pope had used, or had been accustomed to exercise within this realm.

It is evident, upon an examination of the papal appropriation by Innocent, that the abbot and convent of Jumiéges were legally possessed of two parts of all the tithes in the Island of Hayling, and of the right of patronage under their original charter from William the Conqueror, confirmed in the reigns of Henry I and Henry II. It is also evident that the other, or third part alluded to, as then being in the possession of Nicolas de Rye, the rector under the institution of the Bishop of Winchester, had been granted to the abbot and convent in reversion upon the decease of the rector, and probably consisted of the tithes of pulse and oats excepted in the charter of Henry II, which the pope had wrested from the hands of the bishops of Winchester; and this being so, it follows that upon the death of the rector they would become entitled to the tithes great and small of the whole island. Out of this, therefore, the vicarage was carved; the endowment of which consisted of the tithes of hay, the small or ordinary vicarial tithes, the usual oblations and obventions, the rector's residence with the glebe, and from entries on the court rolls and presentments at the visitations, in reference to the mortuaries, it may be presumed that they were left as before, payable to the prior in right of the abbot and convent of Jumiéges.

There is a curious fact to be gleaned from these proceedings bearing upon the original endowment of the church. In the petition presented to Pope Innocent by the abbot and convent of Jumiéges, the claim of the house to two parts of the church and tithes is founded upon the charter of William the Conqueror; that of the third part resting upon a grant obtained from the papal see, without reference to the charter of Henry II. In the suit between the prior of Hayling and Nicolas de Rye, the former maintained in his plea, that the abbot and convent were the parsons, and had been seized of the church and tithes from the Conquest, and that the grant of the Conqueror had been confirmed by the charter of Godfrey de Lucy, Bishop of Winchester, which he tendered as evidence in support of his claim. There is little doubt but that the fact was in truth as pleaded by the prior, and that for some reason the bishop's confirmation was suppressed on the application to Pope Innocent, because I find a direct corroboration of it in an entry in the chartulary of Shene, detailing the nature of certain records then in the possession of the abbey. It runs as follows:—

" The church of Hayling and chapel of Northwood.

" Also the appropriation and confirmation thereof by
" Geoffrey Bishop of Winchester, and pope's bull of con-
" firmation.

" Taxation of the vicarage of Hayling."

Now the taxation was of course that of Pope Innocent, in the year 1253. The "Geoffrey" must have been Godfrey de Lucy, who was consecrated 1st November 1189, and died in 1204, no other bishop of Winchester bearing a similar name; but on what ground the pope's bull of confirmation was superseded by that of 1253 I have hitherto been unable to discover.

It is not improbable but that some compensation was rendered to the see of Winchester for the tithes, which are presumed to have been taken from it and conferred by the pope upon the abbey of Jumiéges, since I have met with mention about this time of a charter of the Bishop of Winchester of quit claim of a certain part of the island of Hayling, a con-firmation by the Bishop of Winchester to the Prior of Hayling of tithes and of tenants, and a charter of Henry Bishop of Winchester upon the quit claim of a certain part of the island of Hayling, concerning which part a controversy had arisen between the church of Winchester and the church of Jumiéges. (*Chart. of Shene.*) This latter charter I take to have been granted by Henry Woodlock, who was consecrated in 1304, and died in 1316.

Among the pleas of juries and assize held before Salomon de Rochester and his companions, justices itinerant at Winchester, on the octave of St. Martin, in the 8 Edward I, 1279, the Abbot of Jumiéges was summoned to answer the lord the king by what warrant he claimed to have free warren in all his demesne lands in Hayling without the will of the lord the king and his predecessors. The abbot, by his attorney, answered, that he and all his predecessors had had free warren in his demesne lands, so that no one might enter into the same to chase or to take anything which to warren pertained, without the will of him and his predecessors. The knights summoned to try the issue between the crown and the abbot found that the abbot and his predecessors, from time whereof the memory of man had run not to the contrary, had had free warren in all their demesne lands, and that no one had entered into the same to chase or to take anything

which to warren pertained in the time of the abbot or his
bailiff; and upon this verdict the abbot was confirmed in his
franchise.

This right of free warren had been the subject of a charter
in the reign of Henry I (*Cartul. of Shene*); but it could only
have been intended to take effect by way of confirmation,
because the grant is not alluded to in the plea of the abbot,
and because the latter justified by general prescription
and not by charter; and we may assume that it had been
exercised by the Conqueror, and that it had passed from
him with the manor to the abbey of Jumiéges. It was a franchise highly coveted when war and the chase engrossed all the
time of the nobility, and was not unacceptable to ecclesiastics,
who hunted like laymen, and whose bishops partook of the
pleasures of the field when making a progress through their
respective dioceses. A kennel of hounds formed part of the
necessary establishment of a bishop, and upon his decease the
"*muta canum*," with various articles of his attire and plate,
formed the mortuary or death-offering to the crown. Free
warren was the right of the lord, exclusive of all other persons,
to keep and take birds of game and animals of chase within
the ambit indicated by the terms of the grant. All dogs
within a manor where the right existed were brought to the
court and lawed, that is, several of the nails and claws of
the fore feet were cut off, so as to disable them from following hares or deer; and in the time of the Conqueror the
penalty upon offenders sporting within a warren was loss of
eyes at least, and sometimes mutilation. (*Baker's Chron.* p. 29;
Matt. Westm. p. 9.) The extent of the warrens of the more
powerful of the nobility was in some instances very great,
that of Stanstead for instance, in our own neighbourhood,
reaching to the forest of Arundel, and exercised in the park
at Goodwood down to the death of Mr. Barwell, when the
right was released for a pecuniary consideration.

William de Whitewey, parker of Stanstead, was accused
before the Treasurer and Barons of the Exchequer of certain
trespasses committed by him in the park whilst the same was

in the hands of King Edward I, by reason of the infancy of Edmund de Arundel, son and heir of Richard Fitzalan, then late Earl of Arundel, and being convicted by a verdict of the country, he was, by judgment of the Court of Exchequer, committed to the Tower of London, where he remained for sentence four years, after which he was brought before the court, the judgment was pronounced, and the remainder of the sentence ordered to be finally executed. (*Trin. Brevia*, 2 E. 2 Rot. 86*b*.)

About the period when the plea of *quo warranto* was tried, the king's son, afterwards Edward II, broke into the park of the Bishop of Chester, for which he was committed to prison, and Piers Gaveston, his companion, banished the realm; and to show to what an extent the matter was at times carried, the Bishop of Chichester, so late as the year 1471, addressed a special mandate to the Dean of Boxgrove, and to all his rectors, vicars, &c., in these words—" We have learnt by " report and from persons worthy of credit, that certain persons, " sons of damnation, seduced by the spirit of the devil, laying " aside the fear of God, whose names and persons we know not, " did, on the 31st day of January, come by night to our park " at Selsey, with hunting dogs, nets, arrows, and other arms " and instruments, and did invade and break into our said park, " and did presume to chase, kill, and carry away the deer and " other wild beasts in the said park; therefore all such " hunters, chasers, and wasters are adjudged to have incurred " the penalty of excommunication, by bell, book, and candle, " and the ceremony is required to be performed in every church " of the deanery." (*Dall. West. Sup.* p. 11.)

We think lightly in these days of ecclesiastical censure, but it was an engine of great and fearful power in the heyday of the Roman Catholic Church. It consisted of the greater and lesser censure: by the former, a person was excluded from the communion of the church, from the company of the faithful, and from the performance of any legal act; the latter merely debarred him from the service of

the church.   An excommunicated person could not serve
upon juries, nor be a witness in any court, nor bring an
action, and by the ecclesiastical law he was not permitted to
have Christian burial.   The form of excommunication is given
in Spelman (*Gloss.* p. 205); and, to show the nature of the
weapon wielded by Master Nicolas and the Bishop of Chichester,
I subjoin it *verbatim* :—

   " By the authority of God, the Father Omnipotent, and of
" the Son, and of the Holy Ghost, and of all the assembly of
" saints, and of the holy and undefiled Virgin Mary, the mother
" of God, and of all the heavenly virtues of angels, archangels,
" thrones, dominions, powers, cherubim and seraphim, and of
" the holy patriarchs and prophets, and of the apostles and
" evangelists, and of the holy innocents who only are thought
" worthy to sing the new song in the presence of the Lamb,
" and of the holy martyrs, holy confessors, and holy virgins,
" and of all the saints and elect of God, We do excommuni-
" cate and anathematize [such an one], and do sequester him
" from the limits of the Holy Church of God, that he may be
" delivered to be tormented by eternal punishments, with
" Dathan and Abiram, and with those who say to the Lord
" God, Depart from us, we will not the knowledge of thy
" ways ; and as fire is extinguished by water, so may his light
" be extinguished for ever and ever, unless he repent and return
" to satisfaction.   Amen !   May God the Father, who created
" man, curse him.   May the Son of God, who died for man,
" curse him.   May the Holy Ghost, who is poured forth in
" baptism, curse him.   May the Holy Cross, which Christ
' triumphing over the enemy ascended for our salvation, curse
" him.   May the holy and perpetual Virgin Mary, the mother
" of God, curse him.   May Saint Michael, the receiver of
" holy souls, curse him.   May all angels, archangels, princi-
" palities and powers, and all the army of the heavenly host,
" curse him. May the worthy company of patriarchs and pro-
" phets curse him. May the holy John, the forerunner and prin-
" cipal baptist of Christ, curse him.   May Saint Peter and Saint
" Paul and Saint Andrew, and all Christ's apostles and other
" disciples, and those four Evangelists who by their preaching

" converted the world, curse him. May the glorious assembly
" of martyrs and confessors, who are found acceptable to God
" by good works, curse him. May the choir of holy virgins,
" who despised the vain things of this world for the honour
" of Christ, curse him. May all the saints, who from the
" beginning of the world to the end of time are found beloved
" of God, curse him. May heaven and earth, and all holy
" things in them, curse him. May he be accursed whereso-
" ever he may be—in the house, in the field, in the way, in the
" path, in the wood, in the water, or in the church. May he be
" accursed, living, dying, eating, drinking, hungering, thirsting,
" fasting, sleeping, waking, walking, standing, sitting, lying,
" working, at rest, in nature's offices bleeding! May he be
" accursed in all the powers of his body. May he be accursed
" within and without. May he be accursed in his hair, skull,
" crown, temples, forehead, ears, eyelids, eyes, knees, thighs,
" nostrils, teeth, lips, roof of his mouth, throat, shoulders, elbows,
" arms, hands, fingers, breast, heart, and all the inward parts
" to his stomach, in his reins, loins, thighs, feet, toes, and
" nails! May he be accursed in every portion of his members,
" from the crown of the head to the sole of the feet, may there
" be no soundness! May Christ the Son of the living God,
" in all the empire of his majesty, curse him. And may
" Heaven, with all its virtues that move therein, rise up to
" condemn him, unless he repent and come to satisfaction.
" Amen! Fiat, fiat! Amen!"

In the 13 Edward I, the sheriff of the county of Southampton was commanded, that having taken with him four
discreet and lawful knights of his county, in his proper person
he should go to the court of the Abbot of Gymmings of
Heylinge, and in full court cause to be recorded that plaint,
which was in the same court by the king's writ, between Alice,
who was the wife of Thomas le Clerk, plaintiff, and Henry le
Palmer, tenant of a messuage and two virgates of land, with
the appurtenances in Mengham, whereupon Alice claimed
that a false judgment was pronounced against her in the same
court.

At the halimote of the Abbot of Jumiéges held subsequently,

the suit was prosecuted to a hearing. It was admitted that one Mabill, the ancestor of Alice, was seized of the tenements as of right, which Mabill died without heir, and that the right descended, and ought to be deemed to have descended, to one Maud, her sister and heiress; and that from Maud the right descended to Alice, who was then sued as daughter and heir. They prayed an inquisition, for which they paid four shillings. Henry le Palmer appeared and acknowledged that Maud was seized of the tenements as in villenage of the Abbot of Jumiéges; but that in her pure widowhood she surrendered them into the hands of the lord to his use, and that he bought the tenements of the lord as his villenage; that Maud the mother of Alice was sold out of the manor as a villain, and that the custom of the manor would not allow any male or female villain sold out of the manor to return and claim their rights. An inquisition was demanded to determine the question; the jurors of which found upon oath, that Henry le Palmer had the greater right of holding the messuage and two virgates of land, with the appurtenances in Mengham, as he held the same in villenage, than Thomas and Alice of having the same. The judgment therefore passed in favour of Henry le Palmer, as the villain of the prior; and Thomas and Alice were remitted to make their demand against the prior if it seemed to them expedient. (*Excheq. Pleas*, 13 Edw. I.)

This trial in the court of the abbot gives some little insight into the tenures of the feudal times, and into the position of the manorial villain. Upon the arrival of the Normans in this country, and upon their seizure of the various manors then existing throughout the kingdom, they found persons in a condition of absolute and unqualified servitude, used and employed in works of the most servile nature, themselves, their children, and effects being the property of the lord, and transferred with the manor, upon sale or decease, like the cattle or stock upon it. These were the " servi" or household slaves mentioned everywhere in *Domesday*. The better of these were admitted by the Norman conquerors to the oath of fealty, which conferred upon them the privilege of looking

to their immediate lord for protection. They then obtained
the name of villains, probably from their domiciles being
in the villages attached to the manorial hall, and were
employed in agricultural works of the lowest order. They
were divided into two classes—villains regardant, that is,
annexed to the manor or land; arid villains in gross, that is,
annexed to the person of the lord, and transferable by deed
from one owner to another. They might not remove without
licence of the lord; and the property they possessed for the
ordinary purpose of sustenance was held at his will, and he
might dispossess them whenever he thought proper. In short,
he might rob, beat, and chastise his villains as he pleased,
provided he did not maim them. (Sir Wm. Temple, quoted
by *Bl.* b. 6, ch. ii.) Alice, the plaintiff in this case, was one
of the abbot's villains in gross. Upon the death of her father,
her mother, then a widow, either for a consideration, which is
not however stated, or on seizure of the abbot, surrendered
into the hands of the latter the property which had been held
by her deceased husband, and she herself was sold out of the
manor and located at Portsmouth. There she married Thomas
le Clerk; and upon applying for the restitution of her lands,
she finds them sold by the abbot to Henry le Palmer, who
by the return of the inquisition and the judgment of the halimote, is confirmed in his purchase.

The accounts in the monasteries of old were kept with
scrupulous exactness, and were rendered to the abbot or his
chief officer at stated periods of the year. The duty of
passing accounts devolved, in a religious house, upon the
treasurer or bursar, whose exchequer was a little stone house,
joining upon the coal-garth pertaining to the great kitchen, a
little distance from the dean's hall stairs. His office was to
receive the rents of the house, and all other officers of the
house made their accounts to him. He discharged all the
servants' wages, and paid all the expenses and sums of money
laid out about any works appertaining to the abbey, or with
which it stood charged. His chamber was in the infirmary,
and his meat was served from the great kitchen to his
exchequer. One of these accounts, containing a large amount

of local information as to the management of the demesne
lands, and furnished by the reeve or bailiff of the manor of
Hayling in the early part of the reign of Edward I, is still
extant.   The reeve was Richard, the son of Philip Heyward;
and he answered, among many other things, for 50s. 5¾d. for
rent of the term of Saint Andrew, together with the fishery;
for 18s. 1d. from the fishery for the term of the close of
Easter; for 16s. 8d. for the farm of the mill for the term of
Saint Michael; for 16s. 8d. for the farm of the mill for the
term of Saint Andrew; for 2s. 9d. for hurdle silver for the
year; and for 2d. of the Prior of Modmeney for the same; for
58s. 6d. for twenty-six rases of barley sold; for 25s. 4d. for
two oxen sold; for 30s. for four heifers sold; for 16d. for one
calf sold; for 5s. 3d. for twenty geese sold; for 2s. 8d. for
sixteen hens sold; for 2s. for the skin of one cow dead of the
murrain; and for 12d. for the hide of one calf (a yearling)
dead of the murrain; and for 13s. 9d. for fifteen skins of
muttons, and six skins of ewe sheep, and ten skins of young
sheep (fleeced) sold; for 3s. for one hundred doves; for 49s.
for one hundred and fourteen cheeses sold, weighing 49 stone;
for 15s. 9d. for twenty-one gallons of butter sold, but nothing
for the hives of honey; for 16s. 3d. from the leet of Hayling,
to wit, of the bakers; and for the sum total of the receipts
with arrears, £41. 2s. 6d.

The reeve took credit for 40s. 1¼d., delivered in the chamber
of the abbot by one tally for rents; and for other sums
delivered in the same way, to the amount of £17. 4s. 8¼d.;
for six bundles and a half of steel bought at 4s. 4d.; for the
purchase of four pairs of wheels, 8s. 6d.; in the purchase of
hoops for the same, 4d.; in the purchase of thirty clout nails
for the axles of the carts, 17d.; in one hundred and twelve
horseshoes, 4s. 8d.; in the purchase of twelve gallons of
pitch for greasing the young sheep, 3s. 6d.; in the purchase
of twenty-one gallons of milk for the lambs, 21d.; in shearing
and washing three hundred and thirty-one two-year-old sheep,
20d.; in wages of one carpenter for the doors of the abbot's
chamber, the granary, and the chapel, three days, 4d; in the
purchase of four rases of oats, 6s. 8d.; in the purchase of four-

teen muttons before shearing, 21s.; in the purchase of fourteen lambs, 9s. 6½d.; in wages for one man inclosing the
wood, ten days at the lord's table, 10d.; in fishes bought for
the pool, 4d.; in the purchase of fourteen ells of cloth, 19d.;
in repairing one weir, 18d.; in payment of mariners engaged
in carrying malt to Ramsey, 17d.; in carrying victuals to
Saint Ives, 6d.; in carrying wool to Ramsey, 18d.; in the
purchase of one flail with the iron thereof, 2d.; in weeding
corn at various places in the field, 32s.; by task in mowing
38a. 0r. 7p. of meadow, 17s. 6½d; in expenses to Ramsey on
this side the feast of Saint Michael with the rents, 8d.; for
the expenses of Robert de Mertone, the bailiff of the dairy,
and one servant, from Pentecost to the feast of Saint Peter ad
Vincula, and one maid-servant assisting in the dairy for the
time aforesaid, in the expenses of the servants of the manor
for one meal at the Nativity of the Lord, and for the expenses
of workmen by the year in the manor, by a tally against
Robert de Mertone, 52s.; in wages of four ploughmen by the
year, 16s.; in wages of one carter and one cowherd by the
year, 8s.; in wages of the bailiff by the year, 3s.; and in
wages of one park-keeper by the year, 2s.

Among the issues of the Grange are found:—The ferryman
of the water by the year, two bushels; for the support of
geese, hens, and capons, three bushels; used for malt 90
rases; in food for the horses of the brother of Simon de Eye
by one tally, three bushels and a half; in provender for the
horses on the holding of the leet, one bushel. And it appears
that at this time the stock at the Grange consisted of three
cart horses, four bullocks, two pack horses, two colts, eighteen
oxen, eleven steers, eleven calves, one bull, twenty-nine cows,
sixteen heifers, four hides, two hundred and forty-four muttons,
ninety-five two-year old-sheep, ninety-seven lambs, one hundred and sixteen ewes, fifty-three hogs, three hundred and
thirty-one wool pelts; sent to Ramsey, four peacocks, six
peahens, eighty geese, twenty capons, twenty-eight hens, a
hive of bees, two hundred eggs of hens, and one hundred and
ten for rent; whereof, in expenses of the house, one hundred;
sent to Saint Ives, two hundred; and for the hens to hatch,

ten ; two hundred and eighty cheeses, thirty gallons of butter, one hundred and ninety-two doves out of the dove-cote, and two pounds of honey. (*Queen's Rem. Off. Carlton Ride.*)

The position occupied by the Prior of Hayling was not an enviable one, for it of necessity involved him at times in the difficulties of both Normandy and England : the latter looked with suspicion on the nominee of a foreign house, whilst the possessions held in France by the English crown were always a source of disquiet and uneasiness to the French monarch. He not unnaturally grudged that an extensive and fruitful domain within his own realm should be the appanage of a foreign power, and longed for an opportunity once more to annex it to his own dominions. Accordingly, in the year 1293, the fire which had long lain smouldering broke out into actual flame, and a cause which at any other period would have been insufficient for such a purpose involved both nations in war. Speed (bk. 9, ch. x, s. 22) tells us, that an Englishman casually killed a Norman, upon which the Normans in revenge slew several English, and that the latter were not slow to make reprisals. In the following year, Edward I seized upon all the alien priories in this country dependent upon the Norman abbeys. Among many others, the Prior of Jumiéges was deprived of his cell at Hayling, with all its possessions ; and the unfortunate head of the house himself was seized into the hands of the king. This course had always been adopted during open hostility and actual war between France and England, the revenues being seized by the crown, and restored again when terms of peace were arranged. In some instances the priors were seized, in others they were called upon to find sureties for their neutrality pending the war.

· But in after times King Richard II and King Henry IV exceeded the equitable limit pursued by their predecessors : they not only detained the revenues of the priories in time of peace, but they diverted them from their proper channel, and bestowed them upon the lay nobility. The crown was but little benefited by the donations ; and Arundel, Archbishop of Canterbury, maintained in the House of Commons, in the presence of the Speaker, "that those kings were not half a "mark the wealthier for those rents thus assumed into their "hands." In the 4 Henry V, in the heat and height of his wars with France, all such alien priories as were not conventual were by act of Parliament dissolved and bestowed upon the king; it being deemed unsafe that men of considerable power and intelligence, identified with a foreign interest and having immediate communication with abbeys situated in a country with which we were at variance, should be maintained in this kingdom, beside which, it tended to the manifest detriment of the state that the alien priories should transport corn and stores into an enemy's country without a corresponding return. Other alien houses which were conventual survived until the general dissolution of English monasteries in the reign of Henry VIII, not being considered to have such a temptation to disloyalty as the others, because, although the monks were strangers in reference to their birth, they were to a certain extent naturalized by education and permanent residence.

Proceeding further into detail, we find that in the 22 Edward I, Simon de Marsham was assigned by warrant, dated from Westminster on the second day of August, to seize into the hands of the crown, "All the priories and other religious houses of the land and power of the King of France," with all their lands and tenements, goods and chattels, in the counties of Oxford, Berks, and Southampton (the Isle of Wight excepted), and safely to keep the same, together with the prior or any other superior of every house; and he was commanded, that upon taking the same into the royal possession, an inventory of the lands and tenements, the price of the same, the goods and chattels seized, should be by him certified to the Treasurer and Barons of the Exchequer, under seal, on the morrow of Saint Michael then ensuing, together with the original writ of seizure.

This was accordingly done, and in the return to the writ, under the head of " Heyling of the Abbey of Gumièges," it is stated, among many other items similar to those contained in the Reeves account, that the prior held a manor and a garden,

with a dovehouse, within the close, worth by the year 50s.;
three hundred and sixty-six acres of waste land in demesne,
worth by the year £12. 4s. 2d.; ten acres of wood, worth by the
year 20s.; one hundred acres for the pasture of sheep, 16s. 8d.;
one water mill, worth by the year 60s. : sum of the whole,
£19. 10s. 10d.; that there were forty-eight customary tenants
holding forty virgates and a half of land, worth £24. 2s. 5d.
at the term of Saint Thomas the Apostle, their works being of
the value of £16. 16s. 9¼d.; Nicolas de Leigh and William
Coleman paying 15d. and five capons of the value of tenpence
at the feast of Saint Michael; foreign rents at Portsmouth,
76s. 2d.; that he held the church to his own proper use,
£80—the whole manor, including the church, being valued at
the sum of £144. 8s. 3½d.   Among the utensils and goods of
the abbey at Hayling are enumerated one palfrey price, 60s.;
one sumpter horse, price 40s.; two asses, price 4s.; also seven
score ewes in the town of Estling (Estoke) in the custody of
Adam Browman, worth 112s. 8d.; in the granary, five quarters
of barley for the household, price 20s.; two quarters of old peas
to be distributed in alms; the crop of one hundred and ten
acres of corn, £19. 6s. 9d.; eighty-six acres of barley, £8. 12s.;
eleven acres and a half of oats, 17s. 3d.; eighty acres of peas,
£4; and the crop of seventy-eight acres and a half of peas,
£78. 6s—the value of the articles enumerated in the inventory
being (beside the tithes) £67. 16s.

The foreign rents here mentioned included various houses
at Winchester and at Portsmouth, a moiety of the whole of
Brockhurst called Hull under the charter of Adam, the son of
Adam the Knight of Portesia, made to Saint Peter of
Jumiéges.

A burgage with a house in the town of Portsmouth, under
the charter of William de Cantonia, made to Geoffrey de
Gonner, chaplain.

A certain piece of waste ground in the town of Portsmouth,
under the deed of Eve, relict of Stephen Wynward, made to
the Prior of Hayling.

A quit claim of two shillings which she held for dower
of land in Brockhurst, under a deed of Petronella, relict

of Adam, the son of Adam of Portsmouth, made to the Abbot of Jumiéges and Prior of Hayling.

A yearly rent of fifteen pence received from a house in Portsmouth, under the charter of William Gynnulph, made to the Prior of Hayling.

One messuage with the appurtenances in Portsmouth, under the deed of William Syward to the Abbot of Jumiéges and Prior of Hayling.

The moiety of the site of a mill there, under two deeds to the Abbot of Jumiéges and Prior of Hayling.

A moiety of the fee of Brockhurst.

A messuage in Portsmouth given to the abbot and convent of Jumiéges by Joan Alicia and Matilda daughters, and heirs of Walter Trogges of Portsmouth.

A house in Portsmouth, situate upon le Peray (the Parade), and of half a windmill, under the charter of William de Lewer and Joan his wife.

An acre of land in Broadcroft.

Three crofts of arable land called the Hull, within the liberty of Portsmouth, for 23s. 4d. yearly, under the deed of John Bewcott, Prior of Hayling.

This return affords an insight into the customs and habits of the times : the prior's household living on barley, the alms of the priory issued in the form of old peas, and the whole produce of 366 acres valued at the sum of £37. 14s. 6d. The most valuable part of the prior's stock seems to have been his horses—the palfrey for his own riding, the sumpter horse for the carriage of necessaries when on a journey—all ecclesiastics as well as laymen at that time adopting horseback as the only means of conveyance.

During the prelacy of John de Pontissera, Bishop of Winchester, further disputes arose between the prior of the church of Hayling and the vicar of the one part, and the parishioners of the chapel of Saint Peter of Hayling of the other part, as to which of them ought to repair and roof in the chancel of the chapel : the parishioners affirming that it was a duty cast upon the prior and vicar ; the latter, on the other hand, declaring "that for certain reasons" the burden

fell upon the parishioners.   In the desire to avoid strife and
matter of dispute, both parties submitted the case for the
judgment of the bishop, who decided that for the sake of
peace he had determined that upon that occasion the prior
and vicar should cause the chancel of the chapel to be
repaired and roofed at their proper charge, in the proportion
of two parts for the prior and one part for the vicar; but so
that through the submission and ordinance no prejudice
should arise to them for the time to come, nor should such act
be adduced as a precedent in time to come, until the bishop
should have an opportunity of inquiring to which of the two
parties the burden belonged, and of making the ordinance
required.

And the bishop ordained, that the vicar and his successors
in time to come should, under canonical punishment, cause the
chapel to be served as it had been served in former times; that
in the weeks of our Lord's Nativity, Easter and Whitsuntide,
and on every feast throughout the year, and on every Sunday,
they should perform a full service, as well in matins, vespers,
and complines, as in masses, and also in every week; on
Mondays, Wednesdays, and Fridays, they should perform mass
only in chapel.   (*Regist. Pontissera*, fol. 42.)

There is no evidence to show on what grounds the parishioners contended for exemption from the burden of repairing
the chancel, or for what " certain reasons" the prior and vicar
sought to impose it upon them.   The prelate who determined
that the latter should do the repairs without prejudice upon
this occasion—intending, as it would seem, to investigate the
matter more fully—did not live to carry his intentions into
effect, but died in the course of the year.

During the reign of Edward II, hostilities between this
country and France were again renewed.   All the French
were banished from England, those even who were in attendance on Queen Isabel, daughter of Philip the Fair, not being
excepted.   All the alien priories were again made the subject
of confiscation, and that of Hayling was among the number.
In the month of January, in the eighteenth year of the reign,
a return was made of the possessions of the priory under the

authority of a writ of inquisition addressed to Ralph de Bereford and Richard de Westcote, keepers of the alien religious houses of the power and dominion of the King of France in the county of Southampton. The Prior of Hayling appeared before the Treasurer and Barons of the Exchequer at Westminster, and earnestly prayed that his house with its appurtenances might be committed to him for safe custody. The crown, conceiving as it is said that such places and chattels might be more fitly kept by the priors and rectors than by others, consented to the petition of the prior, and committed to him the keeping of his house with its appurtenances, and all issues thence received from the date of the seizure, saving to the crown however the prayers of the church and military services when they should happen to be required, and upon condition that all the animals and chattels should be kept in good order and sustenance. The prior was ordered to find sufficient security at the Exchequer for the safe custody of all the animals and chattels; and the escheators delivered the priory up to him, the arrangement being confirmed by an indenture executed between them.

The prior had no sooner obtained possession of the revenues of his house than another and more grievous trouble awaited him. It would seem, that in the same year that the confiscation took place, a very considerable portion of the island of Hayling was swept away by the inundation of the sea. Tradition always ran to this effect, but the proof was believed to be wanting, until, upon search among the records of that particular period, ample evidence was found in corroboration of the fact; but from what cause it arose is not known, neither is it material to the purpose of our history. The whole line of coast from Hayling as far as Hastings suffered severely from the same inroad of the waters; the accounts of the various seaborne villages, comprising the district called the Manwood, speak of the arable and other lands at this time "per mare destructas;" and the harbour of Pagham is supposed to have been formed by this means. The devastation committed by the irruption of the sea in this place is testified by the jurors appointed to assess the ninth fleece in 1345;

and twenty years after this date there is an entry in the Nonæ
Rolls of that year, stating that in the parish of Pagham there
were devastated by the sea 2700 acres, whereof the rector
used to receive £10. 10s.; and in 1332, the dean and chapter
of Hastings petitioned the crown for leave to repair the castle
walls, and to secure their chapel from the devastation of the
sea.   In 1333, further damage was done, for "this yeare, on
"Saint Clement's daie at night, which fell on the three and
"twentieth of November, through a marvellous inundation and
"rising of the sea all alongst by the coasts of this realme, but
"especiallie about the Thames, the sea bankes or walles were
"broken and borne downe with violence of the water, and
"infinite numbers of beasts and cattell drowned, fruitfull
"grounds and pastures were made salt marshes, so as there
"was no hope that in long time they should recouer againe
"their former fruitfulnesse."   (Hol. Chron. vol. ii, p. 601.)

A petition was presented to the crown by the prior, alleging
that the church of Hayling, which he formerly had to his
proper use, and a large portion of his lands and possessions
there, had been inundated by the sea, submersed and destroyed.
On the 8th of March, 18 Edward II, 1324, a warrant issued
for an inquisition to ascertain the truth of the statements
contained in the prior's petition; and in the same month the
inquisition was taken at Hailyngge, before Ralph de Bereford
and Richard de Westcote, described as wardens of the alien
religious houses under the government and dominion of the
King of France, being in the hands of the Lord the King of
England, in the county of Southampton, on Friday next
before the feast of the Annunciation of the Blessed Virgin
Mary, by the oath of Nicholas Stak, Simon le Rous, Geoffrey
de Brockampton, Simon Ingel, Simon Michel, Thomas Stak,
William Stuteville, John the son of Ralph Clark, John de
Hursi, John le Longe, Richard Thomas, and Robert le Eyr,
as to whether the possessions of the priory of Hailyngge were
submersed and destroyed by the sea, as had been asserted by
by the prior, there or not; and if so, then what possessions
were then so submersed, and of what yearly value those possessions were at the time in which the house was in the hands

of the Lord Edward I, by reason of the war then existing between him and the King of France ; and also what and how much the possessions which he then had there were worth by the year in all issues.

The jurors upon oath found, that two hundred and six acres of arable land of the demesnes of the priory had been inundated and destroyed by the sea, since the house was in the hands of the Lord Edward, father of the lord the then king, on account of the war ; and that they were worth at that time £10. 6s. by the year, because the better land of Hayling was nearest the sea ; that fourscore acres of pasture, which belonged to the priory, had been submersed by the sea since the time aforesaid, which were worth by the year twenty shillings ; that six virgates of the land of the customary tenants of the priory had been submersed by the sea and destroyed since the time aforesaid, from which the prior was in the habit of receiving 48s. rent by the year ; that nearly the whole hamlet of Estoke, with the lands pertaining to the same, as well as a great part of the larger hamlet of Northwood, and the greater part of the lands of the same, which hamlets and lands were belonging to the parish church of Hayling, and which the prior had for his own proper use, were submersed and destroyed by the sea, by which the church, as well by the submersion and destruction of those lands which the tenants of the Bishop of Winchester and John le Boteler held, as by the destruction of the lands and tenements which the tenants of the said prior held within the parish, was then worth less than it was at the time when the house was in the hands of King Edward I, by £26. 13s. 4d. by the year ; that two mills pertaining to the priory were by the submersion worth less by 20s. a year, because the tenants used to grind at the same mills ; that the fines and perquisites of court of the prior, by reason of the submersion and destruction of the prior's tenants, and of their lands and tenements, were then worth less than at the time aforesaid by 20s. a year ; and that the annual value of the possessions destroyed by the sea amounted to £42. 7s. 4d., in those days a large sum of money.

And in reference to the possessions which the prior still

28

held there, they found that there were easements of houses, with a garden and curtilage, worth 20s. a year; that there was a dovecote worth 6s. 8d. a year; two hundred and eighty acres of arable land worth £6 a year, of which fifty acres were worth per acre 12d., fifty 6d., and one hundred and eighty acres worth 3d.; also thirty-two acres of pasture worth 8d.; and ten acres of wood worth 3s. 4d.; also rents of assize worth £24. 7s. 1d. a year; the works of customary tenants there worth 10s. a year; the fines and perquisites of court worth 20s. a year; and two mills, one water-mill worth 13s. 4d. a year, and a windmill worth 6s. 8d. a year; a windmill at Portsmouth belonging to the prior, worth 6s. 8d. a year; the church of Hayling, which belonged to the prior, worth £13. 6s. 8d. a year, and not more, because there was a vicar who received a third part of the value of the same church; and that the annual value of the lands, tenements, and church there, amounted to £48. 8s. 5d. (*Records in Queen's Rem. Office, Extents of Alien Priories*, 18 Edw. II.)

On the 20th day of November in the same year, a further commission was issued from the Exchequer by order of the crown, and the escheators were directed, that after the extents were made, if the Prior of Hayling were willing to find security to them that he would not leave the kingdom, then they were to permit him to come and appear before the Treasurer and Barons of the Exchequer, to hear and to do that which might be decreed by the king and council. The extent was accordingly taken at Hayling on the Wednesday next after the feast of Saint Katharine, when the jury returned in substance the same verdict as that contained in the former inquisition, except that the vicar was stated to receive all the tithes "except sheaves," and except that the annual value of the lands and tenements of the prior and the church of Hayling was reduced to £42. 4s. 7d. (*Ibid.*) And this extent was evidently acted upon, as I find that a charter was passed under the great seal subsequently in the same reign, by which Edward remitted to the prior a part of his pension, which he was bound to pay in time of war, on account of the devastation made by the inroads of the sea. (*Chartulary of the*

Abbey of Shene.) He was however, in the 2 Richard II, in accordance with an order of the crown, obliged to find sufficient sureties to prevent communication with the enemy, the Island of Hayling being deemed so conveniently situated for the transport of troops, arms, and munitions of war into Normandy. (*Records relating to the Island of Hayling, Southampton.*) In the 7 Edward III, 1333-4, an act was granted by various prelates and heads of religious houses towards the expenses of the marriage of the king's sister, Eleanor, to Reynold, the second Earl of Guelder. Her portion was £15,000, of which sum the amount paid by the Prior of Hayling was returned at 60*s.* (*Rymer's Fœd.*)

The men of the towns of Hayling, Stoke, East Stoke, Northwood, Mengeham, Southwood, and Weston, were bound to pay for fifteenths and tenths granted from the laity in the first year the sum of £13. 10*s.* 3½*d.* (*Chartulary of the Abbey of Shene*); and in the 2 Richard II, they presented a petition, praying for exemption from a proportion of the taxes levied upon them, in consequence of the loss of a great part of their island by the encroachment of the sea. The king, "piously commiserating their state and misery," commanded that if the said men were really in the indigence stated in their petition, they should be exonerated from a part of their taxation; and among the records of the Lord Treasurer's Remembrancer's Office of the Exchequer, it is said, that in the term of Saint Hilary, John Tichborne Chevalier, and his companions, then lately collectors of two-fifths of the tenths, and of the tenths of the lord the king, granted in the first year of the reign, had a respite for £27. 0*s.* 6½*d.* with which they stood charged for the fifteenth touching the men of Hayling, which being explained to the men of Hayling, they said that they were heavily taxed, as well by the sheriff of Southampton as by the collectors, for the sums to be paid to the king; and this with the less justice, because by reason of the great consumption of their land within the island, and the inundations of the sea, and by reason of various other things to which they were subject before that time, as well for the expense and burthen to which they were put for the defence of the island against hostile invaders, they were brought to such penury that they were wholly unable to pay any sum beyond £6. 15s. 7¼d., to which they were taxed afresh in respect of a fifteenth : and this they were ready to verify.

Moreover, it was found in the memoranda of the fourteenth year of the grandfather of the then king, in the term of the Holy Trinity, viz. after the account of John Roches and William Brockhurst, then late collectors of the fifteenths and twentieths every third year granted to the grandfather of the then king by the laity in the eleventh year of his reign, in the county of Southampton, that there were the towns of Stoke, Estoke, Northwode, Southwode, Myngham, Westiton, and Hayling, within the island of Hayling; and that the greater part of the same island, in the fourteenth year aforesaid, was nearly destroyed and submerged by the inundation of the sea ; that the place where the parish church of the same island was at first erected and built was in the centre of the island ; and being so built within the time of living memory of some then coming thither, it stood by the seashore in good pre- servation, and at that moment was so deep in the sea, that an English vessel of the larger class could pass along there, and that it was then distant from the land about two (leucas) miles ; and so from day to day, on every side towards the sea, the land was destroyed and submerged by the inundation of the sea ; and that on account of such devastation and con- sumption, and labours about the watching and close custody there continually made and to be made, during all the time of the then war between the king and those of France, and the costs of their victualling the men of the neighbourhood coming to their aid to resist the enemies of the king, often coming by the seacoast, they had sustained very heavy losses beyond the sufficiency of their condition, so that they were in no way able to support the charges falling upon their island as they had theretofore been wont to do ; and so the goods and chattels of the men of those towns had been destroyed and consumed, by reason of which destruction and consumption, and of all the burthens aforesaid, very many men, from the pressure of poverty, had withdrawn themselves from those towns.

Upon information of these complaints and grievances, a royal commission was issued to make inquisition into the fact, and the jurors appointed in the 2 Richard II made their return from Havant upon oath, to the effect following:—

"That the men of Hayling, on account of the great destruc-
"tion of their lands in the island of Hayling, and the flux of
"the sea, and by reason of other disasters to which they had
"before that time been subject, as well as from the expense
"and charges which they had been put to for the defence of
"the island against the attacks of the enemy, were brought to
"such poverty that they had not sufficient to pay the tenth.
"And they found that the men of the island had made divers
"walls of piles, earth, and turf, for the preservation of their
"lands in various places within the island aforesaid, at the
"cost of the men of the island of forty marks, which by the
"inundation of the sea were entirely broken down, destroyed,
"and submerged; that three hundred acres of arable land,
"which used to be ploughed and sown, were submerged by
"the sea and entirely destroyed within forty-three years then
"last past; that there was then deep water there, and that at
"every flux of the tide some part of the lands of the island
"was destroyed and overflown, which land, so overflown by
"the tide for five or six years then last past, could not be
"sown nor any profit be taken by feeding of the same land,
"or in any other manner; and that the premises having been
"seen by the Barons, it was considered that a part of the
"taxation should be remitted."

In consequence of this the men of Hayling were exonerated from the payment of £27. 0s. 6½d., being the triennial fifteenth granted in the 47 Edward III, 1372-3. The exemption was again renewed in the 22 Richard II, 1398; and in the 3 Henry IV, 1401, upon a further petition being presented to the king, a remission was obtained, which recited the original submersion, which at that time was still very much on the increase, by which means, and by other impoverishments, many persons of the island had left the island to dwell elsewhere. It also appeared, that they had paid £6. 15s. 7d. for

their tax, but that the Barons of the Exchequer, "not con-
"sidering the perils and matters aforesaid," refused to discharge
them of the sum of £13. 10s. 3¼d., being the difference between
the £6. 15s. 7½d. and the sum of £20. 5s. 10½d., their former
tax, and in respect thereof had grievously distrained the men
of Hayling.   Therefore the king, "with pious affection,
"pitying the miserable state of the same men, of his special
"grace, in reverence of God," had pardoned and released to
the inhabitants of the island aforesaid, their heirs and successors, all manner of sums then respited in the Exchequer.
And "of his more abundant grace, to the effect that the
"persons of the island aforesaid, and others, might have
"greater disposition to dwell in the island and inhabit the
"same," he granted, for the period of five years then next
ensuing, a remission of the fifteenths, which were settled at
the sum of £6. 15s. 7¼d.   (*Pub. Rolls*, 3 Hen. IV, m. 16, in
Tower of London.)   This charter was by writ of privy seal,
and bore date the 24th of January.

It would seem that matters did not mend in the island;
for I find that a further application and remission were made
in the 8 Henry IV, 1406. (*Ibid.* 8 Hen. IV; and *Rolls of
Parliament*, Henry IV, 620); and in the following year "the
"poor liege men of the towns of Stoke, Estoke, Northwood,
"Mengham, Weston, and Hayling," petitioned the crown,
that whereas lately, as in the time of King Edward III and
Richard II, by reason of many of the lands and possessions
of the island of Hayling being laid waste by the sea and
entirely lost, and the inhabitants of the said island having
been thereby in divers ways impoverished and injured, the
said men, upon inquisitions taken by command of the said
king, were discharged in their Exchequer from £13. 10s. 4¼d.
for each fifteenth granted, and which sum had been anciently
paid, as plainly appears by record, &c.   And the said king,
anno 3 Henry IV, considering the above matter, and wishing
the inhabitants to continue in the said island, reduced the
payment of the said fifteenths to £6. 15s. 7d., and so in proportion as is contained in the letters patent, grant, &c.   They
prayed the king to consider the former grants and reductions,

Simon Dubosc.

abbé de Jumièges au 15.ᵉ Siècle.

and as the said island continued daily to waste and be destroyed, so that there was hardly left in any of the said towns a man to be benefited by such grant or reduction, they trusted that they might be entirely quit and discharged from payment of any fifteenths for the relief and preservation of the said island, which otherwise would be entirely destitute or destroyed. (*Records relating to the Island of Hayling, Southampton.*)

The petition was not unheeded, for the king assented to its prayer, and remitted the whole of the taxation (*ibid.*); and in the act of resumption 13 Edward IV, 1472, there is a saving clause that that act be not prejudicial to any grant or grants made by letters patent of the 20 July 8, Edward IV, to the inhabitants in the towns and villages of Stoke, Eastoke, Northwood, Mengham, Weston, and Hayling, within the Island of Hayling, by what name or names the inhabitants or towns in the letters patent might be named or called; but that the same might be good and effectual to the said inhabitants and every of them. During the abbacy of Simon Dubosc, who was elected Abbot of Jumiéges in 1391, and who derived his descent from the Danes under the command of Rollo, it appears (*Histoire de l'Abbay de Jumiéges*, p. 87) that the priory of Hayling was again seized into the hands of the crown. The monks of Jumiéges compelled Dubose to retire to the priory, which it is stated he had obtained a restoration of from the Duke of Lancaster, while he was in France as ambassador endeavouring to arrange terms of peace. Three monks were at this time sent to Hayling to re-establish the discipline there; and Deshayes tells us that they continued to enjoy the revenues of the priory until the year 1413, when alien priories were for the most part dissolved. (*Ibid.* p. 88.) There is no further mention made of the island until the year 1553, when Queen Mary, in the first year of her reign, granted letters patent of confirmation " of divers confirmations "and grants of divers kings to the inhabitants within the " Island of Hayling," shortly after which period the taxation of the country assumed a different aspect, and there was no further necessity for royal charters of exemption.

It appears, by a petition of the Commons in the Parliament 9 Henry IV, that of ancient time, when any tenth, fifteenth, or other general tax, was granted to the king, certain towns were taxed and assessed at certain sums in gross; and that those persons who had lands and tenements within those towns, and their cattle, goods, and chattels there, though they were not inhabitants, were contributory in respect of such cattle, goods, and chattels, to the assessment; but that of late such persons had, on intelligence of any such tax, withdrawn their property from their lands in such towns, until the assessment had been made, and then brought their property back, and thus avoided the charge, and threw the whole burthen on the remaining inhabitants. A general statute, 9 Henry IV, cap. 7, was framed upon this petition, but without reference to the ancient custom stated in the petition. From this proceeding however it appears that these taxes were charged upon the property within each district at the time of the assessment. The grants of tenths and fifteenths at this time therefore differed from the grants in the reign of Henry III, and particularly in this, that, either by custom or special grant of the crown, certain sums were considered as chargeable on certain towns, including a district of land, in respect of a grant of a tenth or of a fifteenth, or other proportion of moveables; whereas in the reign of Henry III, and for some time afterwards, as far as can be collected from existing documents, it appears to have been left to the assessors either to agree for a certain sum in gross for each town, for which the whole would be responsible, or to assess each individual separately in respect of his or her actual property on the spot, as should be deemed most beneficial for the crown.

This change in the mode of assessment is clearly indicated by the letters patent before cited in the reign of Henry IV, purporting that on every grant of a fifteenth to the king or his heirs by the Commons in Parliament, the men of the towns of Hayling should be assessed at £6. 15s. 7d., and on every grant of a half fifteenth at the moiety of that sum, and so in proportion according to the rate of the grant. This the king granted by the advice of the Lords spiritual and temporal in

Parliament, without mention of the Commons: a power which the king possibly assumed under the advice of the Lords, conceiving that the grant being made to him, it was wholly in his own power to determine whether it should be levied or not.

The town of Great Yarmouth appears, by the next entry in the Parliament roll, to have usually paid one hundred pounds upon the grant of a tenth to the king, and sought to be relieved at the same time with Hayling, on payment of sixty pounds only; but to this the king declined to assent. Great Yarmouth was a borough represented in Parliament, and such boroughs were ordinarily charged with a tenth, when the commonalty were only charged with a fifteenth. The towns in the Island of Hayling not being borough towns, were chargeable with fifteenths, in common with the rest of the county of Southampton, and not with the tenth, which seems to have been originally only chargeable by right on the cities and boroughs of which the king was lord, and which he had anciently the power of tallaging by his own commissioners, provided he required only a reasonable tallage. A grant therefore of a tenth, to be levied in cities and boroughs, was originally made by the special representatives of the cities and boroughs charged, and long continued to be so made; and when the commonalty, exclusive of cities and boroughs, were charged with a fifteenth, it was granted by the knights of the shire as the representatives of the towns and lands charged with that tax. The origin of the representation of cities and boroughs in Parliament was therefore a desire on the part of the king to obtain from them more than he could by a reasonable tallage; they contributed in common with the king's other subjects in respect of the general obligation of the subjects of the realm to supply the necessities of the crown, but they contributed at a higher rate, in consequence of their liability to tallage at discretion.

In the early part of the reign of King Henry V, the alien priories throughout England were finally dissolved and seized into the hands of the crown, never again to be returned to their original grantees. Hayling formed one of the number, and in the third year of the reign, was bestowed by the king upon the newly founded monastery of Shene, in the county of Surrey. The royal charter of foundation contained a peroration of considerable length, expressive of the piety of the donor, who thereby disposed, appointed, and founded a certain conventual house of monks, of the Carthusian order, on the north part of the site of the manor of Shene, containing 3125 feet in length and 1305 feet 8 in. in width, which he willed to be for ever called the House of Jesus of Bethlehem at Shene, and which he declared should be held to the prior and monks there, and their successors, in free, pure, and perpetual alms, free and quit from all secular tax and service.

And he granted to them the alien priory of Ware in the county of Hertford ; the priory of Noion, and the alien priory of Newmarket, pertaining to the abbey of Saint Elbœuf in Normandy ; the priory of Lewisham and the alien priory of Greenwich in the county of Kent, pertaining to the abbey of the Blessed Peter at Ghent in Flanders ; and the alien priory or manor of Haylyng, otherwise called Helyng, with the appurtenances pertaining to the abbey of Lire, otherwise called the abbey of the Blessed Peter of Jumiéges ; as well as the priory of Carisbrook in the Isle of Wight, and all lands, tenements, churches, portions, pensions, alms, and any other possessions whatsoever, pertaining or belonging to the alien abbey of Lire in Normandy, within the kingdom of England, and the parts of Wales—the priory of Hynkley in the county of Leicester, which was of the possessions of the abbey of Lire, alone excepted. And also all manner of hundreds, manors, lands, tenements, rents, services, and possessions, knights' fees, advowsons of churches, vicarages, chapels, and hospitals, portions, pensions, tithes, oblations, obventions, and other emoluments and profits whatsoever, to the said priories or manors and each of them, and to the aforesaid lands, tenements, and possessions of the said Abbey of Lire (except as before excepted), in any way whatsoever pertaining or belonging ; together with any reversions after the death of such persons as held the same or any of them in fee tail, or for a term of life or of years, or in any other manner whatsoever, to have and to hold to the same prior and monks and their successors the priories or manors aforesaid, and the said lands, tenements, and possessions of the said abbey of Lire (except as before excepted), together with the reversions aforesaid, and all manner of hundreds, manors, lands, tenements, possessions, rents, services, churches, pensions, portions, knights' fees, advowsons, liberties, franchises, and other commodities and profits whatsoever to the said priories or manors or any of them, and to the said lands, tenements, and possessions of the said abbey of Lire, by whatsoever names the priories or manors aforesaid, or the other possessions aforesaid, might be in any way known, pertaining, appendant, or belonging, as fully and entirely as the persons aforesaid then held the same, or any other persons had had and held the same before that time, without rendering or paying any report, farm account, or reckoning, or any other profit whatsoever to the king or his heirs.

He also granted and gave license to the same prior and monks and their successors, that they might acquire the priories or manors so bestowed, and the land, tenements, and possessions of the abbey of Lire (except as excepted), from the abbots and convents of the abbeys being within the power of the kingdom of France, and the same priories or manors, lands, tenements, and possessions of the abbey of Lire, together with the churches appropriate to the same, if any such there were, to transfer, unite, and incorporate, and that the union, appropriation, and incorporation of the same churches to the same priories or manors, and to the lands, tenements, and possessions of the abbey of Lire, so made, should be entirely dissolved; and that they should be appropriated, united, and incorporated *de novo*, if need were, to the same Carthusian house and the prior and monks there, and their successors, and be held to their proper uses for ever, notwithstanding the Statute of Mortmain.

He also granted to the prior and monks, that if the priories or manors so bestowed, pertaining to the abbey of Lire, should be gained or recovered out of their hands, or those of their successors without fraud or evil device, or if it should happen at any time that they should be taken away from them or their successors, then that the prior and monks of Shene and their successors should have and yearly receive seven hundred marks, namely, one hundred pounds of the issues of the hanaper of the chancery of the king and his heirs, by the hands of the keeper of the hanaper, at the terms of Saint Michael and Easter; and one hundred pounds in the port of the city of London, as well as one hundred pounds in the port of the town of Saint Botolph, one hundred and ten marks in the port of the town of Southampton, and one hundred marks in the port of the town of Bishops Lynn, and forty marks in the port of the city of Chichester, from the custom of wools, hides, and wool fells in the same ports, by the hands of the collectors, at the terms of Saint Michael and Easter, until provision should be made by the king or his heirs to the same prior and monks of lands, tenements, and possessions elsewhere, in a fit place within the kingdom, to the value of seven hundred marks by the year, and so in proportion for any lesser quantity that might be recovered.

He also granted to them Petersham Weir in the river Thames, and two tuns of red wine of Gascony within the port of London, every year at the feast of the Purification of the Blessed Mary; that they should be for ever quit of aids for making the first-born sons of kings knights, and for marrying the first-born daughters of kings, and from all aids and tallages due in respect of their lands; and that whenever the clergy of England, or of the province of Canterbury alone, or of the province of York alone, should grant to the king a tenth or any other proportion of their spiritual and ecclesiastical goods; or the community of the counties of England, or the citizens or burgesses of the cities or boroughs of the counties, should grant the tenth, fifteenth, or any other tax of their lands or goods; or when the king should cause his demesnes to be taxed; or when the lord the pope should impose a tenth or other proportion upon the clergy of England, and should grant the same or any part to the king or his heirs,—the churches and benefices of the prior and monks of Shene, their goods, lands, and chattels should not in any way be taxed; and they should be free of the tax to be levied for the munition and furnishing of men at arms in time of war; that no livery should be made to the use of any person in any of their houses against the will of the prior and monks, and that no one should be lodged there against their will.

He also granted to them, their men, and tenants, that they should be quit of all toll in every market and fair throughout England, and from the toll in all passage of bridges, waters, roads, and sea throughout England; and that they, their men, and tenants, their goods, chattels, and merchandise, should be quit of all pavage, passage, lastage, stallage, carriage, picage, terriage, nonage, pontage, chimniage, ankerage, wharfage, and talliage; of all amercements and fines of counties and hundreds; of all royal works of castles, parks, bridges, and houses; and from suits of counties throughout the kingdom.

He also granted them the goods of felons and outlaws, the returns of writs, fines for trespasses and offences committed within their manors; wreck of sea, waif, and estray; and that they might have free warren in all the lands, lordships, fees, and possessions to them granted, and thenceforth to be granted, wherever they might be, even if they were within the metes of the royal forest, so that no one should enter such lands to chase in the same, or to take any thing which pertained to warren, without the license and will of the prior and monks of Shene, under a forfeiture of ten pounds, the moiety of which was to be levied and returned to the use of the king, and the other moiety to be levied by the prior and monks and their successors, to be applied to their uses; that they might hold the lands then or thereafter to be granted to them, soc and sac, infangtheof and outfangthef, with view of frankpledge, thew, pillory and tumbrel for the punishment of evildoers there, and that they might cause gallows to be erected on the soil of their lands, demesnes, fees, and possessions, and judgment to be done upon the malefactors who should happen to be apprehended there; that they should have leets and lawdays within their lands, a market and two fairs at East Henreth, and that nonuser should not be a bar to the exercise of the various franchises granted at any future time.

This charter was dated on the first day of April, by the king himself at Westminster. (*Chart. Rolls*, 3 and 4 Hen. V, No. 8.)

The privileges granted to the abbey of Shene were very considerable, and they were by their foundation charter exempt from every kind of taxation. The building itself, when completed, endowed as it was with such ample revenues, formed a magnificent structure, such as in those days were dedicated to the honour and service of Almighty God. To this monastery of Carthusians another religious house of the order of Saint Bridget was attached, called the monastery of Sion. The place itself was one to which royalty had been partial ; and there seems to have been a royal mansion at Shene as early as the reign of Edward I, who there received the commissioners for establishing a new civil government in Scotland. Here Edward III, when he had filled up the measure of his glory and life, ended his days with grief for the loss of his brave son, irreparable both to him and to the nation at large. Here likewise died Anne, consort of Richard II, sister of the Emperor Wenceslaus, and daughter of the Emperor Charles IV, who first taught English women the present mode of riding on horseback, and whose death so affected her husband that it is said by Holinshed that he destroyed the palace ; it is however probable that he only suffered it by neglect to fall into decay. In the reign of Henry VII the palace was destroyed by fire ; but that monarch rebuilt it after it was burnt in 1499, and died there in 1509. Queen Elizabeth also died there in 1603. The first religious house founded at Shene was that of a convent of Carmelites, under a charter of Edward II ; but it was removed in about two years after its establishment to Oxford. In the monastery of Henry V Dean Colet died.

In the reign of Henry VII, by the consent of Margaret Duchess of Burgundy, Perkin—a man of mean extraction, of Tournay in France, declaring himself to be Richard Duke of York, who had in reality been slain in the Tower, together with his brother Edward V, by command of his uncle the Duke of Gloucester, afterwards Richard III—

raised a sedition, and after having married Katharine, daughter of the Earl of Huntley, made a descent upon England. Landing in Cornwall, and proceeding to Exeter, he besieged the town, but without success; for on hearing of the approach of the king's forces, he withdrew to Taunton, and made preparations for battle. He fled however before the battle commenced, and threw himself into sanctuary at the abbey of Beaulieu in Hants. Being much pressed by two companies of the king's army, who had been sent to watch for his escape, he voluntarily yielded himself up, was taken prisoner to London, and was confined in the Tower. From thence he contrived to make his escape, and besought the intercession of the Abbot of Shene, in whose monastery he had taken refuge. The abbot complied with his request, and his life was spared; but he was committed for close custody to the Tower, whence attempting his escape a second time, he was retaken and hanged with several of his companions.

In the following reign King James of Scotland, brother-in-law to King Henry VIII, having married the Lady Margaret, eldest daughter of Henry .VII, was killed at the battle of Flodden Field on the 9th Sept., 1513, and his body being on the next day recognized by the Lord Dacres and others, although disfigured with wounds, it was embowelled, embalmed, put into lead, and conveyed to the monastery of Shene, where it was buried. (*Baker's Chron.*, p. 27, 9.) In the month of November, 1542, Queen Catherine, daughter of Edward Howard, Duke of Norfolk, being charged with an evil life, was conveyed to Sion, there to remain till the king's pleasure should be known. She was shortly afterwards removed to the Tower of London, where she was beheaded in the following February.

Returning to Hayling, it will be borne in mind that in the prelacy of John de Pontissera, Bishop of Winchester, an ordinance was made in reference to a dispute which existed between the prior and vicar of Hayling, and the parishioners of Hayling North, on the subject of the repairs of the chancel in the chapel there. The ordinance then made was expressly

stated to be for that occasion only, and the death of the
bishop precluded the possibility of any permanent decree.   It
would seem that the matter remained the fruitful subject of
dispute until the time of Waynflete, Bishop of Winchester,
who was consecrated in the year 1447, and died in 1486,
when the litigation was finally set at rest.   That prelate, in a
very curious and interesting document, entered very fully into
the various points of difference between the parties.   He took
notice of the dispute which had arisen between the parishioners of the chapel of Northwode, in the Island of Hayling,
and diocese of Winchester, of the one part, and Sir Walter
Paye, perpetual vicar of the church of Hayling, of the other
part : the parishioners asserting that Sir Walter, the then
vicar, and his successors vicars, of the church in all time to
come, were bound and obliged to the celebration of Divine
service in the chapel on every double feast happening
throughout year, first and second vespers, matins, and
masses, and on Sundays, and other feasts which were considered and were used to be observed as Sundays, chanted
mass, and on the Rogation, Lent, and on the eves of Easter
and Whitsunday, the due and accustomed service; by reason
whereof they were disposed in many ways to annoy the vicar;
but the latter alleged that he and his successors were by no
means bound to celebrate Divine service in the chapel as
stated, and earnestly requested that perpetual silence should
be imposed upon the parishioners respecting the celebration
and services.   Upon the appearance of the vicar in person,
and the parishioners by their proctors, Ralph Cradocke and
Nicolas Aylwyn, the difference was by common consent
between them thus disposed of :

Sir Walter Paye, then vicar, and his successors in all time
to come, perpetual vicars of the church of Hayling, were to
find for ever, at their proper charges, a suitable chaplain, resident by day and by night at Northwode, to celebrate Divine
service in the chapel of Northwode on all Sundays and holi-
days happening throughout the year, and used to be celebrated by law or custom in other parish churches; but so
that the parishioners, their heirs and successors, should find

for ever, at their proper charges, a house for the habitation of
the chaplain; also paying to the then vicar and his successors,
perpetual vicars of the church, thirty shillings sterling every
year, by equal portions at Easter and Michaelmas; finding at
their proper charges, bread, wine, incense, and all lights in
the chapel (except the five candles for the purification of
women, and one candle for single mass when it should be
celebrated by day, which burthen should fall upon the vicar
and vicarage); also making their due oblations in the chapel on
the day of the dedication of the same for ever, with similar
oblations on the day of the Purification of the Blessed Mary,
and on other days in the year, as the other parishioners had
been accustomed to make them in the mother church of
Southwode; and that all the parishioners of Northwode should
go in procession solemnly and devoutly on the feast of the
relics in all years to come, with the principal cross, their
parochial chaplain and water sprinkler, to the mother church
of Southwode, there to pay their devotions.

And in reference to the question which had arisen between
the prior and convent of the church, and the vicar, of the one
part, and the parishioners of the chapel of Saint Peter of the
other part, as to which of them ought to repair the chancel of
the chapel, and in order to avoid " the circuitous proceedings
" of actions at law," a perpetual composition was entered into,
that the prior and convent should repair two parts of the
chancel for ever, as often as it should need repair in time to
come, and should bind themselves and their successors by
deed, to be executed under their common and conventual
seal; and that the vicar and his successors should repair at
their proper charges for ever the third part of the same chancel;
and that the parishioners of the chapel, their heirs and
successors, should repair the fourth part, in all times to come
for ever.   But if and so often as it should happen that the
then vicar or any of his successors should withdraw the
celebration or services appointed, or should break the arrangement, then it should be in the power of the Bishop of
Winchester or his officials to sequester all the oblations and
obventions of the chapel belonging to the vicarage, and out

of the proceeds to cause the chapel to be served by a fit chaplain, until the vicar should have complied with the terms of the composition so contravened. And if and so often as the parishioners should fail in the payment of the stipend, or should act in contravention of the composition, then the vicar should be at liberty to withdraw the celebration of Divine service, until they had paid the vicar the money in arrear; and the party which should be otherwise guilty should be punished according to the judgment of the bishop or his official.

The deed containing the terms of the composition was duly executed by the vicar in person for himself, his vicarage, and successors; by the proctors of the parishioners, for themselves, the parishioners, and their successors; and by the prior and convent, by the affixing of their common seal: the bishop, with the express consent of the parties and at their request and petition, approving and ratifying the final arrangement.

At the same time, and with a view of obtaining a privilege which was much needed, the parishioners of Northwode presented a petition to the prior and convent of Shene, and to the bishop of the diocese, on the subject of burial at the chapel of Northwood. They stated that they experienced many inconveniences, and ofttimes the most grievous anxieties, through the detention of dead bodies and the corpses of the deceased parishioners of the village of Northwode, in taking the same from thence to the parish church of Hayling or its burial-ground, for the purpose of burial, as well on account of the great distance thereof, as on account of the inundation of the waters; and they besought the prior and convent of Shene, then proprietors of the parish church and chapel of ease, and the then vicar of the parish church, that they considering with godly affection the pains and dangers of the inhabitants of Northwode, which they at that moment sustained, and would probably have to sustain for the then future, owing to the detention of corpses requiring burial, would kindly grant them assent that the inhabitants and parishioners of Northwode might, by the authority of the bishop as ordinary, have free burial in the same chapel and its cemetery for the interment of their corpses.

To the prayer of this petition the prior and convent of Shene and the vicar, for themselves and their successors, agreed to give their consent, by permitting the inhabitants or parishioners of Northwode to have interment in the chapel and in the cemetery as they desired, from the 4th day of the month . . . . 1486 then instant, in all future times for ever, but so that no prejudice should be wrought to the parish and mother church of Hayling touching oblations and other its rights, privileges of themselves and of the church being in all things kept wholly safe and secure ; and this consent was ratified under the common seal of the prior and convent of Shene, and under the ordinary seal of the vicar of the parish : the bishop also, "applauding and approving" the consents of the prior and convent and of the vicar, confirmed them under his authority and the seal of the diocese. (*Regist. Waynflete*, fol. 13S.)

The residence of the chaplain to be provided under the ordinance of the bishop in Northwood, by night as well as by day, was evidently intended to secure the more certain performance of the several services then required : an object which otherwise could hardly have been obtained, if we consider the very defective means of communication even between places not far distant, and the requirement of some of those services at night. The Romish service consisted of matins after one A. M. ; prime at sunrise ; the third, sixth, and ninth, at nine A.M., noon, and three P.M. ; vespers in the evening ; and complines at bedtime. On festivals the appropriate services began in the evening of the preceding day, and were continued over the evening of the day itself, so that in such cases there were two vespers, called the first and second, the first being the more solemn of the two. The seals of the ecclesiastics, alluded to in the confirmation of the ordinances, were used under the authority of the laws of Henry III, by which it was enacted, that not only archbishops and bishops, but likewise their officials, should have seals for the ratification of their acts ; and the privilege was not confined to them alone, but was extended to abbots, priors, deans, archdeacons, and their officials, rural deans, cathedral chapters, and all colleges and convents. In

after times, as arms became more general, archbishops and
bishops impaled the arms of the diocese with those to which
they were entitled in their private capacity, borne either by
right of descent or by special grant from the College of
Heralds.   In compliance with the terms of the composition,
the parishioners proceeded to build a residence for the parochial chaplain.   How long he continued to reside is not
known ; probably however until the period of the Reformation in the reign of Henry VIII, when the mode of Divine
service being altered, and the difficulty of providing a fit
chaplain in the illiterate times which followed, joined to the
withdrawal by the parishioners of the oblations and obventions
upon which he must mainly have depended for subsistence,
might well operate to prevent his "continual abiding" there
both by day and by night.   The house itself, close by the chapel,
and styled the vicarage house, having for many years previously
been tenanted by paupers of the parish, and being in a state
of utter dilapidation, was finally pulled down in the year 1828.
The annual payment of 30s. to the vicar continues to this day
to be made by the churchwardens ; and Divine service is performed in the chapel of St. Peter, alternately with the mother
and parish church of Hayling.

The grounds upon which the division of burthens in the
repair of the chancel was ordered by the bishop, cannot at this
day be determined with accuracy, at least so far as the vicar
and the parishioners were concerned, since the deed of
composition, which would possibly have thrown light upon
the matter, and which appears in the schedule of the records
of the monastery of Shene at a late period, cannot now be
found.   The burthen of the prior and convent of Shene was
in proportion to the interest claimed by the abbey of
Jumiéges, and admitted in the endowment of 1253, as being
that to which the abbot and convent had been entitled from
time whereof the memory of man ran not to the contrary.
That of the vicar was no doubt, in respect to the tithe of hay,
usually a rectorial tithe, with which the vicarage was endowed ;
and that of the parishioners was probably one to which they
consented, either on the original erection of the chapel, or,

with greater probability perhaps, on the grant of the privilege
of interment within the chapel and cemetery of Northwood.
The chancels of both churches are at this time repaired by
the lord of the manor, who is the lay rector of both parishes.

Nothing further of moment occurs in the history of
Hayling during the period that it was held by the abbey of
Shene; and there is every reason to believe that the monks
were indulgent landlords, and that the parishioners during
their lordship enjoyed a time of comparative prosperity.
But in the reign of Henry VIII the cloud, which had long
been gathering over the abbeys and monasteries of the land,
burst with a violence but little to have been expected. In
the year 1539 the smaller religious houses, which were not
clearly able to expend above £200 a year, were granted by act
of Parliament to the king. The preamble of this act was
very curious, being in fact nothing less than an apology for
the suppression. It assumed, as a matter of notoriety, that
manifest sin, vicious, carnal, and abominable living, was committed in religious houses where the congregation consisted
of less than twelve persons, whereby the governors of such
houses and their convent spoiled and utterly wasted the
churches, monasteries, farms, and chattels, to the high dis-
pleasure of Almighty God, the slander of good religion, and
the great infamy of the king's highness. And albeit that
visitations had been made for the space of two hundred years
then past for a reformation of such abominable living, yet
that no amendment had ensued, but the vicious living had
shamefully increased, and by a cursed custom so grown and
infested, that a great multitude of the religious persons in
such small houses rather chose to rove abroad in apostacy,
than to conform to the observation of good religion; so that,
unless they were utterly suppressed, there could be no redress
nor reformation in that behalf. In consideration whereof, the
king's majesty being supreme head in earth under God of the
Church of England, daily studying and devising the increase,
advancement, and exaltation of true doctrine and virtue in the
same church, to the only glory and honour of God, and the
total extirpating and destruction of vice and sin; considering

also that divers and great monasteries, wherein religion was right well kept and observed, were destitute of such full numbers as they ought to keep, the Lords and Commons, by a great deliberation, finally resolved, that it was more to the pleasure of Almighty God that the possessions of such small religious houses not being spent, spoiled, and wasted for increase and maintenance of sin, should be used and converted to better purposes; and thereupon desired the king's highness that it might be enacted by authority of Parliament, that his majesty should have to him and his heirs for ever all and singular such monasteries.

No fewer than three hundred and seventy-five convents were suppressed at this time, and ten thousand persons were, by the dissolution, sent to seek their fortune in the wide world. Some had friends to receive them, others none at all; some had twenty shillings given them at their expulsion, and a new gown. A clear revenue of thirty thousand pounds per annum was acquired by the crown, besides plate and moveables to the value of ten thousand pounds more, although the king enjoyed it but a short time, bestowing it in grants, sale, or exchange, with those who had assisted in the work of spoliation. Most specious uses however were pretended that all should be done to the pleasure of Almighty God, and for the honour of the realm. And particular care was taken by the statute as it is printed, for the reservation of rents and services, corrodies, and pensions to founders, donors, and benefactors. It was also ordered that those to whom abbey lands were granted should keep, or cause to be kept, a continual house or household in the same site or precinct. They were also to occupy yearly as much of the demesnes in tillage as the abbots had done, or their farmers under them, under a monthly penalty of £6. 13s. 4d., which remained in force about eighty years, when the repeal of the conditions annexed to the grants was obtained in the 21st of King James.

This was but the forerunner of the general dissolution under which the whole of the larger abbeys and monasteries throughout England were swept away with an unsparing hand; and the House of Jesus of Bethlehem shared the fate of the rest

The commission of visitation issued by Cromwell, the ready minister of Henry VIII, returned to him an account of the state in which these larger religious establishments were found; and there is extant a "Lettere" from the commis-sioners which will be found in Fuller (bk. 6, sec. iii, No. 8), "certefying the incontynense of the nuns of Syon with the "friores; and aftore the acte done, the friores reconsile them "to God," addressed to the Right Honourable Master Thomas Cromwell, chief secretary to the king's highness; but it is not of a nature to insert here; and it may be added that many such scandals reported by the visitors are believed to have had little foundation in truth, and to have been invented, or at all events greatly exaggerated, for the purpose of showing some justification, however trifling, for the act of dissolution.

Upon the confiscation of the monastery of Shene, the manor and rectory of Hayling passed into the hands of the crown; and in the 32 Henry VIII, I find, by the minister's accounts in the Augmentation Office, that Hayling had been in the farm of John Tawke, the reeve of the crown, whose assignees, Nicolas Cheke and John Kempe, then stood charged with the rent from the feast of Saint Michael in the 31st, to the same feast in the 32d year of the reign. By this document it appears that the farm of the priory yielded £56 for the year; but the water-mill, with various other property, consisting of the courts, wreck of sea, the chief chambers, and one stable, then called the prior's stable, the rectory and tithes, and the vicarage, was in lease to John Tawke, by indenture dated the 11th day of January, 7th Henry VIII, 1515, for a term of fifty-three years, at the rent reserved in the lease. They also rendered 20s. for the farm of a water-mill, with houses and a pool, and 61s. 11d. for the perquisites of court.

They took credit for £4, the amount of the vicar's pension by the year; 20s. for the water-mill, standing waste; and £55. 14s. 7d. for money paid on repairing and newly making the mill of Hailinge; with 100s. for two pair of millstones and divers other necessaries purchased and provided for the repair of the same, in accordance with a bill of particulars then delivered, examined by John Lorymer, surveyor and steward of the late prior of Shene.

In the following year another change took place in the ownership of Hayling. The colleges, not being included within the category of the religious houses suppressed at the general dissolution, for the most part remained untouched until the reign of Edward VI, when many of them were seized and appropriated to the purposes of the crown. The College of Arundel, dedicated to the Holy Trinity, possessed the manor or lordship of Bury, in the county of Sussex; and at the request of the king, by an indenture of the 20th May in that year they conveyed the same with various other lands to him, his heirs and successors. In return for this, or rather by way of exchange, Henry granted to the master, chaplains, and fellows of the college, the manor and rectory of Hallyng, in the county of Southampton, then lately belonging and apper·taining to the then late monastery or priory of Shene, with the tithes, oblations, obventions, fruits, profits, and glebe lands, to the rectory of Hayling belonging or appertaining; and the site, circuit, ambit, and precinct of the then late priory of Hayling, and of the manor of Hayling, then lately belonging to the monastery of Shene, with the water-mill, fisheries, tithes, and all other appurtenances then or lately in the lease and tenure of John Tawke; and the lands, waters, commons, fisheries, vivaries, water-courses, pools, mills, marsh lands—salt as well as fresh, warrens, liberties, franchises, rents, by copy of court roll and customary rents, courts leet, heriots, reliefs, escheats, goods and chattels of felons, outlaws, and persons attainted, and all other the royal hereditaments and possessions in the parishes, towns, hamlets, and fields of Hayling, Chewton, and Winterborne Stoke, reputed as parcel of the manor of Hayling, within the space of four years then last past, as fully and wholly and in as ample manner and form, and with all such-like liberties, franchises, warrens, and privileges, as the last prior of the then late monastery or priory of Shene, or any one or more of his predecessors, priors of the then late priory of Shene, in right of the then late priory, by virtue of the letters patent of the then king, or any of his progenitors before written, or otherwise, or in any other way he or they had had, held, used, or enjoyed, or might or ought to have had, held, used, or enjoyed in the same manor, rectory, messuages, lands, tenements, mills, tithes, and other the premises, with the appurtenances in the county of Southampton, and so fully and wholly, and in as ample a manner and form, and with all such liberties, profits, franchises, warrens, and privileges, as the same manor and premises in any way soever had come to the hands of the crown.

And he granted to the master, chaplain, and fellows of Arundel, the woods, underwoods, and trees within the manor of Hayling, reserving only the advowsons and presentations of churches and chantries belonging to the manor of Hayling: to hold to them and their successors for ever of the king, his heirs, and successors *in capite*, by knight's service of half a knight's fee, and rendering for the manor of Hayling (together with that of Schepley included in the grant) £6. 14s. 10½d. at the Court of Augmentation on the feast of Saint Michael yearly, for all other services and demands whatsoever.

He also granted to them the advowson and patronage of the parish church and vicarage of Haylinge, then lately belonging to the monastery of Shene, together with the views of frankpledge, courts leet, assize and assay of bread and beer, goods and chattels waived, goods and chattels of felons and fugitives, outlaws and attainted, escheats, wreck of the sea, free warrens, liberties, franchises, and privileges, as held by the last Prior of Shene, free from all payments except the reserved rent of £6. 14s. 10½d., and " a certain annuity or stipend of " four pounds sterling from thenceforth yearly, payable to the " vicar for the time being of the parish church and vicarage of " Haylinge." This charter bore date the 18th day of July, 33 Henry VIII, 1541, and was granted at Westminster by writ of privy seal. (1st part *Pat. Rolls*, 33 Henry VIII).

In the latter part of the reign of King Edward III, Richard Earl of Arundel founded a chantry for six chaplains and several clerks and cloisters at Arundel, near the church there,

and bequeathed to it one thousand marks by his will, dated
in 1375. His son Richard obtained of King Richard II
permission that the alien priory of Saint Nicolas at Arundel,
founded by his predecessors, and bestowed by them on the
Benedictine abbey of Saint Martin de Seez in Normandy,
should be extinguished, and that the tithes and lands
belonging to the priory should, together with the bequest of
the earl his father, and various other estates, be appropriated
to the foundation of a collegiate church, styled the College of
the Holy Trinity, for the maintenance of a master, twelve
secular canons, three deacons, three sub-deacons, two acolites,
seven choristers, and two sacrists. In the 26 Henry VIII,
1534, it was found to be endowed with £263. 14s. 9d. in
gross, or £168. 0s. 7½d. net, but did not long survive the
endowment contained in the charter of 33 Henry VIII, for
in the 36 Henry VIII, it was surrendered to the crown, and
was by the king bestowed upon the patron, Henry Earl of
Arundel.

The grant to the earl was very extensive in its terms, and
in the property to which it had relation; for the king, as well
in consideration of the good, faithful, and acceptable service to
which his most dear cousin, Henry Earl of Arundel, had to
him theretofore performed, as in consideration of one thousand marks by the same earl paid, of his special favour, and
of his certain knowlege and mere motion, gave and granted
to the same earl, all the ground, ambit, circuit, and precinct
of the late collegiate church or college of the Holy Trinity of
Arundel in the county of Sussex, otherwise called the
chantry of the Holy Trinity, then dissolved; and the belfry
and cemetery of the college or chantry, and all messuages,
barns, granges, dovehouses, orchards, gardens, ponds, vivaries,
and soil whatsoevor, within the site and precinct of the
collegiate church, college, or chantry, with (among various
other lordships) the manor of Hailing in the county of
Southampton. The general words included dovehouses,
waters, vivaries, fisheries, advowsons, donations, free dispo-
sitions, and patronage of churches, vicarages, chantries,
chapels, and other ecclesiastical benefices, reliefs, courts,

bondmen, and villains, with their suits, leets, view of frank-pledge, estrays, wreck of sea, free warrens, and all things which to free warren pertained, deodands, and all and singular other the royal franchises whatsoever to the same manor belonging and held by the college so lately dissolved.

He also granted to him the rectory of Hailing, tithes, as well great as small, oblations, obventions, pensions, portions, whatsoever belonging thereto, and the advowson, free dispo-sition, and right of patronage of the church and vicarage of Hailing: all which said premises were stated to have come into the hands of the crown by the surrender and confirma-tion of Alan Percy, clerk, the last master of the college of the Holy Trinity of Arundel, and the chaplains of the same, by deed under their common seal, bearing date the 12th day of December, in the 36th year of the reign, and inrolled of record in the Court of Chancery.

And he granted to him the woods, underwoods, coppices, and trees upon the premises, and all such franchises, rights, and privileges as the same college or its predecessors had held at any time before the dissolution thereof, and before it had come into the royal hands, as fully and entirely as it had come into the royal hands by reason of the dissolution of the same college, and of the surrender of the same : to hold all and singular the same premises unto the same Henry Earl of Arundel, his heirs and assigns, of his Majesty, his heirs and successors *in capite*, by knight's service, to wit, by the service of the tenth part of a knight's fee, and the rent of £16. 16s. 0¾d. in the name of a tenth, at the Court of Aug-mentation at the feast of Saint Michael the Archangel in every year, for all other services and demands whatsoever.

And he granted to him, his heirs and assigns, that he and they might hold and enjoy within all the premises, such courts leet, view of frankpledge, fines, profits, the assize and assay of bread, wine, and beer, wardship, marriages, escheats, reliefs, heriots, marts, markets, tolls, customs, fairs, liberties, fran-chises, free warrens, and all that to free warren belonged, goods and chattels warded, chattels of felons, outlaws, fugitives, attainted and put in exigent, deodands, wreck of the sea, rights and jurisdictions whatsoever, as fully and entirely, and in as ample a manner and form, as the college or its predecessors had held the same by reason of any charter, gift, grant, or confirmation, or of any letters patent by the king himself or any of his progenitors to the same college or any of its predecessors in any manner made or granted, or by reason of any lawful prescription, acquisition, use, custom, or otherwise, in whatsoever manner had or done.

And he granted to the earl, his heirs and assigns, that he and they might impropriate and hold in proper uses to him and his heirs, the rectory of Hayling, with its appurtenances and glebe lands, as amply as the college had held the same, with the oblations, obventions, and profits there, and all the charters, evidences, letters patent, and muniments of title of the college to the premises granted, and the bells, lead, goods and chattels thereto belonging. This charter (1st part *Pat. Rolls*, 36 Henry VIII, *Rolls Chapel*), containing the donation of eighteen other manors, several rectories and land at Lumps in the island of Portsea, was given by writ of privy seal at Westminster on the 26th day of December.

This Henry Earl of Arundel stood high in the favour of Queen Mary; and although the grant of Henry VIII was ample—founded partly upon services performed, and partly upon the payment of a pecuniary consideration—yet, in consequence of the tender footing upon which the title of abbey lands then rested, he deemed it of importance to obtain a confirmation from his royal mistress, and additional privileges within the lordships comprised in the charter. Accordingly we find that in the first year of her reign, on account of the faithful ministry which her well-beloved and faithful cousin and councillor, Henry Earl of Arundel, one of her privy council, had shown to the crown in the then late civil war against the then late traitor, Sir John Dudley, knight, and for other causes and considerations, she, of her especial grace, granted to the earl and his heirs, that they for ever should have and hold the returns of all writs, bills, and precepts of the Exchequer, precepts of the justices itinerant, pleas of the crown, common pleas and pleas of the forest, in numerous

manors, and among them in the lordships and manors of
Aulton and Haylinge in the county of Southampton; that
within the same lordships and manors he should hold courts
baron and leet, goods and chattels of felons, view of frankpledge, waifs and strays, deodands, treasure trove and other
things found, and manuopera, wreck of the sea, in whatsoever
coasts and arms of the sea of the lordships, manors, lands,
tenements, possessions, hundreds, liberties, franchises, and
hereditaments of him the earl adjoining, in whatsoever way
arising, and all things which to wreck of sea and deodands
belonged, to his and their use for ever; assize and assay of
bread, wine, and beer, and all other victuals and all things
which belonged to the clerk of the market of the royal household.   And that they for ever should have free warren in all
and singular the lordships and manors of the earl, and in his
demesne lands wheresoever they might be, and free chase in
his lordships and woods, although the same might be within
the metes of the royal forests, so that no forester or other
officer should enter therein without the license of the earl and
his heirs.

And the queen being willing to secure more fully the grant
of the franchises thereby made to the earl, and that he and
his heirs might at all future time quietly enjoy the same,
granted to the earl, that although he or his heirs any of the
grants, liberties, franchises, acquittances, and immunities to
them then granted, from thenceforth, in any case should
happen not to use or abuse, nevertheless it should be lawful
for the earl and his heirs afterwards, from time to time to use
and enjoy the same grants, liberties, franchises, acquittances,
and immunities, without impediment or molestation; and
that upon production of the letters patent then made, or the
inrolment of the same in Chancery before the justices of either
bench, or before the Treasurer and Barons of the Exchequer,
or in any court throughout the realm of England, the same
letters patent should be allowed to the earl and his heirs.
This charter bore date on the second day of February from
Westminster.   (2d part *Pat.* 1 Mary.)

On the 15th of July, 2 and 3 Philip and Mary, 1554, the

earl obtained a grant of the hundreds of Rotherbridge and
Bury, with all their rights, members, and appurtenances, by
virtue whereof, and of the former grants, he became seized in
his demesne as of fee; as well of the hundreds of Rotherbridge and Bury, as of the hundreds of Westbourne, Singleton,
Eastbourne, Box, Stockbridge, Avisford, Westerwich, and
Polinge, and of the manor of Haylinge and hundred of
Redbridge, and of the liberties and franchises expressed in the
letters patent.   It is stated among the *Norfolk Muniments,*
that the earl paid no less a sum than £14,000 for these
grants the privileges being deemed of such value and
importance.   (*Steward's Account Book,* 1657 to 1662;
Norfolk Muniments.)

This Henry Earl of Arundel remained lord of Hayling up
to 1579, when he died.   He was the last of the Fitz Alans,
and was buried in the choir of the church of Arundel, of
which he was patron.   There is a monument to his memory,
erected by John Lord Lumley, his son-in-law and the executor
of his will, the inscription upon which gives an epitome
of his life and services.   It runs as follows :—

"SACRED TO VIRTUE AND HONOUR.

" *The illustrious hero, whose figure you see here and whose
bones rest here below, was Earl of this place (Arundel).
He derived his descent and name from Fitz-Alan, his
honours from Maltravers, lord and baron Clun and
Oswaldestre, oldest companion of the most noble
order of the Garter, only son and successor to William
Earl of Arundel, and heir to all his virtues.   He was
privy counsellor to Henry VIII, Edward VI, Queen
Mary, and Queen Elizabeth, and governor of Calais,
and when King Henry besieged Boulogne in Picardy,
he was chief marshall of his army, and afterwards lord
chamberlain.   At the coronation of his son Edward, he
held the office of marshall of England, and was chamberlain to this king as he had before been to his father.
At the accession of Queen Mary, he was appointed*

high constable for her coronation, and afterwards
steward of her household and president of the council,
as also to Queen Elizabeth, to whom he was also steward
of the household.

" *Thus this nobleman, illustrious by birth, more so by his*
discharge of his several public characters, and most
illustrious both at home and abroad, loaded with
honours, worn out with toil in a good old age, having
reached his 68th year, devoutly and sweetly slept in the
Lord at London, Feb. 25, A.D. 1579."

John Lord Lumley, as I have before stated, married Jane the eldest daughter of the earl, who, from his extravagance, became involved in debt. Lord Lumley extricated him from a portion of his difficulties, and in consequence of this, terms were granted by the earl in his favour out of various manors which were then held by the latter. In the 1 Elizabeth 1558, Lord Lumley had issue by the Lady Jane one son and one daughter, " of young and tender age, and more plenty of " issue was likely by God's grace to have by the said Lady " Jane." In consideration of the marriage, for the better maintenance of the Lord Lumley, and for the especial and hearty favour, love, and affection that he bore to the Lord Lumley, and in consideration of the payment of monies then owing by the earl to persons scheduled in a bill then prepared, the earl, by indenture dated the 9th January 1559, and inrolled in the Court of Chancery, demised to the Lord Lumley the hundreds of Westbourne, Singleton, Eastbourne, Box, Stockbridge, Avisford, Westerwich, Polinge, Bury, and Rotherbridge, and the manor of Haylinge and hundred of Redbridge, with all their appurtenances, liberties, franchises, rents, and other yearly profits reserved : to hold the same to the Lord Lumley, his heirs and assigns, for the term of one hundred years then next following, without impeachment of waste, rendering to the Earl of Arundel, his heirs and assigns, twenty shillings yearly if demanded.

Under this deed the Lord Lumley entered into possession of the manor of Hayling, with the liberties, privileges, franchises, and jurisdictions thereof; and being so possessed, the earl, by certain other indentures dated the 4th Nov. 4 Elizabeth, 1562, and made between the earl of the one part, and Thomas Stoughton, Thomas Bromley, and Roger Daylinder, of the other part, for the love and affection which he bore to the Lord Lumley and Lady Jane his wife, daughter of him the said earl, gave and granted to Stoughton, Bromley, and Daylinder, the reversion of the hundreds and liberties included in the term of one hundred years, and the manor of Hayling and Redbridge in the county of Southampton, to the use of the earl and the heirs male of his body lawfully begotten; and for default of such issue, to the use of Lord Lumley and Lady Jane his wife, and their heirs male lawfully begotten; and in default of such issue, then to the use of the heirs male of the Lady Jane; and in default, to the use of the heirs of the Lord Lumley; and in default of such issue, then to the use of the heirs of the body of the Lord Lumley; and for default of such issue, to the use of him, Henry Earl of Arundel and his heirs for ever.

In consequence of this entail of the reversion, Lord Lumley being in possession of the hundred of Westbourne and other estates, and of Haylinge and Redbridge, for the residue of the term of one hundred years so granted, as I have before mentioned, attorned tenant to Stoughton, Bromley, and Dalynder.

Henry Earl of Arundel therefore was seized in his demesne as of fee tail of the reversion of the hundreds and estates so settled, including the manor of Hayling and hundred of Redbridge; and this being the case, in the year 1576-7, Lady Jane Lumley died without issue, and was buried at Cheam in Surrey, on the 9th of March in that year, and John Lord Lumley surviving her, was in possession of the hundreds, with the manor of Hayling, for the residue of the term of one hundred years. Henry Earl of Arundel on the thirtieth day of December, 22 Elizabeth, made his last will and testament in writing, whereby he confirmed the conveyance made between himself and Stoughton, Bromley, and Daylinder, of the 4th November, 4 Elizabeth, 1562, and he devised the hundreds of Westbourne, Singleton, and other estates, including the manor of Haylinge and hundred of Redbridge, with the various liberties and franchises vested in him, to the Lord Lumley, styled in the will as his son, to hold to him and his assigns for ever.

Upon the death of Henry Earl of Arundel, without heir male of his body, John Lord Lumley became seized of the hundreds of Westbourne and other estates, including the manor of Haylinge and hundred of Redbridge in fee tail, with remainder to himself and his heirs, as appears among the memoranda of the Exchequer of the 23d Elizabeth, 1580, in the records of Hilary Term, in a process touching the then late sheriff of the county of Sussex.

By an indenture bearing date the 17th June, 3 James I, 1604, John Lord Lumley and Elizabeth his then wife (he being stated to be invested with the right, title, and interest of the estates under conveyance made to him of the same by Henry Earl of Arundel deceased), in consideration of sixteen hundred pounds paid to him by Edward Carryll, John Holland, John Cornwallis, and Robert Causefield, granted to them, their heirs and assigns, the hundreds of Polinge and other estates, together with the liberties, privileges, fines, and other franchises, within the same hundreds, and the manor of Haylinge, to hold to the said Carryll, Holland, Cornwallis, and Causefield, their heirs and assigns for ever, in as full and ample a manner and form as the premises had been originally granted to Henry Earl of Arundel, and by the earl granted to him the Lord Lumley, and as he the Lord Lumley and Elizabeth his wife, and the assigns of him the Lord Lumley, then held or enjoyed the same, if the indenture had not been made. Under this conveyance therefore, Carryll, Holland, Cornwallis, and Causefield became seized in their demesne as of fee, in trust for Thomas then Earl of Arundel and Surrey, of the hundred of Polinge, with other estates, including the manor of Haylinge and hundred of Redbridge.

The reversion of the manor of Hayling having thus been traced into the possession of Thomas Earl of Arundel, by the conveyance from John Lord Lumley to his trustees, it becomes necessary to see in what manner the residue of the term of one hundred years, originally granted by Henry Earl of Arundel to John Lord Lumley, was disposed of. Litigation to a very considerable extent has lately arisen out of this lease, and it may therefore be interesting to show the various assignments, so far as they are capable of proof, leaving observation upon the nature of the existing claim as founded under the lease for comment hereafter.

By an indenture bearing date the 1st April, 1st Elizabeth, 1559, John Lord Lumley made a demise of ninety-nine years from the date of the indenture to Thomas Stoughton and Humphrey Lloide; and by another indenture, for a consideration, paid to Lord Lumley, the amount of which does not appear, Stoughton and Loide on the 4th Elizabeth, 1562, demised to one Ralph Henslowe the site of the manor of Hayling, and all lands, tenements, and hereditaments, with all manner of rents arising out of the same tenements, parcel of the manor, as well copyhold as freehold, or in anywise holden of the manor, the water-mills, wards, marriages, reliefs, escheats, wrecks of the sea, courts, fines, waifs, strays, felons' goods, heriots, granting of copies of customary lands and tenements, parcel of the premises, upon which copies the old accustomed rent or more should be reserved, and all the lands and tenements of the said copyholders always excepted and reserved, to Stoughton and Loide, to hold the premises from the feast of Saint Michael 1568, for the term of fifty years, under such articles and agreements as were declared by indentures of the same date as the demise, with a clause of re-entry upon nonpayment of the rents at the days appointed, or within two months after upon demand at the Mansion-house. (*Liber Ro. Spiller*, 1586.)

By indenture bearing date the 4th June, 4 Elizabeth, the Lord Lumley, after reciting that Ralph Henslowe was standing lawfully possessed of the manor place of Hayling, and of divers other lands, tenements, and hereditaments, parcel of the manor, and also of the rectory of Hayling, with the tithes there, for the term of fifty-three years from Michaelmas, 7 Henry VIII, 1515, under a demise from John Jeeborne, some time prior of the dissolved house of Sheene of the order of Carthusians, in the county of Surrey, to John Tawke, of Havant, then deceased, for the yearly rent of fifty-six pounds, of whose estate Henslowe was then lawfully seized. And reciting the lease made by Henry Earl of Arundel to the Lord Lumley, of the 9th January, 1 Elizabeth 1558-9, the lease made by the Lord Lumley to Stoughton and Loide of the 1st April, 1 Elizabeth, and the lease made by Stoughton and Loide to Henslowe of even date, for the term of fifty years from the year 1568, for the yearly rent of £56, confirmed by recognizances inrolled in Chancery, the Lord Lumley ratified and confirmed, as well the former lease made by the prior to Tawke, and the lease made to Henslowe by Stoughton and Loide, as also the estates, terms, and interests for years then to come, which Henslowe then had in the premises, to be good and effectual in the law against the Earl of Arundel, him the Lord Lumley, his and their heirs, executors, and assigns, and against the Lady Anne Matravers and all other the person and persons claiming or to claim under him the Lord Lumley. And the Lord Lumley demised to Henslowe all the premises mentioned in the demise to Stoughton and Loide; and he covenanted to save him and the demised premises harmless from the payment of four pounds yearly, payable to the vicar of Hayling or his successors out of the parsonage, and twenty shillings rent reserved by the Earl of Arundel upon his lease of one hundred years to him the Lord Lumley, his own rent payable by Stoughton and Loide, and all tenths due to the queen's majesty; and Henslowe covenanted during the terms which he held, to find for the steward and officers of the Lord Lumley coming to keep the courts upon the manor, and their servants, convenient meat and drink for them and their servants, and provision for their horses, and that he would find a man and horse for service in the wars at his own charges. The Lord Lumley covenanted that Henslowe should enjoy his term of fifty years against the Earl of Arundel, him the Lord Lumley, and the Lady Anne Matravers. Henslowe covenanted not to alien without licence, and assigned his interest in the former lease of the

rectory to the Lord Lumley, excepting the tithes of the
demesnes. (*Ibid.*)

It seems that Stoughton survived Loide, and demised
twenty-two acres in the parish of Portsea, called Kingston
Pastures, parcel of the manor of Hayling, to Henslowe; and
as the entry in Spiller's book, which gives information of the
fact, has been the subject of so much argument, on the point
of its admissibility to establish the descent of the lease, and of
the lands comprised in it, I give the extract as it is found in
the book itself.

" Tho. Stoughton, by indenture bearing date 14⁰ die Junii
" 12 R. Eliz. resiting one lease made by Henry Earle of
" Arundell, dated 9⁰ Januarii anno 1⁰ Eliz. unto John
" Lo. Lumley for 100 years, and one other lease made by
" the said Lo. Lumley unto the said Stoughton and one
" Humphrey Loyde, declaringe then the said Loyde to be
" deade, and hymselfe to be sole seazed by survivershipp for
" and in consideration of the summe of lxxvˡʰ paid unto the
" said Lord Lumley by Raphe Henslowe Gent. demiseth
" and graunteth unto hym all those pasture groundes
Kingston Pas- " lyinge in Kingston in the pishe of Portzee, pcell.
tures in Por- " of the mannor of Haylinge, contayninge 22 acres,
tize pcell of " &c. to have and to holde from the feaste of St.
the mannor of
Haylinge. " Michell the Archangell before the date there of
" for the term of 51 yeares Reddend. p. annu. at the 2 usual
" feastes xxviˢ. viiiᵈ. A clause of distresse for the rent arere bye
" the space of one monethe. A reentre for not payinge by the
" space of 3 moneths, the same being lawfullye demanded,
" &c. And after endorsed, signed, sealed, and delivered by
" Tho. Stoughton Esq. 13 Maii ano. 13 Eliz. Raphen
" Henslowe by deede indented, bearinge date xxii⁰ Aprilis
" ano. 17⁰ Eliz. resytinge the former deedes, asyneth all his
" interest to Mr. Popiniaye, from whose widow, by speciall
" conveyance, Sr. Edward Cresswell, knighte, claymeth x
" yeares yet to come from the feaste of St. Michael last.

" Entered 22 Nov. 1610."

The lease of the manor of Hayling, together with two other leases of the manors of Alton and Westbrook, all being of the same date were excepted out of the indenture of the 17 June, 3 James I, 1605, under which the manor of Hayling was, among other estates, conveyed to Carryll, Holland, Cornwallis, and Causefield; and, by an indenture bearing date the 6th October, 6 James I, 1607-8, John Lord Lumley, who was therein stated to be lawfully possessed of the manor of Hayling in the county of Southampton, and of divers lands thereunto belonging for divers years then to come and unexpired, and upon divers particular estates thereof expectant, for the special love and affection which he bore unto the Right Honourable Thomas Earl of Arundel and Surrey, and for other considerations, at the nomination of the said earl, assigned to Danyll Pullein and Nicolas Tomson the manor of Haylinge, and all his lands, tenements, and hereditaments thereunto belonging, and the rectory of Haylinge, together with the glebe lands, tithes, oblations, obventions, profits, rights, members, and appurtenances thereunto appertaining or of right belonging, and the reversion of the said manor and rectory, and the rents thereto incident, and the estate, interest, and term of years which he the Lord Lumley had then to come and unexpired in the manor and parsonage, to hold to Pullein and Tomson, their executors, administrators, and assigns for and during all such estate, interest, and term of years as he the Lord Lumley had then to come and unexpired in the manor and parsonage of Hayling.

By this means Thomas Earl of Arundel became possessed of the residue of the term of one hundred years granted by Henry Earl of Arundel to John Lord Lumley in the 1 Eliz. 1559, and of the reversion of the manor, expectant upon the determination of the lease.

The disgrace of the Howard family by Henry VIII is too well known to require comment; suffice it to say that the accomplished Henry Earl of Surrey was beheaded in his father's lifetime, and the Duke of Norfolk was imprisoned in the Tower, having been attainted of high treason by Parliament. He married first, Anne, daughter of King Edward IV, and by his second wife, Elizabeth, daughter of Edward Duke of Buckingham, he had issue Henry above mentioned, and Thomas.

Thomas Howard, son of Henry Earl of Surrey, was restored in blood, his grandfather's attainder having being reversed in the 1 Mary, 1553. He married Mary, coheiress of Henry Fitz-Alan Earl of Arundel, the grantee of the manor of Hayling; and being attainted of high treason, for endeavouring to compass a match with Mary Queen of Scots, was beheaded in the year 1572. His only son by the Fitz-Allan coheiress, Philip Howard, was summoned to Parliament in 1580 as Earl of Arundel, in right of his mother, and by possession of the Castle of Arundel. He was a zealous Roman Catholic; and in endeavouring in 1586 to pass beyond seas without the leave of Queen Elizabeth, he was fined £10,000 in the Court of Star Chamber, and was condemned by his peers in Westminster Hall for practices in reference to his religion, and for countenancing the Spaniards. He was imprisoned in the Tower until his death, which took place in the year 1595.

His son Thomas Earl of Arundel and Surrey, the reversioner of the lease and fee of the manor of Hayling, was, by act of Parliament of the 1 James, 1603, restored to all such titles of honour as his father, Philip Earl of Arundel, had lost by his attainder, and to such dignity of baronies as his grandfather, Thomas Duke of Norfolk, had lost by his attainder. The lands however which formed the baronies of Clun and Oswaldestre had been granted to the Earl of Northampton, had passed from him to the Earl of Suffolk, and were therefore lost to the family of the Earl of Arundel.

In the 2d of James I, 1604, that monarch granted to Thomas Earl of Arundel, his heirs and assigns, the honour and borough of Arundel, in the county of Sussex, and the Castle of Arundel, with its rights, members, and appurtenances, the hundreds of Powling, Eastborne, Eastwith, Westwith, Avesford, and Rotherbridge, in the county of Sussex, and among various other manors, the manor of Hayling, in the county of Southampton, with its rights, members, and appurtenances; and the rectory of Hayling, with its rights, members, and appurtenances, which honour, castle, lordships, manors, hundreds, rectories, and other premises, were stated to have been parcel of the possessions of Henry the late Earl of Arundel, or of Philip, then late Earl of Arundel, or one of them. The general words comprised warrens, fisheries, mines, quarries, marriages, escheats, reliefs, heriots, courts leet, view of frankpledge, profits, advowsons, and rights of patronage ; and all churches, chapels, estrays, bond men and women, villains with their families, markets, fairs, tolls, customs, rights, and all the other appurtenances.

He also granted to him all woods and underwoods, and that he, his heirs, and assigns, from thenceforth for ever, should hold and enjoy, within the premises comprised in the grant, so many, so great, such and the like courts leet, view of frankpledge, law days, assize and assay of bread, wine, and beer, heriots, free warrens, and all other rights and jurisdictions, as fully, freely, and wholly, and in as ample manner and form as the then late Henry Earl of Arundel, or Philip, then late Earl of Arundel, or other person having been possessed of the honour, lordships, and manors, ever had, held, or enjoyed the same, under charter, grant, or confirmation theretofore made, or by prescription, use, or custom, and as fully as the same had come into the hands of the then King, or of Elizabeth, then late Queen of England, by reason of the attainder of Philip Earl of Arundel, and any other way howsoever : To hold the same to the sole and proper use of him, Thomas Earl of Arundel, his heirs, and assigns, for ever, by the ancient rents and services. This charter (*Pat. Rolls*, 2 James) was granted at Westminster, on the 6th day of June, by writ of privy seal.

In the 14th of James I, 1616-17, the Earl of Arundel applied for a special charter of free warren, and the king, in consideration of twenty shillings, and for other good causes and considerations, granted to him, by the description of Knight of the most Noble Order of the Garter, and one of the Privy Council, and to his heirs and assigns, that he, his heirs, and assigns, and every of them for ever, should have

free warren in various lordships and manors situate in the
counties of Cumberland, Westmoreland, Norfolk, Suffolk,
Shropshire, Sussex, Bedford, and Lincoln; and also free
warren within his Island called Haylinge, and in all the lands
and tenements, meadows, feedings, pastures, woods, woodlands, wastes, furze heaths, marshes, commons, and hereditaments of him, Thomas Earl of Arundel and Surrey, within
the island aforesaid, in the county of Southampton; with
liberty to reduce any parcel into severalty, and thereof to
make a park and parks, warren and warrens, and to separate
and inclose the same with ditches, hedges, walls, pales, or in
any other way for a park or warren.

And the king granted to the earl, his heirs, and assigns,
full and entire liberty, license, and authority, all the said
baronies, manors, lordships, lands, tenements, wastes, commons, furzes, heaths, marshes, and hereditaments, as well
inclosed as not inclosed, from time to time to stock with
deer, hares, rabbits, pheasants, partridges, fowl, and other
beasts and birds of whatsoever kind of *feræ naturæ;* and
that no one should enter or presume to enter such park or
free warren, to drive, hunt, hawk, chase, shoot, or in any way
disturb or take any thing which belonged to park or free
warren, without the license of the earl, under the accustomed
penalties, and under a penalty of ten pounds to the use of
the earl, his heirs, and assigns. This charter (15 *Par. Pat.
Rolls*, 14 James I) was granted at Westminster, on the 7th
day of March, by warrant of the commissioners.

It would appear that this Thomas Earl of Arundel was
anxious to keep up, in after times, the *prestige* attached to his
house and lineage. The honour consisted of no less than
eighty-four knights' fees originally; and the earl, in the 3rd
Charles I, obtained an act of Parliament, intituled " An Act
" concerning the title, name, and dignity of Earl of Arundel,
" and for the annexing of the castle, honour, manor, and lord-
" ship of Arundel, in the county of Sussex, with the titles and
" dignities of the baronies of Fitzalan, Clun and Oswaldestre,
" and Maltravers, and with divers other lands, tenements, and
" hereditaments in the act mentioned, being then parcel of the

" possessions of Thomas Earl of Arundel and Surrey, Earl
" Marshal of England, to the same title, name, and dignity of
" Earl of Arundel."

The act was in the form of a petition from the earl to the
king, stating that the title, name, and dignity of Earl of
Arundel was, and, from time whereof the memory of man was
not to the contrary, had been real and local, and had, from
the time aforesaid, belonged unto and been used and enjoyed
by himself and such of his ancestors as had had in them and
enjoyed the inheritance of the castle, honour, and lordship of
Arundel ; and by reason of such inheritance and seisin the
earl and his ancestors, from time whereof the memory of
man was not to the contrary, had been Earls of Arundel, and
had thereby used, borne, and enjoyed the title, name, and
dignity of Earl of Arundel, and thereby also had, from the
time aforesaid, enjoyed their places in parliaments and
councils and elsewhere as Earls of Arundel.

He also stated that the large revenues that were, in former
times, wont to support the title, name, and dignity, had, in
the latter ages, been dismembered and diminished by alienations, and, in future times, might be lessened if not prevented, which could in no way so well be had as by annexing
as well the castle, honour, and lordship, as also divers other
of the baronies, lordships, manors, lands, tenements, and
hereditaments of him, the earl, to the title, name, and dignity
of Earl of Arundel, in such sort as that, thereafter, the castle,
honour, and lordship, with other lands, might continually
remain to those of the blood of him the earl, that should
thereafter have, use, and enjoy the title, name, and dignity of
Earl of Arundel ; that so they might better support the titles,
names, and dignities, and be the more able to serve the
queen's majesty, her heirs, and successors, in their rank and
quality.

And the earl prayed that it might be, and it was accordingly enacted, that the title, name, and dignity of Earl of
Arundel, and castle, honour, and lordship of Arundel, and
the baronies of Lord Fitzalan, Lord of Clun and Oswaldestre,
and Lord Maltravers, and all places, pre-eminences, arms,

33

ensigns, and dignities to the earldom, castle, honour, and baronies belonging, and the borough and manor of Arundel, and various hundreds there. enumerated ; and the jurisdictions, royalties, pre-eminences, liberties, and franchises within divers hundreds, manors, and precincts, in the county of Surrey, Sussex, and Southampton, called "the Earl of " Arundel his liberties," and the manor, rectory, and Isle of Hayling, with the rights, members, and appurtenances thereof, should for ever stand, be, and remain estated, assured, and settled to him the Earl of Arundel and Surrey, and the heirs male of his body lawfully begotten and to be begotten ; and for default of such issue, then to the heirs of the body of him the earl lawfully begotten and to be begotten ; and for default of such issue then to the Right Honourable the Lord William Howard, uncle of him the earl, and son of the Right Noble Prince Thomas, then late Duke of Norfolk, and the heirs male of his body lawfully begotten and to be begotten ; and for default of such issue, then to the heirs of the body of the Lord William Howard lawfully begotten ; and for default of such issue to him, Thomas Earl of Arundel and Surrey, and his heirs for ever.

And it was enacted, that neither Thomas Earl of Arundel and Surrey, nor any of the heirs male or other heirs of his body, nor any other person or persons, his or their heirs male of his or their bodies issuing, to whom any estate of inheritance should thereafter descend under the act, should thereafter give, grant, or otherwise convey away any of the entailed estates, nor any other thing do which might be to the disherison of the heirs inheritable in remainder under the act, or whereby any of them should be barred or put from entry into the estates ; but power was given to lease for a period of not exceeding twenty-one years (excepting as to the castle and parks of Arundel, and the manor-house called Arundel House, in the parish of St. Clement Danes, London) ; and it was declared that all and every alienation, conveyance, gift, grant, bargain, and sale, and every other act whatsover thereafter had, made, or suffered by any of the persons to whom the Arundel estates were limited contrary to the intent of the act, should thereafter, for ever after the decease of the alienor, be deemed in law to be utterly void.

The act provided for the better maintenance of Arundel Castle, and for the repair of the chapel adjoining to the church of Arundel, where the Earls of Arundel lay buried; and that for the better furnishing of Arundel House and the Castle of Arundel, the plate, jewels, hangings, pictures, household stuff, statues, books, arms, armour, and pedigrees, and all other goods and chattels of which Thomas Earl of Arundel and the Lady Alatheia his countess, and the Lord Maltravers, son and heir-apparent of the earl, were possessed, should be the goods of such person as should, under the limitations of the act (*Act of Parl.* 3 Charles I.) be in the enjoyment of the Arundel estates, and should remain as heirlooms of the house of Arundel.

It is particularly observable, in reference to this peculiar act of parliament, that the claim of the earl to the title of Earl of Arundel, as annexed to the castle, manor, and lordship of Arundel, from time immemorial, was not founded upon the general law of the land, but on a special prescription alleged in respect of the particular property and particular dignity. In the 1st, 2d, and 3d of Richard II, John de Arundel was summoned to Parliament by writs directed " Johanni de Arundell;" and Dugdale supposes that these writs were addressed to John, younger son of Earl Richard, who created the entail in the 19 Edward III, 1344, and grandfather of John, who succeeded to the castle and honour of Arundel on the death of Earl Thomas. He married Eleanor, daughter of John Lord Maltravers, the sister and heir of Henry Lord Maltravers, and perished by shipwreck, in the 3d Richard II, 1379, leaving, by Eleanor, John his son and heir, who was never summoned to parliament. He died in 1390, leaving John his son and heir, a minor, who, on the death of Thomas Earl of Arundel without issue in 1415, succeeded to the possession of the castle and honour of Arundel, under the entail of 19 Edward III. Although he was not summoned to parliament, he was styled Earl of Arundel after his death, which occurred 9 Henry V, 1420.

He left John his son and heir, a minor, who, on attaining
his majority, was summoned to parliament, in the 7th of
Henry VI, 1428, by a writ directed "Jo. Arundell de
Arundell, Chivaler." If the dignity of Lord Fitzalan was
annexed to the baronies of Clun and Oswaldestre, which
were included in the entail of Earl Richard, he had also a
claim to that title. If not, it was in abeyance between the
coheirs of Earl Thomas and the title to the dignity of Lord
Fitzalan entailed, by the act of Charles; if it belonged to
the Thomas then Earl of Arundel, it must have been in right
of one of those coheirs.

The lordship of Clun, the ancient possession of the Fitzalan family, and which, by a return found in the Testa de
Nevill, "Quod dominus Johes. fil Alain, tenet Baron de Clun
de domino Rege in capite" (*Salop and Stafford*, 272), appears
to have been a barony, was included in the original entail;
but Earl John did not, in the proceedings of 2d Henry VI,
1432, claim the title of baron of Clun as annexed to the
lordship of Clun; and it does not seem that he ever assumed
any title but those of Earl of Arundel and Lord Maltravers,
except as he was summoned to parliament as John Arundell,
Chivalier.

The legislative provision put an end to all question as to
the title of Earl of Arundel so long as there remained issue
male of Thomas Earl of Arundel. Upon what ground the
title of Lord Fitzalan was so limited, it is difficult to say,
inasmuch as that title, if derived from possession of the
baronies of Clun and Oswaldestre, must have followed the
descent of those baronies, which were not in the possession
of Thomas Earl of Arundel, having passed to another branch
of the family, and therefore not entailed by the act; and if
the title of Lord Fitzalan were a personal dignity, the title
could not have belonged to John Earl of Arundel, who
claimed the earldom under the entail of Earl Richard, as he
was not heir-general of the family; and therefore Thomas
Howard Earl of Arundel, who obtained the act, if one of the
coheirs of Thomas Earl of Arundel and Lord Fitzalan, who
died in the 3d Henry V, 1415, by descent from one of his

sisters, could have no right to the title of Lord Fitzalan as a personal dignity, except by favour of the king, the title being in abeyance. The act, indeed, may be considered as a grant of the crown determining the abeyance, but the petition of the Earl of Arundel assumed that he had in him the title of Lord Fitzalan.

By this act also, the ancient honour of Arundel, which had descended from Roger de Montgomery, and which was of very great extent, with various important privileges and franchises annexed to it, became in effect remodelled. The manor of Hayling became, as we have seen, included in the entail, and from thenceforth it formed parcel of the honour of Arundel, inalienable as to its lands and franchises, except by act of parliament. The act also obviated all difficulty during the continuance of heirs male of Thomas Earl of Arundel and Surrey, and for that period has prevented what a decision in the 2d of Henry VI, 1432, had previously established, that the alienation of the castle, manor, and lordship of Arundel by sale, or by any other means according to the caprice of the person seized in fee of the castle, manor, and lordship of Arundel, would transfer the title of Earl of Arundel, so that one person might have been a peer of the realm by that title on one day, and another person entitled to demand a writ by the same title on the succeeding day.

Thomas Earl of Arundel and Surrey, being so seized in his demesne as of fee tail, viz. to him and the heirs male of his body to be begotten, with remainder as limited, died at Padua on the 4th October 1646; whereupon the castle, honour, and lordship of Arundel, and the manor, rectory, and isle of Hayling, members of the castle and honour of Arundel, with all the various liberties and franchises, descended to Henry Earl of Arundel and Surrey, as son and heir male of Thomas. Henry Earl of Arundel being so seized, died on the 17th day of April 1652; after whose death the entailed estates descended to Thomas Earl of Arundel and Surrey; who being so seized, was, in the 13 Charles II, 1660, restored, by act of parliament, to the dignity and title of Duke of Norfolk, to him and the heirs male of his body, remainder to the heirs male of Henry Earl of Arundel, with other remainders over.

In the 14 Charles II, 1661, Thomas Duke of Norfolk prayed favour of the Barons of the Exchequer, that he might have within the hundreds of Poling, Avisford, Easeborne, and Westerwith, within the liberty of the honour of Arundel, and within the manor of Hayling and the hundred of Redbridge in the county of Southampton, members of the castle and honour of Arundel, and within the hundreds of Rotherbridge and Bury in the county of Sussex, and in every of them, the valuable privileges and franchises granted to his predecessors, Earls of Arundel and Dukes of Norfolk: among them the return of writs and the execution of them, the court of the borough and town of Arundel, and the Sheriffs' turn, fines and amerciaments of his own men, as of all his tenants, in any courts before the king, the barons of the Exchequer, the justices of the Common Pleas, pleas of the forest, justices of assize and of gaol delivery; and of all hereticks, lollards, traitors, murderers, and felons; views of frankpledge, waifs, deodands, treasure trove, wreck of the sea, assize of bread, beer, and wine, and free warren in all his manors.

The earl produced and made profert of the letters patent of the 27th February, 1st Mary, containing the grant of privileges to Henry Earl of Arundel, with free warren and free chase within the manor of Hayling. Also the letters patent of the 15th July, 2d and 3d Philip and Mary, containing a further grant of privileges to Earl Henry, and confirming to him, within the manor of Hayling and other lands, the rights of free warren and free chase, treasure trove, wreck of the sea, and power to make coroners.

He produced and made profert of the indenture of the 9th January, 1st Elizabeth, being the demise of various hundreds, and the manor of Hayling for the term of 100 years, to John Lord Lumley, at the rent of twenty shillings. Also the indentures of the 4th of November, 4th Elizabeth, whereby the earl granted to Stoughton, Bromley, and Dalinder the reversion of the manor of Hayling to the use of him the earl and the heirs male of his body lawfully to be begotten;

remainder to the Lord Lumley and Jane his wife, in tail male; remainder to Lady Jane, in tail general; remainder to Lord Lumley, in tail general; and remainder to him the Earl of Arundel in fee. Also the will of Henry Earl of Arundel, bearing date the 30th day of December, 22d Elizabeth; whereby he devised the manor of Hayling and other estates to the Lord Lumley. Also the indenture of the 17th day of June, 3d James I; whereby John Lord Lumley and Elizabeth his then wife (the Lady Jane his first wife having died without issue) granted the manor of Hayling and other estates to Caryll, Holland, Cornwallis, and Causefield, in trust for Thomas Earl of Arundel and his heirs. Also the entail act of the 3d Charles I. He also proved the descent to Henry Earl of Arundel and Surrey, the descent to Thomas Earl of Arundel and Surrey, his son and heir, and the restoration of Earl Thomas by the act of the 25th of April, 12th Charles II, to the title and dignity of Duke of Norfolk.

Sir Geoffrey Palmer, Baronet, the king's attorney-general, appeared in court, and saw and inspected the documents produced by the duke; whereupon and upon due deliberation had by the Barons of the Exchequer, it was by the barons adjudged that the claimant, Thomas Duke of Norfolk, should, by his bailiffs, have, hold, and enjoy, within the hundreds of Polinge, &c. and within the manor of Hayling and hundred of Redbridge, the liberties and privileges which he claimed, saving the right of the lord the king; and at the request of Henry Howard of Norfolk, brother of the Duke, the barons caused the tenor of their confirmation to be exemplified under the seal of the Exchequer by letters patent. This was done at Westminster, on the 11th day of September, in the 16th Charles II, 1664.

Thomas Duke of Norfolk died without issue; whereupon his brother Henry Howard became Duke of Norfolk; and he afterwards died, leaving Henry, his eldest son (who, after his death, succeeded to the title), the Lord Thomas Howard, and several other children.

The last-named Henry Duke of Norfolk died without issue; but his brother Lord Thomas Howard died in his lifetime, leaving issue, the Honourable Thomas Howard, Henry, Edward, Richard, and Philip Howard. Thomas Howard, on the death of the last-named Henry Duke of Norfolk, became Duke of Norfolk; and dying without issue, was succeeded by his brother Edward Howard (Henry having died without issue). Richard died in the lifetime of Thomas; Philip, the youngest son, had two sons, Thomas and Edward, who, with their father, died without issue, in the lifetime of Edward Duke of Norfolk. Upon the death of the latter, Charles, the great-great-grandson of Charles, the fourth son of Henry Earl of Arundel (who died in 1652), became, pursuant to the entail act, Duke of Norfolk; and as such seized of the castle, honour, and lordship of Arundel, and of the manor of Hayling. He died leaving an only son, Charles, who succeeded him as the eleventh duke, restored the Castle of Arundel, and died in the year 1815.

No material change had taken place in the Island of Hayling during the lordship of the Earls of Arundel and Dukes of Norfolk. They resided at Arundel; the courts were held by their steward, the demesne lands farmed by their bailiffs or let to tenants at a moderate rent. We hear of no complaints of extortion on the part of the lords, nor of further inundations of the sea, and we may therefore presume that the island in some degree recovered from the difficulties with which in former times it had had to contend. But it would however seem that the tenure of the copyhold lands held under the manor, and the payment of the tithes, up to a late period collected in kind, were felt to be a grievance; and an application was in consequence made to the duke to take such steps as might be necessary to enable him to enfranchise the copyholds of the manor, and to sell the tithes, to which, as lay rector, he was entitled.

The duke complied with the request; and in the 37th of George III, 1796, an act was obtained "for the enfranchise-"ment of copyhold and customary lands, parcel of the manor "of Arundel, and other manors entailed by the act of parlia-"ment of the 3d of Charles I, and for the sale of tithes also "entailed by the said act." It recited that a considerable number of the tenants of copyhold and customary tenure were desirous to purchase the freehold and inheritance of their tenements, and the timber thereupon, so that the same might be enfranchised and discharged from all copyhold and customary tenures, and from the payment of all fines, rents, sums of money, and heriots, payable in respect of the same. That within the parishes of Arundel, Rustington, North and South Hayling, there were considerable quantities of land not comprised in or entailed by the act of Charles, which were liable to pay tithe to the duke, and that there was great reason to believe that the owners of the lands liable to the payment of tithes would pay a considerable price for the purchase of the tithes issuing out of, or payable in respect of, their respective lands.

And it was thereby enacted, that it should be lawful for Charles then Duke of Norfolk, during his life and after his decease, for such persons as should for the time being, by virtue of the limitations of the entail act, be seized of the castle of Arundel, or entitled to the rents and profits thereof for a money consideration, by deed or deeds, to be sealed and delivered in the presence of, and to be attested by, two or more witnesses, to make enfranchisement of any copyhold or customary hereditaments, parcel of the manors mentioned, and the timber, trees, and woods thereon, and all such common of pasture, common of turbary, rights of common and other rights, liberties, and privileges, in and upon all and every or any of the commons and waste grounds, parcel of the manors, by copy of court roll or any customary tenure whatsoever; and all such common of pasture, common of turbary, rights of common, and other rights, liberties, and privileges in and upon all and every or any of the commons and waste grounds, parcel of the said manors, as the copyhold or customary tenant was entitled to before enfranchisement, and that, after enfranchisement, the hereditaments so enfranchised should be held in free and common socage of the lord of which they should be held at the time of the enfranchisement; and that out of every such grant, all such franchises, royalties, rights, liberties, and privileges of chase and free warren, hunting, hawking,

fowling, and of chasing and killing of game and beasts of
chase and free warren, and all such ancient piscaries, fishings,
and right of fishing as should have been then before anciently
used, exercised, and enjoyed by the lord or lords of the same
manors respectively, and also all mines and minerals whatsoever within or under the premises, exclusive of all other person
or persons whomsoever, should be excepted and reserved
thereout to the lord for the time being of the manors so
mentioned; save that the person whose lands should be so
enfranchised, and his, her, or their heirs and assigns, tenants or
under tenants, should have full right and liberty to dig for,
raise, and get in or upon his, her, or their own lands, any
stones, lime, slate, clay, turf, peat, or marl to and for his, her,
or their own use and benefit.

It was also enacted, that the same provisions should be
extended to the sale of the tithes, and that every person to
whom the duke should sell and convey the tithes, and the
heirs and assigns of such person, should hold the premises so
to be sold absolutely freed and discharged from the uses and
limitations contained in the entail act of Charles I.

Very many enfranchisements of copyhold estates were
effected under this act. The deeds followed the provisions
of the enactments, and contained a clause, that the tenants of
the enfranchised lands should thereafter have the right of
taking and carrying away in carts and waggons only, sea-sand,
gravel, and sea-beach from South or Beach Common, for the
use and benefit of the enfranchised lands, but for no other
use or purpose whatsoever. The tithes of the greater part of
the island were purchased by and conveyed to the late
Mr. Henry Budd for a large consideration, and he sold them
out to the smaller proprietors as opportunity offered.

Charles Duke of Norfolk died on the 16th December 1815,
and was succeeded in the title and estates by Bernard Edward
Duke of Norfolk, who was descended from Bernard, eighth
son of Henry Earl of Arundel and Surrey.

By articles of agreement, bearing date the 24th February
1825, which recited the entail act of Charles, the act of the
37th of George III, and the act of the 41st of George III,

for enlarging the powers of the enfranchisement act, the Duke of Norfolk contracted with William Padwick the younger, described as then of Warblington House in the county of Southampton, Esquire, for the sale of the manor, rectory, and Isle of Hayling, and the remainder of the tithes then undisposed of, for the price at which the same should be valued by Thomas Drewitt, of Picard's Farm, near Guildford, Surrey, land-surveyor; and in accordance with the terms of the agreement on the 5th of July 1825, an act of parliament was obtained " for vesting the manor, rectory, and Isle of " Hayling, in the county of Southampton, part of the settled " estates of the Duke of Norfolk, in William Padwick the " younger, Esquire, his heirs and assigns, and for applying " the money thence arising in the purchase of other estates to " be settled to the same uses and for other purposes."

It was thereby declared that the Most Noble Bernard Edward Duke of Norfolk, Earl Marshal, and Hereditary Earl Marshal of England, was heir male of the body of Thomas Earl of Arundel and Surrey (the entailer of the Arundel estates); that the sum of one thousand nine hundred and eighty-nine pounds and five pence was then due from the Arundel estates to Henry Howard, of Corby Castle, in the county of Cumberland, Esquire, sole executor of the will of Charles, then late Duke of Norfolk, bearing date the 25th day of November 1815; and that there were no funds applicable to the payment. That the manor, rectory, and Isle of Hayling, together with the tithes then remaining unsold, and the timber and other trees growing and standing upon the said estates, had been valued at the sum of thirty-eight thousand six hundred and fourteen pounds five shillings and five pence.

And it was thereby enacted, that immediately after payment into the Bank of England of the sum of thirty-eight thousand six hundred and fourteen pounds five shillings and five pence, part of which was to be applied to the payment of the debt to the late Duke Charles, and part to the purchase of other estates near Arundel, the fee simple and inheritance, free from all incumbrances of and in the manor, rectory, and Isle of

Hayling, and other the hereditaments, in the county of Southampton, described and specified in the schedule to the act, and the appurtenances thereunto belonging or appertaining, should be and become absolutely vested in and settled upon the said William Padwick, his heirs and assigns, to the only proper use and behoof of him, his heirs, and assigns for ever, freed, discharged, and absolutely acquitted and exonerated of and from all and singular the uses, estates, entails, remainders, limitations, trusts, powers, provisoes, and declarations in and by the act of the 3d of Charles I, limited, created, expressed, or declared of and concerning the castle and manor of Arundel, and the other estates entailed thereby.

The schedule appended to the act, containing a description of the manor, rectory, and Isle of Hayling, included—

The manor of Hayling, in the county of Southampton, with the rights, royalties, members, and appurtenances thereunto belonging. The rectories of North and South Hayling, and the tithes remaining unsold, and the advowson of the vicarage of North and South Hayling.

Hayling manor farm, held by Charles Osborn on lease, for a term of which fourteen years would be unexpired at Michaelmas 1825, at the rent of £575 per annum, and stated to contain 660a. 3r. 33p. in statute measure. The tide-mill and mill-pond included in the rental of the farm held by Charles Osborn on lease for a term of which nineteen years would be unexpired at Michaelmas 1825.

Public-house farm, Sinar Common, and Beach Sinar, held on lease by Joseph Bulbeck for a term of which seven years would be unexpired at Michaelmas 1825, at the rent of £90 per annum, and stated to contain 190a. 3r. 30p. in statute measure.

The Wholsinar, or Shingle Bank, in the occupation of Joseph Bulbeck, Beach Common, containing 121a. 0r. 28p. in statute measure, stated to be then in hand.

A piece of land for Preventive Service House, held by the commissioners of Customs at will, at the rent of one pound per annum, and stated to contain two rods.

Out of which estate a modus of £4. 8s. was stated to be yearly payable to the vicar of Hayling in lieu of vicarial tithes.

The purchase money was paid into the Bank of England on the 8th May 1827; whereupon the manor, rectory, and Isle of Hayling passed absolutely in conformity with the act to the use of William Padwick the younger, his heirs and assigns for ever.

I find the customs of the manor stated by Mr. Walter Butler, who was the deputy steward of the Duke of Norfolk in the year 1817, to be as follows :—

Upon the death of a copyholder intestate, his next heir is admitted; and if a minor, guardianship is granted to his next friend not likely to inherit, upon condition well and honestly to educate the minor, allowing him competent victuals and clothes, and all other necessaries, and keeping the premises in decent repair, and producing a true account of the profits when required.

The widow of an intestate copyholder is admitted to her tenement, to hold so long as she shall live sole, chaste, and unmarried, as her widow's bench, and pays one penny to the lord for a fine.

In default of a tenant surrendering to the use of his will, his tenement descends to his widow for her bench, and then to his heir, which is his eldest son or eldest daughter. (This is altered by the statute dispensing with the necessity for a surrender to the uses of a copyholder's will.)

No tenant can let his lands for a longer term than a year without the lord's licence, and paying a fine. An entail is barred by recovery in the manor court.

I find from a letter written by Thomas Hensloe to Lord William Howard, dated Burhunte, 4th July 1604 (*Howard MSS*. No. 204), that the customary tenants at that time paid yearly thirty-four pounds as rents of assize, "which tenants "had estates of inheritance to them and their heirs, the wife "her widow's estate, and on every tenant's death, a fine *ad* "*voluntatem domini*, but which had usually been three years' "rent full value. The lord to have his heriots and use of the "land during minority."

These customs were set out with greater particularity at a court baron, held for the manor on the 14th July 1778,

when the homage upon their oaths presented that every copyhold tenant, upon death or alienation, ought to pay to the
lord a heriot, to wit, his best beast, and for want of beast his
best in-door goods, and his heir a fine at the will of the lord.
That by the custom of the manor, the eldest son was to inherit
after his father; and in case there were no son, then it
descended to the eldest daughter, and in like manner among
collaterals.   That the widow of every copyholder ought to
enjoy the same after the death of her husband during her
chaste widowhood, upon paying to the lord for a fine one
penny on her admission, and on the death of such tenant, to
pay a heriot as a copyholder.   That all wrecks of the sea,
estrays, deodands, goods of felons, goods of *felo de se*, happening within the manor, belonged to the lord of the manor.
That for every horse turned loose into the lanes the owner
should pay sixpence, for every hog threepence, and for every
sheep twopence, to the lord of the manor.   And that every
person who should cause gravel to be carried from that part
of the land called the Ferry-house Point, should forfeit and
pay to the lord of the manor two shillings and sixpence for
every cart load. (*Hayl. Cot. Rolls.*)

The ancient court leet of the manor of Hayling has fallen
into disuse, and has not been held for many years.   The court
baron, which used in former days to be held at Lady Day and
Michaelmas, is only now convened when occasion requires it.
Various circumstances have tended to produce this: the
transfer of local business from the view of frankpledge to the
quarter sessions; the enfranchisement of so many of the
copyhold estates in the time of Charles Duke of Norfolk,
when, although the accustomed suit and service of the tenant
were retained, yet he was no longer bound to pay heriot, fine,
or quit rent, or to surrender or take admission to his lands,
all of which occurred as a matter of course at the court of the
lord; added to which, the recent statute which has been passed
enabling a court to be held for the purposes of surrender or
admittance without the intervention of the homage, the game
laws, and the improved communication between the island and
the main land, all these things have co-operated to the gradual

decay of these courts; and the powers which were once exercised unquestioned by the lord and his homage would, if revived in the present day, be looked upon as unwarranted, and as a positive invasion of the ordinary rights of the subject. The jurisdiction exercised in early times by the feudal courts, often to a great extent under the immediate control of the lord of the manor, when the feudal system was in the ascendant, may perhaps be deemed excessive in our own time, but they undoubtedly possessed, amidst occasional oppression, the elements of positive good, upon which we have failed to improve. The jury was selected from the residents, the subject matter of inquiry was known to all, the circumstances attending the offence were generally patent, the hearing and the judgment followed immediately upon each other, and a distress upon the lands of the offender, or corporal punishment in the view of his peers, ensured the execution of the sentence. And what, it may be asked, was the cost of all this? Was it, as now, an expensive and ruinous affair, with power of appeal to the several existing tribunals, beginning with the lowest and ending with the highest, so that he whose purse is longest can give the greatest possible amount of trouble and vexation, and prolong his litigation to a period, when the facts of the case have long since ceased to be borne in mind, and when the primary cause of complaint is unknown, except as a matter of tradition? The cost was literally nothing; the steward, who was paid by the lord, officiated in his absence and presided as judge; the homage gave their time and attendance as part of the service by which their lands were held; and questions of descent, of title, of boundary, of municipal right, of custom, and of offences against the common law of the country, were disposed of without appeal, without delay, and without the payment of a single fee.

It is therefore much to be doubted whether, amid the network of modern legislation, we have not in a great measure lost sight of the principle upon which our ancestors founded their practice, and whether, in the endeavour to make a by-path to every village, we have not suffered the high roads to fall into decay. Justice, to give satisfaction, should, as in the

court of pie poudre of old, be afforded on the spot, be always
without delay, and at the same time be final; and if we look
to the demands of the present moment, we shall see that in the
crusades against the forms and technicalities of the law, and in
the establishment of county courts throughout the breadth of
the land, we are in effect confirming the basis upon which the
feudal courts were originally founded, and restoring a system
of judicature peculiarly acceptable to a free and enlightened
people.

The court rolls of the manor of Hayling extend back to a
very early period, some being in the Tower, some in the Rolls
Chapel, some in the custody of his Grace the Duke of Norfolk,
and very many lost on forfeiture to the crown, and on the
dissolution of the alien priory of Hayling, and of that of the
abbey of Shene. The presentments which are found upon
them in reference to timber, wreck of the sea, treasure trove,
free warren, and the fisheries, supply the information omitted
in the customs, to which our attention has already been
drawn. They also contain information bearing upon the
administration of the customary and common law of the land,
as applied to offences happening within the manor, with the
decision of the homage upon questions of descent, distress,
and boundary of lands. It would seem that the tenure of
Harold's lands had always been preserved separate from that
of the manor of Hayling; and it is found that in former days
the courts for the island generally, both of the leet and baron,
were held at the priory, or the manor-house for the time being,
whilst the court baron for Harold's lands was held specially
at Northstoke. It is clear that there never was but one manor
properly so called within the Island of Hayling, the courts,
when held for the manor of Hayling, being headed " Hayling
" or Hayling Priory, the view of frankpledge, with the court
" there holden ;" after which followed the fines and entries for
the tithings of Northney, Mengeham, and Westown, whilst,
when held for the lands of Harold, they are simply headed
" Northstoke, the court there holden," in two instances " of
" Katharine" being added.

These latter rolls, extant only from the year 1371 up to the

year 1406, are not however confined to circumstances or
questions arising within the lands of Harold only, because
I find that in one instance wreck was presented at Saltoners,
in another at Streathend, in another at Mengeham, in another
the repair of the sewer at the creek is mentioned, neither of
which places formed part of the tithing of Northstoke, comprising Eastoke in the south parish, and Westhay or Westney
in the north parish. They also mention pleas of land situate
at Heilyng, between William Palmer of Heilyng, and Isabella
his daughter; and between John Michel and William
Westowne; and I therefore conclude that the owner of these
lands, styled in two or three entries as "the lady" holding
certain privileges within them by special grant, was entitled
to the fines and heriots arising from them, and such wreck as
was seized within the particular boundaries. The grant of
wreck to William le Fauconer, lord of the manor of Lymbourne,
which I have before noticed, was certainly maintained at
different times, from the year 1371 down to the year 1405;
and in one case against the Prior of Hayling by the verdict of
the homage; but I find no instance of user after the latter
period; and I presume that the franchise, which was limited
to Fauconer and his heirs, must have escheated to the crown,
either on failure of Fauconer's heirs, or together with the
lands on the attainder of Sir Thomas Lewknor in the reign
of Richard III, or on the dissolution of the convent of de
Calceto, and the disgrace of Cardinal Wolsey, and have
been included in the general grant of wreck made by King
Henry VIII to the College of Arundel, since which time it has
undoubtedly been exercised, claimed, and allowed by and to
the lords of the manor of Hayling.

The return to the inquisition relative to the inundation at
page 217, which states that nearly the whole hamlet of Estoke,
with the lands pertaining to the same, belonging to the parish
church of Hayling, *and which the prior had for his own proper
use,* had been submerged, proves that Estoke formed part of
the demesnes of the manor of Hayling.

The rolls of the courts held at Northstoke also afford
evidence that the lands of Harold were held under the chief

manor of Hayling, for in a presentment made on the morrow
of Saint James the Apostle in the year 1399, at the time
when " Katharine" was "the lady," William Segar, Henry
Danell, John Aughtman, Richard Estoke, John Landman,
Nicolas Herbard, Thomas Isabella Danell, Richard Alderman,
Thomas Danell, Joan Cantelow, and John Atte Stubbe,
tenants of the lord, acknowledged and attorned to Katharine
for all their rents and services, the homage commanding other
tenants "of the lord" to attend at the next court to acknow-
ledge their rents and services; and at the same time the
homage presented that an acre of bond land of John Landman
had fallen into the hands "of the lord" by the flight of
Robert Harvest, who had married Joan the late wife of
Richard Knott the farmer of the same, and had feloniously
killed her, showing that, although the rents and services were
due to " the lady," yet that the higher franchises of escheat,
&c. were due to the lord of Hayling.

They show also that Estoke was parcel of the lordship of
Hayling; for in the year 1373, at a court held at Northstoke,
there is an entry that Richard Alderman and Richard le
Merleward had mainprized for William Gauntelow towards
the lord, for that he had pulled down his hall at Estoke and
taken away the timber thereof, *upon the lordship of the prior
of Hayling* without license; and the fact of Harold's lands being
so held under the chief manor of Hayling is confirmed by the
general rolls of Hayling, which contain particulars of payments
made to the lord of Hayling by various lands forming the
aggregate of the *terra regis*, which payments have been
made from time immemorial, and are collected to this day by
the tenant of the piece of land called " Martin's Gore," in the
tithing of Stokefield, belonging to the lord of Hayling, in the
following proportions:—Stoke Tithing, Eastock, 1s. 1½d.;
William Carpenter, 1s. 3d.; Mrs. Budd, 1s. 5½d.; Thomas
Rogers, sen., 8½d.; George Rogers, 1s. 3¼d.; Thomas Rogers,
sen., 2s. 8d.; Mrs. Budd, 1s. 1¾d.; Thomas Rogers, 1s. 4d.,;
William Carpenter, 8½d.: Total, 11s. 8½d.

Westney Tithing: Martha Rogers, 1s. 10d.; Mrs. Budd, 10d.;
Widow Rogers, 1s. 4d.; Mary Carpenter, 1s. 2d.; Joseph
Thomas Crasler, 6d.: Total, 5s. 8d.

The payment to the lord of the manor of Hayling by the owners of the lands in Northstoke, Eastoke, and Westney, entered variously as lady's silver, sheriff's tourn, and viscountiel money, is perhaps somewhat questionable in its creation; but, whatever may have been its origin, it implies that the lands themselves and the owners of those lands owed suit and service to the chief lord of Hayling. The difficulty arises from the terms applied to the payment. Lady's silver, which in the reeve's account of the reign of Edward I is called hurdle silver, could not, I think, at that time have been paid except in the shape of a commutation of service, the term hurdle silver pointing to the actual service commuted; and for that reason one is led to conclude that the lands in question, although of ancient demesne, were of the third or lowest order of that tenure. Fitzherbert tells us that tenants in ancient demesne had their tenures from ploughing the king's land, and from the performance of other works towards the maintenance of the royal freehold, on which account they had a grant of liberties; and as the lands of Harold fell into the hands of the Conqueror, it is reasonable to suppose that the services due to himself in respect of the tenure were bestowed upon the Abbey of Jumiéges, and that in after times these services were commuted for lady's silver. An instance of this occurred with the Lords Fitzalan at Bickton, where the inhabitants were bound to perform different manual services for them as lords of Clun Castle in Shropshire; which were afterwards turned into a rent, called " Bickton Silver," whereupon the services ceased.

On the other hand, the terms of sheriffs tourn and viscontiel money indicate that the payment was one primarily due to the sheriff of the county. Vicontiels were certain farms for which the sheriff in early times paid a rent to the king, and he made what profit he could of them. Vicontiel rents came usually under the title of *firma comitatus;* and of these the sheriff had a particular roll given to him, which he delivered back with his account. They were payable on the yearly tourn of the sheriff; and as we have seen that the rents of the tourn were granted to the lord of Hayling within the manor and island, it is possible that they may have arisen from this source; and they were certainly so treated in the year 1778, when Charles Duke of Norfolk, in compliance with the act of parliament obliging Papists to register their estates, returned his within the county of Southampton, as the manor of Hayling and Island of Hayling, with the courts leet, baron, and other courts, rights, royalties, franchises, with the members and appurtenances belonging and therewith held and enjoyed, with the advowson, the quit rents of the manor, amounting yearly to £38. 1s. 10½d., *and* 17s. 4d. *for sheriff's tourn;* Hayling farm, with the tithes of the parish of Hayling, then held by Andrew Bone, as tenant under lease at the yearly rent of £650.

It might also have been that the tenants of these lands were bound in olden time to attend the tourn of the sheriff before it was held in Hayling, Havant being the chief town of the hundred; and that, in order to be relieved from this attendance, they aided their lord of Hayling in the purchase or grant of a court leet, which dispensed with their attendance out of the manor. This view is supported by the fact that for a very long period the tenants of Northney, Mengham, and Westown paid a common fine at the court, the only difference being that in the latter case the fine varied according to the number of residents within the several tithings, and that in the former it was fixed as a rent charge upon the land, and never varied at all.

It was not by any means an unusual thing for the manorial courts in early times to be held at different tithings within the manor, particularly where, as in the case of Hayling, the manor comprised several towns, several tithings, and a large tract of country, in the same way as the sheriffs held their tourns within the hundreds, and the itinerant justices their pleas of assize. I take Northstoke to have been an instance of this. In the manor of Havant the same practice was adopted; and there were separate court rolls, and separate quit-rent rolls, for the separate mesne manors of Hall Place, Leigh, and Brockhampton, which were at intervals entered by the steward of Havant upon the general court rolls of the

chief manor, the mesne lords compounding for the fines and
heriots happening within their separate jurisdictions, with
their chief lord. This practice ceased, so far as regards the
mesne manor of Hall Place, in the year 1800, and as far as
Leigh was concerned, when the mesne manor fell by purchase
into the hands of the chief lord; but in the case of Brockhampton, the distinctive tenure of the mesne lord is still preserved, and a separate quit-rent roll is collected to this day,
the title conferring the latter manor being the admission to
a copyhold estate held under the manor of Havant, analogous
to the title of the mesne manor of Northstoke, which seems
to have been conferred by the admission to the Eastock
farm, held apparently as a copyhold estate of the prior of
Hayling, and subsequent lords down to the period of its
enfranchisement.

This conclusion receives additional confirmation from the
fact that the manor of Hayling is in many of the charters and
records described as the manor and isle of Hayling ; that it
was held of Queen Emma allodially, or subject to no services
in fee (*Spelman's Glossary*, p. 27), and capable of sale or
transmission without reference to the crown; that in the
Testa de Nevill and grants of donation it is said to be held of
the king *in capite;* that the courts of the manor, as held by
the abbots of Jumiéges, the priors of Hayling, and the subsequent lords, comprised the view of frankpledge of the whole
island; whilst, on the other hand, the *terra regis* is never
described otherwise than as "lands in Hayling," or "lands in
"Northstoke, Eastoke, and Westhay;" is never stated to be
held *in capite;* no single separate grant as a manor is found
in reference to it; and in the grant from the abbey of Troarn
to John le Fauconer, afterwards confirmed by the crown, in
the conveyance from Harrison Lattness to Thomas Peckham
of London, in the year 1630, and in the conveyance from
Thomas Peckham to John Peckham, in the year 1665, "the
"service due and accustomed to the chief lord of the fee" is
specially reserved. All these circumstances, coupled with the
existing and long continued payments from the tenants of
Northstoke, Eastoke, and Westhay, seem clearly to indicate

that the lord of the manor of Hayling was that chief lord to whom the reservation of the service due and accustomed was intended to apply.   The only judicial decision, in reference to the soil on the shores of Eastock, that I know of, is that which was given in the case of Hellyer v. Miller, which was an action brought in 1830, by the former, then tenant and lessee of John Williams, who claimed to be lord of Northstoke, Eastoke, and Westhay.   The trespass complained of was the taking of sand and shingle from Eastock beach. The lord of Hayling justified the trespass on the part of Miller ; and on the trial at Winchester, a juror was withdrawn, upon the understanding that the right on the part of the plaintiff was abandoned.   Hellyer however afterwards seized portions of wreck on the sea-shore, and took up boulder stones ; and upon a second action being brought, judgment was suffered to go by default, a writ of inquiry was executed at the Winchester assizes of July 1830, and Hellyer paid the damages and costs.   Another recognition of the tenure of Eastock is to be observed in the pound of Hayling manor, to which all the estrays of the island, including those of Eastock, are driven by the hayward, who receives the accustomed fines on behalf of the lord of Hayling.

Various offences, occurring within the jurisdiction of the leet, are found upon the court rolls ; and on these a small money fine was usually imposed.   On a view of frankpledge with a court held for the priory of Hayling, in the 34th of Henry VI, 1455 (*From muniment-room of Duke of Norfolk*), the homage presented that John Giles, William Hamond, John Belour, William Tabawd, Simon Medway, John Webb, and William Yeman permitted their pigs to be unrung, and to rout up the soil of the lord of the manor at Mengeham ; therefore they were in mercy, and were each amerced one penny.   John Bolour was also fined one penny, for permitting his cow to destroy and consume the trees of his neighbours. In the 12th of Henry VIII, 1520, William Pepson was ordered to build a new barn called Ranstowes, in the tithing of Mengeham, before the feast of Saint Michael 1521, under a penalty of 13s. 4d. ; and the several tenants were ordered to cut the branches of the trees growing over the common ways within the lordship, before the feast of the Nativity of the Lord, under a penalty of forty pence upon each delinquent. In the 24th of Elizabeth 1582 (*ibid.*), it was ordered that no one should permit their cattle to roam through places to the nuisance of their neighbours, under penalty for every defaulter of fourpence per head, twopence to the finder, and twopence to the lord. A penalty was put upon John Cobden, that thereafter he keep not horses, for each default ten shillings; and the tithing men of Northney were ordered not to put any of their cattle in the common fields there, without the assent of the tenants there, under penalty for each offence of ten shillings. Because the statute had not been observed, for placing stocks, therefore each tithing was amerced in 8*s.* 4*d.*, which amounted to ten shillings, whereof five shillings was paid to the lord of the manor, and five shillings to the poor. A day was given to John Colin, Stephen Smyth, John Steyning, Nicolas Payn, Stephen Biggs, and Richard Carpenter to survey a post placed by Henry Milward, near the queen's highway, to ascertain whether it were an impediment or not, before the feast of Philip and James then next coming, under a penalty to each in default of twelve pence; and a day was given to Henry Milward rightly to place the same post, if it stood not rightly, before the feast of Pentecost then next coming, under a penalty of 6*s.* 8*d.* The homage also presented, that because they could not excuse those who exercised unlawful games (*galeris*) on Sundays and on feast-days against the statute, therefore they prayed that the offenders should pay four shillings only for a fine, so that the lord should have two shillings and the poor two shillings; which presentment was adopted. (*Rolls Chapel Augment. Office*, fol. 10, 6, 1582.)

At a court held in the 7th of James, it was ordered that it should be lawful for the inhabitants of Hayling to take and carry away stones from Southmoor for the amendment of the wadeway into Hayling, in all places needful and convenient, so as it be not prejudicial to any of the tenants of Havant. It was also ordered that the inhabitants of the parish of

Havant amend the highway leading from Havant to Langstone, and also so much of the wadeway as lay within the parish of Havant, before the feast-day of Saint James the Apostle. And it was likewise ordered that the inhabitants of the parish of Hayling amend so much of the wadeway leading between Langstone and Hayling as lay within the parish, before the feast-day of Saint James the Apostle then next coming. (*Court Rolls*.)

It appears from the presentments on the rolls, and from the custom, that there is a piece of land in the common field which changes hands every year, the tenant of the same being bound to keep the sewer of the creek clear. All the commons in the island are stinted. That of Stoke contains thirty-two cow commons; that of Northney and Creek twenty-four; Verner twelve; and Gutner, which originally contained twenty, four cow commons. The time of turning out is from the 13th of May to the 12th of November.

By the ancient custom of the manor, a headborough was appointed for each tithing, who was chief of the frank-pledge, and had the principal charge of those resident within his jurisdiction; he rendered the common fine, reported all things amiss in the tithing, and was an important officer within the manor. It seems that they were elected at the court leet of Hayling, and by a presentment made in 1405, that they were obliged to attend the hundred court of Bosmere, in order to take the necessary oath of service.

There are very many presentments of seizure of wreck upon the seashore surrounding the Island of Hayling occurring upon the court rolls of ancient date. Among them are found in the year 1371, a barrel of soap of the value of nine shillings, seized to the use of the lord. An empty cask at Saltomers, taken by William Josayre. In the year 1369, the tithing-man, with his tithing, came to the court, and presented one small boat broken as wreck of the sea, price 40*d.*, and one small trunk of an ash, which the lord gave to William Tyrnold, of the value of twopence. In the year 1395, the whole homage presented that Richard Clere found upon the seashore, at Crakehorde, a dead man, by wreck of the sea,

upon whom were found certain chattels, money to the amount
of 3s. 5d., and clothes of the value of 16d. Also upon
Henry Mulward, found in the same manner, in money 3s. 4d.,
and in other things, 12d. Also upon Roger Bohun, in money,
18s. 4d., and of other things and clothes, 20d. Also upon
John Daniel, in money, 10d., and clothes of the value of 6d.
Also upon John Legard, in money 15d., and clothes of the
value of 4d. Also upon Laurence Roven, in money 16d., and
clothes of the value of 20d., and one silver seal, by weight,
20d. Also one basillard, and one girdle with silver harness,
remaining in the custody of Evyh, servant of Maud Chaun-
deler. Also two obligations, one made to Thomas Waryn,
and the other to Henry Elone of Shoreham. Also three
letters. Also upon Thomas Jurdan, of money 3s., and clothes
valued at 2s. Also upon Roger Litelman, of money, 1½d.
and clothes valued at 6d. Also upon Roger Wade, in money
5s., and clothes of the value of 8d. Also upon Margery Atte
Hasle, in money 4s. 9½d., and clothes of the value of 20d.
Also upon William Wade, in money ¼d., and clothes of the
value of 12d. Also upon Roger Palpaman, in money 2s. 4d.,
and clothes of the value of 12d. Also upon Henry Bohun,
in money ½d., and clothes of the value of 8d., and one dagger
with silver harness. Also upon Nicolas Joie, in money 3s. 4d.,
and clothing of the value of 6d. Also upon Thomas Smith,
in money 9s., and clothing of the value of 12d. Also upon
John Mulward, in money 6d., and clothing of the value of 16d.
Also upon Peter Bedford, in money 9s., and clothing of the
value of 16d. Also upon John Passage, in money 5d., and
clothing of the value of 6d. Also of certain other chattels :
four bags, a pack-saddle, six yards of murrain, and two bits,
price in the whole, 3s. 4d. Also one little boat of the price
of 5s., arising to the lord as wreck of the sea. In the year
1406, the homage presented that two empty pipes, one small
chest, empty, and one trunk called Toppeley, of the value of
20d., arising of wreck of the sea upon the land of the lady
at Estoke, which had been seized by the wrecker of the lady,
and delivered for the stock of the lady at Lymbourne. They
also presented one small empty chest, arising of wreck of the
sea upon the land of the prior of Hayling at the Streathend,

which John Dover, Richard Catell, and Henry Magum had
taken and unjustly carried away, as appeared by the charter
of the lord the king; and they thereupon ordered that they
should be prosecuted by the writ of the lord the then king.
In the year 1402, the homage presented a piece of timber, as
wreck of the sea, of the value of 2d.; that it pertained to the
manor of Lymbourne from time whereof the memory of man
had not run to the contrary; and that John Boket, prior of
Hayling, and William Cattle, had carried away the same
against the custom of the manor of Lymbourne, therefore
they were in mercy.

In the reign of Queen Elizabeth, and in the year 1571,
Nicholas Morys, headborough of Mengham, presented that a
boat called a skiff, which came as wreck of the sea, was in
the custody of John Bacon, and was valued at ten shillings;
and that part of a ship, called a capstan, which came as
wreck of the sea, was in the custody of Elizabeth Carter.
In the year 1582, the homage presented, that John Bill had
found near the seashore a piece of cloth, called webbe, of
the value of 8d. (*Lumley Papers*, Augm. Office); and subsequently to this period there are numerous entries in reference
to the seizure of wreck by the lord of the manor of Hayling,
but none that I have ever seen by the owner of Eastock.

In the year 1759, fifty-six gallons of brandy were picked
up and seized, as wreck of sea, by Budd, the then tenant of
the Duke of Norfolk. The Admiralty obtained possession
of it, and it was taken to the custom-house at Chichester; but
the crown officers afterwards admitted the right of his grace,
and delivered it up on the 8th November 1759. The brandy
was subsequently sold for £19. 12s., and the steward of the
duke debited himself with the sum in his annual account.
(*Norfolk Muni.*)

On the 24th February 1782, three hogshead of wine were
seized by Richard Moaze, a custom-house officer, as a droit of
the crown. The Duke of Norfolk claimed them as lord; the
Admiralty disputed his right to seizure of wreck on the
shores of Hayling, and the duke brought an action against
Moaze. The cause was tried at Winchester; but three
witnesses only were examined on the part of the Admiralty,

· when the latter abandoned the case, and the following rule of
court was entered into :—

"The counsel of the defendant, who appeared for him by
"the direction of the Lords of the Admiralty, admitting that
"the Duke of Norfolk and his heirs, as lord of the manor of
"Hayling in the county of Southampton, are entitled to all
"manner of wreck within the said manor, the right to which
"alone was the subject of the present action, the plaintiff
"consented to withdraw a juror, and this consent be made a
"rule of court."

In the year 1823, the duke's right to sell the sand and
ballast from that part of the seashore called the "Wolsinars,"
was disputed by one Samuel Moore. An action was brought
against the latter by the duke; the cause was tried at the
Winchester summer assizes of that year, when a verdict was
given in favour of his grace as plaintiff. Very many other
instances of seizure of wreck by the lords of Hayling are
found upon record; but those which I have adduced are
amply sufficient to prove the exercise of the right on the part
of the lords, and its maintenance when questioned even by the
crown, from whom groundage has repeatedly been received.
Under the recent act of parliament, in reference to droits,
the present lord receives compensation from the Admiralty in
lieu of the wreck itself.

There are also various presentments bearing upon the right
of the lord of Hayling to the timber upon the copyhold
estates within his manor. Among them are found, at a view
of frankpledge of Halying priory in the 34th of Henry VI,
1455, with a court then held there, that the homage presented
William Couper for cutting an oak growing upon his land, to
the great damage of the lord, for which offence he was
amerced twopence. In the 37th of the same reign, that John
Atte Pitte cut a certain oak upon his tenure, and sold it out of
the lordship, whereupon the farmer came and seized the same
oak. That John Knott had committed waste in cutting
divers trees upon his tenure, and that in the 38th of the same
reign he came to the court and put himself in favour of the
lord in reference to the waste. In the 6th of Henry VIII,
1514, they presented that William Bright cut the trees of the

lord without his license, whereupon he was amerced twopence. In the 13th of the same reign they commanded that
from thenceforth no tenant should cut underwood or coppice
wood within the lordship without license, under a penalty of
6s. 8d. In the following year they presented that Agnes
Marshall had unjustly cut two small oak-trees upon her
tenure without license, whereupon she was in mercy; and
that William Bright had committed waste upon his land in
cutting a small oak there growing, whereupon he was amerced
sixpence. At the same court a day was given to all the
tenants of the lordship, sufficiently to repair their messuages
in timber, the roofs and walls, before the feast of Saint Michael
then next. In the 13th of Elizabeth, 1571, the homage
presented, that Richard Carpenter, and other tenants of the
manor, had unjustly taken the lops of trees which had been
cut down for timber to repair the mill of Hayling, to the prejudice of the lord, whereupon they were in mercy by distress
of the steward, 6s. 2d. and 2s.; and a penalty was imposed
upon each who would not permit the branches of the trees
which had been cut for the repairs of the mill to be taken by
those to whom it was committed by the officer of the lord,
and permit them to remain untouched upon the land, under
penalty of each in default, 5s. They also presented, that
forasmuch as it appeared by the confession of the tenants and
inhabitants of the parish of Southwood, that the lops and tops
of two elms, felled for repairs of the mill, were unlawfully
carried away either in the night or by the sunrising, in
unwise and unlawful manner, contemptuously and spitefully,
and that they, concealing the same, would not utter who were
the doers thereof, therefore they were, by the discretion of the
steward, amerced at the court in twenty shillings, the money to
be levied upon the lands of the copyhold tenants within the
parish of Southwood, and that every one who did not clearly
cut the branches of the trees and hedges growing over the
common ways in the tithing of Westowne before the feast of
Annunciation of the Blessed Mary, should forfeit 40s. (*Lumley
Papers.*)

Several of the court rolls of this period, during the lordship
of Henry Earl of Arundel, are missing; but it would seem

that the customs of the manor, and the rights of the lord in regard to the timber upon the various copyhold estates, were found inconvenient and oppressive, and it is evident that the copyholders came to an arrangement with the lord for the purchase of the timber then growing upon their estates; for in Spillers book there is an examined copy of the agreement so entered into between the lord and the tenants. It runs as follows:—

"Be it known unto all men, that the tenants of Hailinge "have bought of the Right Honble Henrie Earle of Arundel, "all the trees and woods growing and standing in and upon "their copyholds severally, and paid for the same in sort as "they may do it as shall think good. And in witness of the "truth hereof, Edmund Doringe, and John Allewyn of Preston, "woodward to the said earl, have put their hands to this, and "to the record thereof written in the court holden for the "manor of Hailinge the 3rd of October, 20 Eliz. Rnë 1578.

"THOMAS LEWKNER. *Ex. p.* Ricum LEWKNER.
"EDMUND DORINGE. JOHN ALWYN, 22 Junii 1609.
Copia vera. W. H."

The Earl of Arundel, not being possessed of an estate in fee simple in the manor of Hayling at this time, could only as a matter of course dispose of the limited interest in the timber and woods of the copyhold estates to which he was himself entitled; and this is evidently alluded to, by the purchase being "in such sort as they may do it." But this in aftertimes gave rise to the impression that the timber on the copyholds had by some means become the property of the tenants, and the long entail in the Arundel family favoured the conclusion. In consequence of this, and within our own memory, the copyholders assumed the right to cut, and in some cases to dispose of, the timber. This was resisted on the part of the lord, and two actions of ejectment were brought by him: in the one instance, for cutting timber without a license, where he had received a quit-rent subsequent to the alleged act of waste (Doe *d.* Padwick *v.* Rogers), and in the other instance, for cutting five elm-trees without a license (Doe *d.* Padwick *v.* Carpenter), where no act of waiver had occurred. In Doe *d.* Padwick *v.* Rogers, the jury returned a verdict for the defendant, partly upon the ground of waiver; but in the case of Doe *d.* Padwick *v.* Carpenter, where no such waiver existed, and where the court-roll entries were adduced in support of the claim of the lord, Mr. Justice Coleridge, in summing up, directed the attention of the jury particularly to the entries of the reigns of Henry VI and Henry VIII, which had been produced by the lord in support of his claim; since, unless they believed them to be fabricated, no plea of modern usage would avail the defendant. (Quoted from *Southampton Paper Report*, July 20, 1850.) The jury however (a common one), after a brief deliberation, returned a verdict for the defendant; and the court above, on the application for a rule for a new trial, declined to disturb the verdict, stating that if the case were worth the expense of a new trial, and a fresh action were brought against any person who should commit a similar trespass, the jury would be told by the judge who tried the cause, that very little reliance was to be placed to the prejudice of the lord upon the verdict in question; that it was only the inference of the jury drawn from the evidence then laid before them, and if before another jury other evidence were laid, or even the same evidence, and such a statement made which should induce the jury to come to a different conclusion, there was nothing to prevent them from so doing.

Numerous presentments are also found upon the rolls, showing the exercise of the right of free warren by the lord of the manor of Hayling, in confirmation of the franchise claimed by and allowed to the Abbot of Jumiéges under the *quo warranto*, and recognised in the general and special charters from the crown, and the claim of the Duke of Norfolk. In the 46th of Edward III, 1371, William Cantelow, William Purerman, and John Shipman came to the court and engaged to the lord to amend for their daughters taking a litter of conies in the warren of the lord at Estoke; and it was granted to them, each of them paying the sum of 12*d.* for the trespass so committed. In the 3rd of Henry VI, 1424, the hayward of Hayling priory presented that Richard Hamond, John Aldersnape, and John Japes kept destructive dogs in the warren of the lord, wherefore they were amerced sixpence each, and it was commanded that the dogs should be removed. In the sixth of the same reign, the homage presented that Simon Type laid snares and took a pheasant within the warren of the lord, and he was attached to answer the charge. In the tenth of the same reign the homage presented that William Yeman kept a dog to the nuisance of the warren of the lord; he was therefore amerced and ordered to remove the same.

There is a letter in the possession of his Grace the Duke of Norfolk, written by Charles Chute to the Lord Arundel in the 1st of Charles II, 1650, wherein he informs his lordship that "there is one Rogers, keeper of the game in the island, " that sayth your lordship promised him £6. 6s. 8d. yearly, for " wages for looking to the game there; this I humbly conceive " may be paid him."

In the account of Mr. Howe the receiver, there is an entry of payment of £2. 7s. 2d. to one Perrin, that he had laid out for physic for a Dutchman sent to Hayling to make a decoy; and a credit of £6. 2s. 8d. for birds sold by Bennet at the decoy, beyond 440 sent to London and Albery for the use of the lord. There is also a charge for seventy-two quarters and a half of oats received by Mr. Marsh at London, and six or seven measures of grass respited by the knights of parliament, and the barley sent for the decoy ducks, of the value of £192. 8s. 6d.

In the enfranchisements executed by the Duke of Norfolk under the provisions of the act, and in that granted by the present lord, the ancient rights of free warren and free chase were reserved. The franchise was also recognised and acknowledged in an agreement between the lord and the tenant of Estock, at that time the property of John Williams. The deputations for the manor of Hayling included the free warren and free chase; and in the year 1847 the present lord brought two actions against Joseph Thomas Crasler and Joseph Long, for a disturbance of the franchise. The actions were not defended; judgment was suffered to go by default, and the damages were assessed and paid under a writ of inquiry. In the year 1846, under the impression that lands at Leigh called Menghams, which had been alienated by Lord and Lady Lumley with a remainder over, had passed to him under the limitation of the entail as parcel of the manor of Hayling, the lord of Hayling brought ejectments to recover the land so alienated, then the property of Sir George Staunton, and forming the greater part of Leigh farm. He also, at the same time, asserted his right of free warren over Bonvilles, an enfranchised portion of the manor of Hayling on which the right had been reserved in the deed of enfranchisement, and brought an action against Staunton's tenant in Hayling Island for disturbance of his franchise there. Cross actions for trespass were brought against the lord, and the actions proceeded *pari passu* up to notice of trial, when the whole were arranged. It was agreed that Staunton should discontinue his actions; that Padwick should do the same; that the latter should execute a release of claim of the lands in respect of which the ejectments had been brought, and a release of the claim of free warren over Staunton's lands in and out of Hayling; and that each party should pay his own costs. This arrangement was carried into effect, and no other action has since occurred, although persons have been summarily convicted before the justices, for trespass within the Sinah Warren, which is well stocked with rabbits, and some few hares. The lord still continues to exercise the franchise; and since the decision of the judges in the Earl of Carnarvon's case, where the right was established, no one has thought proper to dispute the point.

It will be remembered that two fisheries of the value of twenty pence are mentioned in Domesday, and that in the rental of Edward there is an account of the sums paid in respect of them. I presume that the fisheries were those of the eastern and western shores of the island, including the rifes surrounding and debouching into the main channel, on either side. These fisheries in early times were of very much greater moment than since the period of the Reformation, when fast-days were in a great measure abolished; but mention has come down to us of weirs which show that the harbour must always have been abundantly supplied with fish. In the 1st of Edward VI, 1547, twelve pence was paid for the new rent of " one piece of land and water between Rode " Ryth and Frypole Ryth, wherein to build one weare leased "to William Pepesham for term of his life, by copy of court "roll." For twelve pence, for a fishery there leased to Thomas George. For sixpence, for one other fishery there leased to John Roger yearly. For sixpence, for one wear leased to William Brygg. For sixpence, for a new rent of William Bright for one wear there; and for twelve pence, for one wear there leased to John Seaman. By the court rolls it appears that on the 3d November, 19 Henry VI, 1440, William Hamond came to the court and took of the lord a certain parcel of land within the seacoast (*infra costeram maris*) called Seynor, there to place a certain wear at his own expense, by the rent of sixteen pence yearly, and on the payment of a fine of two shillings. In the 31st year of the same reign, 1452, a grant was made by the steward to Nicolas Aylwin of a waste piece of land (*infra ripam maris*) within the sea-bank, for the construction of a wear in the tithing of Northney, at the yearly rent of twopence. On the 13th December, in the 34th year of the same reign, William Shipman was ordered to repair the wear at Lambard. In the 16th of Henry VIII, 1524, John Roymayn had a license to underlet to Thomas Perkins a sea wear. In the 36th of the same reign, William Pepsham took from the lord a place between Rode Reach and Fryspoolk Reach, to build a dam called a wear, for the term of his life, at the yearly rent of ten pence, rendering other services according to the custom of the manor; but nothing was assessed, by way of fine, as he undertook to build the wear at his own expense. On 6th October, 1708, a grant was made to Edward Mitchell of "A ware for "taking fishes" at the Northwood Point, for the term of his life, at the yearly rent of sixpence. On June 10, 1724, Thomas Duke of Norfolk, then lord of the manor, granted to John Warne a lease of the mill-rife for the term of ninety-nine years, described as then being in the occupation of his grace as lord, where an ancient corn-mill had stood in former times, with liberty to rebuild the mill or to erect a new one; and in the accounts of Abraham Ibbetson, steward to the duke in 1725, there is an entry of "Receipts of Mr. Till for fishery in "Hayling, five shillings, and for the fish-pond there, £1. 2s."

I do not find any further particulars in reference to the wears; nor do there appear to have been any further manorial grants for this purpose. It is possible that the mullet, base, and other fish frequenting the harbour diminished in quantity, from some local cause with which we are not acquainted; and the fishermen seem rather to have turned their attention to the dredging for oysters, and to the clearing of the soil in the rifes, in order to deposit the spat, which was not available until it arrived at a proper size. Various portions, previous to and during the time of the present lord, have been granted to the fishermen; and the requisite notice was given that they had, in conformity with the provision contained in Peel's acts, been formed into oyster-beds. In the year 1842 an inroad was made upon beds held by one Fleet of the lord in the mill-rife, by Cribb and others; and a considerable quantity of oysters was dredged up and carried away. A bill of indictment was preferred at the Hants summer assizes against two of the parties for stealing, and against three for dredging. The former were convicted of felony, the latter of a misdemeanor, by Mr. Baron Rolfe; and, as it was merely sought to establish the right to the bed of mill-rife, no judgment was passed upon them, on their entering into recognizances to appear and receive judgment upon some future occasion. At the Lent assizes of 1844 the present lord brought an action of trespass against Davis, a fisherman, in order to try and establish an exclusive right to the fishery of Hayling. The ancient wears were proved, but from the non-user of the right in modern times, the exclusive right of fishery was negatived by the jury. They however confirmed the right of the lord to the soil of the creeks; and since this time there has not, that I am aware of, been any further litigation on the subject.

The mackerel fishery in the Hayling Bay, on the southern side of the island, commences about the beginning of June, if the wind and weather permit; and the season continues, if there are no strong winds on land, for a month or six weeks; but it not unfrequently happens that their appearance is delayed until the beginning of July. The fish are first observed at a considerable distance from the land, which they approach in such prodigious shoals that many thousands have sometimes been taken at a single haul. The time of fishing is from sunset to sunrise; and they are taken with a long draw-net of an inch and a half mesh, from forty to fifty fathoms in length. One man stands on the shore, holding the rope, while two others row off the boat and drop the net into the sea, which is afterwards drawn on shore. In the season the fish are sold for about one penny apiece; they are from five to nine inches in length, and are considered the finest on the English coast. From their extreme delicacy, they travel badly, and to be eaten in perfection they should be dressed within a few hours after they are taken out of the water.

Among the ancient personal rights of the lord of Hayling was that of fine on the marriage of his copyhold tenants; and in the 22d of Richard II, 1399, William Atte Stone made fine with the lord for having Agatha, then late the wife of Henry Mulward, and paid fifty shillings for the license. In the year 1406 the homage presented that Joan, the daughter of Walter Parson, had married one John Waryn, dwelling within the lordship; whereupon a fine of twelve pence was paid, according to custom; and on the marriage of the daughter of Thomas Estoke within the manor, a similar fine of twelve pence was paid, according to custom.

In the year 1668 the steward accounts as received of Joan Collins, for a deodand, by a cart falling, worth thirty shillings, but only five shillings taken, to " preserve my lord's right to " deodand;" and in the Hayling Priory court rolls of the 33d Henry VI, 1455, there is an entry made of a mortuary paid to the lord on the death of the vicar of Hayling.

The ferry at the western harbour is appurtenant to the manor, and was let by lease to Bulbeck in the time of the late Dukes of Norfolk. Upon a disturbance of the exclusive right of ferry by John Cole, in the year 1842, the present lord brought an action against him, and obtained a verdict in confirmation of his claim, which was subsequently further recognised by an injunction of the Court of Chancery. The ferry at the eastern harbour is also appurtenant to the manor; and after the trial of the action of Hellyer *v.* Miller, the former, then the tenant of Eastock farm, under John Williams, entered into an agreement with the lord, under which a rent was settled for the tithes on Eastock, for the privilege of taking such gravel as he might require, and for the privilege of the eastern ferry-way. The ferry at the northern extremity was free; and the house, which in former days was occupied by the ferryman, was built at the joint expense of the parishes of Hayling North and Hayling South.

In the year 1823 it was considered that the island needed better accommodation of ingress and egress than that afforded by the Wadeway and the northern ferry; and an act of parliament, which received the royal assent on the 2d May in that year, was obtained for building a bridge and making a causeway from Langstone in the parish of Havant to the ferry-house in the parish of Hayling North. If one may trust the preamble of the act, the situation of the islanders must up to this time have been pitiable indeed; for it recited, that from the violence of the winds and sea, the Wadeway was frequently covered by the tide the whole twenty-four hours together, and that boats were often totally prevented from crossing the harbour, by reason whereof any communication between the main land and Hayling Island became impracticable, and that great inconvenience, difficulty, and loss were thereby occasioned, and that the lives of his Majesty's subjects were very much endangered. Be that as it may, the act, which contained considerable powers, enabling the company to construct docks, wharves, and quays, and to levy quay and other dues, was carried into effect. The Duke of Norfolk, earl marshal of England, contributed to the undertaking, and opened the bridge in person on the 8th September, 1824. His grace and most of the resident gentry of the neighbourhood dined together at the Bear Inn, Havant; and Mr. Padwick, who had promoted and carried the bill through the House, received the thanks of the subscribers and a present of plate on the occasion. The bridge has been a great convenience to Hayling. In 1851 an amended act was

THE SALTERNS

THE BRIDGE, WITH THE MAINLAND IN THE DISTANCE.

THE LIBRARY.

THE BATHING HOUSE.

obtained for making a tramway from the bridge to the Havant station of the London, Brighton, and South Coast Railway. This has been allowed to expire, a locomotive line being under consideration; and it is hoped, by the expenditure of a small sum of money in affording better accommodation and greater depth of water for vessels using the harbour, and by the construction of local docks in communication with the Portsmouth Railway, that the local trade of the neighbourhood may be increased and developed, to the benefit of the company in quay dues and tolls for passengers. On the 16th June, 1852, the consent of the Admiralty as conservators of tidal waters, was given to the embankment from the harbour of about three thousand acres of mud land surrounding the island, parcel of the manor of Hayling; it is hoped to commence the work within a comparatively short period, and to reclaim land which will be valuable for agricultural purposes, and afford permanent employment to many of the neighbouring poor.

Subsequent to the erection of the bridge, an endeavour was made to form a watering-place on the southern shore of Hayling. It failed, partly from internal dissension among those whose interests were to preserve peace; partly from the nature of the site, which might have been better selected at a greater distance from the beach; and partly from the misconception of the architect, who carried out ideas of London houses upon a shore where the south-west wind sets almost continually for nine out of the twelve months of the year, and where, of all places, the buildings should have been low and compact. Instead of this, houses of five and six stories meet the eye, without the slightest reference to the wants or the capabilities of the locality, and, as a natural consequence, they are only tenanted when other houses cannot be obtained. That the site would have become a watering-place possessing considerable attractions of sand, of view, of water, and of the purest air, cannot be doubted, had different measures been adopted; and the result of such measures may readily be seen in the permanent occupation of the villa residences north of the beach, which afford ample accommodation for persons of quiet habits and moderate fortunes.

The church of Hayling South, dedicated to the Virgin Mary, is beautiful and very interesting, presenting every appearance of having been founded and completed without interruption, and affording an example of Early English architecture of high character and workmanship. It is of considerable size, adapted evidently for a much larger population than the island now possesses, and comprises a nave, with side aisles and a chancel. The latter is forty-two feet long by eighteen wide, and very lofty, like those attached to monastic establishments. The eastern window contains five lancets united; three windows on either side, deeply splayed, are of the same date and style, and were, till lately, embellished with a profusion of painted glass, now broken or removed: a few squares crusted over by time alone remain. The windows stand up high from the pavement; in one on either side of the altar is a decorated bracket for a lamp or image of the Virgin; and opposite to the communion table, in the southern wall there is a double trefoil piscina. An ancient seat, recently removed with a view of restoration, served to separate the chancel from the nave, exhibiting a quantity of carved work about it: one panel bore a pelican in her piety, vulned proper; another bore an anchor in pale, with a cross of three coils of rope. At the bottom of the seat are two stone coffin-lids, of priests or ecclesiastics, one of them probably of a prior, with a crosier upon it. Tradition assigns it to the last of the priors of Hayling. The arms of the pelican have erroneously been attributed to the family of Tawke, who were farmers of the priory and manor in the reign of Henry VIII. They bore however, according to the visitations of the heralds, confirmed by Dallaway and Berry, Ar. three chaplets in chief vert, in base a capital Roman T gules; and on the seat before alluded to there is a coat bearing these arms. There is no question but that the pelican arms were those of Fox, bishop of Winchester, lord privy seal and counsellor to Henry VII and VIII, the founder of Corpus Christi College, Oxford, who was consecrated in the year 1500, and died in 1528. They are still to be seen in one of the restored windows of Winchester Cathedral, with the motto he adopted, " Est Deo

Enriched Corbel.

Norman Font, with a Battlement.

Niche for the Virgin.

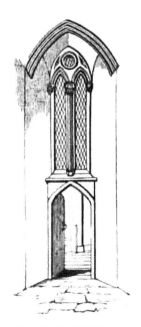

The end of the Side Aisle of
the South Church.

Niche in the splay of a window for a Lamp

Stoups for Holy Water in the Chancel of the Church.

Stoup in the Church.

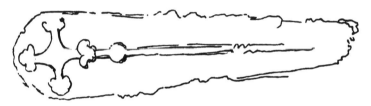

The Prior's Grave.

One half of the Old Barn.

"gracia;" for whom the other coat was intended, cannot be learnt.

The tower or lantern rises between the chancel and the nave with a flight of steps leading into the belfry, which contained originally three bells, one of which bore the date of 1324. These were sold in 1805, and realized the sum of £170. A steeple covered with shingles rises above the tower, and serves as a landmark to passing vessels. This steeple was re-shingled in June, 1734, at a cost of £42; and again in the year 1771. The great west window was blown in by the storm of January, 1734; and was rebuilt in stone, during the same year, at an expense of £52. 15s. (*Parochial Records.*) The font, which stands near the western door, is square, embattled, and of about the date of 1140. The heads surmounting the pillars, having been much injured by time, a restoration has been effected. It has every appearance of being of greater antiquity than the church in which it is placed, and might possibly have been brought there from the priory on its dissolution. About thirty years ago, during the incumbency of the late Mr. Stopford, a very ancient font was discovered in a shallow well in the south parish. It was taken up and removed to Westbourne, but has lately been restored to Hayling South. The lantern itself is twenty-four feet square. The arches are very fine specimens of the Early Decorated; in that between the lantern and the chancel the groove for the screen is still visible; and the brackets which once supported the rood-loft, on which the images of the Virgin Mary and saints were exhibited on festivals, are yet to be seen on the imposts of the arches. The work, which has recently been cleansed from the white-wash of years past, is sharp from the chisel, and remarkably well executed.

The nave is sixty-three feet long, by forty-five wide, including the side aisles; the pavement is laid with square encaustic tiles, intermixed with some of modern date; the former are very ancient, larger than those at Warblington, inlaid with colours and figures of different design, but so much broken and defaced that no pattern can be traced upon

them. There are three lancet windows on either side, deeply
splayed, with depressed arches in the interior. The pillars
separating the nave from the side aisles are octagonal; some
of the capitals bear an ornament of leaves, apparently copied
from nature, one of them being identical with that of
Warmington, which was built about 1280: the corbel of the
westernmost arch represents a serpent, emblematic of the
tempter, and another a horn, or cornucopia. A clerestory
occupies the space between the arches and the roof, with
quatrefoil windows, deeply splayed. The southern oratory at the
east end of the side aisle contains a trefoil piscina; and it is
remarkable that the arches adjoining to the oratory, on the
northern as well as the southern side of the aisles, differ
materially in their span and form from those of the tower and
nave. Beverley Minster, built about the year 1310, has specimens of a similar construction. The corbels are very highly
decorated, that on the southern side, beneath a fretwork
capital, bearing the head of a crowned female, and that on the
northern side, beneath a capital ornamented with *fleurs de lis*
above a wreath of ivy-leaves, bearing the head of a crowned
man. It is natural to suppose that these heads were intended
to represent the king and queen in whose reign the church
was built; and upon referring to the royal portraits of that
period, it would certainly seem that the heads are those of
King Edward I and Eleanor of Castile. The face of the king
is without a beard, and bears a resemblance to that upon his
coins, the crown also corresponding with that he was accustomed to wear. It could not have been intended for that of
Edward II, or of Edward III, as both, but especially the
latter, are always represented with beards, and hair on the
upper lip. The head of the female, although somewhat mutilated, is like that upon Eleanor's monument in Westminster
Abbey, and the crown corresponds as well. Adopting this
supposition therefore, it follows that the South Church of
Hayling was built between the years 1272 and 1291, the
latter being the year in which Queen Eleanor died, at
Herdelie in Lincolnshire. The general style of the architecture is precisely of this period; and, looking to the circum-

New Vicarage House – Hayling, South?

Old Vicarage House. Hayling - Island - South?

stances in connection with its history, there is every reason to believe that the date to which the erection has been ascribed is substantially correct.

The entrance to the church is through an ancient decorated porch of the fourteenth century on the southern side, bricked up half way to the level of the seats, and paved with large stones, broad at one end, but narrowing to the other, which appear from their shape to have served as coffin-lids to some ecclesiastics. The principal entrance, in former days, was by the large door at the west end of the nave, through which the processions of the Romish Church passed on festivals and holy days. There is a low doorway under an arch on the northern side, and a private entrance for the officiating priests on the southern side of the chancel. Near the southern porch stands an immense yew-tree, apparently of greater age than the church itself.

The cemetery, surrounding the church, is unusually large, indicating, like the church, the existence of a larger population than at the present moment. The parishioners of Hayling South bury on the southern, and those of Hayling North on the northern side of the ground. The fences of the cemetery are repaired by different persons proportioned to their interest : for instance, the North parish maintains the northern hedge ; certain lands in West town the western hedge ; Griggs Land, the southern hedge ; the Manor farm, six panels of paling on the east side ; Estock farm, four panels ; and the remaining panels are distributed amongst the various other landed proprietors resident in the parish of Hayling South. It also receives the bodies of those not unfrequently washed on the shore of the island, who were in earlier times buried on the beach where they were first discovered. On digging the foundation of the hotel, bones were found of persons interred in this way ; and the workmen employed at the bridge came upon similar remains in the course of their excavations.

The old vicarage-house of Hayling South parish stood about two hundred yards to the south of the church itself, near the present blacksmith's shop. On the induction of the now vicar, a new vicarage was built on a portion of the glebe, a

part of the expense of which was charged upon the living by
annual instalments extending over a period of several years.
On the eastern side of the church, and close adjoining
it, is a piece of land called "the Church Plot," and anciently described as town land. The tenant of the church
plot has from time immemorial, either washed the vicar's
surplices three times in the year, or has paid a money-rent of
three half-crowns to cover the charge. The lord and lay
rector is the present occupier. It would seem that there had
formerly been a question as to the ownership of this church
plot, and that it had been brought under the notice of the
archdeacon; for at the visitation of Hayling South, in the year
1729, a schedule of the property of the church is set forth, in
which the plot is particularly mentioned, and, for greater
accuracy, I subjoin the schedule verbatim:—

"A schedule of y° goods belonging to the church.
" A communion table-cloth, a carpet, and napkin.
" A silver cup wth a cover, a pewter flaggon, &c.
" Plate of the same metal.
" A church Bible, two common-prayer-books,
" A surplice, a pulpit-cloth and cushion, and a cloth for the
" reading-desk. A Beer.
"There is a plot of ground wch they say belongs to y°
" church, wch the churchwardens for many years past, received
" rent, and is now entered upon by —— ——, Lord of y°
" Manor, as properly his." (*Certified by Jas. Lampard, Dep.*
Registrar, 16 *July*, 1840).

In what way it became the property of the church, is not
known; I cannot think that it could ever have formed parcel
of the glebe; and I conclude, that on the inclosure of the
adjoining lands, which have at no very distant period been the
subject of a common allotment, and the fences of which are
straight—this piece, like that of Havant and other neighbouring places, was appropriated to the purposes of the church,
the wardens of which have always seen that the rent in kind
has been performed.

The church, or chapel of ease, of Hayling North, dedicated
to Saint Peter, and situate in the hamlet of Hayling North-

wood, is a plain unornamented edifice, sixty feet in length by thirty in width, with side-aisles separated from the nave by heavy pointed arches of Early English architecture, with massive columns of the same period, the capitals bearing the spear-head ornament. The northern transept was apparently designed for a chantry, having a trefoil niche to the east for an altar; over the niche is a pedestal, on which an image of the Virgin or the patron saint may have been placed. The chancel is separated from the body of the church by a wooden screen, and contains a piscina for holy water, and an ambry.

The turret springs from nearly the centre of the building. The nave is occupied by strong oak-benches, serving the purpose of seats, some having poppy-heads, others *fleur de lis,* and several devices emblematic of the Holy Trinity, carved upon them. The windows are uniform on either side; and the church is entered on the northern side through a carved wooden porch, of the age of Henry VI.

The pavement of the nave bears the following inscriptions :—

" *To the memory of Matthew Monlas, vicar of Hayling, who departed this life April the 25th, in the year 1703, aged 57 years; and also of Anna his wife, who departed this life August 3rd, in the year 1724, aged 74 years. This stone laid down March 9th, 1765.*"

" *To the memory of John Monlas, gent. and Frances his wife, son of Matthew Monlas, vicar of Hayling, who departed this life January 16th, in the year 1725, aged 39 years. There has been no other remembrance of him for the space of forty years, but what he produced for himself (the best indeed) by his virtue and good works. Such a character, such an example of good works, should never, if possible, be forgotten; and therefore, in justice to. the memory of the deceased, and for the good of mankind, is now renewed.*"

" *Near him lies Frances his wife, a beloved wife, an affectionate mother, and sincere friend; these three*

*important characters she maintained with great credit
to herself, and comfort to her friends. She departed
this life February the 3rd, in the year 1765, aged 69
years. This stone laid down March 9th, 1765."*

In the year 1627, Nicholas Harryson was vicar of Hayling;
Matthew Monlas succeeded him, and died in 1703; Mr. Smith
followed; and in 1741, Mr. Partington was vicar. In 1750,
Isaac Skelton, a gentleman of considerable attainments, was
inducted; at whose death in 1773, the cure was conferred on
John Webster. He was succeeded in 1805 by Mr. Groom;
the latter in 1810 by Peter W. Moore and Dr. Heming.
Thomas Valentine followed; Joshua Stopford in 1817; and
at his decease the Rev. Charles Hardy, the now vicar, was
inducted on the 20th January, 1832, on the presentation of
the present lord. (*Par. Register.*)

In the Valuation of Pope Nicolas, made in the 20 Edward I,
1292, the church of Hayling is thus rated:—

The church of Heylingg . . £80 0 0	£8 0 0
The vicarage of the same . . 14 6 8	1 6 8

In the valuation found in the Nonæ Rolls, which were
compiled in 15th of Edward III, 1340-1, from the returns
made in the 13th year of the same reign, it appears, on the
oaths of Geoffrey Segare, Walter de Southetone, Simon
Osebern, William Landman, William Curps, and Thomas
Cardenille, that the ninth of corn, wool, and lambs of the
parish of Heilynge, was in the thirteenth year of the reign, of
the value of £26. 13s. 4d. And they stated, that the aforesaid
ninth could not amount to the tax of the church in the year
aforesaid, for that the same church was endowed with one
messuage and one hundred and twenty acres of land, which
were worth by the year £9. 12s., and of rents and services of
the yearly value of £6. 12s. 8d. They stated also, that the
tenths of hay, and other small tithes, with the oblations and
mortuaries, were of the yearly value of £12. 19s. 8d.; and
they stated, that very many other tenths belonged to the same
church, which had lately been destroyed by the sea, so that
the tax of the same church was not worth so much as in times
then past. (*Inq. Nonar. com. Suth. Paroch. de Heilynge.*)

The vicarage was valued in 1750 as a discharged living at the clear yearly sum of £47. The tenths, before the discharge took place, were £17 per annum. (*Butler*.) The living of South Hayling is now styled a vicarage, with the perpetual curacy of North Hayling annexed to it, of the annual value, as settled under the Commutation Act, of £211, in the patronage of the lord of the manor. There are 35*a*. 2*r*. 24*p*. of glebe land ;. and there is a tradition, that under a tree standing on part of the glebe in West Lane, a large quantity of money lies buried. It is almost a matter of surprise that ordinary curiosity, and the want of timber for repairs, have not combined to put the truth of the tradition to the test of demonstration. The manor farm, as forming part of the demesnes of the priory of Hayling, is exempt from tithes under the original endowment of Pope Innocent, and the principal great tithes unenfranchised are those on the Eastock farm.

By the census taken in 1811, the north parish contained forty-two houses and two hundred and fifty-four inhabitants ; and the south parish contained fifty-six houses and three hundred and twenty-four inhabitants. By that of 1851, the population in the north parish had increased to two hundred and seventy-two, while that in the south parish had increased to eight hundred and twenty-four.

There is no distinct account of the foundation or erection of either of the three churches which have been built within the Island of Hayling. The first was undoubtedly that which was standing at the date of the Conqueror's grant, and therein mentioned, and which Henry II, who began to reign in the year 1155, confirmed to the church of the Blessed Mary and Saint Peter of Jumiéges, as of the gift of King William, the greater part of the Island of Haringey, with the church and the tithes of the whole island, except the tithes of pulse and of oats in the land of the Bishop of Winchester. By whom this church was erected—whether by Queen Emma, by the Abbey of Hyde, on whom she bestowed the manor, or by the Abbey of Jumiéges on the donation of the Conqueror—cannot now be ascertained ; but, looking to the probabilities of the case, the erection may, I think, be attributed to the Abbey

of Hyde, the precise site of the building being marked out by
the existing Church Rocks to the south of the present shore
of Hayling.   If this be so, the date of the first church would
be about the year 1050; and the ancient font now restored
from West Bourne was no doubt that from which the first con-
verts to Christianity within the island received their baptism.
On this account alone, independent of the ordinary association with the past, the font possesses a peculiar interest to
the inhabitants, and all must be gratified at its restoration to
the present church of Hayling South, as the most appropriate
place for its reception.   .   '

The period at which the church was so injured by the sea
as to render it unfit for service, is pretty well determined by
the return to the Inquisition in the 14th of Edward III,
1339-40, where it was found that the greater part of the
same island was almost destroyed and consumed by inundation of the waters, and that the place where the parish church
had been first built had been in the middle of the island, and
that it was then immersed so deep in the sea that an English
ship of the larger class might pass there.   It is quite clear,
therefore, that the church must have been abandoned some
time before the date of this inquisition.   :

The chapel of Hayling Northwood was built for the convenience of the inhabitants of the northern part of the island,
about the reign of Henry II, the style of the architecture
being of that date, and the *fleur de lis*, still to be seen in the
nave, confirming the supposition; but when the Abbey of
Jumiéges had founded the priory in Tourner Marsh, and
when the original church had become untenable, they naturally
turned their attention to the better accommodation of their
establishment and tenants at Hayling Southwood; and with
this view.they built the existing church to replace that which
the waters had swept away.   It is evident that it was built in
the latter part of the thirteenth century, from the outline of
the ground-plot, the style of the architecture, the ornaments
of the capitals, and the porch at the south door; whilst the
stone coffins of the priors, and the tessellated pavement, presumed to have been laid down under the superintendence of

North Hayling Chapel and Old Vicarage House.

foreign workmen, who were generally employed in works of this description, indicate that it was completed long before the priory was dissolved, and the manor given to the Monastery of Shene, in the year 1418.

It would appear, however, that the ancient burying-place surrounding the original church was used for the purposes of sepulture for some time after the erection of the present edifice. At what precise period it ceased to be the burying-place of the parish there is no evidence to show; but that it so remained down to the year 1486, when the parishioners of Hayling North petitioned the Abbey of Shene for permission to bury in their own cemetery, is clear from their statement, because they speak of taking the dead from the hamlet of Northwood " to the parish church of Hayling, *or* its burying-" ground;" and they urge as a reason, both the great distance and the inundation of the waters. Now, this could not by possibility have applied to the cemetery of the preserved church, which has never been affected by the sea, and must therefore have had reference to that of the original church. It is probable, that soon after the privilege of burial had been conceded to the north parish, a cemetery was added to the present church, inasmuch as the inconveniences which affected the north parishioners affected those of the southern portion of the island to a considerable, though not to an equal extent.

The Island of Hayling must in early times have been a very much larger place, and one, from its position, of much greater importance than has generally been conceived. The six tithings of Northney, Eastney, Stoke, Westney, Menge-ham, and West-town, which have come down to us, show that at a very early period Hayling contained sixty families, exclusive of slaves, and exclusive of the various towns which sprung up in after times; and taking, therefore, each family at ten, the tithings alone give a total of six hundred souls, and upon a fair inference a total probable population of ten times the present population of the island. The various inquisitions throw considerable light upon its size, and the dangers to which it lay exposed, both from the ravages of the sea and from the inroads of the enemy—the open coast

presenting a convenient spot for landing a hostile force.
Looking to the return, which states that the parish church,
which was then being fast washed away, had stood originally
in the centre of the island, we are at once led to the conclusion that, allowing the same extent on the south as on the
north, the island must at the time when the church was
built, and up to the period of the inundation, have reached to
within about two miles of the spot now occupied by the Nab
Light. The word " leuca," which is used in the return to the
inquisition, two of which formed the distance between the
shore and the church, consisted, according to the Roll of
Battle Abbey, of four hundred and eighty perches : Ingulphus
however, who is a good authority, speaks of the Leuca as a
mile. The ordinary mile of England, it will be remembered,
in former times was more of a traditionary than an ascertained
measure ; it was, in fact, nearly a mile and a half of the
present standard. Bloomfield, in his *History of Norfolk*,
renders "leuca" a league, meaning something less than two
miles, which appears to have tallied in the generality of places
which he examined in order to ascertain the correct distance.

Considering also that the best land, as stated, lay nearest
the sea, and that the devastation must, in the course of time,
have swept away a space of no less than nine miles in length
by about five in breadth, this may well account for the depo-
pulation of the place, and for the miserable state to which
the inhabitants were reduced. The ravages of the sea were
not confined to the southern side of the island, but extended
up as far as Hayling Northwood. There is reason to believe,
that formerly there was a ford rather than a channel between
the main land of Havant and Hayling, and that the channel
has become very much deeper within the last seventy or eighty
years. Old persons not long deceased have been heard to say,
that at that time a man on horseback could ride across at almost
any time of tide, by jumping his horse over the channel of the
Wadeway ; and where at low water on the Dobbin Point the
same thing could be done less than a century ago, between
Thorney and Chidham, there is now from fourteen to sixteen
feet of water. The four hides of land, equal to four hundred

and eighty acres, stated in the Testa de Nevill to have been held by Ralph d'Anvers, are never afterwards mentioned; and I conclude they also must have formed part of those lands, although not specifically named, which were inundated and destroyed by the sea; and the reason for this might have been, that they formed no part of the possessions of the prior, being held of the honour of Gloucester. If not so washed away, they must have escheated to the crown, and have been included in the subsequent grants of the manor and isle of Hayling.

After the manor was granted to the monastery of Shene, the priory of Hayling fell, as may easily be imagined, into a state of rapid decay. The prior's stables are alone noticed in the minister's accounts of 32d Henry VIII, 1541; and, as the grange or farm-house of the demesne lands was rebuilt nearer to the centre of the island, this circumstance may also have contributed to the dismantling of the priory itself. At what time the grange, which was pulled down by the late Duke of Norfolk in the year 1777, on the erection of the present manor-house, was first built, does not appear from the records of the manor; but, looking at the state of things in the island at that period, it may be conjectured to have been built out of the ruins of the priory after the dissolution. It is very questionable whether the grange always stood on its present site, because the word Healingey, Helingey, or Halinghei, derived from the Saxon *healle, inge,* and *ey,* signified the place of the meadow in which there was an *aula,* or hall, answering to our word *hall* or *mansion;* or, as all islands were in early times considered objects of sanctity, the name may have been derived from the Saxon *helige,* which signified *holy* or *sacred.* In the return of the lands submerged by the sea, there is mention made of almost the whole hamlet of Estok, with the lands belonging to the same, appertaining to the parish church of Hayling, which the prior had to his own use, being destroyed by the sea—treated, in fact, as the demesnes of the manor; and a presentment, to which I have before alluded, occurs in the rolls where, William Gauntelow is found to have pulled down the ancient hall at Estok, on the lordship of the

39

prior of Hayling. Now, it is not at all improbable but that Harold, who had resided at his manor of Bosham, built this hall at the time when he possessed the Hayling lands, and that on its falling into decay, with the fear of future inundations, from which the island had suffered so grievously, before their eyes, they determined upon changing the site, and removed the grange away from the sea more inland to the then centre of the island, where the manor-house now stands.

There are many reasons why the ancient hall or grange should have been at Eastock. In the first place, it was at a convenient distance from the church; in the next, it must have been near the sea fishery of the eastern harbour and the stews, or fresh-water fishery, called " My Lords " and the Tourner Ponds, with direct access across the harbour to Bosham. It was close to the salterns, then far more necessary to the comfort of a hall than at the present day, both for the curing of fish, and for the salting of beeves; added to which, there was Tourner Bury itself, to which the inmates might have retired for defence in case of invasion. The word Eastock or Estoke signifies east wood, as Northstoke signifies north wood, so called in after times; and the pannage of the hogs was always an important consideration in selecting a manorial residence. The contiguity of the priory too favours the supposition that the hall could not have been far distant. In the reeve's account of Edward I, the wages of the park-keeper are spoken of; and upon the court rolls, " Chapel Park" occurs; the latter was situate to the north of Mengham, adjoining Tourner Bury; and not many years since, a large quantity of old timber was cut on this very spot, the lands having most probably been imparked by the priors in exercise of their franchise of free warren. These circumstances seem to warrant the conclusion that the most valuable of the demesne lands and the ancient manorial hall were at Eastock.

The present manor-house was built by Edward Duke of Norfolk, part only of the former offices and ancient walls being suffered to remain. A moat surrounded it at one time, forming an area of eight acres, which was sheltered on the north by the Home Coppice. A cannon-ball, a key, a knife

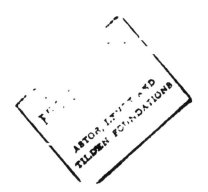

Hayling. Manor House.

studded with *fleur de lis*, and some few coins, were found some years since in cleaning out the moat. The manor barn is a curious structure, having been built from a cargo of German oak, wrecked some centuries ago upon the shore of the island, seized by the ancestors of the Duke of Norfolk as lords, and appropriated to this purpose. The tradition is, that the oak was shipped from the Elbe, and that it was intended for a monastery in France. The huge timbers of the barn have been put together in the same state in which they were cast on shore ; and upon entering it the visitor will be surprised at the immense quantity of timber employed in the construction of the building.

The dovecote of the former grange is still in existence, being capable of containing a large number of pigeons, as the walls are of great thickness, and are perforated for the convenience of the nests. It was held in the case of Boulston *v.* Hardy (*Cro. Eliz.* 548), that dovecotes could be erected by the lord of a manor only, and that if a private person erected a dovecote he was punishable in the court leet for a nuisance. It was clearly a manorial privilege in early times, and formed a considerable item of profit and convenience to the lord.

The Westhay, now corrupted into Westney, might very possibly have been an incident of the right of free warren, as exercised by the abbots of Jumiéges and the priors of Hayling. The word "hay" occurs not unfrequently in the Book of Domesday, and was described as a place where beasts of warren were captured. In Shropshire, at Lege, three hays are mentioned ; at Wirdine a wood in which were three hays. At Leland, in Lancashire, among the lands between the Ribble and the Mersey, it is said the men of this manor and of Salford do not work at the hall of the king, but they make one hay in the wood there ; and among the possessions of Saint Peter of Gloucester, at Hamene and Hortune in Gloucestershire, it is stated that the church had the hunting in three hays there. Beasts were caught by driving them into the hedged or paled part of a wood, as elephants are in India, or deer in North America ; and this in the forest laws of 36th Edward III was called the hay. The well-known Rothwell

Haigh, near Leeds, was the park belonging to the Lacies
within their manor of Rothwell. The out-park of Skipton
Castle is still called the Hawe Park, and that of Knareborough
the Haye Park. (*Whit. Hist. of Whalley*, p. 175.) In the
north parish of Hayling, the north coppice is believed to mark
the site of part of an ancient wood; from which the place,
North Stoke, afterwards Northwood, took its name; the same
may be said of East Stoke and Southwood; and, if we bear
in mind the state of the neighbouring country, it would seem
likely that a clearance of the primeval forests ·must have been
made before a settlement could have been effected. The
entries upon the court rolls point to the existence of a much
greater quantity of timber within the island than at the present
moment; and only in the time of Mr. Budd, the avenue which
reached from the South Church to the Ham Farm was felled;
and it is also said and believed, that not many years before
this event took place, not less than ten thousand pounds' worth
of timber was cut and sold in a single season on the demesne
lands of the Duke of Norfolk.   With abundance of food and
timber, boars and deer were no doubt found in Hayling as in
the forest of Bere, a part of which derived its name from the
boar-hunt; and although the plough has obliterated all trace
of the embankments usually accompanying such an enclosure,
there is no reason to think but that the name signified in
Hayling, where rights of free warren are known to have
existed, what it is clearly proved to have signified in other
places of the same description.

     The shore of Hayling has from time immemorial been
one of great danger to shipping, and there are many tales
throughout the island of vessels which have struck upon the
Wolsinars, and have been totally lost.   In the year 1798, the
Impregnable man-of-war ran upon the Wolsinars, and became
a total wreck, the then Duke of Norfolk receiving his share as
lord, and purchasing largely beside, out of which the Norfolk
Lodge Inn at Sinah was built.   An Indiaman went down
close to the present western ferry-house, and part of her hull
can still be seen at low water.   It does not appear how she
got there, whether driven over the bar by stress of weather or

not; but she went to pieces, and such parts of her as could be recovered were bought by one George How, then a ship-chandler on the Point of Portsmouth. In the year 1805 a vessel, with the Bennett family and other passengers on board, stole away from Gibraltar, bound for Penzance in Cornwall. The authorities of the latter place refused to admit her, as the plague had broken out among her crew; and the master stating that he could pilot her into Chichester harbour, her course was at once changed for that port. A heavy storm came on, and the vessel was driven on the Poles, nearly in front of Eastock. She was obliged to remain in the position where she had at first struck, as the coast-guard had strict injunctions to shoot the first who came on shore, in order to prevent the spreading of the infection. Provisions were passed from the beach without contact by means of a rope. The pestilence increased, and day by day the mortality became greater, until a heavy sea and bad weather set in from the southward, when the ill-fated vessel foundered, and all on board perished. An antique silver spoon, the only vestige of the bark, is still pre-served as a relic by William Barber, of Hayling South, who picked it up among the fragments of the wreck.

Nothing of importance has been discovered within the island, either in the way of coins or pottery; but not long since, a curious matchlock was found in Sinah Warren, covered with sand and much eaten with rust; and upon what is called Abbot's Land, it is said that the father of Mrs. Warren stum-bled upon some money, though not to any great amount.

There is no positive record of any market or fair having been held within the Island of Hayling, and at all events, none has ever been held in modern times. At what period the establishment of public markets first took place in England we are not told, but the constantly increasing severity of the Anglo-Saxon laws against theft probably multiplied their number. To escape this severity, it was necessary that every man, and especially a dealer in goods, should always be able to prove his legal property in what he possessed. In the laws of Athelstan, it was enacted, that no one should make a purchase beyond twenty pennies without the gate, but that such bargains should take place within the town itself, in the presence of the portreeve, or some other person of veracity, or of the reeves in the folkmote.   Although all trace of a market has been lost, yet the manor of Hayling may have had one when it was of greater consequence than at the present moment.   In the charter of Henry to the Abbot of Jumiéges there is a grant of Thol, called some- times Theloneum, which was in fact the privilege to the abbot of buying and selling in his own land.   In the language of the Domesday Survey, it was not merely the liberty of buying and selling or keeping a market, but it meant as well the customary dues or rents paid to the lord for his profits of the fair or market, as well as a tribute or custom for passage (*Bract.* lib. ii, cap. 24, s. 3) ; and under the charter of Henry, I conceive that the ferries at the eastern and western harbours, and the passage money paid to the ferrymen, passed to the Abbot of Jumiéges.   There is a spot called the Townhall Furlong in the north parish, and another called the Fish Shambles at Mengham, consisting of very large and massive stones, on which fish may have been sold at some time, and, in the absence of any further explanation, they may be con- sidered as the vestiges of a market long since passed away.

The freedom from toll and market tallage granted to the tenants of the manor under the various charters from that of Henry I, downwards, and the exemption from service on juries at the sessions and assizes of the county, are still pre- served to the inhabitants ; and upon a question which took place some few years since at Winchester, in reference to the exemption, Mr. Padwick appeared by counsel, and future attendance was excused.   There are two benefit clubs in the island on the usual footing, which hold their annual meetings at the Maypole Inn and the Royal Hotel.

To whatever portion of the manorial history we happen to turn—whether to the Survey of Domesday, to the period of the *quo warranto,* to the time of John le Botiler, to that of the first vicar, to that of the Dukes of Norfolk, or to that of the present lord—litigation in various shapes seems to have formed a staple commodity in the natural produce of the island.

Questions of wreck, free warren, fishery, and custom have all
in turn contributed their *quota*, until one might have imagined
that there was literally nothing left for the present generation to
try. It was some time since however discovered, that certain
lands called "Howard's Furlong," in the parish of Portsea,
covered with houses, and of the estimated value of £200,000,
had been included in the Lumley entail before mentioned,
and that upon the expiration of the original lease of the
manor of Hayling, and of the land at Portsea, parcel of the
manor, the latter had been wholly lost sight of, and in fact
had been wholly unnoticed down to the time of the Purchase
Act of 1825. The reversion of Howard's Furlong having,
as it was contended, vested in Mr. Padwick as lord of the
manor, he in the year 1847, under the joint opinion of three
eminent counsel, brought 600 separate actions of ejectment
for the recovery of the property as parcel of the manor of
Hayling: this he was under the necessity of doing at one
time in order to save the Statute of Limitations. (Doe d.
Padwick *v.* Whitcombe.) The first case was tried at Exeter;
and Spiller's book, which was very material to trace the lease
into and through the hands of Sir Edward Cresswell, on being
tendered in evidence to Mr. Justice Coleridge, was by him
rejected, and the superior court confirmed the view entertained
by the learned judge. In consequence of this, the first case
was disposed of adversely to the plaintiff. A second action
was then tried, where the book was, on the suggestion of the
Court of Exchequer, tendered in a different way, as evidence
of reputation that the lands were parcel of the manor, and
again rejected. A bill of exceptions to the ruling of the
learned judge was thereupon tendered, and the question has
since been decided by the House of Lords adverse to Mr.
Padwick. Many of the defendants in ejectment had com-
pounded the matter by payment of a sum of money, taking
a release of title, as the means of avoiding a protracted and
expensive contest.

Experience of the past, however, is, we trust, likely to
introduce a better order of things within the island, and
litigation is certainly on the decline. There are very many

objects in which a common interest should unite the inhabitants for the benefit of the community, and it is to be hoped that they may no longer, as heretofore, be neglected. The act for the compulsory enfranchisement of copyholds, which has recently received the royal assent, will adjust many little differences and causes of dispute hitherto existing between the lord and the tenant. It will place all upon a just and proper footing in regard to the tenure of their lands. All issues arising out of copyholds, now the subject of judicial inquiry at the assizes and in the courts above, may, under the act, be referred for the opinion of the commissioners, and decisions may be obtained at a nominal expense, whilst the rights and franchises will, on enfranchisement, be finally adjusted. In this way copyholds will gradually diminish in number, and in a few years will become extinct. The heriot or habiliments of war delivered up to the lord on the death of a tenant, to be put into other hands for the service and defence of the country ; the fine paid to relieve the estate and obtain possession of the profits, consisting of horses and armour, till by the assize of arms in the 27th Henry II, it became payable in money ; the mortuary, sometimes of special custom due to the lord, and for which the body of John of Eltham, in 1334, was arrested at the altar by the prior and convent of Westminster, until a composition of one hundred pounds had been paid ; the license to alienate, the license to marry, the annual quit-rent, the suit and service, the homage of the copyhold tenant, and the fealty of the free tenant,—all these will alike for ever cease ; and when the tenure shall have come to an end, and the courts be no longer holden, the chief remnant of the feudal times, the last connecting link between the baron and his vassal, will have passed away, and after an existence of a thousand years, the manors of the land, like the castles they served to maintain, will become a matter of history and mere tradition.

APPENDIX.

I.—NATURAL HISTORY OF HAYLING AND ITS VICINITY.

FAUNA.—FISH.

BASSE.

DELPHINUS, *Phocæna*, Porpoise, only an occasional visitor.

RAIA. *Batis*, Skate.

    Clavata, Thornback.

    Pastinaca, Sting-ray, Sting, frequent in the summer.

SQUALUS, *Squatina*, Angel-fish, Monk-fish, occasionally found, though rare.

    Glaucus, Blue Shark, taken some years since.

    Catulus, Lesser Dog-fish.

LOPHIUS, *Piscatorius*, Fishing Frog, not common.

ACCIPENSER. *Sturio*, Sturgeon, one taken in Emsworth Harbour, in the summer of 1798, weighing eight pounds; rare.

TETRAODON, *Mola*, Short Sun-fish; this curious fish was taken off the harbour of Emsworth.

CYCLOPTERUS, *Lumpus*, Lump-fish; frequently in the spring in dredging for oysters.

SYNGNATHUS, *Acus*, Shorter Pipe-fish, Sea Adder; one was pumped out of a well in Havant, 4th Feb. 1814.

MURÆNA, *Anguilla*, Common Eel.

    Conger, Conger Eel.

AMMODYTES, *Tobianus*, Launce, Sand Eel.

TRACHINUS, *Draco*, Weever, rarely found; one taken 21st July 1808.

GRADUS, *Morhua*, Common Cod-fish, not so plentiful as formerly.

40

GRADUS. *Barbatus,* Whiting-pout, in great abundance; great quantities may be caught with a rod and line close to the shore.

Carbonarius, Coal-fish, Whiting-cole.

Pollachius, Pollack, not common.

Merlangus, Whiting, not so common as some years since.

COTTUS, *Scorpius,* Father Lasher, Bur, commonly taken in the shrimp nets.

ZEUS, *Faber, Dorée,* John Dory; this must now be considered as a rare fish, but formerly was more plentiful.

PLEURONECTIS, *Hippoglossus,* Halibut; we find this fish was taken some years ago, but not of a large size, as is common with the species.

Platessa, Plaice, common and excellent of their kind.

Flesus, Flounder.

Lunanda, Dab.

Solea, Sole; numerous, though seldom of a large size.

Maximus, Turbot, not common.

Rhombus, Pearl, Prill; generally small, but much esteemed.

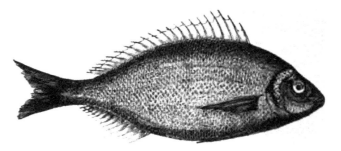

BREAM.

SPARUS, Lesser Sea Bream, Brazen.

LABRUS, *Gibbus,* Gibbous Wrasse, Golden Maid; frequently in the summer.

PERCA, *Fluviatilis,* Perch.

Labrus, Basse.

RED MULLET.

Gasterosteus, *Aculeatus*. Three-spined Stickleback, Minnow.

Scomber, *Scomber*, Mackerel; this species is taken in Hayling
Bay, in July and August, sometimes in great quantities.

    Thunnus, Tunny, Albicore. This is a very rare fish; we
can hear but of one that has been taken, and that at
Emsworth, on 14th October 1779: it was eight feet
in length, and weighed 3 cwt.

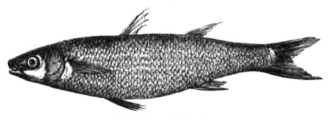

STRIPED MULLET.

Mullus, *Cirris*, Striped Surmullet; not common, generally taken
in summer.

Trigla, *Hirundo*, Tub-fish, Gurnard.

Cobitis, *Barbatula*, Loche.

Salmo, *Salar*, Salmon; has been taken at Emsworth, but not
often.

    Trutta, Sea-Trout, Salmon Trout; frequently in the
summer months.

    Fario, Trout.

Esox, *Belone*, Sea-pike, Gour-fish; common in the summer
months.

Atherina, *Hepsetus*, Atherine, Smelt.

Mugel, *Cephalus*, Mullet; common during warm weather, excellent of their kind.

Culpea, *Harengas*, Herring; sometimes in great quantities
between Michaelmas and Christmas.

    Sprattus, Sprat.

    Alosa, Shad.

Cyprinus, *Carpio*, Carp.

    Tinea, Tench.

    Rutilus, Roach.

    Phoxinus, Minnow.

    Auratis, Gold-fish; naturalized.

REPTILES.

RANA, *Bufo*, Common Toad.
      Temporaria, Common Frog.
LACERTA, *Palustris*, Warty Lizard.
      Agilis, Scaly Lizard.
      Vulgaris, Common Lizard.
COLUBER, *Berus*, Viper.
      Natrix, Ringed Snake.
ANGUIS, *Fragilis*, Blind Worm.

BIRDS.

SEA SWALLOW.

FALCO, *Milvus*, Kite.
      Buteo, Buzzard; generally found in the northern or more
          woody parts. Neither can be said to be common.
      Cyaneus, Hen-harrier, Blue-hawk; not common.
      Tinnunculus, Kestril, Wind-hover.
      Nisus, Sparrow-hawk.
STRIX, *Flammea*, White Owl.
      Stridula, Brown Owl.
LANIUS, *Collurio*, Lesser Butcher-bird: this may be considered as
      a rare bird.
CORVUS, *Corax*, Raven; not common, sometimes a solitary pair.
      Corone, Crow.
      Frugilegus, Rook. There are several rookeries in this
          district, two are in Hayling, one at Ham, and the
          other at the Manor farm.
      Cornix, Hooded Crow, Pied or Grey Crow; visits the sea-
          shores annually in the autumn, and remains the
          winter.

CORVUS, *Monedula*, Jackdaw; not common.

Glandarius, Jay.

Pica, Magpie.

CUCULUS, *Canorus*, Cuckoo.

JYNX, *Torquilla*, Wryneck; one of the earliest summer birds of passage, generally arriving about the middle of March.

PICUS, *Viridis*, Green Woodpecker, Jaffot.

Medius, Middle-spotted Woodpecker.

ALCEDO, *Ispida*, King-fisher. It is said that a nest of this bird has been found in the neighbourhood, but it could not be traced to an authority sufficient to positively assert the fact.

SITTA, *Europæa*, Nuthatch; found only in the more woody parts.

CERTHICA, *Familiaris*, Creeper, Free Runner.

PHASIANUS, *Colchicus*, Pheasant.

TETRAO, *Perdix*, Partridge.

Coturnix, Quail: not common.

COLUMBA, *Ænas*, Wild Pigeon, Wood Pigeon.

Palumbus, Ring-dove.

Turtur, Turtle-dove; not by any means common.

STURNUS, *Vulgaris*, Starling.

Cinclus, Water Ouzle. A solitary individual taken (supposed to have been wounded) at Emsworth in January 1808. Shot at Hayling in 1835.

TURDUS, *Viscivorus*, Mistle Thrush; not common.

Pilaris, Fieldfare.

Iliacus, Redwing; generally appear about Michaelmas.

Musicus, Song Thrush.

Merula, Blackbird.

Torquatus, Ring Ouzle; a rare species was seen on Emsworth Common in March 1807.

AMPELIS, *Garrulus*, Bohemian Chatterer; one shot at Emsworth in the winter of 1779-80.

LOXIA, *Curvirostra*, Crossbill; one shot at Havant in July 1810.

Pyrrhula, Bullfinch. An instance has been stated of a Bullfinch that never attained its proper colours, but was a deep black.

Chloris, Greenfinch.

EMBERIGA, *Miliaria*, Bunting.

Citrinella, Yellow-hammer.

Schæniclus, Reed Sparrow.

FRINGILLA, *Domestica*, House Sparrow.

FRINGILLA, *Cœlebs*, Chaffinch.
>   *Montifringilla*, Brambling; not common; shot near Emsworth in February 1808.
>   *Carduelis*, Goldfinch. We have observed at Emsworth two remarkable changes in the plumage of this bird; in one instance the subject was fed wholly with canary-seed, and became of a beautiful white; whilst another, whose food was hemp-seed, became a deep black. These are striking instances of the effects of food. In the autumn thousands of these birds visit the Hayling Bay.
>   *Linota*, Linnet.
>   *Canaria*, Canary-bird; naturalized, but bred in cages.

MUSCICAPA, *Atricapilla*, Pied Fly-catcher.

ALAUDA, *Arvensis*, Sky-lark.
>   *Pratensis*, Tit-lark.
>   *Petrosa*, Rock-lark, a newly discovered species; (vide Linn. Trans. v. iv. p. 41;) visits the shores of Emsworth harbour in winter.
>   *Arborea*, Wood-lark.

MOTACILLA, *Alba*, Pied Wagtail, Moll-doll; congregate in the autumn, chiefly in the evenings, on sedge; many of this species at this season emigrate, only a few remain the winter.
>   *Flava*, Yellow Wagtail.
>   *Luscinia*, Nightingale.
>   *Modularis*, Hedge Sparrow.
>   *Salicaria*, Sedge-bird, Reed Sparrow.
>   *Sylvia*, Whitethroat.
>   *Passerina*, Lesser Faucette, Wall-bird.
>   *Œnanthe*, Wheat-ear; more plentiful in the autumn; they do not appear to breed here.
>   *Byhetra*, Winchat, Furze-chucker: not common.
>   *Rupicola*, Stone-chat; not common.
>   *Atricapilla*, Black-cap, or Oxeye.
>   *Phœnicurus*, Redstart.
>   *Rubecula*, Redbreast.
>   *Troglodytes*, Wren.
>   *Regulus*, Golden-crested Wren.
>   *Trochilus*, Willow Wren.

PARUS. *Major*, Greater Titmouse, Tom-tit.
>   *Cœruleus*, Blue Titmouse.
>   *Ater*, Coal Titmouse.

PARUS, *Caudatus,* Long-tailed Titmouse, Pudding.

Biarmicus, Bearded Titmouse.

HIRUNDO, *Rustica,* Chimney Swallow.

Urbica, Martin.

Riparia, Sand Martin; appear only on their first arrival in the spring, do not breed here.

Apus, Swift.

CAPRIMULGUS, *Europæus,* Goat-sucker, Night-hawk.

ARDEA, *Major,* Heron, Jack Heron.

Stellaris, Bittern; shot at Emsworth in January 1809.

SCOLOPAX, *Arquata,* Curlew; common in the harbours.

Phæopus, Wimbrel. We are rather inclined to think that this bird frequents the harbours in the autumn, and is known by the name of Titrel; generally supposed to be the young Curlew.

Rusticola, Woodcock.

Gallinago, Common Snipe.

Gallinula, Jack Snipe.

TRINGA, *Vanellus,* Lapwing, Peewit.

Hypoleucas, Common Sand Piper.

Ochropus, Green Sand Piper.

OX-BIRD.

Cinclus, Purre, Grey Sand Piper, Ox-bird. The birds of this genus, and that of Scolopax, are so various at different stages of growth, and their habits so obscure from common observation, that even with the best ornithologists their history is involved in much uncertainty.

HÆMATOSSUS, *Ostralegus,* Oyster-catcher, Olive.

RALLUS, *Crex*, Land-rail; not common.

    Aquaticus, Water-rail, Water-runner.

FULICA, *Chloropus*, Water-hen, Moor-hen.

    Atra, Coot.   These birds were so plentiful some years since in the harbours, when the weather was severe, that it was not uncommon to see the mud covered with them for the space of several acres.

COLYMBUS, *Minutus*, Little Grebe, Daberchick.

RECURVIROSTRA, *Avasetta*, Avoset; killed in Emsworth harbour in the month of April 1806,[1] and again in the same month in the following year: never before noticed.

COLYMBUS, *Troit*, Guillemot.

LARUS, *Canus*, Common Gull.

    Nævus, Wagel.

MERGUS, *Castor*, Dun-diver Spear-duck; not common, found only in severe weather.

LITTLE AUK.

ANAS, *Cygnus*, Wild Swan.   These birds are sometimes particularly numerous in severe weather.   In the winter of 1800 it was no uncommon circumstance to see a hundred in a flock in Emsworth harbour.

    Olor, Tame Swan.   This species frequents the harbours when their usual haunts are frozen up.   In the winter of 1739, one was shot at Emsworth, with a brass collar on its neck, bearing the letters R. V. I. cut through the brass; this collar was at the time sent to the Duke of Richmond for his inspection, but never returned.

---

[1] For an account of the Avoset, see the Penny Cyclopædia.

WIDGEON.

Anas, *Tadorua*, Shieldrake, Beergander; frequently a few solitary individuals, in severe weather, in the harbours.

Anser, Wild or Grey Goose.

Bernicla, Brent Goose, Bran Goose. There are few winters, however mild, in which the harbours are not visited by these species, and sometimes in great plenty.

GREEN PLOVER.

ANAS, *Nigra*, Scota; we have noticed but one instance of this bird being found in the neighbourhood.

> *Baschus*, Common Wild Duck : in frosts, when the usual haunts of this species are frozen,—they are common in the harbour.

> *Penelope*, Widgeon.   These birds are sometimes so plentiful in severe weather, that two persons firing at the same instant have killed sixty birds out of one flock.

> *Crecca*, Teal; in general a scarce bird.

PELICANUS, *Carbo*, Corvorant; found in the harbours at all seasons.

> *Bassanus*, Gannett.   An individual of this species taken alive off Emsworth harbour in the summer of 1806, the only instance of this bird approaching our shores that has come to our knowledge.

SHELLS.

MULTIVALVE.

CHITON, *Crinitus;* Langstone harbour, on oysters.

> *Lævis;* frequently in Emsworth harbour, affixed to stones.

LEPAS, *Balanoides*, barnacle; common in Emsworth harbour.

> *Conoides*, ditto; bottoms of ships from the Mediterranean.

> *Rugosa ;* posts in Hayling wade-way.

> *Elongata?* ditto.

> *Anatifera ;* drifted wood, and bottoms of ships from South of Europe.

> *Anserifera*, ditto.

> *Sulcata?* ditto.

PHOLAS, *Dactylus;* Emsworth harbour, in clay and mud.

> *Candidus*, ditto.

BIVALVE.

MYA, *Truncata;* Emsworth harbour.

> *Arenaria;* Emsworth harbour.

SOLEN, *Vagina*, razor shell; mouth of Emsworth harbour; rare.

> *Vespertinus ;* off Emsworth harbour; rare.

> *Siliqua*, ditto.

> *Ensis*, ditto, Langstone harbour; rare.

BIVALVE SHELLS FROM HAYLING BEACH.

TELLINA, *Lactea;* Emsworth harbour; common.
    Solidula, ditto.
    Amnica; Emsworth mill-pond; rare.
    Cornea, ditto; common.
CARDIUM, *Echinatum;* Emsworth harbour; rare.
    Exiguum, ditto.
    Lævigatum; off Emsworth harbour, dead; rare.
    Edule, common cockle; Emsworth harbour; common.
    Fasciatum; salt-water pool at Slipper Marsh.
MACTRA, *Stultorum,* ditto, dead; not common.
    Subtruncata, ditto; common.
    Lutraria, ditto; not common.
    Listeri, ditto; mostly dead.
    Tenuis, ditto.
VENUS, *Verrucosa,* ditto; common.
    Islandica, ditto, dead; not common.
    Escoleta, ditto.
    Decussata, pulder, ditto; very common.
    Pullastra, ditto.
    Virginea, ditto.
    Aurea, ditto.
OSTREA, *Varia, Squius,* Emsworth harbour; common.
    Edulis, common oyster; ditto.
ANOMIA, *Ephippium,* crow oyster; ditto.
    Squamula, ditto, on the shell *Mytilus edulis,* &c.
MYTILUS, *Edulis,* common muscle, Emsworth harbour, common.
    Pellucidus, ditto, off Emsworth harbour.
    Modiolus; young shells off Emsworth harbour.

UNIVALVE.

Cypræa, *Pediculus*; Emsworth harbour; not common.

UNIVALVE SHELLS.

About the 4th of September the oyster-dredging commences in Langstone and Chichester harbours, both which places are famous for the quantity and quality of their fish.   They are sold at one shilling the hundred.   At the commencement of the fishing season, about fifty sail may be there seen, all occupied with dredging.

Bulla, *Hydatis*; Emsworth harbour: dead on the shore, with the animal, after gales of wind.

    Akera; Emsworth harbour, dead on the shore, with the animal, after gales of wind.

    Fontinalis; Emsworth mill-pond.

    Hypnorum; in ditches.

Voluta, *Denticulata;* found amongst the rejectamenta of the sea in Emsworth harbour after gales of wind.

Buccinum, *Lapillus;* off Emsworth harbour: this species contains the celebrated Tyrian purple of the ancients.

    Undatum, whelk; Emsworth harbour.

    Reticulatum, ditto.

    Variety of, ditto.

Strombus, *Pes pelecani;* Emsworth harbour, dead; rare.

Murex, *Erinaceus;* off Emsworth harbour; common.

    Antiquus, ditto.

Trochus, *Magus;* off Emsworth harbour; common.

    Lineatus, ditto; not common.

    Zyizphinus, ditto: common.

Turbo, *Jugosus*, ditto; rare.

    Littoreus, perriwinkle; common.

    Rudis; not common.

    Ulvæ; common.

    Labiatus; ditto.

    Elegans; Rowland's Hill and Portsdown.

    Fontinalis; Emsworth mill-pond.

    Nautilus, ditto.

    Clathratus; off Emsworth harbour; rare; allied to the Turbo.

Turbo, *Scalaris*; that rare and valuable shell the wenteltrap.

Truncatus; among the rejectamenta of the sea after gales of wind.

Subtruncatus, ditto.

Nigricans; stems of willow-trees; Emsworth.

Laminatus; Portsdown; rare.

Perversus; stems of willow-trees; Emsworth.

Muscorum; Emsworth, amongst moss in woods.

Helix, *Lapicida*; Rowland's Hill; rare.

Planorbis; Emsworth mill-pond and ditches.

Vortex; Emsworth ditches; common.

Contorta; Emsworth mill-pond; not common.

Alba, ditto.

Fontana; Emsworth mill-pond and ditches; common.

Paludosa; Warblington marshes; rare.

Ericetorum; Rowland's Hill; not common.

Virgata, ditto.

Caperata; not common.

Rufescens, ditto.

Pantiana; not common.

Nitens; in moss; not common.

Radiata; Emsworth; not common.

Arbustorum; common, generally under the shade of the *Urtica dioica*; common nettle.

Nemoralis, ditto.

Hortensis, ditto.

Elegantissima, among the rejectamenta of the sea after gales of wind.

Sybrica; Emsworth; not common.

Palustris, common.

Fossaria, ditto.

Succinia, ditto.

Putris, ditto.

Tentaculata, ditto.

Lævigata; Emsworth harbour; rare.

Nerita, *Glaucina*; Emsworth harbour.

Palidula, common.

Littoralis, not common.

Patella, *Vulgata*, limpet; frequently on stones in Emsworth harbour.

Oblonga; Emsworth mill-pond, on the stalks of the *Iris pseudacorus*.

Græca; Emsworth harbour, dead; rare.

Dentalium, *Entalis*; sands off Emsworth harbour, dead and rare.

Serpula, *Spirorbis;* Emsworth harbour, on the *Fucus serratus;* common.

      Triquetra; stones and shells, Emsworth harbour.

Teredo, *Navalis;* on drift-wood on the shores; not common.

PLANTS.

MARITIMA, OR SEA-HOLLY.

Salicornia, *Herbacea,* marsh samphire; Emsworth.

Veronica, *Officinalis?* common speedwell.

      Pseudacorus, yellow iris, or fleur-de-lis; common.

Galium, *Verum,* yellow bed-straw; Emsworth.

      Mollugo, great hedge bed-straw; ditto.

      Aparine, goose-grass, or cleavers; Emsworth.

Plantago, *Major,* greater plantain; ditto.

      Maritima, sea plantain; ditto.

      Coronopus, buck's horn plantain; ditto.

Lithospermum, *Officinale,* common gromwell.

Symphytum, *Officinale,* common comfrey; ditto.

Borago, *Officinalis,* common borage; Warblington and Bedhampton.

Primula, *Vulgaris,* common primrose; the banks under the hedges are filled with them.

PRIMULA, *Elatior*, great cowslip; Emsworth; not common.

    Veris, common cowslip; ditto, common.

ANAGALLIS, *Arvensis*, scarlet pimpernel; ditto.

CONVOLVULUS, *Sepium*, greater bind-weed; ditto.

    Arvensis, small bind-weed; ditto.

VERBASCUM, *Thapsus*, great mullein; ditto.

HYOSCYAMUS, *Niger*, common henbane; ditto.

ATROPA, *Belladonna*, deadly nightshade.

SOLANUM, *Dulcamara*, woody nightshade; Emsworth.

BETA, *Maritima*, sea-beet; ditto.

CUSCUTA, *Epithymum*, lesser dodder; Emsworth Common.

ERYNGIUM, *Maritima*, eringo, or sea-holly; Hayling beach.

DAUCUS, *Carota*, wild carrot; Emsworth.

CONIUM, *Maculatum*, common hemlock; ditto.

CRITHMUM, *Maritimum*, sea samphire; once found on the shore at Warblington.

CHÆROPHYLLUM, *Sylvestre*, smooth cow-parsley; Emsworth.

PASTINACA, *Sativa*, wild parsnip; ditto.

ANETHUM, *Fœniculum*, common fennel; ditto.

APIUM, *Graveolens*, smallage, or wild celery; ditto.

SAMBUCUS, *Ebulus*, dwarf elder; Warblington and Havant.

STATICE, *Armeria*, thrift; Emsworth.

    Limonium, sea-lavender; Emsworth sea-shore.

RUMEX, *Aquaticus*, great water-dock; Emsworth mill-pond.

    Acetosa, common sorrel; Emsworth.

ERICA, *Vulgaris*, common heath; Emsworth common.

AGROSTEMMA, *Githago*, corn cockle; Emsworth.

LYCHNIS, *Flos-cuculi*, ragged-robin; ditto.

LYTHRUM, *Salicaria*, purple loosestrife; ditto.

EUPATORIA, *Agrimonia*, common agrimony; ditto.

RESEDA, *Lutea*, wild mignonette; ditto.

SEMPERVIVUM, *Tectorum*, common houseleek; ditto.

SPIRÆA, *Ulmaria*, meadow-sweet; ditto.

GEUM, *Urbanum*, common avens; ditto.

CHELIDONIUM, *Majus*, celandine; Emsworth and Warblington.

    Luteum, yellow-horned poppy; Hayling beach.

PAPAVER, *Rhœas*, common red poppy; Warblington.

NYMPHÆA, *Alba*, white water-lily; ditto.

    Vulgaris, common columbine.

ANEMONE, *Nemorosa*, wood-anemone; Emsworth Common.

VERBENA, *Officinalis*, common vervaine; ditto.

MENTHA, *Arvensis*, common mint; ditto.

GLECHOMA, *Hederacea*, ground-ivy; ditto.

LAMIUM, *Album*, white archangel; ditto.

YELLOW HORNED POPPY.

GALEOBDOLON, *Luteum*, yellow dead-nettle; found between Emsworth and Havant.

BALLOTA, *Nigra*, stinking or black horehound; Emsworth.

ORIGANUM, *Vulgare*, common marjoram; ditto.

RHINANTHUS, *Crista-galli*, yellow rattle; ditto.

EUPHRASIA, *Officinalis*, eye-bright; Emsworth Common.

DIGITALIS, *Purpurea*, purple foxglove; ditto.

THLASPI, *Bursa pastoris*, common shepherd's-purse; ditto.

CRAMBE, *Maritima*, sea-kale; Hayling beach; rare.

SISYMBRIUM, *Nasturtium*, water-cresses; Havant and Emsworth.

ERYSIMUM, *Officinale*, common hedge mustard; Emsworth.

MALVA, *Sylvestris*, common mallow; ditto.

SPARTIUM, *Scoparium*, common broom; ditto.

ULEX, *Europæus*, common furze; ditto.

ONONIS, *Arvensis*, rest harrow; Warblington.

ORNITHOPUS, *Perpusillus*, common bird's-foot; Emsworth.

HYPERICUM, *Androsæmum*, tutsan; Emsworth Common.

SONCHUS, *Arvensis*, corn sow-thistle; ditto.

　　　　　　Oleraceus, common sow-thistle; ditto.

LEONTODON, *Taraxacum*, common dandelion; ditto.

　　　　　　Palustre, marsh dandelion; ditto.

CARDUUS, *Marianus*, milk thistle; ditto.

ARTEMISIA, *Maritima*, sea-wormwood; ditto.

TUSSILAGO, *Farfara*, colt's-foot; ditto.

SENECIO, *Jacobæa*, common ragwort; ditto.

INULA, *Dysenterica*, common flea-bane; ditto.

URTICA, *Urens*, small nettle; ditto.

　　　　　Pilulifera, Roman nettle, ditto.

　　　　　Dioica, great nettle; ditto.

ARUM, *Maculatum*, cuckoo-pint; ditto.

SALIX, *Repens*, dwarf willow; ditto.

RUSCUS, *Aculeatus*, butcher's broom; ditto.

II.—THE COTTON FAMILY.

FROM the memoir of Henry Fitzroy, Duke of Richmond (*Cam. Mis.* vol. 3) it appears that Richard Cotton was clerk comptroller of the Duke's household in 1525. His brother, George Cotton, was the Duke's gentleman usher and governor; and it would seem that there existed a considerable difference of opinion between George Cotton and Doctor Richard Croke, the Duke's tutor, as to the course of instruction which it was necessary for the Duke to pursue. Cotton had no taste for Latin, and he is charged by Croke with putting off the lessons, and withdrawing the Duke to out-door amusements. He positively refused to permit the Duke to rise at six, or to learn at all before mass, and he almost entirely set aside the arrangement of time prescribed by Cardinal Wolsey. Croke complained by petition to the Cardinal, stating, among other things, that the latter would hardly believe how great a quantity of the Prince's corn, malt, wine, ale, beef, mutton, veal, venison, salt meat, and every kind of provision, had, within the past two years, been squandered by the Cottons, as well in presents to their friends as especially in providing for the family of Parr, of all which not a fifth part appeared in the Prince's accounts; and that this had occurred by the fraud of Richard Cotton, the clerks of the Duke's kitchen could prove, provided they were bound by oath under the Cardinal's authority to do so, as otherwise they would not dare whisper in a business of such importance. The upshot of this was that Croke eventually retired, and the Cottons remained about the person of the Duke until the period of his death, which happened on the 22nd July, 1536.

After the death of the Duke of Richmond, King Henry VIII made George Cotton bailiff of Boston Martock and Sampford Peverell, and steward and receiver of Holt and Chirk, and keeper of Merslay Park. Richard Cotton was also made steward, bailiff, master, and keeper of the game of Bedhampton, with the farm, paying the rents thereof per annum £10. 13s. 4d., and bailiff and keeper of the park of Bovytracy. William, George, Richard, Ralph, Robert, and Thomas Cotton were sons of John Cotton, of Cotton, county of Salop; and from George Cotton, who received a grant of the Abbey of Combermere, according to Ormerod's *History of Cheshire*, descended the family now represented by Viscount Combermere. This George Cotton figured as a favourite companion of King Henry VIII in his exercises of archery, and won at three several times the sums of 46s. 8d., £3, and £7. 2s.

at the butts or rounds in Tothill-fields, near Westminster. Three
of the brothers also won of the King's grace, in Greenwich Park,
£20 and 6*s.* 8*d.*

From two letters of Richard Cotton to the Lord Privy Seal
Cromwell, among the Cromwell correspondence in the State Paper
Office, it appears that in 1536 he was the commander of a company
of soldiers sent to repress the rebellion in Linçolnshire. He was
knighted on the coronation of King Edward; and, having held for
some time the office of Treasurer of Boulogne, he was one of the
commissioners for the delivery of that city to the French in 1550.
In 1551, he occurs as one of council for Wales. He was M.P. for
Cheshire in 1 and 2 and 2 and 3 Philip and Mary. He died on
2d October, 1556, and was buried at Warblington. Machyn's
Diary states that in " 1556, October, was buried Sir Richard Cotton,
Knight and Comtroller to K. Edward VI of his honorable household, with a herald of arms and a standard, penone, and coat of
arms, and a 6 dozen of ' Skochyons,' and buried at Warlbrylton."
King Edward's *Diary* mentions that the Queen Dowager of Scotland
had lodged at Warblington on the 28th October, 1552. George,
the son of Sir Richard Cotton, was knighted and was living at
Warblington in 1596.

In the *M.S. Harl.* 2083, art. 16, will be found the copy of a
letter of the commissioners appointed to inquire into the value of
the lands of George Cotton of Warblington, convicted of recusancy.

III.—JUMIEGES.

THERE are numerous traditions and superstitions connected with
the early history of the Abbey of Jumiéges, some of which have
come down to our own times. Among the most singular is that of
the " Loup vert," an account of which is given in a little work published at Rouen, and the substance of which is as follows :—

Saint Philibert, the founder of Jumiéges, founded also the
Monastery of Pavilly, situated at a distance of four leagues from the
abbey, and of which Ausheberthe became the first abbess. This
pious woman being employed with her nuns to wash the linen of
the sacristy of Jumiéges, an ass carried it regularly without a guide
from one monastery to the other. One day a ravenous wolf de-
voured the ass as he was crossing the forest, and the abbess, having
arrived on the spot at the moment, loaded the wolf with the ass's

Procession du Loup-Vert.

burden, and ordered him to carry it to its proper destination. The wolf not only obeyed the order, but continued from that time to present himself for service at the appointed hour, and to acquit himself of his sacred functions with a zeal and fidelity beyond all praise. In the eighth century a chapel was erected on the spot where the ass was killed. After the lapse of some centuries, this edifice, commemorative of the early legend, was replaced by a cross of stone, known by the name of the *Ass's Cross :* this was destroyed some eighty years ago, since which several wooden niches contain- ing statues of the Virgin have been placed in a neighbouring oak, now bearing the name of the *Ass's Oak.* The procession of the "loup vert," still kept up at Jumiéges, appears to have been insti- tuted in commemoration of this tradition. On the 23rd of June, the eve of St. John the Baptist's day, the brotherhood established under the patronage of this saint go to seek in the hamlet of Conihout the new master of their devout society, who cannot else- where be legally elected; this person, who is called the "loup vert," being muffled up in a large green coat, and a brimless high-pointed cap of the same colour, marches at the head of the brethren singing the hymn of St. John to the sound of crackers and muskets, and preceded by the cross and banner, they go to the place called Chouquet, where the curate with his clergy joins them, and thence conducts them to the parochial church, where vespers are chanted. A repast composed of meagre dishes is prepared at the house of the *loup vert,* after which dancing begins, and is kept up until the hour arrives for lighting the fire of St. John. After singing the *Te Deum* around the pile, which is lighted with much solemnity by a boy and girl crowned with flowers, and to the tolling of bells, one of the assistants sings a hymn in the Norman dialect, whilst the *loup* and the brethren in costume, with the chaperon on their shoulders, run round the fire holding each others' hands, after the person chosen to be *loup* the following year. Of these strange huntsmen only the first and last of the string have a hand at liberty; they must how- ever surround and catch the future *loup* three times, without which he would not be considered chosen, he in his flight striking all in his way with a long stick with which he is provided. When the brethren succeed in catching him, they carry him in triumph and pretend to throw him into the fire. After the conclusion of this strange ceremony, they proceed to the house of the *loup,* where they sup on meagre fare as before. The least word immodest or foreign to the solemnity of the moment is signalized by the noisy sound of the bells placed near one of the assembly who officiates as judge, the ringing being in effect a decree which condemns the offender to recite, aloud and standing, the Pater-Noster ; but at midnight the most entire liberty follows this restraint : bacchanalian songs succeed to religious hymns, and the harsh notes of the village minstrel are scarcely heard above the discordant voices of the riotous company. At last they retire for the night ; but on the following day the feast recommences ; an enormous consecrated loaf, surmounted by green branches and ornamented with ribbons, is carried in procession, after which the bells are placed on the steps of the altar, and are confided to the *loup vert* chosen for the succeeding year, as the emblems of his motley honour.

INDEX OF PERSONS.

Donewych, Peter de, 103.
Donovan, Daniel, 67.
Dormer, Lord, 63.
Dorynge, Edmund, 285.
Dover, John, 282.
Downe, Thomas, 139.
Downell, Robert, 109.
Drewitt, Thomas, 267.
Dubosc, Simon, 223.
Dudley, Sir John, 245.
Dugard, Samuel, 127.
Durham, William Bishop of, 183.

Earle, John, 66.
Earwaker, Charles, 29.
Edgar, 5, 6, 165.
Edge, Peter, 54.
Edilwalke, King, 5.
Editha, 5.
Edward the Confessor, 9.
      King, 2, 4, 6, 7, 91, 92, 104.
Egitha, daughter of Earl Godwin, 159.
Ella, 156.
Elleswik, Alexander de, 102.
Elone, Henry, 281.
Elsi, Abbot of Ramsey, 173.
Eltham, John of, 312.
Emma, Queen, 156, 165.
Estneye, Phillis de, 91, 122.
Estoke, Richard, 274.
Estonhille, Robert, 185.
Ethelbert, King, 8.
Ethelred, King, 49, 156.
Evans, Dorothy, 21, 26.
      John, Bishop of Meath, 17.
Ewer, Robert le, 91.
Eyles, James, 193.
Eyr, Robert le, 216.

Faith, Saint, 8.
Fauconer, Henry, 151.
      John le, 186, 189, 277.
      William, 187, 189, 273.
Featherstonehaugh, Sir Matthew, 66.
Ferries, William, 185.
Field, S. P. 132.
Fitzalan, Henry, Earl of Arundel, 23, 254.
Fitzherbert, Henry, 87.
      Matthew, 90, 91, 121.
Fitzwalter, Viscount, 192.
Forbes, Alexander, 54.
Forde, Sir Edward, 63.
      Sir William, 64.
Foster, Francis, 22.
      John, 138.
      Thomas Land, 22.
Franceis, John le, 102.
Francis Maud, daughter of Sir Adam, 94.
Franklin, Joseph, 24.
      Thomas, 24.
      Thomasin, 24.
Franks, Thomas, 28.
Frating, Catherine de, 104.
Frederick, Emperor, 7.
Fulco the Dane, 86.

Galley, William, 145.
Garrett, William, 19, 27.
Gatere, John, 63.
Gaveston, Piers, 203.
Geldernet, William, 40.
Gerold, 86.
Giffard, Walter, 86.
Giles, John, 278.
Giselham, William de, 90, 107.
Girman, John, 139.
Glamorgan, Robert de, 101.
Godfrey, Nicolas, 39.
Godwin, Abbot of Hyde, 166.
      Earl, 84, 156, 165.
Gold, John, 14.
Golden, John, 139.
Goodchild, John, 40.
Gonner, Geoffrey de, 212.
Gounter, Colonel, 68.
Gouthard, Abbé, 167.
Grant, Sir Richard, 58.
Green, Thomas, 40.
Grey, Forde, Earl of Tankerville, 63.
      Lady Jane, 97.
      Lord of Werk, 63.
Gulderhugg, Roger, 188.
Gynnulph, William, 213.

Hall, Gregory, 36.
      John, 12, 75.
      Richard, 12.
Halsey, Elizabeth, 22.
      John, 21.
      Nathaniel, 21.
Hammond, Henry, 59.
      John, 28, 42.
      Richard, 286.
      Walter, 188.
      William, 278, 289.
Hannam, John, 39.
Hardy, Charles, 68.
Harold Harefoot, 157.
Harris, William, 41.
      Thomas, 194.
Harrison, John, 127.
Harryson, Nicolas, 300.
Hart, Reuben, 42.
Harvest, Robert, 274.
Hasle, Margery Atte, 281.
Hatchard, Thomas Goodwin, 57, 59.
Hawker, John, 62.
Hayling, Prior of, 182, 194, 212, 213.
Heather, Harry, 40.
      Thomas, 40, 43.
Hedger, Richard, 137.
Hedley, 80.
Hellyer, John, 29, 193.
Henry, King I, 8, 174.
      II, 175.
      III, 2, 87, 104, 186.
      IV, 95.
Henslowe, Ralph, 250.
      Thomas, 269.
Herbard, Nicolas, 274.
      Thomas, 188.

INDEX OF SUBJECTS.

F I N I S.

TUCKER AND CO., PRINTERS, PERRY'S PLACE, OXFORD STREET.